Great Orchestral Music

Great Orchestral Music

A TREASURY OF PROGRAM NOTES

Edited by JULIAN SEAMAN

Volume V of the series
THE FIELD OF MUSIC
edited by Ernest Hutcheson, *President Emeritus*
of the Juilliard School of Music

RINEHART & COMPANY, INC.

NEW YORK • TORONTO

ILLUSTRATED BY ROY COLONNA

TO ELAINE

A lady of strength and purpose, who
plays Strauss waltzes divinely.

INTRODUCTION

The program annotator pursues a thankless calling. He devotes endless hours to research—checking dates, reconciling flatly contradictory statements by eminent authorities, and in general racking his brains to think up new ways of saying things that have been said a thousand times before. The notes that are the outcome of these labors are printed in the programs of the orchestra for which he happens to be working, where they are hastily skimmed by the many and read by the few. After that, aside from a brief recrudescence when the conductor repeats a given piece, they are consigned to oblivion.

Such was the annotator's fate until Julian Seaman came along. When I read the proofs of this unique book I was struck by the frightening amount of reading that must have gone into its compilation. For here under one cover is the work, not of one commentator, but of a score or so, selected from the programs of the finest orchestras this country can boast. Here you will find notes by men and women of nationwide reputation—men like John N. Burk, whose biography of Beethoven is a source book, Alfred Frankenstein, Herbert Peyser, Felix Borowsky—together with picked examples of the work of departed experts such as Philip Hale of the Boston Symphony and Pitts Sanborn and Lawrence Gilman of the New York Philharmonic-Symphony. In addition you will find material (no less excellent for being anonymous) culled from programs, magazine articles, essays, and newspapers.

Mr. Seaman's treasury is unusual in another respect. As a rule, program notes, or collections of program notes, confine themselves largely to the music. Whatever biographical material they contain is severely factual, being generally confined to the birth, death, and career dates that any musical dictionary could provide. Here, every biography is as exhaustive as the importance of the subject demands, well and entertainingly written (by the modest author-editor himself) and providing the sidelights that so rejoice the lay listener. Needless to say, such a book carries a formidable weight of authority. The reader can safely assume that its facts *are* facts, that its opinions are those of experts.

The author mentions the value of this book to the radio listener. He might also have stressed its enormous usefulness to the record collector. With a very few exceptions, the music mentioned herein has been recorded, much of it many times. The possessor of a record library who likes to assemble his own recorded symphony concerts will find this treasury an invaluable adjunct. He can, literally, curl up with a good book and doubly enjoy the music.

DEEMS TAYLOR

FOREWORD

Listening to music can be fun, as I have learned in my years of doing it for a living. Writing this book has been fun, too; especially the day I became so enmeshed in the life and loves of an obscure Russian composer that I turned out thirty-two pages, and quit only when somebody locked up the typewriter.

This book is intended for those who also think serious music is fun. It should be a guide to listening; it should fill in that empty moment called "intermission," when the lights come up and one feels disinclined to join the crush in the foyer and the gabbling powwow.

I commend it, also, to the student who seeks history and background and a glimpse or two of composers as human beings, long before he hears the sounding note and darkening chord. The radio listener, sitting before his "symphonic hour," may leaf it through, supplementing where the hearty announcer left off.

In compiling a book of this kind, the author and his assistants have been forced to do a shocking amount of sober reading, for program notes often have been too scattered and indefinite to provide adequate information for the reader's questing mind.

The program notes included here have been chosen either for their preciseness and brevity, or for some unusual feature in the writing. Many of the notes considered were too long—though perhaps more informative—or were diffuse. In some instances, there were two of equal caliber—in which case, a coin was flipped.

I will not pretend that the research has been all mine. In fact, but for the intelligent and careful assistance of several people, the book would have been impossible to do.

I should like to express my obligation to the kindness of Miss Gladys Chamberlain, of the Music Library in New York, for her suggestions and cooperation; to Louis Lane, Music Librarian of the National Broadcasting Company; to Paul Affelder, former annotator of the Pittsburgh Symphony Orchestra; to Alfred Frankenstein, of the San Francisco Symphony Orchestra and to the managements of the Philharmonic-Symphony Society of New York, the Philadelphia Orchestra Association; the Baltimore, Boston, Chicago, Cincinnati, Cleveland, Detroit, Indianapolis, Kansas City, Los Angeles, Minneapolis, New York City, Rochester, Seattle, St. Louis and other major orchestras of the entire United States, for permission to quote their program notes.

Nor can I forget the kindness of Mrs. Lawrence Gilman, who graciously allowed me to make use of the Philharmonic and Philadelphia program notes written by the late Mr. Gilman.

And, though not as a postscript, my deepest gratitude to Helen Kaufman and to Richard and Kyra Hubbell.

JULIAN SEAMAN

New York
January 1950

CONTENTS

Great Orchestral Music

ANTON STEPANOVITCH ARENSKY

(Born in Novgorod, Russia, August 11, 1861—died
in Terijoki, Finland, February 25, 1906)

CONTRARY to the sour prediction of his teacher, Rimsky-Korsakoff, Arensky has not been entirely forgotten today. His music lays no claim to wisdom or eloquence, yet it does hold grace and charm, melodic originality and haunting beauty.

Both of Arensky's parents were musical; his father, a doctor, played the 'cello, and his mother was an excellent pianist. Consequently, when the child showed an aptitude for music at a reasonably early age, he was encouraged.

He began the private study of music in St. Petersburg and entered the Imperial Conservatory at the age of eighteen. He became a pupil of Rimsky-Korsakoff and of Johansen, and won the Conservatory Gold Medal for composition in 1882. A first symphony and a piano concerto won him immediate attention, and in the same year he was appointed professor of harmony and counterpoint at the Conservatory in Moscow.

There Arensky came in contact with Tschaikowsky, who formed a warm regard for the young composer, and was to exercise a decided influence upon the style and texture of his music.

His first opera, *The Dream on the Volga,* was finished in 1890 and produced in Moscow the same year. M. Montagu Nathan, in his *Short History of Russian Music,* tells us that from 1889 to 1893 Arensky held a position on the Synodal Council of Church Music in Moscow and that during this period he refused the post of director of the Tiflis branch of the Russian Musical Society. Instead, he became conductor of the Moscow Choral Society, and director of the St. Petersburg Imperial Chapel.

3

Rimsky-Korsakoff seems to have entertained a poor opinion of his former pupil. In his memoirs he remarks that "Arensky's life ran a dissipated course, between wine and card-playing, yet his activity was most fertile. His mode of life undermined his health, and he died of galloping consumption as a final result . . . In his youth, he did not entirely escape my own influence (as a composer). Later, he fell under Tschaikowsky's. He will be soon forgotten."

Arensky was a comparatively young man when he died in Finland of what today would be called tuberculosis. In the gallery of composers from the past century, he is regarded as prolific but hardly discriminating. Among his best-known works are a ballet, *A Night in Egypt;* a second opera, *Raphael;* a fantasy, *The Foundation of Baktchissarai,* for solo voices, chorus and orchestra; a piano quintet; a second quartet in A minor; and an Intermezzo for Strings.

Variations on a Theme by Tschaikowsky (for String Orchestra) Opus 35-A

When Tschaikowsky died, several Russian composers—associates and former pupils—wrote commemorative pieces. Anton Arensky, who early came under Tschaikowsky's influence, incorporated his tribute in a string quartet. Among Tschaikowsky's lyric works were *Sixteen Children's Songs,* with piano accompaniment, grouped as Opus 54. From them Arensky chose the seven variations, dedicated "to the memory of Peter Ilich Tschaikowsky." In the final variation the melody, seemingly a new theme, appears in reverse. Arensky is supposed to have alluded here to the practice of holding guns upside down at military funerals. After the theme is announced, *moderato,* by the first violins, to pizzicato support, the seven variations and coda follow:

Variation 1: (*Un poco più mosso*) the theme goes from minor to major, and back to minor.
Variation 2: (*Allegro non troppo*), violas and 'cellos take up the theme against repeated sixths, mostly in the high violins.

Variation 3: (*Andantino tranquillo*), the melody is given out serenely in the major.

Variation 4: (*Vivace*) bristles with telling pizzicato effects.

Variation 5: (*Andante*), while 'cellos and basses discourse the theme, violas and violins chant a different melodic pattern. Later the roles are reversed.

Variation 6: (*Allegro con spirito*), arpeggi and tremoli almost conceal the theme in places.

Variation 7: (*Andante con moto*) the first violins reverse the melody. Apart from the basses, largely heard in pizzicato, all strings are muted. The coda reverts to the *moderato* marking of the opening.

Rimsky-Korsakoff and others give sharp pen-portraits of Arensky as a gambler, drunkard and roué, who dissipated himself into consumption and an early death. Riesemann adds he was lazy, hot-tempered and abusive. His pupil Scriabin hated him cordially.

"Drinking bouts—card-playing—galloping consumption—a period of dying in Nice—and then death in Finland," runs Rimsky-Korsakoff's terse obituary of a former pupil.

Louis Biancolli, *New York Philharmonic-Symphony Society*

JOHANN SEBASTIAN BACH

(Born in Eisenach, Germany, March 21, 1685—died
in Leipzig, Germany, July 28, 1750)

For more than two hundred years, the Bachs were a family of successful musicians. From all accounts, the family originated in Wechmar, Thuringia (a one-time duchy in Germany). Veit, a baker, was the first known ancestor of the family, and he traveled to Hungary to settle. But Protestants were hardly welcomed there, so Veit journeyed back to Wechmar, rather than change his faith.

Ambrosius Bach, father of Johann Sebastian, a musician in the service of the Town Council of Eisenach, died when the boy was ten, and he was taken into the home of his elder brother, Johann Cristoph. Undoubtedly he had already received some musical instruction from the parental home, and his brother continued these lessons.

Johann also was enrolled in the town school, where he advanced steadily. At fifteen, he was admitted to the church choir of St. Michael's, in Lueneburg, and thereby earned his schooling by song. Also seizing the opportunity to study the keyboard instruments, he visited Hamburg where a famous organist, Feinken, played.

He failed at seventeen to get the post of organist at Sanger-hausen. But he did obtain a minor post at the Court of Weimar, and was soon promoted to the rank of *Konzertmeister,* though he drew the salary of a *Kapellmeister.*

But Johann was not to enjoy the eminence of this title until some years later, when he became *Kapellmeister* to Prince Leopold of Anhalt-Coethen. At the age of twenty-two he had married, in 1707, Maria Barbara Bach, who presented him with seven children. She died in 1720, three years after he had moved to Coethen and in the following year he married Anna Magdalena Wilcken, by whom he had thirteen more Bachs.

Johann joined the Court of Coethen in 1717 and remained there until 1723, six of the happiest years of his life. We are told that "Prince Leopold was truly musical and was Bach's good friend and patron." He played in the orchestra under Bach's direction, but, unfortunately, the prince married an unmusical princess and his interest in the art waned.

About this time the position of cantor of the Thomas-Schule in Leipzig and director of music in the principal churches of the enterprising city became vacant. The post was a plum but Johann hesitated to give up his position at Coethen.

The Leipzig Council at length decided to engage him and he resigned his post at Coethen, to enter upon a long and exhausting period of struggle and frustration. He spent the remainder of his days there, despite sporadic attempts to place himself elsewhere. Although constantly embroiled in feuds and wrangles with the Town Council, gradually he was able to shift from his shoulders the most irksome of his many duties.

In the spring of 1747 Bach made a second journey to Potsdam in response to repeated expressions of King Frederick's desire to receive him. It was the king's custom to hold a private concert in the evening, playing the flute himself. On such an evening, when the musicians were at their desks, a chamberlain entered with a list of passengers newly set down by the coach. Frederick, running his eye down it, rose suddenly in some excitement. "Gentlemen, old Bach has arrived," he announced. A summons brought Bach from his son's lodging in his traveling dress, having been forbidden time to put on his cantor's black gown. High compliments were exchanged, the concert was abandoned, and, accompanied by the king and his musicians, Bach passed from room to room, trying Frederick's new Silbermann pianofortes, and extemporizing on them to the king's admiration. At Bach's invitation, Frederick played him a subject to treat *ex tempore*. Frederick then asked for a fugue in six parts. Bach forthwith improvised one and on his return to Leipzig developed Frederick's interesting theme in a similar manner. Judiciously including a Trio for flute, violin and clavier, he despatched the gift to Frederick as a "musical offering" with a dedication to "a sovereign admired in music as in all other sciences of war and peace."

His last work, besides a revision of the Eighteen Choral Preludes, was the Art of the Fugue. Blindness finally overcame him after an unsuccessful operation performed by John Taylor, physician-surgeon to Händel. Bach suffered a paralytic stroke and died in Leipzig, July 28, 1750.

"His obscure grave," writes Charles O'Connell, "was forgotten and neglected until 1894, when it was located and positively identified. His ashes were entombed in a crypt beneath the altar of St. John's Church in Leipzig, in 1900, on the one hundred and fiftieth anniversary of his death."

Fate decreed rather bitterly that the two greatest musicians of their time, Bach and Händel, should never meet. Bach sought Händel at Halle in 1719 but found he had returned to England. Ten years later, when Händel was again in Halle, Bach was not well

enough to travel, but sent an invitation to Leipzig by the hand of his eldest son, which Händel was unable to accept. Händel's last visit to Halle, in 1750, coincided with Bach's fatal illness.

Passacaglia in C minor for organ
(Symphonic Transcription by Leopold Stokowski)

The word *passacaglia* is a Spanish term which came into France as *passaccaille* after operas were introduced there. It means a "street song." But it is also a slow dance of three-beats-to-a-measure, originating in Spain or Italy, and not to be distinguished at this late day from a chaconne. The two dance rhythms and forms were taken into music as a basis of instrumental composition, and the two terms were used interchangeably, which has led to endless disagreements among the doctors.

As a musical form it is a sort of theme and variations. The theme is a constantly recurring bass, in this instance a phrase of eight measures, over which a changing musical structure is made as elaborate as the composer's ingenuity can devise. Musicians of the seventeenth and early eighteenth centuries made frequent use of the form, and there are fine examples from Frescobaldi, Buxtehude, Couperin and Händel, as well as the more familiar ones from Bach. A fashion set by Lully and followed by Rameau and Gluck was to write the finale of an opera in this form. English composers used the form if not the term; they preferred to call it a "ground" or "divisions on a ground." Beethoven's Thirty-two Variations for the piano and the Finale of Brahms' Fourth Symphony are later examples of the same kind of thing.

Bach composed the *C minor Passacaglia* originally for a two-manual clavicembalo with pedals. He wrote the version for organ later, presumably during the latter part of his stay at Weimar, about 1715. He borrowed the first half of his theme from a *Trio en passacaille* by Andre Raison, a French organist of the time of Louis XIV. Upon this "ground" he constructed a series of twenty variations.

Mr. Stokowski first performed his transcription of this work at the Philadelphia concert of February 10, 1922. He then contributed the following paragraphs to the program-book:

"Bach's *Passacaglia* is in music what a great Gothic cathedral is in architecture—the same vast conception—the same soaring mysticism given eternal form. He left us no orchestral works of this grandeur, probably because the orchestra was too little developed in his time. His *Brandenburg Concerti* and the orchestral Suites are more intimate works written for the salon. The most free and sublime instrumental expressions of Bach are his greater organ works, and one of the greatest of these is the *Passacaglia in C minor*. Unfortunately, we do not often enough have opportunity to hear it, and so to bring it nearer to those who love Bach's music I have made this symphonic transcription.

"This *Passacaglia* is one of those works whose content is so full and significant that its medium of expression is of relative unimportance. Whether played on the organ, or by the greatest of all instruments—the orchestra—it is one of the most divinely inspired contrapuntal works ever conceived."

RALPH McCOMBS, *Philadelphia Orchestra*

Toccata and Fugue in D minor for organ

The Toccata and Fugue in D minor for organ (not to be confused with the "Dorian" Toccata and Fugue in the same key) dates from the early part of Bach's residence at Weimar, where for nine years (1708-1717) he was Court Organist and *Kammermusiker*.

The word "toccata" was derived from the Italian *toccare:* to touch, to strike, move, excite, play upon. When the term found its way into the nomenclature of music, it was used at first to describe a composition designed to display the characteristics of music written for keyboard instruments, chiefly the organ, and especially to exhibit the touch and execution of the performer. According to the definition of Michael Praetorious, it meant originally a free prelude, or introduction. In old examples by Andrea Gabrielli (1510-1586) and Claudio Merulo (1533-1604), the Toccata begins with full harmonies, followed by running passagework interspersed with brief fugal periods; thus exhibiting its essential character as a brilliant showpiece, generally with the suggestion of an improvisation.

The organ toccata descended through Claudio Merulo, the great master of the Venetian School, and reached its highest point of development in Italy in the works of Frescobaldi. In Germany, the toccata stems from Dietrich Buxtehude (1637-1707); but it was Bach who, in his toccatas, cast into the shade all previous experiments in this form—if form it may be called. For it must be remembered that the old composers applied the term to various types of compositions—Georg Muffat, for instance (*circa* 1645-1704), affixed the label to what is really a five-movement suite, comprising a stately *Alla breve,* a rapid *Fugato,* a canonic *Adagio,* an *Andante,* and a jiglike *Fugato* finale in 12-8 time. Yet this work exists as one of the toccatas in Muffat's *Apparatus musico-organistus* (1690). The form of the toccata, indeed, suffers from "faint individuality," as Corder remarks in his essay on the subject.

Not all of Bach's cantatas are improvisational in style—the famous one in F major, for example, is not; although the one on this program (D minor) indisputably is.

This D minor Toccata, with its appended Fugue, constitutes one of the most brilliant of Bach's concert works of the virtuoso type; and it is also an extraordinarily dramatic, imaginative and distinguished piece of music.

The opening Toccata is one of those fiery and rhapsodic movements which Bach handled with such consummate effectiveness. Written under the influence of Buxtehude, it is nevertheless unmistakably Bach: in the freshness and vitality of its invention, in its enormous strength, and especially in those contrasts of dazzling bravura passages (in this case, rushing semiquaver passages on the different manuals) and great chordal masses of titanic breadth and power.

"The Fugue, although very free in appearance," as Marcel Dupré remarks of it, "contains the essentials." It is based on a subject the melodic form of which is outlined through swirling and broken harmonies. At the eighty-fifth measure, Bach begins to work back to the mood of the Toccata, and winds up with a coda of overwhelming power.

PHILIP HALE, *Boston Symphony Orchestra*

Prelude and Fugue in E minor for organ

This is a transcript of No. 3 of Bach's *Acht Kleine Prae-ludien und Fugen* for organ. It is sometimes assumed that these Eight Short Preludes and Fugues were very early works; but Harvey Grace in his admirable study of Bach's organ music asserts that there can be no doubt that Bach wrote them "after he had been settled at Weimar for a considerable time—long enough to have gathered round him a few pupils. We may well understand," says Grace, "that good teaching material—brief pieces, employing two manuals and with a definite and moderately difficult pedal part—must have been scarce at that time. Bach endeavored to supply this deficiency, and the result was so successful that this collection —at least, the final part of it—has taken a high place in the curriculum and is not likely to be superseded."

Mr. Grace believes that the general excellence of the writing in these Short Preludes and Fugues proves them to belong to a period when Bach was approaching maturity (his stay at Weimar was from his twenty-fourth to his thirty-third year). "Even their simplicity and brevity indicate a fairly late date; for youthful genius is not usually inclined to be simple and unpretentious. A further hint as to the date of these works is to be found in the Preludes, which remind us that in his early Weimar days Bach was much attracted by the concertos of Vivaldi."

The finest of this set of Preludes and Fugues is, by general agreement, that which is performed at this concert in Mr. Stokowski's version for orchestra in which is to be found, thinks Mr. Grace, "the real Bach spirit."

LAWRENCE GILMAN, *Philharmonic-Symphony Society of New York*

Chaconne from Partita in D minor for unaccompanied violin
(Transcribed for orchestra by Leopold Stokowski)

Bach's *Chaconne* for solo violin is the concluding movement of the second (*D minor*) partita for violin. It belongs to the period (1717-1723) during which Bach dwelt at Coethen as *Kapellmeister* of Prince Leopold of Anhalt-Coethen. The oldest known manuscript of the violin partitas and sonatas dates from about 1720 —which narrows the probable date of the composition of the *Chaconne* to the three years 1717-1720, so that Bach could not have been over thirty-five when he wrote this marvel of polyphonic skill and imagination.

The manuscript in question, discovered at St. Petersburg in 1814 by Georg Polchau, Librarian of the Singakademie, Berlin, is not, as Polchau thought, in the handwriting of Bach, but in that of his wife, the incomparable Anna Magdalena, whose script resembled closely that of her husband.

Both Mendelssohn (in 1847) and Schumann (in 1854) wrote piano accompaniments for the *Chaconne*. Brahms wrote a piano version for left hand and Busoni a concert transcription for piano. Raff arranged the *Chaconne* for orchestra in 1874; and in 1911, Maximilian Steinberg, son-in-law of Rimsky-Korsakoff, made an orchestral version of the piano transcription by Busoni. An orchestral transcription of Bach's original (generally attributed to an eminent Philadelphia musician*) was introduced to the repertoire of the Philadelphia Orchestra in the season of 1930-1931.

A transcription for orchestra, made in 1924 by Mr. A. Walter Kramer, the distinguished American composer, critic and editor, was performed by the Seattle, Cincinnati and Cleveland orchestras in the season of 1931-1932.

PHILIP HALE, *Boston Symphony Orchestra*

The Choral Preludes

More than a third of the music that Bach composed for the organ is of the kind known as *Choralvorspiel*—Choral Preludes— short compositions on the melody of a congregational hymn. There are extant one hundred and forty-three examples in this genre. The majority are in Bach's own autograph, or in copies engraved and published under his direction and with his consent; a few have come down to us in transcript by his pupils or amateurs of his work. Bach himself compiled four collections: The *Orgelbuechlein*

*Stokowski.

—Little Book for the Organ—The Schuebler Chorales, the Eighteen Preludes, and the Catechism Preludes.

". . . . The little volume (*Orgelbuechlein*) is, in fact, a condensed hymnary, based on the hymnbook authorized for use in the Grand Duchy of Weimar, in 1713. Its arrangement follows that of the hymnal; Part I contains hymns relative to the seasons and festivals of the Church; Part II comprises those that illustrate the various aspects and aspirations of Christian life. The booklet was undertaken at Weimar; afterwards, at Coethen, Bach made a fair copy of it. The work is only about a third complete.

"Bach had planned to write one hundred and sixty-four Preludes; sixty in the first part, one hundred and four in the second. Actually, he completed thirty-six of the first group, and only ten of the last. He disposed the chorales so that those of the Nativity form a small-scale Christmas oratorio, those of Passiontide a Passion and those of Easter time an Easter oratorio. The title of each chorale is carefully inscribed on the page on which it is to appear. Evidently, they were all intended to be brief like the few that were completed, the longest of which counts only twenty bars. The resource and imagination that Bach brought to these little movements is extraordinary. His profound love for this music, with which he was associated so intimately all his life, is here revealed in all its tenderness. Each Prelude offers some new artistic scheme, worked out with infinite care and delicate fancy. In some the tune alone is given, others are in variation, charmingly embellished; some have simple figures which run throughout, some display admirably contrived canons, others are treated contrapuntally. According to the sentiment expressed in the text or melody, the figure in the accompaniment expresses now tenderness, now sorrow, now liveliest animation. Here, if ever, we find Bach communing with his God, discoursing with Him in speech all can understand."

LOUISE BECK, Philadelphia Orchestra

The Suites

Bach was thirty-two when he became *Kapellmeister* (musical director) for Prince Leopold of Anhalt-Coethen. During the six years Bach held this post (1717-1723), he had to renounce his self-appointed duty "to dedicate his art to the service of God." The Coethen court was "reformed" and only stern Calvinist psalms were heard in its chapel. There was no call for church cantatas or chorales. Also there was no organ worthy of the talents of the most famous organist of that time.

Bach had at his disposal a small group of instrumentalists and his duty was the entertainment of the young prince in his palace. So the music of the Coethen-period is entirely secular and instrumental.

The four orchestral suites were probably composed at Coethen. All four are groups of dances of the period, preceded by an overture. The lively dances "however gay or merry, never lose the distinction of noble art. Nobody but J. S. Bach ever succeeded in presenting such sparkling gayety and fun in such fine and manly terms. However freely they sparkle and play they are never trivial." (Parry)

Schweitzer, another Bach-authority, writes: "in the dance melodies of these suites, a fragment of a vanished world of grace and eloquence has been preserved for us. They are the ideal musical picture of the rococo period."

Indianapolis Symphony Orchestra

Brandenburg concerti

Bach completed in March 1721, six concertos written for Christian Ludwig, Margrave of Brandenburg, a prince who had met Bach when that composer, either in 1718 or 1720, had accompanied Prince Leopold of Anhalt-Coethen to Carlsbad.

An edition of the concertos was published for the first time by Peters, in 1850, the works having been edited by Siegfried Wilhelm Dehn, at that time librarian of the musical section of the Royal Library, Berlin. This authority testified that "the exterior of the manuscript forms in several ways, a rare exception to such other manuscript forms by Bach as are known. In comparison with these the notes are written with extraordinary neatness, even the bar-lines being drawn with the aid of a ruler, so that the writing surpasses in elegance the autograph scores of the *St. Matthew Passion* and the first part of the *Well-Tempered Clavichord,* which, among the many other original manuscripts by J. S. Bach, are treasured in the musical department of the Library at Berlin."

The set of six concertos bears a dedication—in French—to *Son Altesse Royal, Monseigneur Cretien Louis, Margraf de Brandenbourg,* etc., etc., etc., This inscription, dated Coethen, March 24, 1721, was probably not composed by Bach, but by some helpful associate at the Court of Coethen. It bore, however, that servility of expression which characterized the letters of dedication inscribed by authors and composers in the eighteenth century who offered the fruits of their genius to those whose rank was high. Bach entreated the Margrave "very humbly" not to judge the imperfections of the concertos by the severity of that fine and delicate taste which everyone knows that he possesses; but rather to see in them, by his kind consideration, the profound respect and the very humble allegiance which they seek to convey." . . . . their keys (are) arranged as follows: No. 1, F major; No. 2, F major; No. 3, G major; No. 4, G major; No. 5, D major; and No. 6, B flat major.

FELIX BOROWSKI, *Chicago Symphony Orchestra*

SAMUEL BARBER

(Born in West Chester, Pa., March 9, 1910—now
living in Westchester County, N. Y.)

THIS RISING young composer, whose music has been gaining steadily in the esteem of musicians and the lay public, here and abroad, is the son of a physician. His mother is a sister of the late American contralto, Louise Homer.

Barber began to study music at the age of six, and entered the

Curtis Institute at thirteen. He studied piano with Isabella Vengerova, singing with Emilio de Gogorza, and composition with
Rosario Scalero.

He was graduated in 1932 and in 1935 was awarded the Prix
de Rome and the Pulitzer Prize for Music. A year later, he won
the Pulitzer Prize again, the first time that it has been conferred
twice on the same musician.

Barber continued to compose while serving in the Army Air
Force during the Second World War and his Second Symphony is
dedicated to this branch of the service. Another of his popular
wartime compositions is a score for male chorus, "A Stop Watch
and Ordnance Map." His works have been played by most major
American orchestras, also by the Vienna Philharmonic and British
Broadcasting Company orchestras abroad.

Unlike many young composers today, Barber is not a radical,
but composes skillfully in familiar and conservative terms.

Overture—*The School for Scandal*

The Overture, according to Arthur Loesser, program annotator of the Cleveland Orchestra, "is said not to be intended as a
prelude to an actual performance of Sheridan's famous comedy of
the same name, but merely as a musical reflection of the play's
spirit. Its sprightly character, coupled with its classical pattern,
demonstrates its affinity for its original." Mr. Barber supplied this
description for the initial performance:

"The Overture begins with a very rapid figure for the full orchestra, except trombones, followed by a lilting melody in 9-8 time
in the first violins, which is developed somewhat by other instruments of the orchestra. A second figure in the piccolo and flutes
then appears, a phrase which plays an important part later in the
Overture. There is a change to a slightly slower tempo, and the
second subject, a melodious tune, is played by the oboe, followed
by a new figure in the first clarinet, with an accompaniment in the
strings reminiscent of the oboe melody.

"This leads through the flutes and strings, the latter in very
rapid figuration, back to the first subject and in the original
tempo. The second theme, first announced by the oboe, now re-

turns in the clarinets and violas and later in the first violins. There
is a return of the triplet figure, and the Overture closes with a
joyous rush in the full orchestra. The music is in keeping with the
spirit of the Sheridan comedy, itself a great stage classic."

Boston Symphony Orchestra

Adagio for Strings

The . . . . *Adagio for Strings* was first performed on November 5, 1938, by Arturo Toscanini at a broadcast concert by the
NBC Symphony Orchestra. The work was derived, writes Mr. Barber, "from a string quartet first played by the Pro Arte Quartet in
Rome in 1936. After that it was arranged for full string orchestra.
The composition is built entirely on one figure, which is first sung
by the first violins and then by the violas in extended canonic imitation. Later it is given to the 'cellos and is gradually carried up
into the very high strings. There is a pause and the first violins
and violas repeat the theme in octaves before coming to a 'pianissimo close.' "

Lawrence Gilman, *Stadium Concerts—New York*

Essays for Orchestra

In 1937, Samuel Barber composed his *Essays for Orchestra,*
which was first performed by Arturo Toscanini and the NBC
Symphony Orchestra in 1938. It was then described as having been
suggested by the literary form; the themes were concise and were
developed within the limits of the essay form.

The *Second Essay,* completed in March of this year (1944),
follows along the same lines, but is for larger orchestra and somewhat broader in scope. The main theme is announced at once by
solo flute; a second theme by violas and a third figure by the brass.
A fugal section follows, beginning in the woodwind and developed
in the full orchestra, with the intertwining of the first two themes.

After a stretto and a fortissimo statement of the first theme, a Coda built on the ostinato third figure brings the work to a broad conclusion.

ROBERT C. BAGAR, *Philharmonic-Symphony Society of New York*

Capricorn Concerto—for flute, oboe, trumpet and strings

This Concerto, named after the composer's house in Mt. Kisco, N. Y., was written in 1944, especially for the Saidenberg Little Symphony, Daniel Saidenburg, conductor, which group was responsible for its premiere at the Town Hall (New York) on October 8, of that year. It is scored for flute, oboe, trumpet and strings, the three winds behaving in the manner of the Bach "Brandenburg" Concertos as a solo group against the massed strings. . . . . .

ROBERT C. BAGAR, *Philharmonic-Symphony Society of New York*

BELA BARTOK

(Born in Nagyszentmiklós, Hungary, March 25,
1881—died in New York, September 26, 1945)

BEGINNING to compose at eight, and appearing as a pianist at ten, one could say that Bartok was a musical child. His father, a government official, was an excellent pianist and 'cellist; his mother, a schoolteacher, was an amateur singer.

By the time he finished high school in 1899 and entered the

Liszt Academy of Music in Budapest, Bartok had composed a two-movement violin concerto. He began the study of opera and chamber music and during his subsequent years at the academy yielded more and more to the influence of Brahms and Dohnanyi. Here, too, he first encountered the scores of Richard Strauss and became fascinated by *Zarathustra*.

In the latter years of his study at the academy he found time to compose a sonata for violin, and a scherzo for orchestra, that was evidently part of a contemplated symphony.

Bartok also wrote his symphonic-poem *Kossuth,* which Hans Richter conducted in Manchester, England, in 1903. A Quintet for piano and a first Suite for orchestra belong to this period. He and Zoltan Kodaly collaborated in a set of Hungarian folk songs, published in 1906.

His subsequent output, for the next ten years, made little use of accepted idioms in the musical literature of Western Europe, but developed a new tongue of daring dissonance. A storm of comment arose, and the lack of adequate outlet to afford complete performances of these new works led Bartok, Kodaly and other young musicians, to form the New Hungarian Music Union. But the new group could not remedy this defect, nor was it able to break a wall of public indifference and prejudice. It soon dissolved.

Bartok went to North Africa in 1913 to study Arabian folk music. He also presented to the Romanian Scientific Academy his collection of Romanian folk songs. Outbreak of the First World War temporarily halted his work of composing, which he did not resume until 1917. His pantomime, *The Carved Wooden Prince,* performed in the Royal Opera House in Budapest, and a one-act opera, *Prince Bluebeard's Castle,* brought him world-wide fame.

He appeared in New York first in 1927, as pianist-composer, went back to Europe and returned in 1940 with his wife, the pianist Ditta Pasztory. They gave several joint concerts of Bartok's works. For some time immediately before his death, Bartok worked at Columbia University on the Millman Parry Collection of Yugoslav folk music. Reception of his music at the outset was cool, for often the idiom of his expression seemed obscure and bewildering; yet the public at large has come to value and understand his musical speech in the years following his untimely death.

Concerto for Orchestra

The Concerto for Orchestra was composed in October 1945, for the Koussevitzky Musical Foundation, as a memorial tribute to Natalie Koussevitzky. It was performed by the Boston Symphony Orchestra at an afternoon concert in Boston, December 1, 1944, Serge Koussevitzky conducting. The same band was responsible also for its New York Premiere in Carnegie Hall on January 10, 1945.

ROBERT C. BAGAR, *Philharmonic-Symphony Society of New York*

Romanian Folk Dances

Bartok's multifarious research into the folklore and folkmusic of the countries of the Balkan peninsula has won for him the reputation of being a founder and leader of a new school of Hungarian national music. . . . The tale is told of how Bartok's interest was piqued when he heard a servant sing one of these ancient airs while he was visiting a friend in the country. He at once knew that here he had to do with something quite different from what was currently passing for Hungarian music. Bartok recorded all the old tunes that the serving-woman could remember, and he resolved to gather as much of this authentic material as he could, seeking it out at its source, which was among the peasants themselves. . . . The Romanian Folk Dances. . . . Mr. Bartok tells us, were collected between 1909-1914. The first and fourth were played to him by a gypsy violinist, the fifth, sixth and seventh of the group by a Romanian peasant fiddler; the second and third by peasants on their native flute. They were first transcribed for piano in 1915, and in 1918 Mr. Bartok orchestrated them for small orchestra. In this form they have been played by various musical groups in this country. . . ."

LOUISE BECK, *Philadelphia Orchestra*

LUDWIG VAN BEETHOVEN

(Born in Bonn, Prussia, December 16, 1770—died
in Vienna, Austria, March 26, 1827)

LUDWIG's grandfather, Louis, the son of a baker and born in
Antwerp, December 23, 1712, left home at nineteen. He settled
two years later in Bonn, on the Rhine, as a wine merchant and
bass singer in the service of the Elector of Cologne.

His wife, with whom he was unhappy, bore him two babies
who died in infancy. She presented him with a third, Johann, and
took to drink. She ended her days in a Cologne cloister, a hopeless
dipsomaniac. Louis, however, flourished. He served the Elector for
forty years and in 1761 was appointed *Kapellmeister.*

But Johann, weak and disposed to drink like his mother, soon
ruined whatever modest chances he may have had for a career. He
sang in the Elector's chorus, played in the theater orchestra and
married Maria Magdalena Haym, a widow hardly twenty. Her
father was head cook in the castle of Ehrenbreitstein.

Schauffler calls her "gentle, hard-working, amiable and tactful. It is reported that no one ever saw her smile. The children of
Maria Magdalena were three sons—Caspar Anton Carl, Ludwig,
and Nikolaus Johann.

Doubt as to the exact date on which Ludwig was born has
troubled scholars. It was the custom in Rhenish cities of that day
to record the date of baptism but not of birth. Ludwig was chris-
tened on December 17, 1770, according to official record, hence it
may be assumed in view of prevailing custom that he was born on
December 16.

Ludwig was the second child of the Beethovens. He might
never have been a musician at all, for he showed no early bent in
that direction. But his father, Johann, tenor in the service of the
Elector, literally ground the rudiments of music into the dreamy
consciousness of his son, forcing him "to pound the piano or
scratch the fiddle."

Finally, at seven, Ludwig was expert enough to play the piano
in public. For a time he was cymbalist in the theater orchestra—

without salary—then he was appointed assistant court organist. When Elector Max Friedrich died, the theatrical company was disbanded and the new Elector decided to economize; so it was that for three years Ludwig had no duties other than organist.

He went to Vienna in the spring of 1787 and played for Mozart, who was complimentary. The last illness of his mother brought him back to Bonn, for he loved this fine woman deeply.

The official theater was reorganized and Beethoven rejoined the orchestra as a violinist, a post he held for four years, adding substantially to the family income.

While Beethoven was studying violin with Ries, a famous artist of the day then resident in Bonn, one of his fellow-pupils was Stephan von Breuning. The two boys became fast friends and Ludwig was a constant visitor to the Breuning house. Stephan's mother, Frau von Breuning, widow of the court councillor, treated Beethoven as one of the family. It is said that she could manage this lonely, awkward, moody young genius when no one else could approach him.

Probably Count Waldstein, another friend of this period, was responsible for an eventual migration to Vienna, ostensibly for study under Haydn. At any rate, the Elector granted his permission for this move. Fate decreed that Beethoven would never return to his native Bonn.

His fame as a pianist had preceded him and this protege of the Elector was well-received, particularly by the Elector's nephew, the Emperor of Austria. Ludwig found himself in great demand, as teacher, pianist, improviser and composer. He could play the viola as well as the piano and violin, and soon he was earning a good income, helping to support his two brothers, and enjoying a few personal luxuries by way of contrast to the penury of his earlier years.

He did study with Haydn, but the aging music master of the Esterhazy clan could spare him little time and turned him over to an assistant, which seemed to irk the tempestuous Ludwig.

Throughout his long life, apparently, Beethoven fell in and out of love several times—always violently. In the Bonn days, he became infatuated with several of his pupils; later pressed the beauteous Magdalena Willmann, singer at the Vienna Opera, to become his wife; conceived an ardent passion for the Countess Guicciardi; proposed to her cousin, the Countess Therese von Brunswick; to Amalie Sebald and many others, besides the mysterious "Immortal Beloved" to whom he addressed that beautiful and touching letter found in a secret drawer after his death.

The first symptoms of the deafness that was to become the tragedy of Beethoven's existence appeared about 1799. He ignored the symptoms at first, yet they persisted and finally he was forced to give up the idea of touring as a pianist. He tried to conceal his affliction for a while, fearing his enemies in Vienna would use it to his detriment. The malady grew steadily worse. He spent a summer at Heiligenstadt, near Vienna, and there, in despair, penned an extraordinary document, known as the *Heiligenstadt Testament*. It was addressed to his brothers, but never sent to them.

His one and only opera, *Fidelio,* ill-rehearsed and poorly cast, was produced in Vienna in 1805 with indifferent success. This has been blamed as much upon the advance of the French towards Vienna as upon the details of inadequate performance.

His nephew Carl, wayward son of his brother, plagued him through his life. His brother's will appointed Ludwig and the widow joint guardians of the boy. He detested his brother's wife, brought charges of immorality against her and obtained full guardianship from the courts. Subsequent wranglings with the boy's mother forced the court to remove him. He was reinstated in his trust, finally, but an attempt at suicide by young Carl brought matters to a crisis.

As soon as Carl was convalescent, Ludwig took him to visit his Uncle Johann, an apothecary grown wealthy by selling medicines to the French army, at his estate at Gneixendorf. They returned to Vienna in an open carriage in the dead of winter and Beethoven thereby caught a chill. He arrived home really ill, yet tried to ignore his serious condition for several days.

But in the week or two after his return he had pneumonia, then jaundice and dropsy. He was tapped four times between December 20, 1826 and February 27, 1827. The death-struggle had begun in earnest by the last week of March. Beethoven died at five o'clock on the afternoon of March 26, 1827.

Overture to *Leonore* No. 3

A biography of Beethoven by August Goellerich, published with a preface by Richard Strauss, in 1903, gives its own history of *Fidelio*. It seems that Beethoven had long and eagerly sought for the text of an opera. In a fit of irony over his vain search, he wrote to Kotzebue (the playwright), stipulating that the subject must be "romantic, entirely serious, masterful, comic or sentimental." An order from Shikaneder, director of the Theater-an-der-Wien, led to the discovery of the libretto founded upon Bouilly's *L'Amour Conjugal,* based, in turn, upon a Spanish story. The author was Josef von Sonnleithner, registrar of the theater.

Beethoven was seized by the ideal of the tale—Leonore's noble love, unyielding resolution and heroic rescue of her husband from unjust imprisonment.

With great enthusiasm the master began his Opus 72, that was to bring him more sorrow than any other of his works; he moved into lodging, free of rent, in the theater, and he was to receive a tenth from the returns of the first ten performances.

In the overture, the first *Leonore,* he expressed the essence of Leonore's character; Florestan appears only in shadowy lines. But the work was condemned by Lichnowsky, and was not produced until 1832, as Opus 138.

The title *Leonore* was rejected, as it had lately been used by the composer Paer; and the opera was produced under the name *Fidelio,* November 20, 1805, under Beethoven's direction, with an overture (the "Leonore" No. 2) that excited the rebellion of the wind-players. A week earlier the French had entered Vienna, and thus the greatest German opera since *The Magic Flute* was played to an audience of French officers. Moreover, offense was taken in higher circles at the pathos with which Beethoven had treated the theme of political imprisonment. After three performances, Beethoven withdrew the work. . . .

In 1813 Beethoven was once more persuaded to rewrite the music, in order, as he expressed it, "to build anew the neglected ruins of an old castle." The first performance was given with the overture, *The Ruins of Athens,* May 23, 1814, in the Kaernerthor Theater. Schubert, who had sold his textbooks to buy his ticket, exclaimed at the end of the last act, "He [Beethoven] can do every-thing." For the second performance, in the Court Theater, a new overture in E was ready, the one that is nowadays usually played before the first act under the name *Fidelio* Overture. Beethoven was heard to say at the time: "With this opera I earn my crown of martyr."

PHILIP H. GAEPP, *Philadelphia Orchestra*

Overture to *The Creatures of Prometheus*

Die Geschoepfe des Prometheus, a ballet composed by Bee-thoven, was produced for the first time at the Hoftheater, Vienna, March 28, 1801. The work was conceived and put upon the stage by Salvatore Vignano. This author was well-known as a ballet dancer and as an arranger of works for stage dancing. . . . Bee-thoven's music to the ballet consisted of an overture and sixteen other numbers. We know that at least one number—a song en-titled *"Ich denke Dein"*—had been intended for inclusion in the ballet, but that Beethoven withdrew it. Eight years later than the production of *Prometheus* the composer made a present of the song to his publishers, Breitkopf and Haertel. It would seem that Beethoven was not satisfied with Vignano's share in the unfolding of *Die Geschoepfe des Prometheus,* for in a letter to Hofmeister of Leipzig, written April 22, 1801, he said, "I have written a ballet, in which, however, the ballet master has not made the best of his part."

. . . . In his biography of Beethoven, Ludwig Noll . . . . de-clares that the success of the ballet "determined Schikaneder, well-known to the readers of the life of Mozart, who at this time had the direction of the newly-built theater in Vienna, to engage Bee-thoven at a large annual stipend."

Die Geschoepfe des Prometheus was published, with a dedica-tion to Prince Lichnowsky, in June 1801, by Artraria of Vienna. Only the pianoforte score, however, was brought out. In 1804 the overture was published in the orchestral parts by Hofmeister and Kuehnel. In the finale of the ballet there are two themes which

Beethoven employed in other works. One, in E flat major, was introduced into a *Contretanz;* the same subject also was employed as the theme of the Fifteen Variations and Fugue, written in 1802, and as the theme of the finale of the Eroica symphony, composed in 1804. It has been doubted by some whether this subject really appeared first in *Prometheus,* but it is clear from a letter written by the composer to Breitkopf and Haertel in 1803, that it did so appear.

FELIX BOROWSKI, *Chicago Symphony Orchestra*

Overture to *Egmont*

This overture was composed in 1810; it was published in 1811. The music to Goethe's play—overture, four entr'actes, two songs sung by Claerchen, *Claerchen's Death, Melodrama* and *Triumph Symphony* (identical with the coda of the overture), for the end of the play, nine numbers in all—was performed for the first time with the tragedy at the Hofburg Theater, Vienna, May 24, 1810. Antonie Adamberger was the Claerchen.

When Hartle took the management of the two Vienna Court Theaters January 1, 1808, he produced plays by Schiller. He finally determined to produce plays by Goethe and Schiller with music, and he chose Schiller's *Tell* and Goethe's *Egmont*. Beethoven and Gyrowetz were asked to write the music. The former was anxious to compose the music for *Tell*; but, as Czerny tells the story, there were intrigues, and, as *Egmont* was thought to be less suggestive to a composer, the music for that play was assigned to Beethoven. Gyrowetz's music to *Tell* was performed June 14, 1810. It was described by a correspondent of a Leipzig journal of music as "characteristic and written with intelligence." No allusion was made at the time anywhere to Beethoven's *Egmont*.

. . . . Long and curious commentaries have been written in explanation of this overture. As though the masterpiece needed an explanation!

PHILIP HALE, *Boston Symphony Orchestra*

Overture to *Coriolanus*

The Coriolanus of Beethoven's tonal portrait is not the tragic hero of Shakespeare's version of this ancient tale, but the hero of a drama by Heinrich Joseph von Collin, a playwriting contemporary of Beethoven. The Overture, composed in 1807, was published in the following year. The original manuscript was thus inscribed: *"Ouvertura (zum Trauerspiel Coriolan), composta da L. v. Beethoven, 1807"*; though the parenthetical phrase was afterward struck out.

In their main outlines, the plays of Collin and of Shakespeare are alike, with, however, this difference; the Coriolanus of Shakespeare is slain, while the death of Collin's hero is self-inflicted.

The accomplished Sir William Smith considered the tale of Coriolanus "one of the most beautiful of the early Roman legends." Its hero received the surname "Coriolanus" because of the valor which he displayed in the capture of the Volscian town of Corioli. But the arrogant attitude of Coriolanus toward the Commons excited their hatred and apprehension, and in B.C. 491 he was impeached and condemned to exile. He took refuge among the Volscians, and promised to help them in war against the Romans. Attius Tullius, King of the Volscians, appointed him general of the army, and Coriolanus took many towns, advancing without resistance until, in 489, he reached the Cluilian dyke, near Rome. Here he encamped, and the Romans, in panic, sent to him numerous embassies, consisting of the most distinguished men of the state, who sought to placate him. But Coriolanus was obdurate. Then the noblest matrons of Rome, headed by Veturia, the mother of Coriolanus, and Volunia, his wife, with his two children, visited him in his tent, and, by dint of copious weeping and warm reproaches, as was even then the practice, turned his will to water. Whereupon he led away his army, and abode innocuously in exile among the Volscians until he died a natural death; though another tradition relates that he was killed by Volscians upon his return to their country.

LAWRENCE GILMAN, *Philharmonic-Symphony Society of New York*

Overture *Consecration of the House*

This overture was composed for the opening of the Josephstad Theater in Vienna, which took place October 3, 1822.

The slow and majestic introduction to the Overture enlists the solemn strain of the trombones, of which no further use is made. The "motif" on which the whole of the Allegro is built, derives from five notes corresponding to those of the words . . . "is the king of" in the phrase "He is the King of Glory" in the chorus, "Lift up your heads" in Händel's *Messiah*. Beethoven sometimes referred to this work as the "Overture in Händel's Style." In one form or another, the thematic bit is repeated over two hundred times. In the hands of a lesser master than Beethoven this would undoubtedly tend toward monotony. In this work, however, there is no such suggestion.

LAWRENCE GILMAN, *Philharmonic-Symphony Society of New York*

Symphony No. 1 in C major (Opus 21)

Beethoven, giving his first public concert in Vienna "for his own benefit," on April 2, 1800, after making due obeisance to the past with a symphony of Mozart and airs from Haydn's "Creation," submitted his popular septet, and one of his piano concertos, playing, of course, the solo part; he also improvised upon the pianoforte. Finally, he presented to the audience his newly-completed Symphony in C major. The concert was received with marked interest, and a certain amount of critical approval. Indeed the young man was not without a reputation in Vienna as a pianist with almost uncanny powers of improvisation, who had written a number of sonatas, trios, quartets and sets of variations. In the orchestral field he had not yet committed himself, save in two early cantatas and in two piano concertos (in B-flat and C) which he had written a few years before for his own use.

The critic of the *Allgemeine Musikalische Zeitung,* while commending parts of the concerto, and the septet as a work of "taste and feeling," felt called upon to administer a mild rebuke upon the young man who had stepped out with rather too much temerity and confidence upon the hallowed ground of the symphony which Mozart and Haydn had cultivated in such careful and orderly fashion. The writer admitted in the symphony "much art, novelty, and wealth of ideas," but added: "Unfortunately, there was too much use of the wind instruments, so that the music sounded more as if written for a wind band than for an orchestra." It was after a performance in the more conservative Leipzig Gewandhaus about a year later that a critic found in the symphony "a caricature of Haydn pushed to absurdity." Opinions such as these from Beethoven's contemporaries give pause to us of later days who are inclined to accept this particular symphony as fundamentally docile to the traditions of the century which had just passed—bold in many matters of details certainly, but even there not without precedent in the symphonies of Haydn.

JOHN N. BURK, *Berkshire Symphonic Festival*

Symphony No. 2 in D (Opus 30)

Those who insist that a work of art necessarily mirrors the mental condition of the artist who created it find a hard nut to crack in Beethoven's Second Symphony. Gloomy and despairing, he wrote here a work that bubbles over with spontaneous merriment, is filled with the spirit of delight, showers "pleasing badinage."

The Second Symphony is the product of a singularly difficult year. In 1801 Beethoven's deafness, which had begun with a roaring of the ears, increased. He also suffered acutely from colic. After consulting one physician after another he settled on Professor J. A. Schmidt. But previously he had tried a variety of herbs and potions and even blisters, baths hot or cold, the treacherous oil of the almond. Galvanic remedies aroused his curiosity. Still, in the face of discouragement and distress he could write: "I shall as far as possible defy my fate, although there must be moments when I shall be the most miserable of God's creatures. . . . I shall grapple with fate; it shall never pull me down."

Dr. Schmidt insisted that he should spare his hearing by living quietly in the country and so sent him to Heiligenstadt, which at that time was a restful little village near Vienna, with an outlook across the meadows to the Danube and the distant Carpathian Mountains. And Heiligenstadt could boast a history of long extent. It was said the Emperor Protus planted there the first vines of Noricum, and a mineral spring, gushing waters of miraculous virtue, had received the blessing of St. Severinus, who died in the village.

The house Beethoven occupied stood apart on a hill in the outskirts, commanding a noble view of the valley. He scrupulously obeyed his doctor's orders about isolation, seeing only Schmidt and occasionally his pupil Ferdinand Ries. During this residence at Heiligenstadt, in the summer of 1802, he commenced his Second Symphony.

In addition to the physical ills, the stress and anguish of this period were aggravated by the marriage of Giulietta Guicciardi. Like her cousins the Countesses Josephine and Therese von Brunswick, this "little minx" of seventeen was a pupil of Beethoven, and of the three she was the first to make captive his heart. Whether or not the "Immortal Beloved" letter was addressed to her we shall probably never know; but in any case, the impressionable and turbulent Beethoven seems to have fallen deeply in love with her, and her marriage to Count Gallenberg was a crushing blow.

On October 6, Beethoven penned that profoundly pathetic document known as the *Heiligenstadt Testament,* which was designed for his brothers in what he felt to be the shadow of his impending death. Whether he was so ill that he actually expected death or whether he had not altogether mastered the temptation to suicide, one of his most recent biographers. . . . doubts our finding out.

PITTS SANBORN, *Philharmonic-Symphony Society of New York*

Symphony No. 3 in E flat major (Opus 55, *Eroica*)

One evening at Nussdorf, in the summer of 1817, when Beethoven and the poet Kuffner were enjoying a fish dinner together at the tavern "Zur Rose," Kuffner made bold to ask the Titan—

who happened to be in an amiable mood—which of his symphonies was his favorite (there were then, of course, only eight).

"Eh, eh!" responded Beethoven, in great good humor, "the *Eroica.*"

"I should have guessed the C minor," remarked his interrogator.

"No," insisted Beethoven, "the *Eroica.*"

The *Eroica* was then thirteen years behind him; he had finished the Eighth almost five years before; five years later he was to complete the Ninth.

With his preference for the *Eroica,* many will find themselves in sympathy. Yet it seemed to some who in 1808 heard the work for the first time that the symphony "often lost itself in lawlessness—that it contained much that was glaring and bizarre. (The first public performance of the *Eroica* was at Vienna, April 7, 1805; but there had been a private performance at Prince Lobkowitz's in December, 1804.)

A correspondent of that time divided the *Eroica's* hearers into three classes: there were those, "Beethoven's particular friends," who kept a tight upper lip and predicted that after a thousand years have passed it will not fail of its effect; another faction saw in it only "an untamed striving for singularity"... "strange modulations and violent transitions"... producing "a certain undesirable originality without much trouble—but genius proclaims itself not in the unusual and the fantastic, but in the beautiful and sublime." A third party, the middle-of-the-roaders, admitted that the symphony contained "many beauties," but deplored "its inordinate length" and feared that "if Beethoven continues on his present path he and the public will be the sufferers." Beethoven himself, who conducted the first performance, came in for some blame because of "discourtesy" toward his hearers; for it appears that "he did not nod his head in recognition of the applause which came from a portion of the audience."

. . . . The vast passions of the *Eroica* constitute "such a tornado," remarks Sir George Grove, "as would burst the breast of any but the gigantic hero whom Beethoven believed himself to be portraying, and who was certainly more himself than Bonaparte" —which is Sir George's shrewd and psychologically plausible comment on the celebrated tale that associates the symphony with Na-

poleon; for though "it may," as he says, "have been a portrait of
Bonaparte, it is as much a portrait of Beethoven himself; but that
is the case with everything that he wrote."

LAWRENCE GILMAN, *Philadelphia Orchestra*

Symphony No. 4 in B-flat major (Opus 60)

Robert Schumann compared this symphony to a "Greek
maiden between two Norse giants." The Fourth, overshadowed by
the more imposing stature of the *Eroica* and the Fifth, has not
lacked champions. "The character of this score," wrote Berlioz, "is
generally lively, nimble, joyous, or of a heavenly sweetness."
Thayer, who bestowed his adjectives guardedly, singled out the
"placid and serene Fourth Symphony—the most perfect in form of
them all."

This symphony was completed in 1806 and dedicated to the
Count Franz von Oppersdorf. The first performance was in March
1807, at the house of Prince von Lobkowitz in Vienna. It is scored
for flute, two oboes, two clarinets, two bassoons, two horns, two
trumpets, timpani and strings.

It has been noted that in all of his even-numbered symphonies, Beethoven was content to seek softer beauties, reserving his
defiances, his true depths of passion for the alternate ones. There
may well have been something in his nature which required
this alternation, a trait perhaps also accountable for the thematic
alternation of virility and gentleness, of the "masculine" and the
"feminine" in his scores of this period. For the years 1804-1806
were the years of the colossus first finding his full symphonic strength, and glorying in it, and at the same time the years
of the romantic lover, capable of being entirely subdued and sub-
jugated by feminine charm.

They were the years which produced the *Eroica* and C minor
symphonies, and the "Appassionata" sonata on one hand; on the
other, the Fourth Symphony and the Fourth Piano Concerto, not
to mention *Fidelio* and the three *Razumovsky Quartets*. It may
have been some inner law of artistic equilibrium which induced
Beethoven, after drafting two movements for his C minor sym-

phony in 1805, to set them aside and devote himself, in 1806, to the gentler contours of the Symphony in B-flat, which, completed in that year, thus became the fourth in number.

JOHN N. BURK, *Boston Symphony Orchestra*

Symphony No. 5 in C minor (Opus 67)

There is no date on the manuscript of Beethoven's C minor Symphony, but the first performance is on record as having taken place December 22, 1808, when the Sixth (*Pastoral*) Symphony was also heard for the first time. The sketchbooks indicate that he worked long and intermittently over this symphony. The Fifth and Sixth must have been finished about the same time. It is certain that Beethoven laid his C minor aside to compose the idyllic Fourth, in 1806, the year of his engagement to Therese von Bruns-wick. Thayer attributes the earliest sketches for the Fifth Symphony to 1800 and 1801, which would put its inception even before the *Eroica*, of 1802. But the first sketches show no inkling of the significant matter to come. He apparently took it up occasionally while at work upon *Fidelio* and the Fourth Piano Concerto (1804–1806). But the Fifth Symphony may be said to have made its real progress from 1805 until the end of 1807, when it was finished near Heiligenstadt. It was dedicated to Prince von Lob-kowitz and the Count Razumovsky. It was published in April 1809.

Beethoven's Fifth Symphony, like other scores once considered subversive but long since sanctified by custom, both bewildered and amused its first audiences, not to speak of the orchestras and leaders who were destined to be the first purveyors of its ringing message. It is also to be recorded about the Fifth Symphony, however, that its forceful challenge almost immediately dispelled the first befuddled impressions.

When the Philharmonic Society of London first tried over the C minor Symphony, the players laughed openly, and the "conductor," in reality the concertmaster, laid it aside as "rubbish." This leader, who was none other than J. P. Salomon, lived to make a brave retraction. Two or three years later, after another trial of the first movement, so relates Thayer, "Salomon laid his violin upon the pianoforte, walked to the front and, turning to the orchestra said (through his nose): 'Gentlemen, some years ago I called this symphony rubbish; I wish to retract every word I then said, as I now consider it one of the greatest compositions I have ever heard.' "

The very first performance, which Beethoven conducted at the Theater-an-der-Wien on December 22, 1808, seems to have made no recorded impression. The Leipzig public, which had received the *Eroica* with much understanding in 1809, did at least as much for the Fifth. A careful and appreciative analysis appeared in the *Allgemeine Musikalische Zeitung* (July 14, 1810). . . .

Let us turn back. . . . to the curious Akademie in Vienna. . . . when Beethoven labored, with rather pitiable results, to present his C minor Symphony to the world. The programme, according to modern custom, was itself rather forbidding in bulk. . . . Misfortunes beset Beethoven. There was high feeling between him and the orchestra, on account of an outbreak of temper at a concert in November. He quarreled with the soloist, the young and inexperienced singer who took her place grew terrified and gave a miserable exhibition at the concert. . . .

JOHN N. BURK, *Boston Symphony Orchestra*

Symphony No. 6 in F major (Opus 68, *Pastoral*)

There are many who like to think that this symphony is the truest instance of Beethoven's instinct, or perhaps intuition, that kept him from allowing mere delineation to become his ideal. In it is the eternal charm of the country, the deathless voice the composer heard in brook and breeze, in wind and wood, the eloquent mystery which steps ever in the heart of man. He was one able to break through the dumb worship of most of the human kind, and sound its golden melody.

. . . . Vincent d'Indy thinks the second movement, *Andante molto mosso* (B-flat major, 12-8) the most admirable expression of true nature in musical literature. It contains imitations of sounds and sights in nature; the rippling of the brook (strings) is the basic movement; there is the muttering of thunder (contrabasses in their lower register), flashes of lightning (violins); the bassoon of an old peasant sitting on a barrel, and able to play but three tones; and the song of the nightingale (flute), quail (oboe) and cuckoo (clarinet).

Ries, pupil and somewhat inaccurate chronicler of Beethoven, assures us the master laughed at the idea of "musical painting," although the composer did contemplate a definite argument when he composed; with reference to this particular symphony Beethoven insists he is not attempting to "paint." Yet the *Sinfonia Pastorale* is program-music, and the composer himself was good enough to furnish the titles for the movements.

In Beethoven's sketchbook, with sketches of the first movement, it is referred to tentatively as "Characteristic Symphony. The recollections of life in the country." To which is added as a note: "The hearer is left to find out the situations for himself." However, when the symphony was first performed in 1808, it was described on the program:

First piece.

Pleasant feelings which awake in man on arriving in the country.

Second piece. Scene by the brook.

Third piece.

Jovial assemblage of the country-folk, in which appear suddenly

Fourth piece.

Thunder and storm, in which enter

Fifth piece.

Beneficial feelings connected with thanks to the Godhead after the storm.

CYRIL ARTHUR PRYOR and W. K. KELSEY, *Detroit Symphony Orchestra*

Symphony No. 7 in A (Opus 92)

The first sketches of this symphony were made by Beethoven probably before 1811 or even 1810. Several of them in the sketchbook that belong to Petter of Vienna, and analyzed by Nottebohm, were for the first movement. . . .

Thayer states that Beethoven began the composition of the Seventh Symphony in the spring of 1812. Prod'homme believes that the work was begun in the winter of 1811-1812. The autograph manuscript that belongs to the Mendelssohn family of Berlin bears the inscription: SINFONIA, L. *v.* BTHVN 1812 13TEN M. A clumsy binder cut the paper so that only the first line of the M is to be seen. There was therefore a dispute as to whether the month were May, June or July. Beethoven wrote to Varena on May 8, 1812: "I promise you immediately a whole new symphony for the next Academy, and, as I now have opportunity, the copying will not cost you a heller." He wrote on July 19: "A new symphony is now ready. As the Archduke Rudolph will have it copied, you will be at no expense in the matter." It is generally believed that the symphony was completed May 13, in the hope that it would be performed at a concert of Whitsuntide.

The score of the symphony was dedicated to the Count Meritz von Fries and published in 1816. The edition for the pianoforte was dedicated to Elizabeth Alexiewna, Tsarina of All the Russias.

The first performance of the symphony was at Vienna, in the large hall of the university, on December 8, 1813.

PHILIP HALE, *Boston Symphony Orchestra*

Symphony No. 8 in F major (Opus 93)

Early in October 1812, the *Linzer Musikzeitung* thus announced the arrival of a distinguished visitor to the town of Linz: "We have had the long wished for pleasure of having within our metropolis for several days the Orpheus and greatest musical poet of our time. . . . and if Apollo is favorable to us, we shall also have an opportunity to admire his art and report upon it to the readers of this journal."

The Orpheus in question was Ludwig van Beethoven, whose wanderings in the year 1812 had brought him to Linz, (probably from Teplitz via Prague and Budweis) where he purposed to spend a few weeks with his brother Johann, the apothecary. Ludwig's fraternal host gave him a large and pleasant room with a view of the Danube and the lovely country beyond, and there Beethoven settled down and proceeded to make music and trouble. For it was then and there that he completed the Eighth Symphony, and (as even the usually soft-spoken Thayer is forced to put it) took it upon himself to "meddle in the private concerns of his brother" which "he had no more right to do than any stranger."

Beethoven appears to have gone to Linz with the firm intention of breaking up the undiplomatically cordial entente that existed between his brother and Therese Obermeyer. For Therese, who possessed "a pleasing, though not beautiful face," had won the affections of Johann van Beethoven. He had made her his housekeeper—"and (as Thayer is forced to put it) something more."

Ludwig was enraged by the situation, and had no scruples about thrusting a rudely Comstockian nose into his brother's bourgeois romance. Johann seems to have entertained the quaintly perverse notion that his inspired device for retaining a servant was none of his brother's business, and he refused the proffered regulation of his ways. Ludwig, greatly exercised, and with what Thayer calls "an indefensible assumption of authority," betook himself to the police authorities and the bishop, and arranged for the forcible ejection of Miss Obermeyer from the town of Linz; whereupon the amorous apothecary very considerably checkmated Ludwig's maneuver by hastily marrying the lady.

It was during this turbulent period that the Eighth Symphony came into being—it was completed, according to Beethoven's autograph inscription, at Linz, in October 1812. Sir George Grove thinks that Beethoven's excitement at the time "no doubt considerably colored" the music, though he wisely observes that "it is exceedingly hazardous to attempt to connect Beethoven's music with the simultaneous events of his life." . . . . "At this time of life [writes Sir George] his love of fun and practical joking had increased so much in him as to have become a habit. . . . And as what he had in his mind was bound to come in his music, ... this comes out in the Eighth Symphony more than anywhere else; indeed, the work might with propriety be called the Humorous Symphony. . . .

". . . . But there was another humor which was as dear and natural to Beethoven as fun was—the intense love of beauty; and this is also found in the Allegretto, than which nothing is more lovely in the world; in the Minuet, especially the return to the subject by the bassoon—in the *cantabile* passages in the Trio; and in the serenely beautiful second subject of the Finale."

LAWRENCE GILMAN, *Philharmonic-Symphony Society of New York*

Symphony in D minor No. 9 (Opus 125, *Choral*)

"The *Choral Symphony*," Debussy has said, "has been enveloped in a fog of high-sounding talk and epithets. It and the celebrated 'smile of La Gioconda,' to which there has become affixed forever the label of 'mysterious,' are the two masterpieces that have generated the greatest amount of foolish talk; one is astonished that the symphony has not remained buried under the mass of prose it has called forth."

Perhaps no composition in all musical literature, from the time of its first performance, to the present day, has provoked as much discussion as has the Ninth Symphony. The bone of contention is not the main body of the work, but the musical value of the choral ending. . . . The master himself seems to have been doubtful of the fitness of ending his symphony with a choral movement. He voiced these misgivings even while writing the present last movement. After the first performance of the symphony, he is said to have told friends that he was convinced that the vocal ending was a mistake, and that he intended substituting an instrumental one for it.

The symphony was first produced at the Kaernthnerthor Theater, Vienna, on May 7, 1824. Schindler, Beethoven's biographer, tells us that the composition was received with a frenzied outburst of joy. But what did the press have to say? Not until the issue of July 1, 1824, did the *Allgemeine Musikalische Zeitung*, the leading Viennese musical periodical, offer a review. After dwelling on the ovation Beethoven received, it goes on to say: "The Symphony can boldly measure up to its sister symphonies. Its originality suffices to prove its paternity, but everything in it is new. . . . art and truth celebrate here their absolute triumph, and one can say in all justice *Non plus ultra!*"

. . . . In England, the Symphony had its premiere with the

Philharmonic Society of London, March 21, 1825. The work met with but little favor with public and critics alike. . . . Schumann, in reviewing a concert which included the Ninth Symphony, says: "It seems as if one were finally understanding that in this (Symphony) the great man has given us his greatness."

Philadelphia Orchestra Journal

Symphony in C major *(Jena)*

In 1909, Professor Stein found in the archives of the Academic Concerts in Jena a symphony in C major. There was no score but a complete set of parts of which two bore the name of Beethoven in the copyist's handwriting. Some of the corrections seem to be in Beethoven's handwriting. Stein's opinion that the work was written between 1787 and 1790 while Beethoven was still in Bonn has been widely accepted. Aside from casual echoes that might have been Haydn or Mozart there is much that points to later Beethoven. Unconventional modulations, bold climaxes and unexpected turns of harmony, melody and rhythm—definitely out of the sphere of the eighteenth century—resemble the other nine symphonies, in spirit.

From the PROGRAM MAGAZINE, *Saratoga Spa Music Festival*

Concerto for violin in D (Opus 61)

Beethoven's one contribution to the literature of the violin concerto was written in 1806. The earlier portion of that year had been devoted to the composition of the Three String Quartets (Opus 59) dedicated to Count Razumovsky and to the Fourth Symphony (Opus 60); it may therefore be surmised that the Concerto for violin was created late in the year. It is reasonably certain that the completion of the work was not brought about until the end of December 1806, for Beethoven's concerto was written for the violinist, Franz Clement, who played it for the first time at his concert in the Theater-an-der-Wien on the twenty-third, and who, as the piece had not been finished in time for the rehearsal, performed it at sight. . . .

The concerto would seem to have been received with considerable enthusiasm by the audience. There was, however, a conservative element in the gathering which found itself unable to
follow with comfort Beethoven's flight into the rarefied regions of
art and inspiration, whither his genius had borne him. "Concerning Beethoven's concerto," wrote Johann Nepomuk Moeser in the
then newly-founded *Theaterzeitung*, "the judgment of connoisseurs
is unanimous; its many beauties must be conceded, but it must also
be acknowledged that the continuity is often completely broken,
and that the endless repetitions of certain commonplace passages may easily become tedious to the listener. . . . . ."

There is little reason to doubt that the concerto as given to
and performed by Clement in 1806 differed in many details from
the work familiar to modern audiences. The manuscript, now in
the possession of the Vienna Library, contains a mass of corrections put in with ink and pencil and red chalk, these being in
Beethoven's hand. Some of these in the solo part were probably
suggested by Clement after the performance. At the head of the
first page there stands the following punning title in the composer's
uncouth handwriting:

*"Concerto par Clemenza pour Clement, primo Violino e
direttore al theatro a Vienne."*

(Clement was appointed conductor for the Theater-an-der-
Wien in 1802, which position he held for nine years.)

Although completed in 1806, the Concerto was not published
until 1809, in which year it appeared with a dedication, *"a son
Ami Breuning, Secretaire Aulique au Service de sa Majeste L'Em-
pereur d'Autriche par Luis van Beethoven."* In August 1808,
Beethoven had brought out the work, arranged by himself as a
Concerto for piano, for which he composed a cadenza for the
first movement, with an obbligato part for the kettledrum, and a
shorter cadenza for the rondo. The piano arrangement the master
dedicated to Breuning's wife. (It would seem that Beethoven had
some intention of composing a second concerto for violin; for on
the title of the piano arrangement it is stated that the work is
arranged from "his first concerto for violin by Ludwig van
Beethoven." There is a fragment of a violin Concerto in C major
preserved in the library of the Gesellschaft der Musik-freunde in
Vienna.)

The orchestral accompaniment of the Violin Concerto is scored for one flute, two oboes, two clarinets, two bassoons, two horns, two trumpets, kettledrums and strings.

FELIX BOROWSKI, *Chicago Symphony Orchestra*

Piano concerto No. 1 in C major (Opus 15)

Of the five piano concertos established in the Beethoven canon the First, in spite of the numbering, was composed second, dating from 1797, whereas the one known as Second, in B flat major, Opus 19, was finished no later than March 1795.

The orchestral part of the C major Concerto is richer and fuller than that of the B flat, as befits a more mature work. It calls not only for flute, two oboes, two bassoons, two horns and the usual strings, but also for two clarinets, two trumpets and kettledrums.

Both concertos are alike in this, however, that they belong to the Haydn-Mozart period of the composer's youth. The C major is dedicated to the Princess Odescalchi and was probably performed first at a benefit concert given by Beethoven in Vienna in the spring of 1800.

The opening movement of the Concerto (Allegro con brio, C major, 4-4) starts off with a brilliant orchestral tutti, which presents the first and the second themes and deals with them at some length before the entrance of the piano. In the development section the voice of a Beethoven no longer subservient to his elders is heard unmistakably. Midway in the last tutti there is the traditional pause for the cadenza.

The second movement is a Largo (A-flat major, 4-4), graced with a flowing Mozartean melody principally for the piano. Here and there the clarinet takes up the theme, giving the piano an opportunity for delicate ornamental weavings. It has been held that in no other early work by Beethoven is the clarinet treated so sympathetically.

For the Finale (Allegro scherzando, C major, 2-4) Beethoven has recourse to the rondo form, so much favored by Haydn for sympathetic conclusions. The chief subject is deliciously suggestive of Haydn in its rhythmic capriciousness, and again and again in this movement the listener cannot but be reminded of Beethoven's own First Symphony (1799-1800), also in the key of C major, which abounds in humor and high spirits. The rest of the thematic material is delightful, too. There are three pauses for cadenzas.

PITTS SANBORN, *Philharmonic-Symphony Society of New York*

Piano concerto No. 2 in B-flat major (Opus 19)

The first performance of the B-flat Concerto took place at a benefit concert given on March 20, 1795, at the Burg Theater in Vienna, for the Widows' Fund of the Artists' Society, at which Beethoven was the interpreter of the solo part—his first public appearance in Vienna. The Second Concerto was published in 1801, with a dedication to *"Monsieur Charles Nikle, noble de Niklesberg, Conseiller Aulique de sa Majeste Imperiale et Royale."*

Beethoven did not consider this concerto one of the works of which he had most reason to be proud. In writing of it to the publisher Hofmeister in Leipzig, he put the work down among others which he wished to dispose of as "a pianoforte concerto which I really do not give out for one of my best," but he hastened to add: "Still it will not disgrace you to print it."

In another letter, written in the following month, Beethoven made a second reference to the composition: "The concerto," he said, "I value only at ten ducats, because as I have already written I do not give it out as my best . . . ."

FELIX BOROWSKI, *Chicago Symphony Orchestra*

Piano concerto No. 3 in C minor (Opus 37)

According to the inscription on the manuscript of this concerto, it was composed in 1800, the year of the First Symphony, the E-flat septet, the first six string quartets, the piano sonata in B-flat, Opus 22, and perhaps the ballet *Die Geschoepfe des Prometheus* and the oratorio *Christus am Oelberg*. It was not brought out, however, till Beethoven gave the astonishing concert of April 5, 1803, at the Theater-an-der-Wien in Vienna. On that occasion the Second Symphony and *Christus am Oelberg* were also performed for the first time, and the program included further the First Symphony. As if all that were not enough for one session, still other works had been rehearsed but were omitted lest the concert should be too long! However, it began at the suitably early hour of six in the evening.

Of the single rehearsal, which had started that morning at eight, Ferdinand Ries writes amusingly: "It was a terrible one, which lasted two hours and a half and left Beethoven more or less discontented. The Prince Karl Lichnowsky, who had been present from the beginning, ordered large baskets of bread and butter, cold meat and wine to be brought in. He invited in a friendly manner everyone to partake, and all helped themselves with both hands. As a result everybody grew good-humored."

In those days, and for long afterward, it was not the custom for a pianist to play without the music before him. Though Beethoven was the pianist in his own concerto and the manuscript of the piano part consisted only of a few notes scattered here and there, Beethoven played from such notes as were there and to turn each page when he gave the signaling wink he even had the Ritter von Seyfried. It is interesting to learn that according to the critic of the *Zeitung für die Elegante Welt* the Concerto was less liked by the audience than either of the symphonies, and though Beethoven had long been recognized as an admirable pianist, the performance failed completely to satisfy the public.

In the C minor Concerto we observe Beethoven's style in transition from its first period to its second . . . . The work is dedicated to Prince Louis Ferdinand of Prussia, and the orchestral part calls for flutes, oboes, clarinets, bassoons, horns and trumpets in pairs, besides kettledrums and the usual strings.

PITTS SANBORN, *Philharmonic-Symphony Society of New York*

Piano concerto No. 4 in G major (Opus 58)

The exact date of composition of this Concerto is not known. It has been attributed to the years 1804, 1805 and 1806. The first performance was at one of two private subscription concerts in

March 1807, at the house of Prince Lobkowitz in Vienna. The first public performance was at the Theater-an-der-Wien, December 22, 1808. Beethoven was the soloist on both occasions. . . . . It is dedicated to the Archduke Rudolph.

There is a striking similarity of mood between Beethoven's violin concerto of 1806 and the Fourth Piano Concerto which was probably completed in the same year. They are both conspicuously lacking in mere surface brilliance, and they require soloists, as well as conductors and instrumentalists, of taste and sensitivity to bring to life their spacious and dreaming moods. No doubt it is for these very reasons that both concertos were long neglected. Many years passed before the violin concerto made its way, and so it was with the Fourth Piano Concerto which assumed its rightful place with the more obviously impressive third and fifth only after a lapse of years.

It was Mendelssohn, champion of many a neglected score, who resurrected the forgotten G major Concerto. He himself played it with the orchestra of the Gewandhaus Concerts in Leipzig on November 3, 1836. Schumann, who was present, preserved the thrill of discovery in moving words:

"This day Mendelssohn played the G major Concerto of Beethoven with a power and a finish that transported us all. I received a pleasure from it such as I have never enjoyed, and I sat in my place without moving a muscle or even breathing—afraid of making the least noise."

If the origin of this concerto is mysterious, there is a fairly full account of its first public performance at the Theater-an-der-Wien, December 22, 1808. Beethoven had advertised the concert a week ahead in the *Wiener Zeitung,* but the theater was not filled. The small audience huddled in cloaks and furs in the extreme cold from half-past six till half-past ten—four hours!—to hear, in addition to this concerto, the first performances of the fifth and sixth symphonies, the aria *Ah, perfido,* a Latin hymn for chorus and solos, a fantasia for solo piano, the Fantasia for Piano, Chorus and Orchestra and the *Sanctus* from the C minor Mass. There had been trouble at the rehearsals, and Beethoven went to the concert in a difficult frame of mind. The audience was so completely lacking in Viennese notables that he called out to the sole representative of the aristocracy, Prince Wielhorsky, when he walked to his seat, and made him an elaborate bow which was as ironical as it was friendly. . . .

Reichart, however, who was present, has left us a pleasant word about the composer's performance of his own concerto:

"He played a new fortepiano concerto of enormous difficulty with astounding cleverness in the fastest possible *tempi*. The Adagio, a masterly movement of beautifully developed song, he sang on his instrument with a profound melancholy that thrilled me."

GEORGE H. L. SMITH, *Cleveland Orchestra*

Piano concerto No. 5 in E-flat (Opus 73)

This, the last of Beethoven's five concertos for piano and orchestra, was composed in Vienna in 1809. A sixth was planned, and nearly all of the first movement was scored in 1814–1815, but Beethoven set it aside and never finished it. Perhaps this form of expression no longer appealed to him. Indeed, he appears to have been in no haste either to have the Fifth Concerto published or performed. It was played for the first time more than two years after it was completed—November 28, 1811, at Leipzig, by Friedrich Schneider. And it was played again by Beethoven's pupil, Karl Czerny, February 12, 1812, at Vienna, without making much of a stir, chiefly because of the nature of the program and the audience.

This concert was a benefit for the Charitable Society of Noble Ladies for Fostering the Good and Useful. Doubtless the good ladies were in the audience, together with some of those to whom they had sold tickets. And doubtless it was an audience pleased by the scene and aria from Mayr's *Adelasia ed Aleramo,* the aria from Gugliemi's *Debora e Sisera,* and the violin variations on the march from Mayseder's *Aline.* It was still more delighted by the "living pictures" interspersed between the musical numbers— Raphael's *Queen of Sheba,* Poussin's *Esther Fainting Before King Ahasuerus,* and Troyes' *Arrest of Haman.* It was scarcely the most appropriate occasion for the presentation of a "grand new concerto for pianoforte, dedicated to Archduke Rudolph," and played by a

gentleman whose name was misspelled on the program as "Cserny."
One critic complained that the concerto was too long. No doubt it
was for an audience impatient to see one of the noble ladies in the
role of the fainting Esther. Nevertheless, the concerto survived and
public appreciation of it grew, until someone dubbed it *The Emperor* to give it rank among its kind.

It is likely that Beethoven never played this concerto in a
public concert. Thayer marks his appearance in December 1808,
as "the splendid close of his career as a virtuoso." He was growing
increasingly deaf, and he had been criticised for playing too pow-
erfully—as it was natural that he should, being unable to judge
the loudness of sounds. But he seems to have played in 1814 at a
benefit for Schuppanzigh. Perhaps he turned *The Emperor* over
to Czerny because he was a little afraid of the Noble Ladies and
their program.

Cyril Arthur Player and W. K. Kelsey,
Detroit Symphony Orchestra

HECTOR BERLIOZ

(Born at Cote-Saint-Andre, France, near Grenoble,
December 11, 1803—died in Paris, March 9, 1869)

Had Berlioz become a doctor, like his father, music would
have lost one of its most romantic, passionate and original figures.
What medicine might have gained is another matter.

From all accounts he was a precocious and moody boy; a
handsome and willful young man. His mother, like Schumann's,
took the bourgeois attitude that musicians, theater folk and writers
were children of evil, and that no son of virtuous parents should
be identified with such shadows of Satan.

Unfortunately for Mme. Berlioz's peace of mind, a passion for music bloomed when Hector was scarcely quit of the schoolroom. An old flageolet, found in the attic, fascinated him and he made his father teach him the mechanism and the rudiments of playing it.

He prevailed upon his father, probably the more sensitive and artistic of his parents, to let him take lessons on the flute and guitar. He even tried to compose, without instruction, certain little pieces which were played by himself and a circle of amateur friends. And to the end of his days Berlioz played no other instruments except, as he said, "a little on the snaredrums!"

His father hoped ardently that he would follow his own profession and sent him to Paris to study medicine. But he nourished a guilty secret—he was taking private lessons in composition from Jean-Francois Lesueur. He spent his allowance by going to the opera and passed many an hour in the library of the Conservatoire, studying scores.

The crisis that finally drove Berlioz to a musical career was his first introduction to the dissecting room. He was so horrified that he jumped through a window in a panic of disgust. And when he fled shuddering to the opera that night, and heard Gluck's *Iphigenia in Tauride,* the die was cast.

Despite bitter opposition from his mother, he was allowed to enter the Conservatoire, but the first important test, a competition for the *Prix de Rome,* was a failure. His father threatened to cut off his allowance, his mother disowned him. Yet he had the courage to go home and plead for another chance. He won another year's respite.

Meanwhile he was composing and had brought out a mass for which he had contracted a debt of 1200 francs. He gave a first concert of his own works in the hall of the Conservatoire and won second prize, then failed once more in the race for the *Prix de Rome.* Meanwhile, an impatient creditor had informed his father of the debt of 1200 francs, which Berlioz had been trying to pay off from his allowance.

Dr. Berlioz, really exasperated and heeding more acutely the bitter lamentations of his wife, paid off Hector's debt and cut off his allowance. If his erring son would renounce music and return home all would be forgiven. But Hector resolved to stand by his art, come what may. He sang in the chorus of the theater, gave lessons and managed to eke out a scant living. He continued to study at the Conservatoire, tried again for the *Prix de Rome* and failed. A fourth trial in June 1830, finally won the prize. Apthorpe, in a program note for the Boston Symphony Orchestra, published on March 16, 1893, remarks:

". . . . he won the *Prix de Rome* with his cantata 'Saradana-pale.' This was tantamount to graduating with highest honors from the Conservatory; but to him it was important only for the five years' pension it brought him, a pecuniary benefit which was considerably lessened in his eyes by its entailing a three-years' residence at the Academie de France in Rome. He had already made no little stir in the Paris musical world as a composer, and would have far preferred staying there."

One need not set down all the details of his love affairs with Camilla Moke (afterward the pianist, Camilla Pleyel) and others, or of his marriage with Henrietta Smithson, the Irish actress of Macready's company or of his later one with Maria Recio; or of his returning adoration for Mme. Fournier, with whom he had fallen in calf-love at the age of ten.

Nevertheless, let us pause and regard Miss Smithson, if for no other reason than that she is the "Beloved" of the *Symphonie Fantastique.* From all accounts at the source, she was talented but far from a great actress. She had come down to Paris with the English company of William Macready for a season of Shakespeare at the Odeon. Berlioz saw the first performance and fell madly in love with the lady. The cumulative effect of one performance after another must have been psycopathic. Louis Biancolli writes that "once the sight of Henrietta in a stage lover's arms sent him screaming insanely out of the theater. Repeatedly rebuffed by his idol, Berlioz went into a prolonged fit of wild, wandering gloom. He walked the streets in a daze. He whined and whimpered through the countryside. He was haunted day and night by a composite image of Ophelia, Juliet and Henrietta. Who could blame the Irish girl for being startled out of her wits?"

She held out for six years and finally gave in. Berlioz had torn himself away from his idol long enough to embark upon his first tour of duty in Rome as a student at the Academie de France. Upon returning to Paris, he found Miss Smithson crippled by an accident and well-nigh bankrupt by the collapse of her own theatrical venture. So she finally yielded to his advances and they were married.

The union was unhappy from the start. She was given to moods and reproaches, he to wild outbursts of temperament and despair. The result was anything but serene. Crisis after crisis developed and at length they separated.

By the time he had done with the *Prix de Rome* and returned to Paris for good, Berlioz had become a famous figure in the musical world. Incurably romantic, yet touched with the wand of genius, he had transformed the stodgy orchestra of the day into a glittering, flexible instrument, incredibly sensitive and full of iridescent and prismatic hues. He was in truth the forerunner of modern orchestration as such, and his book on scoring and orchestral devices still is held in esteem by modern teachers and students.

Paganini commissioned him to write a concerto for a famous Stradivarius viola. The result was *Harold in Italy,* a piece at first rejected by the great Italian as giving insufficient expression to his priceless instrument. Yet Paganini withdrew his objections, apologized and sent Berlioz twenty thousand francs after he had played the work and studied it closely.

Berlioz also was commissioned by the government to write a Requiem commemorating the victims of the Revolution of 1830 and was appointed Librarian of the Conservatoire. Toward the end of 1842 he set out on his first concert tour to Germany, where he met with flattering success—and some criticism. He went to London to conduct the first season of the New Philharmonic Concerts in 1852.

An intestinal malady caused Berlioz untold suffering in his later years and the death of his only son, Louis, in 1857 was almost fatal to his fading health. He died in Paris in 1869 after a brief illness.

For many years Berlioz was musical critic for the *Journal des Debats,* was elected to succeed Adolphe Adam at the Institut de France in 1856 and was a Chevalier of the Legion of Honor.

Overture *The Roman Carnival* (Opus 9)

Berlioz's opera, *Benvenuto Cellini*, was performed in 1838, "was hissed with admirable energy and unanimity," according to the composer. "It was given three times. . . . and the work disappeared from the bills. . . . not to reappear till long afterwards."

Ten years later Berlioz wrote the *Roman Carnival Overture*, using material from the "unlucky" opera, and conducted it himself. The audience was delighted with the brilliant music: "The audience cried, 'Bis!' We played the overture over again."

The principal theme of the overture is taken from the *saltarello* which was danced and sung in the second act of Berlioz's opera.

Indianapolis Symphony Orchestra

Overture to *Benvenuto Cellini* (Opus 23)

The opera *Benvenuto Cellini*, was begun in 1834, but it was not until 1837 that we find the poet Heinrich Heine writing: "From Berlioz we shall soon have an opera. The subject is an episode from the life of Benvenuto Cellini, the casting of his Perseus statue. Something extraordinary is expected, since this composer has already achieved the extraordinary."

Excited over Cellini's swashbuckling memoirs and a short story, *Salvator Rosa,* by the German, E. T. A. Hoffman, Berlioz had appealed to the French poet, Alfred de Vigny, for a Cellini libretto. De Vigny, deep in other matters, referred the appeal to Leon de Wailly. The latter agreed to supply the text, but only after August Barbier consented to collaborate with him. De Vigny supervised the process, freely criticising and revising. Whatever the reason—perhaps a plethora of poetic gifts—the result was far from brilliant. "Audiences and critics almost to a man have found it ineffective, a bore," wrote Pitts Sanborn.

. . . . The novelty, produced at the Paris Opera on September 10, 1838, was accordingly a fiasco. Caricaturists flailed Berlioz as the composer of *Malvenuto Cellini.* . . .

Louis Biancolli, *Philharmonic-Symphony Society of New York*

Dramatic Symphony, *Romeo and Juliet* (Opus 17)

Ironically, Berlioz set to work on his symphony in the midst of a fresh crisis in his relations with Henrietta. The roles were reversed. As Madame Berlioz, Henrietta was now fanatically jealous. She was against his going on foreign tours. She reviled his friends. Her theatrical appeal was a thing of the romantic past, and so was her beauty. She finally took to drink. In short, Shakespeare had become drab, domestic routine. Henrietta leveled recurring charges of infidelity at her erratic spouse. These accusations "became so intolerable" that Berlioz "determined to justify them," as J. H. Elliot cynically observes. . . .

The dramatic symphony for solo voices, chorus and orchestra was composed between January and September in 1939. The great violin virtuoso Nicolò Paganini has been credited with the 20,000,-franc grant made to Berlioz at this time. Whether the money came from the pocket of the notoriously tight-fisted Italian or some unnamed benefactor, at least it was Paganini who brought the sum in person. Berlioz, assuming Paganini to be the donor, asked him to name the subject of his, Berlioz's, next composition. "I cannot advise you," said Paganini. "You know best what suits you best." Berlioz later records that after long deliberation, he "fixed on a choral symphony on Shakespeare's *Romeo and Juliet*, and wrote the words for the choral section, which Emile Deschamps. . . . put into verse for me."

. . . . Dedicated to Paganini, the symphony was performed at the Conservatoire in November 1839. Its success was immediate. Berlioz himself conducted an orchestra numbering 160 and a chorus of ninety-eight. Two further performances followed in December.

Louis Biancolli, *Philharmonic-Symphony Society of New York*

Symphony No. 1 in C major (*Fantastique*)

This symphony forms the first part of a work entitled *Episode de la vie d'un artiste (Episode in the Life of an Artist)*, the second part of which is the lyric monodrama, *Lelio, ou le retour a la vie (Lelio, or the Return to Life)*. Berlioz has published the following preface:

A young musician of morbid sensibility and ardent imagination poisons himself with opium in a fit of amorous despair. The narcotic dose, too weak to result in death, plunges him into a heavy sleep accompanied by the strangest visions, during which his sensations, sentiments and recollections are translated in his sick brain into musical thoughts and images. The beloved woman herself has become for him a melody, like a fixed idea which he finds and hears everywhere.

(The five movements are entitled: (1) Dreams, Passions; (2) A Ball; (3) Scene in the Fields; (4) March to the Scaffold; (5) Walpurgisnight's Dream)

In a preamble to this programme, relating mostly to some de-tails of stage-setting when the *Episode de la vie d'un artiste* is given entire, Berlioz also writes: "If the symphony is played separately at a concert . . . . the programme does not absolutely need to be distributed among the audience, and only the titles of the five movements need to be printed, as the symphony can offer by itself (the composer hopes) a musical interest independent of all dramatic intention."

. . . . The symphony is dedicated to His Majesty, Nicholas I of Russia.

WILLIAM APTHORPE, *Boston Symphony Orchestra*

LEONARD BERNSTEIN

(Born in Lawrence, Mass., August 25, 1918—now living in New York)

MR. BERNSTEIN may be called an infant prodigy among conductors, for he became assistant to Artur Rodzinski of the Philharmonic-Symphony Society of New York at the age of twenty-five. At sixteen hours' notice, without adequate rehearsal, he conducted a Sunday afternoon broadcast when Dr. Rodzinski was taken suddenly ill.

Since then he has conducted the New York City Symphony Orchestra, the Boston Symphony Orchestra, the orchestras in Cincinnati, Pittsburgh, St. Louis, Montreal and Vancouver, the Palestine Symphony Orchestra in Tel-Aviv, and others.

Mr. Bernstein also is among the brightest in a galaxy of young composers, and in his brief career has captured the fancy of his contemporaries, as well as the sincere regard of seasoned and celebrated musicians.

He attended the Boston Latin School and Harvard, where he majored in music, studying composition with Edward Burlingame Hill, A. Tillman Merritt and Walter Piston. He studied piano with Helen Coates and Heinrich Gebhard. Then he studied for two years at the Curtis Institute in Philadelphia—conducting with Fritz Reiner, orchestration with Randall Thompson and piano with Isabella Vengerova.

He continued his studies in conducting at the first two sessions of the Berkshire Music Center at Tanglewood, Massachusetts, under Koussevitzky and returned as his assistant in conducting for the third year. His symphony, *Jeremiah,* was given the award of the Music Critics' Circle of New York as "the most outstanding orchestral work by an American composer" heard in New York during the season of 1943-1944.

Symphony *Jeremiah*

Mr. Bernstein supplied the following information for the premiere performance on January 28, 1944 by the Pittsburgh Symphony Orchestra under the direction of the composer:

"In the summer of 1939 I made a sketch for a Lamentation for Soprano and Orchestra. This sketch lay forgotten for two years, until in the spring of 1942 I began a first movement of a symphony. I then realized that this new movement, and the Scherzo that I planned to follow it, made logical concomitants with the Lamentation. Thus the Symphony came into being, with the Lamentation greatly changed, and the soprano supplanted by a mezzo-soprano. The work was finished on December 31, 1942, and is dedicated to my father.

"The Symphony does not make use to any great extent of actual Hebrew thematic material. The first theme of the scherzo is paraphrased from a traditional Hebrew chant, and the opening phrase of the vocal part in the Lamentation is based on a liturgical cadence still sung today in commemoration of the destruction of Jerusalem by Babylon. Other resemblances to Hebrew liturgical music are a matter of emotional quality rather than of notes themselves.

"As for programmatic meanings, the intention is again not one of literalness, but of emotional quality. Thus the first movement ('Prophecy') aims only to parallel in feeling the intensity of the prophet's pleas with his people; and the scherzo ('Profanation') to give a general sense of the destruction and chaos brought on by the pagan corruption within the priesthood and the people. The third movement ('Lamentation') being a setting of a poetic text, is naturally a more literary conception. It is the cry of Jeremiah, as he mourns his beloved Jerusalem, ruined, pillaged and dishonored after his desperate efforts to save it. . . . .

Three Variations from *Fancy Free*

The composer has supplied the following description of the Jerome Robbins ballet for which the music was written:

"From the moment the action begins, with the sound of a juke box, wailing behind the curtain, the ballet is strictly young America of 1944. The curtain rises on a street corner with a lamppost, a side-street bar, and New York skyscrapers picked out with a crazy pattern of lights, making a dizzying backdrop. Three sailors explode on the stage; they are on shore leave in the city and on the prowl for girls. The tale of how they meet the first one, then a second girl, and how they fight over them, lose them and in the end take off after still a third, is the story of the ballet.

"The variations are heard during the scene in the bar. The sailors have succeeded in finding two girls. After a scuffle over who dances with whom, each of the three contestants for the two female companions presents a solo. It is in the nature of a competition. The first sailor (in the Gallop) aims to appeal with a kind of acrobatic, vaudeville showiness; the second (in the Waltz) with a mock gentility, abruptly shifting to bumps and dance-hall devices; the third (in a Danzon, modeled on the Cuban pattern), with seductive, Latin-American gestures, grotesquely parodied. The term 'variations' is used in its ballet sense, but the music also is in variation form, and the composer points to the opening notes of the Waltz as the nuclear subject of the three dances. Echoes of one of the main motives of the ballet as a whole also are heard in the course of the excerpts."

ARTHUR V. BERGER, *New York City Symphony Orchestra*

GEORGES (ALEXANDER CÉSAR LÉOPOLD) BIZET

(Born in Paris, October 25, 1838—died in Bougival, near Paris, June 3, 1875)

SON OF AN artisan turned singing-teacher, and of an amateur pianist, sister of the wife of Delsarte, this "simple, brave, honest man," as Philip Hale describes him, led a life of continual disappointment. At thirty-six he exclaimed: "It is extraordinary that I should feel so old." He died soon after, of overwork and heart disease.

Bizet's greatest masterpiece, *Carmen,* was a fiasco and not until some twenty-five years later, after innumerable performances elsewhere, did it gain a place of favor in the standard repertoire of the Opéra Comique in Paris where it had forty-seven performances in 1875.

Bizet's first teachers were his parents. He entered the Conservatoire at nine, to study under Marmontel, Benoist, Zimmerman and Halevy. He won his first prize before he was eleven, and many others thereafter; in 1857, he won his first *Grand Prix de Rome.*

Piano lessons and hack-work for music publishers occupied Bizet in the first years after his return from Italy. He yearned for the stage, and wrote four operas and three operettas, none of which was successful. In the full exuberance of his youth and hope, before the frustrations of his short life aged him prematurely, he wrote two symphonies full of gaiety and grace.

L'Arlésienne Suites Nos. 1 and 2

Alphonse Daudet's tragic drama of the French Midi, *L'Arlesienne,* (*The Woman of Arles*), was originally produced at the Théâtre du Vaudeville, Paris, on October 1, 1872. A feature of the production was the musical score provided by Bizet, who had already to his credit the operas *Les Pecheurs de Perles, La jolie fille de Perth* and *Djamileh,* though *Carmen* was still two and a half years in the future.

A peculiarity of Daudet's play is that the actual heroine never appears. The fatal Woman of Arles, for love of whom the youthful hero takes his life, illumines the whole action with her malignant flame, but only the report of her envenoming beauty comes like an incantation to Rose Mamai's farm from the unseen city on the Rhone. The tormented figure of Rose Mamai, the luckless boy's mother, stands out as the chief protagonist.

Of Bizet's score Camille Bellaigue has well said; "Everything is alive; even inanimate objects have a voice and tears. At night, the burning plain, before it falls asleep, responds to the cry of the shepherds calling home their flocks. A lament arises from the pool of Vaccares and hangs over the waters. Finally, at the nocturnal hour when the youth, mad with love, carries out his terrible suicide, the belated guests at his tragic wedding feast go their way singing. They sing that old Provençal air, the 'March of the

Kings,' in a lugubrious key—already it has an almost fune-real sound—and the shadow and deathlike stillness seems to engulf it like a last sigh, a last gleam of life."

Pitts Sanborn, Philharmonic-Symphony Society of New York

Symphony in C

The . . . . Symphony in C major dates from Bizet's seven-teenth year, and was virtually lost till a few years ago. According to Paul Bertrand, writing in *Le Menestral* of November 11, 1938, the work was found by the French musicologist Jean Chantavoine in the Conservatoire archives. Yet, when the Viennese edition was brought out in September 1935, a preface in three languages ex-plained that the Glasgow critic, D. C. Parker, had "called the at-tention of General Music Director Felix von Weingartner" to the autograph preserved in the Paris Conservatoire library. Where-upon Weingartner examined the score, and, keenly interested, conducted the belated world premiere of the eighty-year-old sym-phony at Basel, Switzerland, on February 26, 1935.

Performances quickly followed in Vienna, Paris and London. The symphony also formed part of the Bizet Centenary celebra-tion in Paris in October 1938. Two years later, on October 20, 1940, it entered the New York Philharmonic-Symphony repertory at a Carnegie Hall concert led by John Barbirolli. Sir Hamilton Harty had already introduced it to America with the Rochester Philharmonic in January 1936.

Stadium Concerts, New York

ERNEST BLOCH

(Born in Geneva, July 24, 1880—now living at
Agate Beach, Ore.)

BLOCH's name became familiar to musical Bostonians, in
particular, soon after the Flonzaleys introduced his quartet in B
minor to American ears. Subsequently, Philadelphia and New
York began to know him, too. When the Boston Symphony Orchestra gave the premiere performance of his Three Jewish Poems,
dedicated "to the memory of my father," Bloch conducted. This
was in March 1917, and in May of the same year, Bloch conducted
the Society of the Friends of Music in New York in a program
comprising the *Three Jewish Poems;* the premiere of the Hebrew
Rhapsody, *Schelomo;* the *Psalms 137 and 114;* and the *Israel Symphony.* He repeated this program with the Philadelphia Orchestra in January 1918.

Bloch's studies began at fourteen in Geneva, with Jacques-
Dalcroze, and he took violin lessons from Louis Rey. Four
years of this and he entered the Brussels Conservatory to study
with Eugene Ysaye, Schoerge and Francois Rasse. His next stop
was the Frankfort Conservatory under Ivan Knorr, of whom he
says: "He taught me to teach myself."

After Frankfort came Munich, with Ludwig Thuille, then
Paris. But his parents—his father had been a clock merchant—
were aging and needed a helping hand, so Bloch returned to Geneva, "where he decided to help run his father's business," says
Hall, "and to carry on with composition in his spare time."

Much to his surprise, the Opéra Comique in Paris decided to
produce his opera, *Macbeth.* After the premiere on November 30,
1910, critical blame and praise were strangely mingled.

Romain Rolland, who had seen the manuscript score of the
C-sharp minor Symphony and had heard *Macbeth,* went to Geneva and found Bloch working in his father's shop. It was through
Rolland, primarily, that the C-sharp minor Symphony, lying
fallow since his student days, finally came to performance in 1915.

Bloch came to the United States in the summer of 1916, as
conductor of an orchestra formed to tour with the dancer, Maud
Allan. He conducted a concert of the orchestra in Aeolian Hall,

59

New York, on October 21, 1916 and the last item on the program was his own youthful *River-Printemps*—probably the first public performance in America of any Bloch composition. But the tour collapsed heavily and Bloch found himself stranded in Ohio, seemingly without friends or money. Musicians heard of his plight and rushed to the rescue, arranging the various concerts aforementioned.

He taught in New York at the David Mannes School from 1917 to 1919 and won the Elizabeth Sprague Coolidge Prize in 1919 with his Viola Suite in Four Movements. Then he was appointed as director of the Cleveland Institute of Music, a post which he held until 1925.

He was invited to head the San Francisco Conservatory and in the following four years attained his greatest stature as a teacher of such distinguished figures as Roger Sessions, Randall Thompson, Douglas Moore, Bernard Rogers, Theodore Chanler, Herbert Elwell and Isadore Freed.

Bloch was able to devote the ten years after 1930 entirely to composition, by reason of an endowment, and embarked for Europe to compose a Sacred Service for the Reformed Synagogue on commission from Gerald Warburg. This occupied two years, and he returned to America late in 1938. Since then he has produced comparatively little, but these few scores, like the rest, are of first quality.

Upon his return, Bloch lived first in California, teaching at the University of California in Berkeley, then moving to Agate Beach, Oregon, where he now resides.

America: An Epic Rhapsody

This Rhapsody was unanimously selected as the winning composition among ninety-two manuscripts submitted in *Musical America's* "symphony contest." The prize was awarded to Bloch in June 1928. The jury, consisting of five conductors Messrs. Walter Damrosch, Hertz, Koussevitzky, Stock and Stokowski, agreed upon "December 20 and 21 as the dates of the first performances in New York, San Francisco, Boston, Chicago and Philadelphia."

PHILIP HALE, *Boston Symphony Orchestra*

The title page bears the inscription from Whitman: "O America, because you build for mankind, I build for you." On another page is found the dedication:

"This Symphony has been written in love for this country. In reverence to its past, in faith in its future, it is dedicated to the memory of Abraham Lincoln and Walt Whitman, whose vision upheld its inspiration."

The Symphony embodies a conception indicated by the composer: "A Union, in common purpose and under willingly accepted guidance, of widely diversified races, ultimately to become one race, strong and great. But, said Whitman: 'To hold men together by paper and seal or by compulsion is of no account. That only holds men together which aggregates all in a living principle, as the hold of the limbs of the body or the fibres of plants.' "

New York *Times,* November 11, 1928

Israel: A Symphony for Orchestra

Israel was composed during the interim of 1912-1915 and comprises only half of Bloch's original intention. Bloch proposed to supplement this meditative portion with an elated eulogy in celebration of the redemption of the Hebrews. For some reason the composer never wrote the second half and recently asserted that he never will do so. The first performance of the Symphony was given as part of an all-Bloch program by the Society of the Friends of Music at Carnegie Hall on May 3, 1917. The composer conducted.

. . . . The beginnings of *Israel* in 1912 constitute the commencement of a definite, salient era in Bloch's life. This is the period recording the sympathies kindred to the Jewish spirit. To it as well as the *Israel Symphony* belong *Trois Poemes Juif,* for orchestra; *Schelomo,* a rhapsody for 'cello and orchestra; a suite for viola; a string quartet and *Avodath Hakodesh,* a sacred service. . . .

Israel is a musical epoch intimating the perennial persecution of a noble race, blessed in tradition, scholarship and practical wisdom. The Symphony is not Jewish in the familiar concept of the name. It is void of such scenes as the contaminated ghetto; the corpulent, uncouth, greedy commission merchant; the gaudiness of a greed, determined to outdo the neighbor; instead, it vivifies the glory chronicled in the Scriptures.

. . . . The Symphony has two distinct movements, prefaced by a brief introduction; played, however, as a single unit. The work is dedicated to Mrs. J. F. D. Lanier.

Essay on Ernest Bloch, *La Revue Musicale*, April, 1923

Schelomo (Solomon): Hebrew Rhapsody for Violoncello and Orchestra

Schelomo was composed at Geneva, Switzerland, in the first two months of 1916. . . . It was performed in New York at a concert of the Society of the Friends of Music on May 3, 1917, Hans Kindler, violoncellist. The orchestral score was published in 1918. The piece was performed in Philadelphia by the Philadelphia Orchestra, Mr. Kindler, violoncellist, on October 27, 1922. The first performance in Boston was at a concert of the Boston Symphony Orchestra, Jean Bendetti, violoncellist, on April 13, 1923.

The *Musical Quarterly* of January 1921, published a translation by Theodore Barker of Guido M. Gatti's estimate of *Schelomo* contributed to *La Critica Musicale* of April-May 1920:

"The Hebrew rhapsody for solo violoncello with orchestra bears the name of the great king Schelomo (Solomon). In this, without taking thought for development and formal consistency, without the fetters of a text requiring interpretation, he has given free course to his fancy; the multiplex figure of the founder of the Great Temple lent itself, after setting it upon a lofty throne and chiseling its lineaments, to the creation of a phantasmagorial entourage of persons and scenes in rapid and kaleidoscopic succession. The violoncello, with its ample breadth of phrasing, now melodic with moments of superb lyricism, now declamatory and with robustly dramatic lights and shades, lends itself to a reincarnation of Solomon in all his glory, surrounded by his thousand wives and concubines, with his multitude of slaves and warriors behind him. His voice resounds in the devotional silence, and the sentences of his wisdom sink into the heart as the seed into a fertile soil. . . .

PHILIP HALE, *Boston Symphony Orchestra*

Concerto Grosso: String Orchestra with piano obbligato

The first performance of the Concerto Grosso was a semi-private one at Cleveland, Ohio. Carl Engel heard it on this occasion and brought it to the attention of Birchard who published the score. Since then it has been played at the Hollywood Bowl by the Los Angeles Symphony Orchestra with the composer conducting; by the Chicago, Boston and Philadelphia orchestras; and in Germany, Italy and England. The first New York performance was under the direction of Koussevitzky, who later played it in Paris.

Bloch conducted the work at the Washington Chamber Music Festival in October 1926.

HENRY BELLAMANN, *Society of the Friends of Music*

ALEXANDER PORPHYRIEVICH BORODIN

(Born in St. Petersburg, Russia, November 12, 1833
—died in St. Petersburg, February 28, 1887)

THIS TALL, dark florid man, with his drooping mustachios and air of detached melancholy, was a little bit of everything in his time. Frederick H. Martens calls him "a kind of human musical paradox . . . a great musician, who was only a musical amateur; an eminent physician and chemist, an unwearied philanthropist, an ardent defender of woman's rights (and in Russia, at that) at a time when the whole movement for the emancipation of women was in its infancy."

Borodin was born the natural son of Prince Guedeanoff. The family lived comfortably on a government pension and Alexander's father "indulged his early leaning toward music."

Beginning to compose at nine, at thirteen he had written a concerto for flute and piano and, just to be sure of polite approval in the musical vein of the time, a Trio for two violins and 'cello on themes from Meyerbeer's *Robert le Diable*.

But his father must have thought the life of a musician hardly commensurate with his illustrious name. He entered his son at the Academy of Medicine, doubtless hitting upon this as a useful and dignified calling.

So he began his study of *materia medica* in 1850, the while attending concerts and cultivating the 'cello and flute. Naturally, his teachers feared that music and medicine did not mix very well, but apparently he was able to keep them apart, for he was graduated and appointed surgeon to an army hospital in 1856, and obtained his degree as a qualified physician two years later.

In Heidelberg, where he was doing postgraduate medical work, he met his future wife, Catherine Sergeievna Protopova. His return to Russia in 1862 coincided with his appointment as assistant lecturer at the St. Petersburg Academy of Medicine; and in the following year he married Catherine Sergeievna.

It was at this time that Borodin began to devote more time to music. While studying with Balakireff, he started his First Symphony in E-flat. Though it took him five years to write, it was the first of his works to bandy his name in melodic circles outside Russia, after its premiere by the Russian Musical Society in 1869. About this time, too, he discovered the song as a short effort with a quick return. Of a round dozen or so, three or four stand out, notably "The Fairy Garden," "The Sleeping Beauty," both dedicated to Rimsky-Korsakoff, and a noble ballad, "The Sea."

Prince Igor, the four-act opera that one may call his lifework, was begun in 1871 and was still uncompleted when he died. Rimsky-Korsakoff and Glazounoff orchestrated most of the work and filled in the gaps. "The overture," says Martens, "had never even been set down in notes, but fortunately Glazounoff had heard Borodin discuss it and play it so frequently on the piano that he was not only able to reproduce it faithfully, but could also develop the orchestration in accordance with Borodin's own wishes. To Rimsky-Korsakoff and Liadow, according to the former's memoirs, is due the brilliant instrumentation of the *Prince Igor* dances."

As a scientist he was a pioneer. "He made his mark," says Grove, "in the world of science no less clearly than in that of art, leaving not only numerous important treatises on chemistry, but taking an active part in founding the School of Medicine for Women, where he lectured from 1872 until the day of his death."

He was induced by Balakireff, his one-time teacher, to join what became the "Famous Five" of St. Petersburg—Cesar Cui, professional military man and formalist; Moussorgsky, described as "the greatest of all musical amateurs," and Rimsky-Korsakoff, who began life as a sailor.

Borodin lived almost like an anchorite. He had an apartment, a wide and rambling sort of place from all accounts, on the ground floor of the St. Petersburg School of Medicine. He and his wife were always adopting destitute or otherwise unfortunate children and bringing them up.

Their hospitality and generosity were limitless. Money was a convenience but really meant very little to them. They had an uncomfortable little cottage in the country and when they went there they lived like peasants and went about barefoot, ate the simplest fare and wore peasant clothes. In the winter, Madame Borodin's health failed and usually she sought the drier climate of Moscow. It was during one of these separations that Borodin died suddenly.

Martens says that "on the last evening of Carnaval, in 1887, he had gathered a group of friends at his home in Petrograd (*sic*), and was entertaining them. He sang and played portions of the Third Symphony for his guests, and smiling and full of gaiety, needed no urging to take part in the informal dancing which had begun. Then, having entered upon an animated conversation, he suddenly grew pale, tottered and fell full-length, before his friends could hasten to his support. He was lifted from the ground dead—having passed away as the result of aneurysm of the heart.

His mausoleum, in the cemetery of the Alexander Nevski Convent, where Rubinstein and Tschaikowsky are buried, is a curious monument. From the rail which surrounds the tomb are suspended two wreaths; on one are graven some musical themes; but the other bears the formulas of chemical bodies, the titles of scientific books. For both the essay on fluorite of benzoin and the invention of the nitrometer, as well as *Prince Igor* and the second symphony were achievements of the same genial brain!"

Orchestral Sketch: *On the Steppes of Central Asia*

Prefacing the score of this Orchestral Sketch is the following description of the picture Borodin sought to evoke:

"Out of the silence of the sandy steppes of Central Asia come the sounds of a peaceful Russian song. Along with them are heard the melancholy strains of Oriental melodies, then the stamping of approaching horses and camels. A caravan, accompanied by Russian soldiers, traverses the measureless waste. With full trust in its protective escort, it continues its long journey in carefree mood. Onward the caravan moves. The Songs of the Russians and those of the Asiatic natives mingle in common harmony. The refrains curl over the desert and then die away in the distance."

We have Borodin's word for it that whatever European prestige he enjoyed as composer he owed to this tone picture of the Asiatic plain. To his friend Gavrouschkiewitch he wrote in May 1886: "The most popular of my works abroad is my symphonic sketch, *Dans les steppes de l'Asie Central*. It has made the rounds of Europe from Christiania to Monaco. In spite of its patriotic program—the success of Russian arms in Asia—the work has been encored almost everywhere and often repeated by request, as at the Strauss concert in Vienna and the Lamoureux concerts in Paris."

Borodin wrote the "sketch" in 1880 for the twenty-fifth anniversary of the reign of Czar Alexander II, which explains the reference to "patriotic program." Among the imperial festivities was an exhibition of *tableaux vivants* (living pictures) drawn from episodes in Russian history.

Central Asia, with its teeming legend and brooding expanse,

long fascinated Borodin. His opera *Prince Igor*, is a tribute to the exotic mystery and mingled culture of the region. In much of Borodin's music we sense the ominous stillness of the vast waste, with its wandering tribes and plodding camels, and remember Shelley's line—"the long and desert sands stretch far away."

A year after composing *On the Steppes of Central Asia*, Borodin paid his second visit to Liszt at Weimar. Thoroughly enchanted with the work, Liszt persuaded Borodin to make a four-piano arrangement before he tackled anything else. The dedication of the "Orchestral Sketch" is to "Dr. F. Liszt". . . .

LOUIS BIANCOLLI, *Philharmonic-Symphony Society of New York*

Symphony in B minor No. 2 (Opus 5)

. . . . The alert searcher of new paths, Franz Liszt, was one of the first westerners to ferret out the nationalist group, and to follow their early gropings. When Borodin brought him his new score in 1877, Liszt was delighted—advised him to alter nothing, to pay no attention to the suggestions of those who found it "strange.". . . .

The Symphony made its way readily into general favor. It was much liked when performed in the early Eighties in Germany and Belgium. Yet it took more than twenty years to reach America. A performance is on record in Cincinnati, in the season of 1898-1899. Artur Nikisch introduced it to Boston at a concert by the orchestra January 4, 1890.

. . . . Borodin lingered over his Second Symphony for six years (1871-1876.) He had put aside the opera *Prince Igor* (which he never finished) to compose the symphony. After completing the first movement, in 1871, he paused to plunge into the project of the operatic ballad *Mlada* which Gedeunov, director of the Russian Opera, wished to mount. . . . the venture fell through, owing to the expense involved. . . .

. . . . The first performance of the Symphony had a doubtful success. Ivanov, in the *Novoe Vremya*, wrote: "Hearing this music, you are reminded of the ancient Russian knights in all their awkwardness and also in all their greatness. There is heaviness even in the lyric and tender passages. These massive forms are at times tiresome; they crush the hearer."

JOHN N. BURK, *Boston Symphony Orchestra*

Excerpts from *Prince Igor*

Ironically, Borodin did not complete *Prince Igor* himself though he had devoted years to research into the history, customs and vagaries of the Polovtsians, a people of Central Asia around whom the dramatic subject evolves. It was completed by Rimsky-Korsakoff and Glazounoff, both of whom labored long and lovingly on the remaining unorchestrated portions, as well as on the development of certain sketches made by Borodin.

The idea for the piece was suggested to Borodin by the Russian critic Vladimir Stassoff. That was in 1869. Twenty-one years later, on November 4, 1890, *Prince Igor* was given its premiere performance at St. Petersburg. Borrowing a good deal of the thematic material for the dances and choruses from actual mleodies of tribes, Borodin placed them in the second act of his work.

Borodin and Stassoff collaborated on the libretto, which is mostly derived from the *Epic of the Army of Igor,* an apocryphal early Russian poem which appeared in 1800 and was regarded by many Russian scholars as a literary fraud.

The action of the opera takes place in twelfth-century Russia. Prince Igor Severski, setting out on a campaign against the Polovtsians, leaves his wife, Jaroslavna in the care of his brother-in-law, Prince Galitzky. Igor's son, Vladimir, accompanies him on the expedition. During their absence Galitzky, together with two deserters, concocts a plot for the overthrow of the government, and when Jaroslavna hears of it she denounces him. Almost at the same time the news arrives announcing Igor's defeat.

Igor and his son, in the meantime, are being regally entertained by their conqueror, the Khan Konchak. And Ovlour, a Polovtsian convert to Christianity, even offers Igor and Vladimir an avenue to escape. But the prisoners refuse, at first, being too honorable for such underhanded devices. Not the least important reason, however, is the fact that Vladimir has fallen in love with Konchakovna, the Khan's daughter.

When some Polovtsian warriors return from Igor's capital city, Poultivle, with many prisoners and much booty, the royal captives change their minds and make the break for freedom in the company of Ovlour. But Little Konchakovna, who is informed of the attempt, turns them in, loving Vladimir as much as she does. Vladimir is captured, but Igor and Ovlour get away. The last scene shows the return of Igor to his wife, "who is weeping amid the ruins of her palace."

The dances, which are so well known in the concert hall, take place in the opera during the festivities in honor of Igor and Vladimir at the Polovtsian camp.

ROBERT C. BAGAR, *Philharmonic-Symphony Society of New York*

JOHANNES BRAHMS

(Born in Hamburg, May 7, 1833—died in Vienna,
April 3, 1897)

BRAHMS' grandfather was a tavernkeeper and his father ran away from home to be a musician. Papa Brahms ended up as the bass-viol player in a theater orchestra in Hamburg, where he married a woman seventeen years older than himself. They had three children—Elisabeth Wilhelmine Louise, who died in 1892; Johannes and Friedrich, for many years a successful music teacher in Hamburg, who lived until 1886.

Johannes, born in "a fine old six-storied house now called No. 60 Speckstrasse," led a fortunate and rather uneventful life.

Here is no tale of poverty and woe, no Beethoven despair or Schubert frustration. Rather did the life of Brahms, despite the efforts of friends to entangle it in strife and wranglings, resemble some deep and placid stream, moving gently and with dignity beside the forest aisles.

The usual early leanings toward music found ready encouragement. Naturally, his first lessons came from his father.

While studying the piano at this time, he was composing very much in secret, although Marxsen was supervising all of his theoretical work. As a graceful acknowledgment of his debt to this wise and beneficent instructor, Brahms dedicated to him the Second Piano Concerto in B flat (Opus 83).

He gave his first concert at sixteen with Theodore Wachtel, and a recital of his own a month later, April 1849, at which he played the Beethoven "Waldstein" sonata and a "Waltz" fantasy of his own.

Brahms and the gypsy violinist, Remenyi, toured North Germany in 1853. When they got to Hanover, Remenyi brought Brahms to see Joseph Joachim, who recognized immediately that the boy had an unusual gift. It was a fortunate meeting, for Joachim asked him to come again; Brahms did and subsequently met Liszt and Schumann through his host.

It was Schumann's famous article in the *Neue Zeitschrift für Musik* that really launched Brahms upon his career. For the article provoked the first of many published controversies concerning his music.

"Many new and remarkable geniuses have made their appearance," wrote Schumann. "I thought to follow with interest the path-ways of these elect. There would, there must, after such promise, suddenly appear, one who should utter the highest ideal expression of the times, who should claim the mastership of no gradual development but burst upon us fully equipped, as Minerva sprang from the head of Jupiter. And he has come, this chosen youth over whose cradle graces and heroes seem to have kept watch. His name is Johannes Brahms."

The encouragement of such eminent figures as Liszt and Schuman induced Brahms to give up the tour with Remenyi. He need an official post at this time, a connection that would give him practical experience with the orchestral and choral repertoire. And as always when Brahms needed something, he got it. Two tempting offers came along, "one," says Grove, "with the Cologne Conservatorium, which he refused, and one from the Prince of Lippe-Detmold, which he accepted."

For four years he was director of the court concerts and of the choral society. These unexacting duties gave him plenty of time for composition and the development of his artistic nature. Upon his resignation, he returned to Hamburg. His public appearances were few and at none of these concerts did he play anything new, until the advent of the D minor Piano Concerto at a Gewandhaus concert in Leipzig on January 27, 1859. Opposition rose in a cloud and it took nearly twenty years of playing all over Germany by himself and Clara Schumann to gain for it a measure of public favor.

He went to live in Vienna in 1862, attracted probably by an interest in Hungarian music which had been awakened by Remenyi. There he gave several important concerts and was appointed conductor of the Singakademie. He "threw himself with characteristic devotion into the congenial work of giving fine performances of the choral works of Bach, Beethoven, Schumann and others," says Grove. He gave up the appointment after a year, subsequently became conductor to the Gesellschaft der Musikfreund in Vienna for three years, then undertook a memorable series of concerts with Joachim in Germany and Switzerland.

"Otherwise," says Grove, "the record is one of peaceful, honored work in his apartment at Karlsgasse No. 4 (third floor), varied by holiday journeys often to Italy, and in later years to such resorts as Thun, Ischl, Baden-Baden or Carlsbad."

He and the Schumanns were fast friends and when Robert became mentally ill and was taken to an asylum after an attempt at suicide, Brahms and Clara sought comfort and counsel from each other. She was a famous pianist at the time and a tireless champion of Brahms' music.

At the funeral services for Clara Schumann, whom he loved, Brahms caught a chill. He was already very ill of cancer of the liver and the consequent cold aggravated the malady of which he finally died.

Academic Festival Overture

There are the makings of a first-rate short story in the circumstances surrounding the composition and first performance of this Overture. Somewhat exaggerated, they are as follows:

In the year 1880 the musical politics of the German-speaking world were divided sharply in two camps. Those who rallied around Wagner anointed themselves with the oil of liberation and progressivism. They stood for freedom and the "art of the future." Those who rallied about Brahms flew the banner of classicism, the tried and true, and the "precious heritage of the past."

So, therefore, when the University of Breslau conferred upon Brahms an honorary degree, it was lending its corporate authority on behalf of the conservative party, and was by implication (at least for purposes of this short story) administering a corporate rebuke to the Wagnerians. Brahms responded to the honor with the composition of an overture which he conducted on the occasion of the conferring of the degree.

Picture then the faculty of Breslau in solemn convocation assembled, in the full dignity of its robes and beards, to listen to the work dedicated to it by the blond lion of German conservatism. Picture the faculty's anticipation of something learned, massive, polyphonic, ingenious with canons and ponderous with fugues. Picture, also, the expressions behind the beards when the first melody of the overture turns out to be that of a freshman beer-drinking song, followed by a long string of tunes and ditties known in all the saloons and taverns of the German university towns, and all this put together with much emphasis upon what Prof. Tovey calls the Great Bassoon Joke. Picture, finally, the smile on the face of the lion.

ALFRED FRANKENSTEIN, *San Francisco Symphony Orchestra*

Tragic Overture, Opus 81

Brahms often published his compositions in pairs of an antithetical character—well illustrated in the case of the *Academic* and the *Tragic* overtures. One is all joy and exuberance; the other profound tragedy.

The very naming of the *Tragic Overture* invites search for a story, a "program" but nothing is further from the practice of this composer. In fact, one must always turn to the music itself for its own explanation. Nowhere do we find less correspondence between the life of an artist and his work than in the case of Brahms. Between the unspectacular and generally prosperous and successful life of the composer with its almost commonplace events, and the deeply brooding, pitying, somber and sometimes tragic music there seem to be no points of contact. It was characteristic of the man that the only revelation of the strange depths beneath his difficult exterior should be in his music.

The *Tragic Overture* tells us more of Brahms than all of his biographies.

It opens in a major key. The preludial atmosphere—a rising curtain on an empty stage—is maintained by the utterance of the great theme which is heard later from the trombones. Maitland speaks of this opening as having "the hush of expectation." Thereafter it is not a tragedy, but tragedy that moves through the scenes of this imaginary drama. It is abstract tragedy—the deep, unanswered questions which Life asks of Destiny, and still unanswered, rises to the dignity of acceptance of the unknown.

Society of the Friends of Music, New York, 1929

Symphony No. 1 in C minor (Opus 68)

When Levi conducted the C minor Symphony at Munich a year after its premiere, the second movement and third were hissed; nor was it the Wagnerites, said Levi, who did the hissing, but the "classicists" so-called. The ineffable John S. Dwight, hearing the Symphony in Boston in 1878, brushed it aside as a work not to be mentioned in the same day with any symphony of Mendelssohn: "It will not be loved," he declared, "like the dear masterpieces of genius!"

Alas for critical prophesy! We no longer hiss the C minor of Brahms; and we most reprehensibly do love it. . . .

Brahms was middle-aged before this Symphony was finished (though it had been maturing for a decade and a half.) He completed it in September 1876, when he was in his forty-fourth year. Its ripeness and its confident mastery are evident throughout. If Matthew Arnold had been as responsive to music as to poetry he would have hailed this symphony as an imposing manifestation of "the grand style."

. . . . From the first notes of this Symphony we are aware of a great voice, uttering superb poetic speech. The momentous opening. . . . is among the unforgettable exordiums of music—a majestic upward sweep of the strings against a phrase in contrary motion for the wind, with the basses and timpani reiterating a somberly persistent C. The following Allegro is among the most powerful and draconian of Brahms' symphonic movements.

In the deeply probing slow movement we get the Brahms who is perhaps the most to be treasured; the musical thinker of long vistas and grave meditations, the lyric poet of inexhaustible tenderness, the large-souled dreamer and humanist—the Brahms for whom the unavoidable epithet is "noble."

. . . . The third movement (the *Pocco allegretto e grazioso* which takes the place of the customary Scherzo) is beguiling in its own special loveliness; but the chief glory of the Symphony is the Finale.

Here—if need be—is an appropriate resting-place for that diffident eagle among epithets, Sublimity. Here there are space and air and light to tempt its wings. The wonderful C-major song of the horn in the slow introduction to this movement, heard through a vaporous tremolo of the muted strings above softly held trombone chords persuaded William Foster Apthorpe that the episode was suggested to Brahms by "the tones of the Alpine horn, as it awakens the echoes from mountain after mountain on some of the high passes in the Bernese Oberland."

This passage is interrupted by a foreshadowing of the majestic chorale (trombones and bassoons) which, at the climax of the movement, takes the breath with its startling grandeur. And then comes the chief theme of the Allegro—that whole-souled and joyous tune of which even the loyal Miss Florence May says that it undoubtedly recalls to everyone who hears it the famous theme in the Finale of Beethoven's Ninth. Regarding this matter, however, Mr. Apthorpe spoke sanely. "One cannot call it a plagiarism," he remarked, "it is two men saying the same thing.". . . .

Of the culminating moment in the Finale—the mighty proclamation of the chorale in the coda. . . . even pedestrian and earthbound imaginations will know what he means; though this overwhelming peroration may remind them of the magnificent affirmation of Jean Paul: "There will come a time when it shall be light; and when man shall awaken from his lofty dreams, and find his dreams still there, and that nothing has gone save his sleep."

LAWRENCE GILMAN, *Philadelphia Orchestra*

The Famous Horn Call (Symphony in C minor)

In April of that year (1876) he (Brahms) was invited by Cambridge University to accept, with Joachim, the honorary degree of Doctor of Music. Brahms considered the offer, but eventually, for reasons variously given, declined it. Nor did Brahms, when the university repeated its offer, in 1893, of conferring doctors' degrees simultaneously upon him and Giuseppe Verdi, accept, saying that he was too old to stand by the side of the ever-youthful genius of Verdi. The degree, according to the traditions of Cambridge, could not be conferred *in absentia*. In 1877, the year after the premiere of the work at Carlsruhe, Brahms, as a token of good-will and appreciation of the honor offered him, sent Joachim to Cambridge, with the score and parts of the new symphony, which was played under Joachim's direction on the eighth of March.

The performance of an overture of Joachim and the Symphony of Brahms, which made the second part of the program, were conducted by the violinist. The rest of the program . . . was conducted by Charles Villiers Stanford, who has recounted the event in an article . . . later reproduced in the volume which Sir Charles published under the title of *Studies and Memories* in 1908. In that chapter he remarks:

"The Cambridge performance of the C minor Symphony attracted almost every musician of importance in England, and much interest was excited among Cambridge men by the curious coincidence that the horn theme in the introduction of the last movement was nearly note for note a quotation of the famous hour chimes of St. Mary's (the university church) bells."

. . . . Now, the pretty Cambridge theory is wrong. So are those wrong—and they are legion—who persist in maintaining that the horn theme is original with Brahms. . . . How can this be proved? The answer is devastatingly simple. . . . Correspondents have given us the lead. The horn theme may be found in the correspondence of Brahms and Clara Schumann. . . . There are six words in a letter from Brahms to Clara dated September 12, 1868 and evidently intended as a birthday greeting—Clara's birthday was the thirteenth. The sentence, without prefatory form of address, reads as follows: "Thus blew the Alpine horn today." Then follows a melody in notation, and under the melody a line of verse. The melody is note for note that of the horn motive of Brahms' finale.

OLIN DOWNES, *New York Times*, April 19, 1931

Symphony No. 2 in D (Opus 73)

After withholding the uncompleted manuscript of his First Symphony for fourteen years, Brahms followed this one with another in short order. The First he gave to Carlsruhe for performance November 4, 1876. Almost exactly a year later, Brahms entrusted his Second to the more important Vienna Philharmonic, through which, on December 30, 1877, Hans Richter first disclosed it to the world.

Brahms, who in his obscure twenties had been proclaimed by Schumann as the destined custodian of the symphonic tradition, bore his responsibility with unease. Knowing full well that the Weimarites were awaiting his first attempt at a symphony with poised and sharpened pens, he approached the form with laborious care, revising and reconsidering, doubly testing the orchestral medium. . . . The second came forth with apparent effortlessness and dispatch. Brahms sought no advice this time, but surprised his friends with a full-rounded manuscript.

Following the premiere, which took place late in December (probably on the thirtieth), Hans Richter conducting the Vienna Philharmonic, Brahms himself led the second performance which was given at the Leipzig Gewandhaus on January 10.

Eduard Hanslick, a pontifical spokesman of Brahms in Vienna, wrote a review which showed a very considerable penetration of the new score. Any helpful effect upon the understanding of his readers, however, must have been almost completely discounted by the following prefatory paragraph, a prime example of jaundiced Beckmesserism:

"It is well known that Wagner and his followers go so far as not only to deny the possibility of anything new in the symphonic form—i.e., new after Beethoven—but they reject the very right of absolute instrumental music to exist. The symphony, they say, is now superfluous since Wagner has transplanted it into the opera: only Liszt's symphonic poems in one movement and with a determinate practical program have, in the contemplation of the modern musical world, any vitality. Now if such absurd theories, which are framed solely for Wagner-Liszt household use, again need refutation, there can be no more complete and brilliant refutation than the long row of Brahms' instrumental works, and especially this Second Symphony."

In this way did the critics of that embattled period industriously increase the obscuring smoke of partisan controversy.

JOHN N. BURK, *Berkshire Symphonic Festival*

Symphony No. 3 in F (Opus 90)

The Third Symphony was completed in 1883 when Brahms was fifty years old. It was first performed December 2, 1883 at a Philharmonic concert in Vienna with Hans Richter directing.

Ferdinand Schaefer (conductor and friend of Brahms) calls the Third Symphony the *Wiesbaden Symphony,* as Brahms himself named it in a letter to his friend von Beckerath. Dr. Schaefer has supplied the following details:

In May 1883, Brahms attended the Music Festival at Cologne where he played his new Piano Concerto and conducted his Second Symphony, which was also rather new at the time.

"He had planned to spend the coming summer at Lake Zurich, but during the Festival he received an invitation from his friend von Beckerath to come to Wiesbaden. Brahms arrived in

Wiesbaden on May 17. He spent the summer in the villa of Frau von Dewitz and wrote of his 'perfectly fascinating quarters.' The villa was known for its wonderful high-ceilinged music salon.

"Here in this magnificent home, surrounded by the lovely forests of the Taunus Mountains, Brahms spent the whole of the summer working on his new symphony—the Third in F major. The emotional essence of his experiences and emotions during his long, lonely walks through the shades of the forest, the master put into the score of this work. He must have felt quite happy and content, judging from the mood of the first and second movements— the third and particularly the fourth—that is a different story.

"The working on a symphony he kept strictly a secret. Not even Clara Schumann, whom he visited in nearby Frankfurt, knew anything about it except a casual remark Brahms made to her, that he had worked on a new symphony. He left Wiesbaden for Vienna on the second of October, the finished score of his Third Symphony safely tucked away in his pocket.

"On November 27 he wrote from Vienna to his friend von Beckerath:

"'Dear Friend: I think you should be somewhat curious about my *Wiesbaden Symphony*. Next Sunday it is going to sound with timpani and trumpets; think a little of me here in Vienna.'"

Dr. Schaefer adds: "Many a time I have walked in the beautiful Taunus forests. Many a time I sat on the 'Brahms Bench' hidden in the forest loveliness. I felt if I were a composer, the spirit might have moved me and given me a motive for a tune or a theme."

The influence of the out-of-doors in the symphony is noted also by Dowans, who writes of the first and last movements as being "heard against a background of mountains, sky and singing winds."

Older, outmoded appraisals of Brahms refer to his "muddiness" of orchestral colors. Bakker writes: "Criticism showing such ignorance on the part of critics concerning the orchestra were made for the most part years ago and dwindled as soon as conductors had learned how to interpret Brahms' works and the orchestra how to play them. . . ."

LENORA COFFIN, *Indianapolis Symphony Orchestra*

Symphony No. 4 in E minor (Opus 98)

The last of Brahms' four symphonies proclaims the autumn of the master's career, that final period which, extending from his Third Symphony to the end of his life, shows him definitely formed. As he advanced in years, he no longer sought to conquer new fields, but devoted himself to the subtilization of familiar processes and the development of an ever higher degree of concentration. . . .

. . . . During the summers of 1884 and 1885 when he was writing the E minor Symphony Brahms read the tragedies of Sophocles. This reading may have influenced his creative work at that time. Max Kalbeck, whose fertility in inventing fanciful interpretations for Brahms' work is notable, was unable to see anything but gloom in the Fourth Symphony and he held Sophocles responsible. But other influences may have conspired to counteract the baneful effect of the composer's heavy literary diet and thus account for qualities in the symphony which Kalbeck failed to get. There were the delightful surroundings of the summer abode at Murzzusschlag, long excursions on the Semmering railway through lovely Styria, the happy visits of friends from Vienna, and the engrossing correspondence with the Herzogenbergs, to whom Brahms appealed for criticism. . . .

It was Brahms' practice to submit manuscripts to friends for approval. He usually accompanied them with some jocularly disparaging remarks as to their intrinsic worth. In letters to Buelow and Elisabet von Herzogenberg he intimates that the Fourth Symphony may have suffered from the same climatic phenomenon which caused the cherries never to ripen in the locality where he was staying. The reserve with which the new work was received by his friends at a private two-piano audition gave the composer real concern. He was almost dissuaded from trying to produce it publicly. "If persons like Billroth, Hanslick and you do not like my music," he said to Kalbeck, "whom will it please?" In spite of the uncertainty produced by the misgivings of his little circle he felt that he had written the symphony with conviction, so he resolved to "eat up the broth he had cooked for himself," and see the thing through.

. . . . A rehearsal was arranged with Buelow's orchestra at

Meiningen in October 1885. At Buelow's invitation a few distinguished musicians were present, among them The Landgraf of Hesse, Richard Strauss, then second conductor of the Meiningen Orchestra and the Scottish pianist, Frederic Lamond. Brahms arrived to conduct a private performance on October 25. The symphony was repeated by Buelow on November 1, and conducted several times again by Brahms on a tour through Germany and the Netherlands. Contrary to expectations the tour was a triumph and the Symphony was received everywhere with the warmest enthusiasm.

HERBERT ELWELL, *Cleveland Orchestra*

Violin concerto in D (Opus 77)

Brahms' Concerto for solo violin and orchestra is from the golden harvest years of his life, the time of his symphonies, his violin sonatas and other great chamber music. Moreover, it is the ripe fruit of the composer's lifelong friendship of the great violinist, Joseph Joachim. Indeed, the work was not completed until after he had had numerous consultations with this outstanding interpreter, whose advice and suggestion concerning violinistic practicality must have been invaluable, since Brahms himself did not play fiddle.

What is more, this is the only one of Brahms' four concertos in which a "time-out" period is especially designated for an old-fashioned cadenza, in which the soloist is expected to disport himself *ad libitum,* unattended. The ostensibly improvised concerto-cadenza, that showy mutilation of the musical form for the enhancement of the virtuoso's vanity, was a late eighteenth century fad, a sort of musical hoop-skirt. . . . .

It seems clear that he was setting a place here for his beloved friend, Joseph Joachim. Unfortunately, Brahms' loyalty and his appreciation of Joseph Joachim's musicianship led him to overrate the latter's creative ability. Joachim did not dare to improvise a cadenza, but carefully wrote one out. Later he had it published. Two generations of pious violinists, aware of its history, have dutifully played it; however, it has been generally felt that it represents a strain of inferior texture in Brahms' noble fabric. Other violinists, including Franz Kneisel and Fritz Kreisler, have also written cadenzas for this work—but it is difficult to supplant the living force of genius. There stands the concerto, one of the greatest masters' greatest works, with a piece of removable bridge-work.

ARTHUR LOESSER, *Cleveland Orchestra*

Concerto for violin and violoncello (Opus 102)

Once upon a time it was fashionable to say that Brahms' music is coldly intellectual, that his orchestration is "thick" and that his tone-coloring is gloomy. These were the critical dicta written and spoken, when Brahms was alive and writing down music to the limit of his genius. Some of the more determined reactionaries continued to speak and write these things long after the composer was dead, and long after the music-going public had accepted the music as superbly romantic, in the best sense of that word.

It is again becoming that fashion to say that, while Brahms knew how to write a song (although his essential vocal style never improved from first to last), he didn't know how to sustain a major work. He had vast technical resources, of course, but his "inspiration" was uneven. The "Double Concerto" has been the particular butt for these animadversions. It is "dry," say some. It is sheer technical trickery, say others. It has a few pleasant passages, but mostly it is dull, say still others. This commentator disagrees with all these statements: he believes it is superb music. So does Donald Francis Tovey, who is an eminent authority on practically all music.

Says Mr. Tovey, with characteristic frankness and humor:

"An important work for an unfamiliar combination of instruments is always at a disadvantage, mainly for the reasons which make the combination unfamiliar. One 'chinoiserie' by Ravel does not make an art-form of duets for violin and violoncello, and the sound of this combination of extremes is inherently strange without a middle part to bridge the gap. But the strangeness is not an absurdity, such as the combination of a violin and the double-bass would be. It is, when properly handled, a powerful stimulus to the musical imagination, alike of listeners, players, and composers.

"When Brahms brought the resources of his ripest experience to the handling of this combination together with an orchestra in the last of his orchestral works, the novelty for many years completely puzzled even those critics who took an official attitude of apostleship toward his music. The explanation of the difficulty is simple enough.

"Brahms did not make the new work a systematic display of the charms of the new combination, but simply expressed some of his most powerful and dramatic ideas, for all the world as if the combination of instruments was perfectly familiar. His critics and his admirers had, in short, to deal with Brahms' most powerful ideas as well as the unfamiliar combination, and it is pathetic to see the struggle of such a critic as Hanslick with this excursion beyond the lines laid down by him in his apostleship.

"The most familiar features of Brahms' way of developing themes, as for instance in the middle of the finale, where the phrases of the heroic middle episode are, in their restatement, dramatically interrupted by echoes through which the solo instruments are heard with their own ornamentation, similar devices in the middle of the slow movement as a whole—these and other equally normal features impressed Brahms' friends, as well as his hostile critics, just as if they were technical immaturities.

"There is no other explanation for this than the fact that everybody expected in a modern double concerto to hear as much of the violoncello, as if there were no violin, and as much of both as if there were no orchestra. In the meantime, Brahms did as Mozart and Beethoven always did: he treated his orchestra symphonically. Accordingly, the orthodox complaints became, first, that the solo parts were enormously difficult; secondly, that it was impossible to hear them; and thirdly, that there was not nearly enough of them. As for the pathos and the poetry of the work, all this general disappointment made it out of the question to speculate whether such qualities existed at all.

"It is to be hoped that at this distance of time there may be less difficulty in taking the work as it really comes. Any one who has made a study of musical first impressions in general and all concertos in particular, knows at once that the complaints described above are 'illusions'."

Mr. Tovey concludes his essay: "It is the privilege of works in sonata form that they can without weakening or falsifying tragic issues, bring their finales to a happy ending. The tragedy of the first movement has been told without flinching, but told within the quarter of an hour which contains symphonic movements on a large scale. Within that quarter of an hour, we have not time to see enough of the world in which such tragedies take place; and we are allowed to see its glorious melodies, its humors, its capacities for happiness in other movements. And so the whole concerto leads up to the wonderful tenderness of this last page, which finally breaks into joyful triumph, and brings the great work to an end."

WALTER WHITWORTH, *Indianapolis Symphony Orchestra*

Piano concerto No. 1 in D minor (Opus 15)

"Brahms to see me (a genius)"—Robert Schumann wrote in his diary September 30, 1853. Brahms was twenty years old, Schumann forty-three. . . . The next year Schumann's career came to a sudden and tragic end. Early in 1854 Schumann wrote to Joachim, "Night is beginning to fall." The persistent ominous melancholy, despair and mental confusion increased. Darkness closed in on his clouded mind. After attempting suicide, Schumann was removed at his own request, to a sanatorium where he died two years later.

The effect of this tragedy is said to be reflected in the first movement of Brahms' First Piano Concerto which he had started to compose that same year. The music of the Concerto was planned originally as a symphony. Then it became a sonata for two pianos. Later Brahms was persuaded by a friend that the work did not possess a form suitable to the dignity and worth of the music and turned the music into a Concerto for piano and orchestra. The first and second movements of the sonata became the first two movements of the Concerto, while the third movement became eventually a part of Brahms' *German Requiem*.

. . . . The Concerto in D minor was first performed at a court subscription concert in Hanover, January 22, 1859. Brahms played the piano part. Five days later, he played it for a larger audience in Leipzig. Brahms wrote Joachim: "It was a brilliant and decisive—failure. . . . In spite of everything, the Concerto will meet with approval when I have improved its form. . . . But the hissing was too much, wasn't it?"

There were three distinctive new features in the Concerto, which may account for the dismay of its first public audience. All technical display of the soloists as an end in itself is suppressed, as the themes and passages, embellishments etc., develop organically out of the whole. Second, an equal footing is maintained by both soloist and orchestra. Instead of being spotlighted, the soloist is a member of the orchestra, with no subordination of one to the other. And last, the Concerto approximates a symphony in the breadth, seriousness and beauty of its content and its lack of triviality.

Indianapolis Symphony Orchestra

Piano concerto No. 2 in B-flat (Opus 83)

In the spring of 1878 Brahms made a journey to Italy, of which he had long dreamed. Two good friends were with him, Carl Goldmark, the composer, and Theodore Billroth, eminent surgeon and excellent amateur musician, who was one of Brahms' few intimates. Goldmark went to Rome to supervise final rehearsals of his opera, *The Queen of Sheba,* but the other two went to Naples and Sicily, returning by way of Florence and Venice. Brahms confessed that he found the music of Italy ghastly (he said he heard an opera which consisted wholly of final cadences), but he could shut his ears to it, feasting his eyes upon cathedrals and palaces, upon sculptures and paintings. He wrote to Clara Schumann: "How often do I not think of you, and that your eyes and heart might know the delight which the eye and heart experience here. . . . We still have the best time of the year before us. It is quite early yet and everything is gradually coming out. You can have no conception of how beautiful it is, and you have only to take a little trouble to enjoy it in comfort. Next year you must see that you are free at the end of March, when I shall be able to be with you on the whole of the journey—by that time I shall have become a thorough Italian, and shall be able to be of use to you."

. After this first one, which occupied nearly a month, he returned to one of his favorite Austrian summer places, Poertschach, with its blue lake reflecting snowclad Alps. There, on the evening before his forty-fifth birthday, he sketched out themes for a second piano concerto, but he carried the project no further at that time.

Three years later, again at the same season, he made another visit to Italy. He returned to Vienna on his birthday, refreshed by the sights and sounds and scents of the Italian spring. The repetition of circumstances turned his attention again to the concerto sketches. He retired to Pressbaum, west of Vienna, on May 22. There, on July 7, he completed the work. . . .

Brahms, after his whimsical habit, made a mystery and a joke of the new work. He talked to Billroth about "some little piano pieces," and wrote to Elisabet von Herzogenberg the very day he had finished his task: "I don't mind telling you that I have written a tiny, pianoforte concerto with a tiny, tiny wisp of a scherzo. It is in B flat and I have reason to fear I have worked this udder, which has always yielded good milk before, too often and too vigorously. . . ."

The first public performance was in Budapest, November 9, 1881. Brahms was the pianist. Alexander Erkel conducted the orchestra of the National Theater for him, and Brahms later took over the baton to conduct his *Academic Festival* overture and his First Symphony. . . .

Brahms dedicated his B flat major Concerto "to his dear friend and teacher, Eduard Marxsen," which gives us a glimpse of a long and affectionate relationship.

R. L. F. McCombs, *Philadelphia Orchestra*

Hungarian Dances

Brahms wrote for the pianoforte (four hands) four sets of Hungarian Dances which are without an opus number. Books I and II were published in 1869; Books III and IV in 1880. Various settings have been made of them; among them one for violin and piano by Joachim; one from Nos. 5 and 6 by Pauline Viardot for two voices and piano.

Book I (Nos. 1, 3) and Book II (No. 10) were scored for orchestra by Brahms; Book II (Nos. 5-10) by Albert Parlow. Parlow, born at Torgelow, near Uckermuende, in 1822, died at Wiesbaden in 1888. At first a bandmaster, he became conductor of a great concert orchestra at Hamburg.

In 1853 Brahms, as a pianist, made a concert tour with the violinist Remenyi, whose real name was Hoffman, born in 1830 at Heves, Hungary, brilliant, eccentric, in appearance a French *abbé* of the eighteenth century, and in his youth a pupil of Joseph Boehm at the Vienna Conservatory. "He played the airs and dances of his native country with a fire and abandon that excited his hearers to wild enthusiasm," and, having genuine artistic endowment, played works by "the classical masters well, if somewhat extravagantly."

There is no doubt that he influenced Brahms in his love for Hungarian music; a love shown in many of his compositions. . . .

The dances, for the most part, if not all of them, are based on dances by Hungarian composers, Pecsenyansky, Sarkozy, Windt, Rizner, Merty, Keler-Bela, Travnik and others, or are paraphrases of them. Brahms was accused of taking unfair advantage of wandering musicians and enriching his fame and purse at their expense. Remenyi was loud, at the time of the publication and in his later years in the United States, in accusing Brahms of plagiarism; but very few of the tunes originated with Brahms; most of them were truly Hungarian, and Brahms put on the title page of the piano version "arranged for the piano." He made no reply, but the publisher Simrock made stir and bustle with affidavits and other documents, as well as protests. The names of the composers of the first ten dances were published in the *Allgemeine Musikalische Zeitung* of 1874 (p. 348).

PHILIP HALE, *Boston Symphony Orchestra*

MAX BRUCH

(Born in Cologne, January 6, 1838—died in Berlin,
October 3, 1920)

BRUCH was fortunate in his mother, a distinguished singer who came of a well-known and gifted musical family of the Lower Rhine. His father was a minor government official.

In his first theoretical studies at Beethoven's birthplace, Bonn, he showed unusual ability and won a scholarship to the Mozart Foundation at Frankfurt-am-Main, at the age of fourteen. He continued his studies under Hiller, Reinecke and Breuning at Cologne. His development was enhanced further by long visits to various musical centers and he finally settled down as a teacher in Cologne from 1858 to 1861. An operetta, *Scherz, List und Rache*, set to Goethe's text, was produced.

He met the poet Geibel in Munich and set his *Lorelei*, written for Mendelssohn, to music.

Bruch was appointed musical director of the Konzert-Institution of Coblenz, then *Kappelmeister* to the Prince of Schwarzburg-Sondershausen, a post he held from 1865 until 1870. Then he resigned to live independently, first in Berlin and later at Bonn, devoting himself entirely to composition.

He returned to Berlin in 1878 to succeed Stockhausen as director of the Stern Singing Society. Then came an offer to conduct the Liverpool Philharmonic Society which he accepted and spent the next three years in England.

The next twenty years were passed in Germany, conducting and teaching in Breslau and Berlin, but in 1910 he withdrew from public life and lived in retirement until his death in 1920. His reputation in this country would seem to rest upon the violin Concerto in G minor, although he is favored abroad for his choral and orchestral creations.

Concerto for violin No. 1 in G minor (Opus 26)

The first sketches which Max Bruch made for his G minor Concerto were set down as early as 1857, but the serious labor upon the work was done in 1865 and 1866, at Coblenz and Sondershausen. The first performance took place April 24, 1866 at the last winter concert of the Musik Institute at Coblenz. The performance had been twice postponed, owing to the illness of Johann Naret-Koning, concertmeister of the Mannheim Orchestra, who was to have given the first interpretation of Bruch's work. At the last moment Otto von Konigslow, concertmeister of the Gurzenich Orchestra and violin teacher in the Conservatory of Cologne, was called in, and he gave the first performance of the Concerto, Bruch directing the orchestra. Following the concert the composer thoroughly revised and overhauled the work, and in the summer of 1866 he sent it to Joseph Joachim for his criticism and advice.

That distinguished violinist did not forward any observations concerning the concerto until August 17, 1866, when he submitted a lengthy list of suggested alterations. It would seem that Bruch had doubts as to the expediency of calling his composition a concerto. In consequence of the constructive freedom of the opening movement, he bethought himself to term the work a "fantasie." Joachim opposed this notion. "I find," he wrote, "that the title 'concerto' is fully justified; for a fantasie, the last two movements are too completely and symmetrically developed. The different sections are brought together in beautiful relationship, and yet—and this is the principal thing—there is sufficient contrast. Spohr, moreover, called his *Gesangscene* a 'concerto.'" Bruch made a number of changes in the work, and in the revised form it was brought out for the first time by Joachim at Bremen, January 7, 1868, the conductor of the orchestra having been Karl Reinthaler, the director of the Singakademie there. An informal and not public rehearsal of the Concerto had previously been made in October 1867, at the Royal Theater, Hanover, with Joachim as soloist and with Bruch as conductor. The Concerto was published in 1868 with a dedication to Joseph Joachim, to whom Bruch also inscribed his third concerto, Opus 58.

FELIX BOROWSKI, *Chicago Symphony Orchestra*

ANTON BRUCKNER

(Born in Ansfelden, September 4, 1824—died in
Vienna, October 11, 1896)

AMONG the handful of musical pioneers still zealous in the
cause of neglected masters is F. Charles Adler, protege of Gustav
Mahler and Felix Mottl, and lately the conductor of the Saratoga
Spa Music Festival. Among Mr. Adler's continued enthusiasms is
the music of Anton Bruckner.

Some years ago (1938) Mr. Adler delivered a radio broadcast
entitled "Anton Bruckner; Genius and Saint." Because the text is
succinct and informative, and therefore suited admirably to the
purposes of this volume, I take the liberty of quoting a part of it:

"Half a century ago a sick old man sat at his desk in Vienna
and wrote a note of dedication into his still unfinished Ninth Symphony. The man was Anton Bruckner whose creative genius has
been hailed as successor to that of Beethoven, and the words that
he scribbled into this, his last symphony, were 'To Dear God!' So,
in a just phrase Anton Bruckner epitomized himself as a man and
as an artist.

"Born in a tiny village near Linz in 1824, Bruckner came of
a family of peasant schoolteachers, and he unquestioningly accepted this calling as his own. However, as a child, his leaning toward music was unmistakable, so that at his father's death, when
Anton was three, he was sent as *Saengerknabe* to the secular music
school of the monastery of St. Florian." The religious impact of
this school left its mark on the rest of Bruckner's life.

"His piety was genuine—the vital mainspring of his entire
life. It is no doubt true that the natural bent of his character was
toward the simple credulity and earnestness of a peasant, but
these years at St. Florian left him forever the believer, the man
who trusts his fellow men as he does his God.

"But the years of protected existence were short and at seventeen Bruckner faced the world to start his career as a village
teacher whose earnings were to be about 80 cents a month. The
story of the years till 1868 are the story of a conscientious music
student carrying studies to unprecedented lengths.

90

"Bruckner spent twelve years in academic exercise in composition, harmony and counterpoint, until finally, in his extreme earnestness, he insisted on being examined. Judges were chosen from among the learned of Vienna who met at the Piaristan church where Bruckner (who was one of the greatest organists of the world) was given themes for fugue and free phantasy. He passed his test and one of the judges, Herbeck, exclaimed: 'He should have examined us!'

"In the meanwhile, in 1856, Bruckner had been appointed organist to the cathedral in Linz and there he spent the happiest years of his life. During this period he finished his self-inflicted studies and began to compose. It was also here that he came to a real turning point in his life.

"Bruckner had, of course, been composing all the time, but in the smaller forms. In 1863 he heard for the first time a performance of Wagner's *Tannhäuser* and from that moment his fate was sealed. No one can question the fact. Bruckner, who was hailed by the Wagnerian camp as doing for the symphony what Wagner did for opera, literally worshipped the Master of Wahnfried. He held him in such awe that it was said that when Bruckner visited Bayreuth and went walking in the fields he always carried his frock coat lest he should meet the master unaware and should be forced to appear in unsuitable garments."

Several triumphs followed in Linz, including the mass in D. . . .

"As a result of this, Bruckner, at the age of forty-four, was offered the post of professor of composition of the Vienna Academy of Music. It was with many misgivings that he accepted. Always a timid man, he distrusted the capital and preferred the peace and seclusion of his life at Linz. But his friends urged and the bishop promised that he could always return and finally he went to Vienna. . . .

". . . . Hans Richter told me that he sat next to Bruckner during the first *Die Walküre* performance at Bayreuth. 'Beautiful, marvellous,' whispered Bruckner, 'but do tell me afterwards what it is all about."

"Now up until the time when Bruckner dedicated his third symphony to Wagner, his sailing, while not exactly easy, was not too rough. His Mass in F was well received in Vienna and the

Mass in E was enthusiastically heard in Linz. He also had fine notices for his first two symphonies, although it is true that he had to pay to have them performed.

"But it was after Wagner had espoused his cause, accepting the dedication of his Third Symphony and hailing him as the greatest symphonic writer after Beethoven, that his trials really began. The critics who had praised his early efforts turned, and could find no words virulent enough to express their distaste. One went so far as to say: 'Bruckner composes like a drunkard!' Orchestras and conductors refused his works as unplayable. Everywhere fun was poked at him and his music. To a man of Bruckner's timidity it was nearly fatal. But somehow he did survive it.

"There were a few friends and faithful ones and then there were his students. . . . Among these students were the great interpreters of the next generation through whom Bruckner's genius finally came to be known: Mottl, Mahler, Nikisch, Muck, Seidl. . . . At the tragic first performance of the 'Romantic' or Fourth Symphony, when at the end there were barely ten people left in the house, it was Gustav Mahler who was one of the first to rush up and console the master, who had been forced to conduct himself.

"That was in 1877. The next five years were gloomy indeed, enlivened only by visits to Bayreuth for communion with the master. But in December 1884, the tide changed at last when the young Nikisch gave the first performance of the Seventh Symphony at the Gewandhaus in Leipzig. It was a triumph. From city to city the news went and performances followed in Munich, in Hamburg, in Holland, in New York and finally, just ten years after the fiasco of the Fourth Symphony, in Vienna. Bruckner lived till 1896 to enjoy his peace and the united acclaim of the musical world."

Symphony No. 7 in E major

Bruckner, like Brahms, was late getting started with his symphonies. He was forty-two when his first was completed and was still working on the Ninth when death stayed his hand. There are some moments, for example the instance of the three trumpets rising in triads at the end of the Seventh Symphony, when his music seems transported into supramundane realms, defying description in words, requiring the experience in performance. In return for these transcendental moments, the analytical listener may find a variety of weaknesses.

Bruckner has been criticized as being long-winded and tiresome, spending twice the time necessary to express what he has to say. He indulges in the disconcerting habit of piling up climaxes until he reaches a state demanding a breathing spell, then inserts a couple of measures of silence (the notorious Bruckner "grand pause"), with a resultant anticlimax afterward. He was sometimes overdevoted to the craft of his art, spending hours working out the technical niceties of a petty contrapuntal device, and forgetting the general structure of a passage and its relation to the whole composition. The number of revised manuscripts from Bruckner's own hand and the cuts and alterations which appear in the early published scores, indicate that both the composer and his well-meaning editors were aware of these structural faults, yet their efforts have only served to obscure the composer's original intent.

Some of these defects may be apparent in the Seventh Symphony, yet it is one of his most popular works. It was begun in 1881 and completed September 5, 1883, about six months after Wagner's death. Bruckner, writing to Felix Mottl, explained that he was led to the composition of the Adagio in this symphony by a premonition of Wagner's demise: "I thought to myself that it would be impossible for the Master to live long; and at that time the Adagio in C-sharp minor came into my head."

The full score of the Seventh bears a dedication: TO HIS MAJESTY, THE KING, LUDWIG II OF BAVARIA, IN DEEPEST REVERENCE —the same eccentric monarch who befriended Richard Wagner when he was most in need of assistance. The first performance took place in Leipzig on December 30, 1884, with Bruckner's friend and pupil, Arthur Nikisch, conducting.

. . . . An interesting diversion from the usual scoring is found in Bruckner's use of the set of "Bayreuth Tubas" designed by Wagner for use in *The Ring* scores. Only the contrabass instrument is a true tuba; the others, two tenor instruments in B-flat and two bass instruments in F, are modified horns with a funnel mouthpiece, permitting a more refined and easily blended tone than the cup mouthpiece of the genuine tuba family.

DONALD L. ENGLE, *Philadelphia Orchestra*

Symphony No. 8 in C minor

. . . . Bruckner began work on his Eighth Symphony in Vienna some time in 1884, finishing the original version of the opening Allegro during the winter of that year. In the course of the next six years he returned to the Symphony again and again, revising it repeatedly, until it was completed in 1890. Hans Richter conducted the world premiere of the new work at a concert of the Vienna Philharmonic on December 18, 1892. Hanslick, still unrepentant as Bruckner's sworn foe, was obliged to report the stupendous ovation given Bruckner: "Boisterous, rejoicing, waving of handkerchiefs from those standing, innumerable recalls, laurel wreaths." It is possible he did not witness the demonstration himself, for the story is that he beat a hasty but conspicuous retreat before the Finale. Max Fiedler introduced the Symphony to America at a concert of the Boston Symphony Orchestra in Boston on March 13, 1909. On March 18 the visiting band performed the work in Carnegie Hall in New York. And one month later Fiedler was prompted to repeat the new symphony in Boston "by request."

. . . . The dedication of the Eighth Symphony reads: To His Imperial and Royal Apostolic Majesty Francis Joseph I of Austria and Apostolic King of Hungary in deepest reverence . . . During the premiere of the Symphony in Vienna, Philharmonic patrons were edified by descriptive clues in the printed program. They were told, for example, that in listening to the first theme of the first movement they should envision the *Prometheus Bound* of Aeschylus. Other portions of the opening Allegro were intended to depict "the greatest loneliness and silence." The Aeschylean hero suffers something of a letdown in the Scherzo, according to the Viennese annotator. There "the deeds and sufferings of Prometheus are reduced in the way of a parody to the smallest proportions." In short, the Scherzo was entitled: *Der Deutsch Michel*—a far from complimentary reference usually denoting an upper-Austrian yokel or clodhopper. One is scarcely surprised to find Hanslick remarking sarcastically: "If a critic had spoken this blasphemy, he would probably have been stoned to death by Bruckner's disciples; but the composer himself gave this name, 'the German Michael,' to the Scherzo, as may be read in black and white in the program."

. . . . In all fairness to Bruckner, who may have been intimidated by Hanslick's gibe, it should be added that the rustic motto does not appear in the published score. . . .

A vast array of instruments is called for in the scoring of the Eighth Symphony. This consists of three flutes, three oboes, three clarinets, three bassoons (one interchangeable with double-bassoon), eight horns (horns 5-8 interchangeable with tenor and bass tubas), three trumpets, three trombones, contrabass tuba, kettle drums, triangle, cymbals, three harps and the usual strings.

Louis Biancolli, *Philharmonic-Symphony Society of New York*

ALEXIS EMMANUEL CHABRIER

(Born in Ambert, Puy-de-Dôme, France, January 18, 1841—died in Paris, September 13, 1894)

Like Hector Berlioz before him, Chabrier was intended for a calling other than music. For sons of the provincial *bourgeoisie,* born in nineteenth century France, did not follow such a vagabond profession as music.

Chabrier's father, a lawyer, intended that his son should follow the same career. He had already begun the study of law when the family moved to Paris in 1857. Of old Auvergne and Bourvonnais stock, he began the study of music in his native town, but his family preferred a legal career for him and his father obtained an appointment in the Ministry of the Interior for him in 1862.

But he also managed to continue his musical studies without neglecting his law duties. His letters at this time reveal that on one occasion, at least, he obtained a leave of three days to attend a performance of *Tristan* at the Hoftheater in Munich, an incident, says Prod'homme, that "had a decisive influence upon his life as an artist."

In 1882, he made a journey through Spain with his wife. In letters to his friends he writes of hearing "national music of an incomparable richness. This excursion produced the rhapsody *España*.

In this same year, he resigned his post at the Ministry of the Interior to become assistant to the conductor Lamoureux in Paris and proved of great assistance in the early performances there of Wagner, to whose music, remarks the English critic, Percy Scholes, "he was greatly devoted."

In his mid-thirties he produced a comic opera with some success. His *Gwendoline* was refused by the Paris Opera but another, *Le Roi malgré lui* was produced and is still performed. But the most successful of his works and the one upon which his lasting fame rests is the Rhapsody.

He died almost in mid-career of paralysis, "brought on by temperamental excitement," to quote Scholes.

Rhapsody *Espana*

For a long time, most of the best and best-known composers of Spanish orchestral music were anything but Spanish. To this day, it is strangely interesting to note how the Russians—such as Tschaikowsky and Rimsky-Korsakoff—and the Frenchmen—including Debussy, Bizet and Ravel—have outstripped their Spanish fellow-composers. Bizet's *Carmen* is an outstanding example.

Another Frenchman, Alexis Chabrier, has written one of the most popular of all Spanish orchestral works, *España*; and it was this colorful work which first drew public attention to its composer, who was educated as a lawyer and who was essentially a self-taught musical amateur.

It seems likely that all the melodies in *España* (except one—played by trombone—which was original with Chabrier) were collected by the composer from the native songs and folk dances of Spain when he visited that country in 1882.

Two Spanish dances, the *Jota* (related to the waltz) and the
Malagueña (also in 3-4 time, but livelier in tempo) form the basis
for this composition and into these two dance forms, Chabrier
poured a number of thoroughly captivating tunes and rhythms.
The work, much admired for its felicitous orchestration, ends in a
blaze of instrumental color. (Lamoureux conducted the first performance in Paris, November 4, 1883.)

GEORGE SCHAUN, *Baltimore Symphony Orchestra*

ERNEST AMEDÉE CHAUSSON

(Born in Paris, January 21, 1855—died in Limay,
June 10, 1899)

ONE NEED not apologize today for liking the music of Chausson, as did several French critics thirty-odd years ago. A post-Wag-
nerian and apostle of Franck, his master, Chausson blazed no trails
into the unknown, yet his music bespeaks a sincerity and nobility,
and the figure of his musical speech is quite his own.

He, too like Schumann, was destined for the law, though his
wealthy parents were aware of his predilection for music. He studied for and was admitted to the bar and, by reason of family connections and influential friends, could have entered upon a lucrative practice.

But he preferred the career of a composer and at twenty-five
entered the Conservatoire, to study under Massenet. He showed no
marked progress under this master, but fortunately Cesar Franck
also was on the staff. The kindly Franck took Chausson into his
little group of intimate students and for three years he acquired
Franckian wisdom and knowledge.

He was diffident and modest to a fantastic degree and this reticence and lack of confidence, together with "the French preoccupation with music for the opera and the stage," seem to explain a long neglect of his music.

The great Russian conductor, Artur Nikisch can be said to have "discovered" Chausson and to have championed his music. Eugene Ysaye, Belgian violinist, and Colonne, French musician and conductor, also aided the cause.

It is said that when he went with manuscripts of his own to the offices of publishers, he offered also the works of struggling composers and pleaded for their music, too.

"For a time," writes Percy Scholes, "he was secretary of the French National Musical Society, which has done splendid and continuous work for a revival of serious music in France."

Chausson was beginning to be known as a composer, and his works were finding some favor with the public, when his untimely death occurred. He had lost control of a bicycle he was riding on his estate at Limay, coasted downhill and smashed into a stone wall. He died of a fractured skull.

Two months after his death, his friend Camille Mauclair wrote of him in *La Vogue,* Paris: "Ernest Chausson presented the appearance of a man of the world without ostentation, amiable, gay, peaceful. In reality few knew him. He did not care for the world, his amiability masked his seriousness, his gaiety was often a deference shown to others, and his peaceful air dissembled a soul moved to sadness by human suffering."

Poème: for violin and orchestra (Opus 25)

The *Poème* for violin and orchestra was composed in 1896, and was performed for the first time at a Colonne Concert in Paris April 4, 1897. The solo violinist was Eugene Ysaye. The orchestral portion of the work is scored for two flutes, two oboes, two clarinets, two bassoons, four horns, two trumpets, three trombones, bass tuba, kettledrums, harp and strings.

FELIX BOROWSKI, *Chicago Symphony Orchestra*

Symphony in B-flat (Opus 20)

Debussy had numbered the seven-years-older Chausson among his friends ever since his return from *Prix-de-Rome* studies in 1887. A song of 1881 is dedicated to Chausson, and there are letters in which Debussy discussed his String Quartet and early stages of *Pelleas et Melisande*. When Debussy was writing critical articles for the press, D'Indy and Chausson escaped the asperity he meted out to others. Vincent d'Indy, four years older than Chausson, was a lifelong friend and champion, as were Faure and Duparc (they were also some years Chausson's senior) and the younger Debussy and Dukas. Of these men, all but Debussy long survived the First World War and by their writing and teaching and enthusiasm fostered French music in the tradition that Chausson had been influential in establishing.

A Philadelphia audience was the first in America to hear Chausson's Symphony. Vincent d'Indy, as guest conductor, introduced it at a Philadelphia concert of the Boston Symphony Orchestra on December 4, 1905. Its indifferently-received premiere had been at a concert of the Societe Nationale in Paris, April 18, 1891, but it took Nikisch in 1897 to awaken the composer's countrymen to its qualities. The Symphony came into the repertory of the Philadelphia Orchestra at the hands of a French guest conductor, Alphonse Catherine, January 31, 1919.

R. L. F. McCOMBS, *Philadelphia Orchestra*

FRÉDÉRIC FRANÇOIS CHOPIN

(Born in Zelaswowa-Wola, Poland, February 22,
1810—died in Paris, October 17, 1849)

HOWEVER tradition may cavil to the contrary, the Chopins
were French people exiled by the merest accident to Poland, a
country they adopted as their own. But for the fact that Frédéric's father, Nicholas, born near Nancy, in Lorraine, accepted a
friend's offer of a bookkeeping post in a tobacco factory at Warsaw, the Chopins might have stayed French and Frédéric, had he
been born at all, would have stayed the humble grandson of a
wheelwright.

Fortunately for the heritage of music, Nicholas did take the
job and in Warsaw met his future wife, Justina Krzyanowska,
daughter of an impoverished noblewoman. They were married
June 2, 1806, settled in a village twenty-eight miles away and had
four children,—three daughters and one son, Frédéric. The youngest, Emilia, lived but fourteen years and died of tuberculosis. Frédéric bitterly mourned her death.

Nicholas and his wife were sympathetic to music—he played
the flute, Justina sang. But the baby Frédéric burst into tears at
the mere sound of music, particularly on the piano. It was some
time before they realized that these were not tears of antipathy
but of passionate enjoyment.

When he was four and his eldest sister, Louise, seven, she gave
him his first lessons. His progress was so marked and immediate
that his parents looked around for a teacher and finally hit upon a
seasoned musician, Adalbert Zywny, a Czech *emigré* who began
life as a violinist.

Here was Chopin's first and only teacher of the pianoforte.
Probably Frédéric's first public performance was on his eighth
birthday, a charity concert. "The boy's success was so complete,"
writes Murdoch, "and his personality so charming that he at once
became the 'lion' of the aristocracy, with invitations to the houses
of many princely families."

An increasing desire to compose impressed Frédéric's father
with the necessity for instruction in this phase of musicianship, so

Joseph Elsner, who had been music director of the National Theater in Warsaw and director of the Conservatorium, was engaged. Elsner, a prolific if mediocre composer, was to be Chopin's only guide in the laws and forms of music.

At fourteen Frédéric entered the Warsaw Lycée, hoping to complete a course of academic study in one year instead of two. He did not pass his final examination and finally went to Reinertz for his health.

His parents realized that nothing could prevent him from becoming a musician. Consequently, they did not object too much when Frédéric, recovering his health, again took a final examination and at seventeen just managed to pass. But he had other, if less important gifts, too. He could have become a great actor, a mimic or caricaturist. He was witty and charming and full of fun at this time, still some years from the sharp-tongued, complaining invalid that he became just before his death.

He fell in and out of love with equal facility, notably with Marie Wodzinska and the singer, Henrietta Sontag, Constantia Gladowska and the Countess Potocka. After various sojourns in Vienna, Munich and elsewhere in Europe, and a return to Warsaw, Chopin saw Paris first, then the world's center of art, in the third week of September 1831. He was never to leave it for long.

He met Liszt and Ferdinand Hiller, Schumann, Thalberg and a host of other lights. He was a frequent caller at the joint salon of Mme. D'Agoult and Aurore Napin Dudevant, alias George Sand, having met her through Liszt at a party in his own rooms. A strange friendship sprang up between them. He was frail, sensitive, foppish, inclined to be morbid and already suffering from the malady that killed him; she, after a harried and none too savory past, brusque, masculine, swarthy and with beautiful and "stupid eyes," to quote Balzac.

It was a last quarrel over George Sand's daughter, Solange, that terminated the strange intimacy. "Chopin," says Murdoch, "was exactly the type for which her soul was yearning—the ready-made prey for all this odd mixture of vulture and vampire."

Their friendship endured for ten years; the details are too many and exhausting to set down in this brief sketch. The journey to Majorca was unfortunate, for it brought Chopin's illness to an acutely dangerous stage. They returned to French soil—he broken,

weary and financially worried; she, exasperated yet still held by a
maternal affection.

For a time Chopin recovered, even undertook a trip to Italy,
then to the Sand château at Nohant and eventually back to Paris.
Artistic Paris, upon hearing they had returned to the city, paid
visits in the afternoons and evenings. Chopin, although increasingly feeble and coughing, taught for hours "with a patience, per-
severance and zeal which were admirable." During this period he
produced some of his finest works for piano, and he grew immeasurably as an artist.

The breach with George Sand came gradually. It began with
a growing hostility between her son, Maurice Dudevant, and Chopin, and fed upon an engagement between Solange and a young
sculptor for whom Chopin conjured an acute dislike. A growing
coolness on the part of George Sand found a response in Chopin
himself.

They met once after the breach, at a reception, when Chopin
was able to give her news of Solange's first child. They never met
thereafter. Chopin went to London, played for Queen Victoria and
visited the Stirlings in Scotland. He played in Manchester, Glasgow
and elsewhere, visited here and there about the Scottish countryside, grew rapidly worse in the London fogs and the bleak airs of
Scotland and finally decided to return to Paris. "But what am I
going back for?" he asked in a letter.

Those last days of 1849 showed a rapid decline. At times he was
barely able to breathe. Yet he tried to resume his teaching, even a
new "piano method," but his strength was unequal to the effort.
He implored his sister Louise to come, even if she had to borrow
the means. "I am stripped too bare to send you any."

Louise, with her husband and daughter, did arrive, but
Chopin was almost too feeble to speak, yet Louise nursed him tire-
lessly. His death came peacefully, in the early hours of October 17,
1849. His heart was sent to Poland.

Concerto for piano No. 1 in E minor (Opus 11)

Harboring high ambitions of winning fame as a virtuoso, the
youthful Chopin doubtlessly thought it expedient to go armed
with a concerto or two in confronting the musical world of his

time, enthralled as it was by the vogue of virtuosity for virtuosity's sake and presided over by such lions as Thalberg, Kalkbrenner and Liszt, who with dazzling transcriptions, grand fantasies and acrobatic variations held their audiences spellbound. Chopin was later to outstrip them at their own game. Before setting out for Paris he wrote two piano concertos, one in F minor, the other in E minor.

The F minor Concerto, although numbered Opus 21 and published in 1836, three years later than the E minor, was composed first. Chronologically the E minor is really Chopin's second concerto, and was written between March and August 1830. It was first performed in Warsaw, October 11, 1830, by Chopin himself. This was Chopin's third and last concert in Warsaw. According to the custom of the time the Concerto was not played in sequence. An aria was sandwiched in between the first and second movements.

The germs of Chopin's second period are already extant in this Concerto. The music is not stifled by an excess of ornament as might easily be the case in a work born of footlight fever and written to comply with an exaggerated taste for embellishment. Its general character is episodical, but there are episodes of rare worth and originality containing passage work whose design is of a distinctly superior quality. The first movement follows out the specifications of conventional sonata form with the customary variations. The development is somewhat in the nature of a technical study. The rondo is "frolicksome, tricky, genial and genuine piano music." Of the second movement, Chopin wrote: "The adagio is in E major, and of a romantic, calm and partly melancholy character. It is intended to convey the impression which one receives when the eye rests on a beloved landscape that calls up in one's soul beautiful memories, for instance, of a fine moonlit spring night. I have written for violins with mutes as an accompaniment. I wonder if that will have a good effect. Well, time will show."

This expression of doubt concerning his instrumentation is characteristic of Chopin's attitude toward the orchestra. He was never able to bring to it that feeling of exquisite adaptability which he had for the piano, and his knowledge of other instruments remained limited. The orchestral part of the Concerto has been bolstered up by both Tausig and Burmeister to a point where Chopin's responsibility for it now seems rather doubtful.

The idea of expressing himself in broad terms was not consistent with Chopin's nature, anyway. As Huneker says; "His lungs were too weak for the pace in seven-league boots, so often required in a score. . . ."

HERBERT ELWELL, *Cleveland Orchestra*

Concerto No. 2 in F minor for piano and orchestra (Opus 21)

Poetically embedded in the slow movement of Chopin's F minor Concerto is the name Constantia Gladowska. The girl was a voice pupil at the Warsaw Conservatory in 1829 when Chopin fell madly in love with her, raved to his friends about her, and never so much as uttered a word to her in the first six months of his adoration. "God forbid," he wrote to a friend who was delegated to act as intermediary, "that she should suffer in any way on my account. Set her mind at rest and tell her that as long as my heart beats I shall not cease to adore her. Tell her even that after my death my ashes shall be strewn under her feet."

To his friend, Titus Wojciechowski, he confided that in Constantia he had found his ideal, that he worshipped her "faithfully and sincerely," adding that a whole half-year had gone by without his having "exchanged a single syllable with her of whom I dream every night." Once in Vienna he dined with a Mrs. Beyer merely because the lady bore the name of Constantia, and he confessed tingling with pleasure whenever a pocket handkerchief or napkin marked "Constantia" came into his hands. Writing to a friend about his idol, he stopped abruptly after the syllable "Con-" remarking: "No, I cannot complete her name, my hand is too unworthy."

. . . . When he wrote to Titus, "Whilst my thoughts were with her, I composed the *adagio* (Larghetto) of my concerto," his thoughts, of course, were with Constantia Gladowska. We have the more sober authority of Franz Liszt that the girl was "sweet and beautiful." Like many others, Chopin greatly admired Constantia's voice.

. . . . The romance, such as it was, remained largely an epistolary affair—between Chopin and his friends. The young pianist-composer left Warsaw and Constantia soon became the wife of a Polish tradesman. A few years later we find the susceptible youth once more playing the role of rejected suitor, the girl this time being Maria Wodzinska. He finally had to be satisfied with a lady known as George Sand, who was not famous for her beautiful voice.

Louis Biancolli, *Philharmonic-Symphony Society of New York*

AARON COPLAND

(Born in Brooklyn, November 14, 1900—now living in New York)

Among the more pertinent of American composers today is Aaron Copland. Once hailed as a leader of the "New School of Younger American Composers," the passing years have established his reputation firmly, relinquishing something of his former distinction to newer and younger talents.

Copland is a serviceable composer, in that his music is always good, always worthy of performance and unpretentious in the sense of aspiring to greatness. His short career has been full of rewards and success, but he is modest enough to realize that final success in an art is never really achieved.

He is verily a child of the pavements. He grew up in populous, crowded Brooklyn, in a Russian-Jewish home. The family had been Kaplan in Russia. "It seems," explains Oscar Thompson, "that the father, emigrating by way of England, had the spelling of his name changed for him en route by some official who was misled by the way Kaplan was pronounced. So it was as a Copland that the future composer entered the world at the turn of the century."

He began to study music at thirteen—piano with Clarence Adler and Victor Wittgenstein; harmony and composition with Rubin Goldmark. Four years later he joined the American students at Fontainebleau, and came under the tutelage of Nadia Boulanger in Paris.

He is in constant demand today as teacher, lecturer and writer, as well as composer. Probably the first work to bring him to the notice of the music world was the *Cortege Macabre,* an excerpt from an unperformed ballet.

Copland was the first composer to obtain a Guggenheim Fellowship (1925-1927). He and Roger Sessions organized the Copland-Sessions concerts in 1928, to focus attention upon the work of still younger composers. He also launched the American Festivals of Contemporary Music at Yadoo, Saratoga Springs, New York.

His *Dance Symphony,* contrived from a one-act ballet called *Grohg,* won a $5,000 prize from the RCA Victor Company, which had announced a prize of $25,000 for a symphonic work. Copland had intended to submit his *Symphonic Ode,* but did not finish it in time. But he extracted three dances from the aforesaid ballet as a last-minute expedient. The judges decided to give $5,000 each to Copland, Louis Gruenberg and Ernest Bloch, and $10,000 for two compositions to Robert Russell Bennett.

Some of his more recent works are a score for the ballet *Billy the Kid, Music for the Theater, Quiet City, Saga of the Prairies, El Sálon México; Vitebsk,* a study on a Jewish melody; a school opera, *The Second Hurricane;* music for various motion pictures; including *Our Town;* three symphonies; the score for a ballet, *Appalachian Spring*—and the end is not yet.

Symphony No. 3

Completed September 29, 1946, this Symphony was commissioned by the Koussevitzky Music Foundation and is dedicated "to the Memory of My Dear Friend Natalie Koussevitzky."

Mr. Copland wrote his first symphony (for orchestra with

organ) in 1924-1925. It was performed by this orchestra February 20-21, 1925, when Mlle. Nadia Boulanger played the organ part. The composer revised this symphony as an orchestral work without organ, and in this form it was performed by this orchestra February 15-16, 1935. His Second Symphony, entitled *Short Symphony,* is a work of great rhythmic complexity. It was performed in 1934 in Mexico under the direction of Carlos Chavez. It was repeated there in 1941 and 1946. There has not been a concert performance of this symphony in America, but a broadcast performance was given by the NBC Symphony Orchestra on January 9, 1944, under Leopold Stokowski. Copland's *Symphonic Ode* written for the fiftieth anniversary of the Boston Symphony Orchestra and his *Dance Symphony,* which is really a symphonic compilation from the ballet *Grohg,* are not considered by their composer to be symphonic in any strict sense of the word.

Mr. Copland divulges that he had been "collecting themes over a period of years with the idea of some day writing a symphony." When he received his commission from the Koussevitzky Music Foundation in 1943, he began actually to plan the symphony. He began work upon the score in August 1944, during a summer stay in a small Mexican village. The first movement was completed in April and the second in August of the following year. The third movement was finished in January 1946, and the Finale on September 29, barely in time for the necessary copying of parts for the first performance.

"Inevitably the writing of a symphony," says Mr. Copland, "brings with it the question of what it is meant to express. I suppose if I forced myself I could invent an ideological basis for my symphony. But if I did, I'd be bluffing—or at any rate, adding something *ex post facto,* something that might or might not be true, but which played no role at the moment of creation. Harold Clurman put my meaning well when he wrote recently that music is a 'reflection of and response to specific worlds of men; it is play, it is speech, it is unconscious result and conscious statement all at the same time.' Anything more specific than that in relation to so-called absolute music is suspect. In other words—to use a well-worn phrase—I prefer to let the music speak for itself.

"One aspect of the Symphony ought to be pointed out: it contains no folk or popular material. During the late Twenties it was customary to pigeonhole me as a composer of symphonic jazz, with emphasis on the jazz. More recently I have been catalogued as a folk-lorist and purveyor of Americana. Any reference to jazz or folk material in this work was purely unconscious. . . ."

JOHN N. BURK, Boston Symphony Orchestra

A Lincoln Portrait

During those crucial weeks that followed our entrance into the Second World War, countless Americans became acutely aware of the many facets of their national heritage which make the United States a great nation. In pondering these matters, the conductor André Kostelanetz gave considerable thought to a means by which music could be used "to mirror the magnificent spirit of our country." As he explained later, it seemed to him that "the greatness of a nation is expressed through its people and those people who have achieved greatness are the logical subjects for a series of musical portraits."

Mr. Kostelanetz shared his idea with three leading American composers, and the result was a triptych of three musical characterizations: <i>A Lincoln Portrait,</i> by Aaron Copland; an orchestral portrait of Mark Twain by Jerome Kern; and a portrait of the late Fiorello H. La Guardia, by Virgil Thomson. In discussing the selection, Mr. Kostelanetz said: "The qualities of courage, dignity, strength, simplicity and humor which are so characteristic of the American people are well represented in these three outstanding Americans."

Aaron Copland's portrait was completed early in 1942 and received its premiere at a Pension Fund concert of the Cincinnati Symphony Orchestra on May 14, 1942, André Kostelanetz conducting. Since then it has enjoyed numerous hearings, not only in this country, but by leading European and Latin American orchestras.

"The first sketches," says Mr. Copland, "were made in February and the portrait finished on April 16. The orchestration was completed a few weeks later. I worked with musical materials of my own, with the exception of two songs of the period; the famous 'Camptown Races' and a ballad that was first published in 1840 under the title 'The Pesky Sarpent' but is better known today as 'Springfield Mountain.' In neither case is the treatment a literal one. The tunes are used freely, in the manner of my use of cowboy songs in *Billy the Kid*."

Philadelphia Orchestra

Music for the Theater

The Suite was begun in May 1925, in New York and completed there in September. It was composed for the most part during the summer months at the MacDowell Colony, Peterboro, New Hampshire.

The composer had no play or literary idea in mind when writing "Music for the Theater." The title simply implies that, at times, this music has a quality which is suggestive of the theater.

The first performance was in Boston by the Boston Symphony Orchestra on November 20, 1925.

PHILIP HALE, *Boston Symphony Orchestra*

El Sálon México

El Sálon México had its first performance August 27, 1937 by the *Orquestra Sinfonia de Mexico,* under Carlos Chavez. It was repeated at a free concert for workers on September 12 by the same orchestra. There was a broadcast performance at the studios of the National Broadcasting Company in New York, May 14, 1938, Sir Adrian Boult conducting as guest. The work was chosen as one to represent the United States at the Festival of the International Society for Contemporary Music which was held in London last summer.

The title of *El Sálon México* and the circumstances under which it was written have been kindly supplied by the composer:

"During my first visit to Mexico, in the fall of 1932, I conceived the idea of writing a piece based on Mexican themes. I suppose there is nothing strange in such an idea. Any composer who goes outside his native land wants to return bearing musical souvenirs. In this case my musical souvenirs must have been very memorable, since it wasn't until 1933 that I began to assemble them into the form of an orchestral work.

"From the very beginning, the idea of writing a work based on popular Mexican melodies was connected in my mind with a popular dance hall in Mexico City called Sálon México. No doubt I realized, even then, that it would be foolish for me to attempt to translate into musical sounds the more profound side of Mexico; the Mexico of the ancient civilizations or the revolutionary Mexico of today. In order to do that one must really know a country. All that I could hope to do was to reflect the Mexico of the tourists, and that is why I thought of the Sálon México. Because in that 'hot spot,' one felt, in a very natural and unaffected way a close contact with the Mexican people. It wasn't the music I heard, but the spirit that I felt there, which attracted me. Something of that spirit I hope to have put into my music.

"I followed no general rule in the use of the themes I treated. Almost all of them come from the *Cancionero Mexicano* by Frances Toor, or from the erudite work of Ruben Campos, *El Folk lore y la Musica Mexicana*. To both authors I owe thanks. Probably the most direct quotation of a complete melody is that of El Mosco' (No. 84 in the book by Campos) which is presented twice, immediately after the introductory measures (in which may be found fragments of *El Palo Verde* and of *La Jesusita*)."

JOHN N. BURK, *Boston Symphony Orchestra*

Statements for Orchestra

The *Statements,* begun in 1933 and completed in 1935, were commissioned by the League of Composers for performance by the Minneapolis Symphony Orchestra. Only the Jingo and Prophetic sections were played by the orchestra under Eugene Ormandy in an NBC broadcast on January 9, 1936, but the New York Philharmonic gave the first complete performance under Dimitri Mitropoulos on January 7, 1942.

Of the *Statements,* he (Mr. Copland) says:

"The title 'statement' was chosen to indicate a short terse orchestral movement of a well-defined character, lasting about three minutes. The separate movements were given suggestive titles as an aid to the public in understanding what the composer had in mind when writing these pieces.

"The 'militant' statement is based on a single theme, announced *unisono* at the beginning by three flutes, two oboes, bassoon and strings. The 'cryptic' statement is orchestrated for brass and flute along with an occasional use of bass clarinet and bassoon. The 'dogmatic' statement is in tripartite form, the middle section quotes the theme of the composer's *Piano Variations*. The 'subjective' statement is scored for strings alone, without double basses. The 'jingo' statement utilizes the full orchestra. It is built in rondo form on a chromatic melody with occasional bows to a well-known tune. The final section, a 'prophetic' statement, is rhapsodic in form and centers about a chorale-like melody sung by the solo trumpet."

HOWARD SHANET, *New York City Symphony Orchestra*

Suite from the ballet: *Rodeo*

The Ballet Russe de Monte Carlo commissioned the choreographer Agnes de Mille and composer Aaron Copland to collaborate on the creation of a Western ballet for its 1942-1943 season. Originally subtitled *The Courting at Burnt Ranch*, *Rodeo* was first produced at the Metropolitan Opera House in New York on October 16, 1942, with scenery by Oliver Smith and costumes by Kermit Lowe.

The idea for the ballet was devised by Miss De Mille who described it as follows: "Throughout the American Southwest, the Saturday afternoon rodeo is a tradition. On the remote ranches, as well as in the trading centers and the towns, the 'hands' get together to show off their skill in roping, riding, branding and throwing. Often, on the more isolated ranches, the rodeo is done for an audience that consists only of a handful of fellow-workers, women-folk, and those nearest neighbors who can make the eight or so mile run-over.

"The afternoon's exhibition is usually followed by a Saturday night dance at the ranchhouse.

"The theme of the ballet is basic. It deals with the problem that has confronted all American women, from earliest pioneer times, and which has never ceased to occupy them throughout the history of the building of our country; how to get a man."

The music was written in June and orchestrated in September 1942. The composer subsequently extracted an orchestral suite from the ballet score for concert performance under the title: *Four Dance Episodes from Rodeo.*

> *Boosey & Hawkes,* publishers of Mr. Copland's scores
> (Used by permission of Boosey & Hawkes, Copyright owners)

Suite from the ballet: *Billy the Kid*

At the suggestion of Lincoln Kirstein, director of the Ballet Caravan, Aaron Copland set to work on a score for a native American ballet, whose subject was to be the young desperado of the Wild West, Billy the Kid. Mr. Copland had doubts, at first, concerning his own qualifications as a cowboy composer, but insistence on the part of Mr. Kirstein brushed aside all misgivings. The resultant work has proved one of the most popular in the Ballet Caravan's repertory.

Mr. Copland admits that he was torn between the use and non-use of cowboy songs as a foundation for his music. He found certain obstacles to overcome, the major ones having to do with making an orchestral speech of the simple unaffected tunes, and another none-too-negligible obstacle being his own distaste for cowboy music as such.

Mr. Kirstein in the meantime, assured the composer that it made no difference whether or not the songs were employed, but, even as he said so, he tucked a sheaf of them under Mr. Copland's arm. In Paris, the following summer, the composer began working on the outline of the scenario, and, *mirabile dictu,* he found that his attitude toward the songs had changed considerably; so much so, in fact, that the completed score carries, in full or in part, such eminent examples of musical cowboyiana as "Great Grandad," "Git Along Little Dogies," "The Old Chisolm Trail," "The Dying Cowboy" and others. Mr. Copland did not interpolate "Home on the Range," for as he puts it, "I had to draw the line some place."

ROBERT C. BAGAR, *Philharmonic-Symphony Society of New York*

Orchestral suite from the ballet, *Appalachian Spring*

In its original scoring for thirteen instruments, this music was first heard in New York on May 14, 1945, when Martha Graham and her company presented the new ballet *Appalachian Spring*, at the National Theater. Mr. Copland promptly set to work on an arrangement for symphony orchestra. Printed at the head of the published score is the following information:

"*Appalachian Spring* was composed in 1943-1944 as a ballet for Miss Martha Graham on a commission from the Elizabeth Sprague Coolidge Foundation. It was first performed by Miss Graham and her company at the Coolidge Festival in the Library of Congress in Washington, D. C., on October 30, 1944.

"The original scoring called for a chamber ensemble of thirteen instruments. The present arrangement for symphony orchestra was made by the composer in the spring of 1945. It is a condensed version of the ballet, retaining all essential features, but omitting those sections in which the interest is primarily choreographic.

"The action of the ballet concerns a pioneer celebration around a newly-built farmhouse in the Pennsylvania hills in the early part of the last century."

Stadium Concerts

Piano Concerto

Around 1925 Aaron Copland entered what may be considered a second phase of his evolution as a composer. . . . "I had," he tells us in his book *Our New Music*, "experimented a little with the rhythms of popular music in several earlier compositions, but now I wanted frankly to adopt the jazz idiom and see what I could do with it in a symphonic way."

The outcome of these speculations was "Music for the Theater" for small orchestra, and in 1926, he further developed jazz elements in his Piano Concerto. This work, though partly based on themes conceived at an earlier date, was begun in January in New York, continued during the summer months in a Basque village in France, and completed here in November. The premiere took place with the Boston Symphony Orchestra under Koussevitzky on January 28, 1927. . . . Many Boston Symphony auditors were so profoundly shocked by this work after its premiere that cabals were promptly formed by its defenders, on one hand, and its opponents, on the other.

Koussevitzky, who we now know to be one of the most active protagonists of native contemporary music, was ironically accused of actually disliking America's contribution to art and of playing the Copland, therefore, to show how bad our music is. H. T. Parker, who had voiced his disapproval of the concerto in no uncertain terms, nevertheless defended in the pages of the *Boston Transcript,* its right to appear on a Boston Symphony program:

No doubt like most of us, he [Koussevitzky] finds America and things American sometimes amusing. But to assert that he played Mr. Copland's Concerto with such derisive purpose is comic nonsense."

ARTHUR V. BERGER, *New York City Symphony Orchestra*

ACHILLE-CLAUDE DEBUSSY

(Born in St. Germain-en-Laye, August 22, 1862— died in Paris, March 25, 1918)

CLAUDE DE FRANCE," as he once was dubbed, was born in the picturesque old residential town of French royalty, St. Germain-en-Laye, a few miles from Paris. In childhood, his musical talents were far from obvious, and his parents, who kept a china shop, were not aware of them. One may lay the "discovery" of his musical proclivities to Mme. Mantet, mother-in-law of the Bohemian poet, Verlain.

His parents had destined him for the navy, as a "respectable" and secure occupation, though at nine his father grudgingly gave him piano lessons.

The advent of Mme. Mantet, however, induced his parents to change their minds about a musical career. At fifteen, he entered the Conservatoire, and there he remained until his twenty-third birthday. Ambroise Thomas, composer of *Mignon,* was then the director. Debussy won three prizes in piano, yet his efforts in harmony met with signal failure. In fact, during the whole tenure of Debussy as a student, he was engaged in continuous battle against rules for the sake of rules.

He took a brief vacation from his studies and went to Russia, as a sort of parlor pianist, music teacher and protege of Madame Nadejda von Meck, that strange woman who was to support Tschaikowsky for some years without ever exchanging a word with him. Of Debussy, Mme. von Meck remarks in a letter:

"Two days ago a young pianist arrived from Paris, where he has just graduated at the Conservatoire with the first prize in the class of M. Marmontel. I engaged him for the summer to give lessons to the children, accompany Julia's singing, and play four hands with myself. This young man plays well, his technique is brilliant, but he lacks any personal expression. He is yet too young, says he is twenty but looks sixteen."

Debussy returned the following year, and the year after that. One might have thought these visits would have widened his acquaintance with Russian composers. On the contrary, this acquaintance remained limited, yet he came to know rather intimately the cabaret byways of Moscow, thanks to the assistance of Nadejda's eldest son, Vladimir.

He resumed his studies at the Conservatoire and won a prize for improvisation, yet he would not attend the organ classes of Cesar Franck. He won the *Prix de Rome* with his cantata "L'Enfant Prodigue." Many a gray head wagged, yet the work undoubtedly had been contrived by an original and well-equipped composer.

His first official clash with the conventional came with his obligatory *envois* to the French Institute. His orchestral suite, *Printemps,* was fiercely denounced and performance was refused. And so the war was on, to last some thirty years.

Returning from Rome, he came across the original and unedited score of *Boris Godounov,* and was deeply impressed. It was to influence much of Debussy's important composition, particularly *Pelleas et Melisande.* He went to Bayreuth in 1889 and was moved to tears by *Tristan* and *The Ring.*

The wife of Maurice Maeterlinck, Georgette, had been a professional singer and conceived the idea of turning the play of *Pelleas et Melisande* into an opera and singing the principal role herself. She hit upon Erik Satie for the job of providing the music but to her dismay Satie demurred, deeming himself incapable of such a task.

It was Satie who broached the matter to Debussy and long did that arch-rebel of harmonic lore muse upon the prospect. Debussy determined first to read the book and in the summer of 1892, says Oscar Thompson, he was strolling along the Left Bank and passed a bookstall. Browsing idly among some worn and shabby volumes, he picked up a copy of Maeterlinck's play *Pelleas et Melisande.* He stuck it in his pocket and forgot it until he hung up his coat at home and took it out. He became absorbed in it and read it from cover to cover that night. He was fired with the idea of setting it to music.

After some difficulty, Debussy obtained the permission of Maeterlinck, and for the next ten years worked assiduously on the score. It is a peculiar departure perhaps, that he began upon the duo of the fourth act, and that the whole opera stems from this beginning.

Pelleas was first performed April 30, 1902, at the Opera Comique in Paris and aroused a storm of controversy. The purists held that it violated every canon of accepted form and harmony, that it ignored the holy tradition of opera, as the Wagnerian music-dramas had done before him, and that this simply was "not music." By an opposing faction he was hailed as a pioneer and a trailblazer.

The influence upon *Pelleas* of his Russian journeys, his contact with and interest in Russian music, particularly that of Moussorgsky's *Boris Godounov,* is apparent.

Debussy died in Paris shortly before the end of World War I in 1918, after a long and troublesome illness of a cancer which might have been cured today under scientific treatment.

Prelude to *The Afternoon of a Faun*
(After the epilogue of Stephane Mallarmé)

Debussy completed his Prelude to *The Afternoon of a Faun* in the summer of 1894. The Prelude was performed at the concerts of the Societe Nationale, December 22, 1894, Gustave Doret conducting. It was published in 1895. . . . The first performance in the United States was by the Boston Orchestral Club, Georges Longy conductor, April 1, 1902. . . . The Prelude did not find its way into the concerts of the Paris Conservatoire until the end of 1913.

It was in 1893 that musical Paris, or at least the more discerning part of its audiences, began to awaken to the special qualities in Claude Debussy, for it was in that year that his String Quartet and *La Demoiselle Elue* were first performed. A result of these performances was the arrangement of an all-Debussy concert in Brussels (where he was as yet unknown) on March 1, 1894. The affair was under the direction of Eugene Ysaye. The new works above named and two songs were to be performed, also at the end of the programme an unpublished manuscript score: *Prelude, Interlude, et Paraphrase Finale pour 'L'Après-midi d'un Faune'.* This work was withdrawn by the composer as not ready for performance. Debussy, following the trait that was to stay with him through life, subjected his first purely orchestral score to much revision, minute reconsideration and painstaking care in detail. He had been working on it two years when in the summer of 1894 he was ready to yield it for performance and publication. The second and third parts, which had not gone beyond the stage of fragmentary sketches, have been abandoned. Debussy's piece was performed under its present title of "Prelude" at the concerts of the

Societe Nationale. Charles Koechlin reports that the acoustics of the Salle d'Harcourt were poor and the performance bad, the rehearsals having been inadequate. Nevertheless, the Prelude had an immediate success, and at the first performance had to be repeated. André Messager and Edouard Colonne soon put it on their programmes, and on its publication in 1895 the piece made its way abroad.

The Prelude seems to have survived its attacks and imitations without loss of its particular charm and beauty in the forty-two (now forty-six) years since it appeared. As for the "violation" done upon it by Diaghilev's Ballet Russe in 1913, the disapproval of Debussy was foreordained fact, as the disapproval of Mallarmé would have been. The arbitrary and highly stylized visualization of Nijinsky, however admirable as an adventure in choreography, inevitably shattered the fragile and elusive dream-picturing of the poet, and no less its subtle and reverent translation into tones.

Mallarmé had published his eclogue, *L'Après-midi d'un Faune* in 1876 in pamphlet form, with illustrations by Manet, after its refusal by the *Parnasse Contemporaine*. Debussy was probably following his best instincts in scrupulously avoiding anything like an interlinear depiction of the poem. His music stands carefully aside from the delicate and tentative dream images of the poet, and sets its own remoter reflection as if apart, in anticipation or preparation. Mallarmé was enthusiastic about the score, and is quoted by Debussy (in a letter to Jean Aubry) as having said: "This music prolongs the emotion of my poem and fixes the scene much more vividly than color could have done."

JOHN N. BURK, *Boston Symphony Orchestra*

La Mer: Three Symphonic Sketches

It was the absence of the old, familiar Debussy as much as the advent of a more robust one that disturbed the composer's admirers when the three symphonic sketches which make up *La Mer* —*The Sea*—finally appeared in March 1905. Ever since the triumph of his opera, *Pelleas,* partisans and adversaries alike had been anticipating the great symphonic work which had been occupying the composer since 1903. His friends recalled pleasur-

ably the exquisite sea-music of the grotto scene of the second act of
Pelleas, and they hoped that these new sea pieces would be conceived in the same vein. Their hopes were dashed. *La Mer* proved
to be an entirely new type of work. Here was a masterpiece of
brilliance and splendor. The impressionistic fancies, undulating
rhythms and delicate, ethereal effects of his previous compositions were replaced by more complex and compact motives,
strong rhythms and vivid colors. Debussy had renewed his art with
the result that the musical public was upset because it would now
fit in no pigeonhole of its neatly ordered mind.

Concertgoers seem to have let the first performance of *La
Mer,* which was given at the Concerts Lamoureux, on October 15,
1905, go by without too much to-do. This was probably due to
the uninspired interpretation of the work which the conductor,
Camille Chevillard, gave. However, when Debussy himself directed
the sketches at the Concerts Colonne, on January 19, 1908, interest at once quickened. Friends applauded loud and long; there
were catcalls and hisses from the anti-Debussyites. For a quarter of
an hour, bravos mingled with abuses. Order was restored long
enough for Jacques Thibaud to begin Bach's Chaconne; then suddenly the din began again. It raged with such fury that the violinist was forced to stop playing. A fortnight later, in London, at a
Queen's Hall concert, Debussy again conducted *La Mer* with
marked success and with no offensive noises from the audiences.

Interminable controversy at once arose in the press on the
subject of these symphonic sketches. Two schools of thought
gradually emerged; the one openly or tacitly reproached Debussy
for abandoning his early style; the other congratulated him on
the way he had regenerated his art. That this score was a development of the third Nocturne, *Les Sirenes,* which they had applauded
four years earlier, seems to have completely escaped the critics of
both camps.

LOUISE BECK, *Philadelphia Orchestra*

Nocturnes: *Clouds—Festivals—Sirens*

The Nocturnes by Debussy are three in number. The first
two, *Nuages* and *Fetes,* were produced at a Lamoureux Concert in
Paris, December 9, 1900, and they were played by the same or-

chestra January 6, 1901. The third, *Sirenes,* was first produced—in company with the other two—at a Lamoureux Concert, October 27, 1901. The third is for orchestra with chorus of female voices. At this last concert the friends of Debussy were so exuberant in manifestations of delight that there was sharp hissing as a corrective.

The first performance of the three Nocturnes in the United States was at a Chickering "Production" Concert in Boston on February 10, 1904, when Mr. Lang conducted. The Nocturnes were played twice at this concert. Nocturnes Nos. 1 and 2 were played by the Boston Symphony Orchestra, led by Vincent d'Indy as guest, at Philadelphia, December 4, 1905. . . .

Debussy furnished a programme for the suite; at least, this programme is attributed to him. Some who are not wholly in sympathy with what they loosely call "the modern movement" may think that the program itself needs elucidation. Debussy's peculiar forms of expression in prose are not easily Englished, and it is well-nigh impossible to reproduce certain shades of meaning.

"The title 'Nocturne' is intended to have here a more general and, above all, a more decorative meaning. We, then, are not concerned with the form of the Nocturne, but with everything that this word includes in the way of diversified impression and special lights.

"*Clouds*: the unchangeable appearance of the sky, with the slow and solemn march of the clouds dissolving in a gray agony tinted with white.

"*Festivals:* movement, rhythm dancing in the atmosphere, with bursts of brusque light. There is also the episode of a procession (dazzling and wholly idealistic vision) passing through the festival and blended with it; but the main idea and substance obstinately remain—always the Festival and its blended music—luminous dust participating in the universal rhythm of all things.

"*Sirens*: the sea and its innumerable rhythms; then amid the billows silvered by the moon the mysterious song of the Sirens is heard; it laughs and passes."

. . . . Debussy, before his death, made many changes in the instrumentation of these Nocturnes.

The score is dedicated to Georges Hartmann, the late music publisher and librettist. Jean Marnold contributed an elaborate study of these Nocturnes to *Le Courrier Musical*, Paris, ...

PHILIP HALE, *Boston Symphony Orchestra*

Rhapsody for orchestra and saxophone

Debussy was reluctant to write this Rhapsody, but since it had been "ordered, paid for, and eaten," he eventually persevered, at least to a certain point. About 1901, Mrs. Richard J. Hall of Boston commissioned Debussy to write a piece for saxophone with orchestral accompaniment. Mrs. Hall for reasons of health had taken up the saxophone, which had not yet gained prominence through jazz. Wishing without regard for cost to build up a repertory for herself, she had ordered compositions from various musicians. "Debussy," so says M. Vallas, "was very dilatory in the matter; he was almost incapable of composing to order, and, besides, he knew very little about the technique of this solo instrument."

To André Messager, Debussy wrote on June 8, 1903; "The Americans are proverbially tenacious. The saxophone lady landed in Paris at 58 Rue Cardinet eight or ten days ago and is inquiring about her piece. Of course I assured her that, with the exception of Rameses II, it is the only subject that occupies my thoughts. All the same, I have had to set to work on it. So here I am searching desperately for novel combinations calculated to show off this aquatic instrument. . . . I have been working as hard as in the good old days of *Pelleas*."

When, the next year, Mrs. Hall played a work by Vincent d'Indy, Debussy "thought it ridiculous to see a lady in a pink frock playing on such an ungainly instrument; and he was not at all anxious that his work should provide a similar spectacle." In a letter to the poet Pierre Louys, Debussy poses the gentle question of "whether the saxophone indulges in romantic tenderness like a clarinet."

While the composer continued to procrastinate, Mrs. Hall became insistent. And, after all, had not the work been "ordered, paid for and eaten?" So in 1905, Debussy sketched a piece for saxophone and piano but not until 1911 did he attempt to orchestrate it. Then he did so only fragmentarily, and the script that he forwarded to Mrs. Hall before the end of the year could not be used. Though the solo part was complete, such was not the case with the instrumentation.

In 1919, after Debussy's death, Roger-Ducasse filled out the orchestral score. This was first performed on May 11, 1919, in Paris. With the solo part transferred to an English horn, the Rhapsody emerged in Boston at a concert of the Boston Symphony Orchestra on February 12, 1932. . . .

PITTS SANBORN, *Philharmonic-Symphony Society of New York*

Iberia: Images for Orchestra No. 2

Iberia is the second in a series of three orchestral compositions by Debussy entitled *Images.* . . . The first performance of *Iberia* in the United States was by the Philharmonic Society of New York, conducted by Gustav Mahler, on January 3, 1911. . . .

Debussy wrote on May 6, 1905 to Jacques Durand, his publisher, that he was preparing these compositions for two pianofortes: I, *Gigues tristes;* II, *Iberia;* III, *Valse.* In September of that year he hoped to finish them. . . . Debussy wrote on December 4, 1910, from Budapest, where he gave a concert of his works, that *Iberia* was especially successful. "They could not play *The Sea,* no more the 'Nocturnes,' from want of rehearsal. I was assured that the orchestra knew *The Sea,* for it had been played through three times. Ah! my friend, if you had heard it!. . . . I assure you to put *Iberia* right in two rehearsals was, indeed, an effort. . . . Don't forget that these players understood me only through an interpreter—a sort of Doctor of Law—who perhaps transmitted my thought only deforming it. I tried every means. I sang, made the gestures of Italian pantomime, etc.—it was enough to touch the heart of a buffalo. Well, they at last understood me, and I had the last word. I was recalled like a ballet girl, and if the idolatrous crowd did not unharness the horses of my carriage, it was because I had a simple taxi. The moral of this journey is that I am not made to exercise the profession of composer of music in a foreign land. One must consent to a sort of compromise which decidedly repels me."

PHILIP HALE, *Boston Symphony Orchestra*

FREDERICK DELIUS

(Born in Bradford, England, January 29, 1862—
died at Grez-sur-Loing, France, June 10, 1934)

HE WAS the son of a wool merchant who had emigrated from Germany and a business career was carefully planned for him. But two years of "preparation" in the Manchester offices of a relative were enough for Delius. He expressed a wish to go to America, possibly to work in an orange grove. In later years, he confessed the idea to be entirely romantic. He had no notion of an orange grove or what such "work" would entail.

So his father bought him the "orange grove" in Florida and Frederick came along to manage it—but not for long. What leisure he could muster from his duties as a planter—and later accounts seem to describe his spare time as considerable—he devoted to the study of piano, harmony and counterpoint. Finally, he abandoned all pretense of business, went to Danville, Virginia, to teach and then gained a post as an organist in New York.

There came a time when he had saved enough to go to Leipzig and study at the Conservatory under Sitt, Jadassohn and Reinecke.

His father died and left him adequate means, and in 1899 he bought a country home at Grez-sur-Loing, France, and settled there for the rest of his life, composing some important scores in the next thirty years.

A young concertgoer was once heard to remark, after he had listened to one of Delius' compositions: "It doesn't get anywhere." The same remark might be applied to Delius himself because, measured by the usual standards, he did not get anywhere. He composed much music during his lifetime, some of it of great artistic worth, but somehow his scores were too often returned by conductors with "unplayable" chalked upon them. In Germany, where he did his serious work as a student of composition, his ability was recognized early, and in France, Floreut Schmitt and Ravel transcribed parts of his operas for piano. It was not until Delius was thirty-six years old, in 1899, that his music was heard in London. The critics were kindly and, as Heseltine said, "acquitted themselves with more sanity and sobriety of judgment than they had displayed on many subsequent occasions." Eight years went by before another Delius composition was played in England; even after Sir Thomas Beecham became his champion, the public remained apathetic. Finally in 1929, there was a London festival of his music, and he was decorated by King George V, but this hardly furthered his reputation in England.

"Perhaps the public should not be censored too severely for its indifference," to quote a program note of the Philadelphia Orchestra by R. F. L. McCombs and Louise Beck. "Its reaction was merely a sign of the times—today's world has use only for the useful. The creative artist cannot sell his goods unless it (he) is backed up by much ballyhoo by press, critics or patrons; the alternative is to slink off in 'lonely splendor' and pursue his ideal. Delius did just this. He withdrew to the little village of Grez-sur-Loing, near Fontainebleau to live in seclusion and write according to his creed: 'It is only that which cannot be expressed otherwise that is worth expressing in music,' He lived as he composed, 'not to be understood, but for those who understand.' "

His final years were tragic. Paralyzed and blind, entirely dependent upon his wife, Delius continued to compose, dictating to a disciple, Eric Fenby, his last works, note by note. He died on June 10, 1934, and his body was transferred to Southern England and "buried in Limpsfield to the accompaniment of Delius music performed in a nearby church under the direction of Sir Thomas Beecham."

On Hearing the First Cuckoo in Spring

This short tone-poem, along with its companion piece, *Summer Night on the River,* was composed during 1912-1913 and came to performance in a concert of the London Philharmonic Orchestra on January 20, 1914, Willem Mengelberg conducting. The score is dedicated to the English composer Balfour Gardiner; it was published, together with a transcription for the piano, by Gerard Bunk in 1913.

Some have seen in this composition an abstract of Delius' life, others merely his great love for Norway, where he spent eighteen idyllic summers with Edvard Grieg and Frants Beyer.

Two themes are used: one, which is original with Delius is "a sequence of phrases that echo each other, like distant cuckoo calls." The second is that of a Norwegian folk song *I Ola Dalom* (*In Ola Valley*), which we find Grieg using in a group of pianoforte pieces, "Norwegian Melodies," Opus 66.

Philip Heseltine who wrote the Keats cycle, *The Curlew,* under the pen name, Peter Warlock, has given us a very sensitive appreciation in his life of Delius. Of *On Hearing the First Cuckoo in Spring,* he says:

"Associated with the song is the legend of an old woman who, thinking her son had been kidnapped by the bogies and bugaboos of the hills, rang the bells of the neighboring church in the hope of releasing him from their power. But Delius chose the theme for its musical beauty, without any thought of its traditional associations and, using it as a motif, has painted in unforgettable tones the emotions of one for whom spring is not so much a season of riot and exuberance, fresh hopes and renewed vitality, as a vision of such sweet and tender loveliness that the heart stands still in contemplation of it and the old unrest of the soul is put to sleep."

Heseltine goes on to speak of the sadness that is mingled with the serenity and sweetness of the conception of spring as Delius has portrayed it in his tone-poem, for "it is a spring of the soul that cannot blossom until autumn has come, that has so little time to stay. And so we are again confronted with the paradox of past and present. The very desire to recapture and embalm the past is a longing that strives to overlap time's limitations, for time is the great enemy of the soul that longs for the infinite."

LOUISE BECK, *Philadelphia Orchestra*

Intermezzo, "The Walk to the Paradise Garden" from *A Village Romeo and Juliet*

Delius composed *A Village Romeo and Juliet,* lyric drama in six pictures, in 1900 and 1901. The libretto was written by the composer and his wife, who based their text on a tale in Gottfried Keller's *Die Leute von Seldwyla* (*The folk of Seldwyla*). The opera was first produced in Germany as *Romeo and Julia auf dem Dorfe* at the Komische Oper, Berlin, under the direction of Fritz Cassiver on February 21, 1907. Sir Thomas Beecham introduced the work to English audiences in English at Covent Garden in London on February 22, 1910. There was a revival at Covent Garden in March 1920, also under Sir Thomas.

The Walk to the Paradise Garden, the interlude between the fifth and sixth pictures of the music-drama, has been edited for concert performance by Sir Thomas. These instruments are used:

Two flutes, oboe and English horn, two clarinets, two bassoons, four horns, two trumpets, three trombones, tympani, harp and strings.

Delius tells in his opera, *A Village Romeo and Juliet,* the story of a modern pair of lovers in a rural setting. Sali and Vrenchen are Delius' counterparts of the immortal characters of Shakespeare! They seek only one happy day together, but even this seems impossible. At the end of the fifth tableau Sali says:

"I know another place not very far from here where we will be quite unknown. In the Paradise Garden we will dance the night away. Come! Let us go!" The curtain falls and the hushed music of the intermezzo begins. The couple walk hand in hand through the moonlit countryside. Only in their walk do they find a full measure of happiness, but it is to lead them only to frustration and death. Philip Heseltine writes of the Intermezzo in his biography of Delius:

"Between the fifth and sixth scenes occurs the miraculously lovely orchestral interlude which is in itself an epitome of the whole dream."

GEORGE H. L. SMITH, *Cleveland Orchestra*

Brigg Fair: An English Rhapsody

Brigg Fair. . . . was inspired by an old Lincolnshire folk song. Percy Grainger is credited with having discovered this folk song and to him Delius has dedicated the work. *Brigg Fair* is a series of variations, sometimes *a la passacaglia,* on that folk song. The interesting tang of the Doric mode in which the folk song moves, as much as Delius' rich harmonic texture, is responsible for the pronounced character of *Brigg Fair.*

The text of the folk song follows:

> It was on the fifth of August,
> The weather fine and fair,
> Unto Brigg Fair I did repair,
> For love I was inclined.
>
> I rose up with the lark in the morning,
> With my heart so full of glee,
> Of thinking there to meet my dear,
> Long time I wished to see.
>
> I looked over my left shoulder,
> To see whom I could see.
> And there I spied my own true love,
> Come tripping down to me.
>
> I took hold of her lily white hand,
> And merrily was her heart,
> And now we've met together,
> I hope we ne'er shall part.
>
> For it's meeting is a pleasure
> And parting is a grief,
> But an inconstant lover
> Is worse than a thief.

The green leaves they shall wither
And the branches they shall die
If ever I prove false to her,
To the girl that loves me.

Brigg Fair. . . . was first played in Liverpool in 1908. The first American performance was in 1910.

CARL PAIGE WOOD, *Seattle Symphony Orchestra*

Concerto for pianoforte

Delius' only piano concerto was written in 1897 and revived in 1906-1907. When Percy Grainger played it for the first time in the United States in 1915, he gave the following information to the editor of the program:

"The work," he said "was conceived in Florida, where Delius as a very young man went to manage a plantation belonging to his father and where the untutored singing of the Negro workers so captivated his imagination that he resolved to become a composer. Out of these promptings the concerto was born. 'Darky' feeling is particularly noticeable in the slow movement, and the beauty and poetry of this section alone are sufficient to immortalize the work, which throughout, is remarkable for the wonderfully telling way in which the rippling and percussive nature of the solo instrument is blended with or contrasted against the singing, melodic quality of the orchestral treatment."

BARBARA DUNCAN, *Rochester Philharmonic Orchestra*

PAUL ABRAHAM DUKAS

(Born in Paris, October 1, 1865—died in Paris, May
18, 1935)

PAUL DUKAS has been considered a glittering ornament of
French modern music and his name has been linked with the revolt of contemporary composers against artistic formalism.

From his earliest childhood he showed a singular bent for
music. His family was too poor to provide instruction, but he
tinkled the keys of a neighbor's piano whenever the chance afforded.

He entered the Paris Conservatoire in 1882, where his musical appetite, according to his instructors, was enormous. He soon
became an outstanding student, for he studied and practiced night
and day. He won the second *Prix de Rome* in 1888 with a cantata,
"Velleda."

Like all young Frenchmen of military age, he had to give up
the Conservatoire for a time for the life of the field and garrison.
But he always considered this a valuable period, for he had leisure
to study the scores of the classics, page by page, thereby gaining a
new insight into composition.

His stint in the army done, the young composer began work
on an overture, "Polyeucte," his first composition to be performed
publicly. But his renown became international with the performance of *The Sorcerer's Apprentice,* of which more later.

He composed two operas, *The Peri* and *Ariadne and Bluebeard,* the latter, on a text of Maeterlinck, has been described as
"second only to *Pelleas* in French opera of the twentieth century."
He has written a symphony in C major and many important piano
works.

The Sorcerer's Apprentice

The story of *The Sorcerer's Apprentice* was originally written
by the Greek satirist Lucian, in the Second Century A. D., as part
of a dialogue entitled *The Lie-Fancier,* which ridicules the magi-

129

cians and pseudoscientists of that time. About sixteen hundred years later, in 1796, Goethe made Lucian's story the subject of a little comic ballad. Just a century after Goethe, Dukas transposed the idea into musical terms.

The story concerns a sorcerer who had a magic formula for turning a piece of wood into a living servant which would then perform all sorts of menial tasks. One day while the sorcerer was not at home, his apprentice, who had overheard the magic words through which this transformation was accomplished, decided to experiment on his own. He ordered a broom to bring water from the lake, which the obliging utensil did until all the receptacles in the house were filled. Then the apprentice discovered that he did not know the formula for restoring the broom to its original form. Meanwhile, bucket upon bucket was diligently brought and the house was flooded.

At length, the apprentice picked up a hatchet and cleft the broom in two, and this only made matters twice as bad, for now both parts of the stick seized buckets and went to the lake. At the height of the confusion the sorcerer himself returned, uttered the formula for calling off the broomsticks and restored his house to order.

The tone-poem begins quietly, but with mysterious hints of the subject matter to come, as if to suggest the apprentice's plans. At last the sorcerer goes and the coast is clear. A famous bassoon melody sends forth the broomstick on its errand. The water rises and the brainless water-carrier grows more furious in its attention to duty. The apprentice cries out and eventually there is a sudden suspense-filled pause as the hatchet is wielded. Then the water-carrying starts again with redoubled energy. At the end the sorcerer's return and the restoration of the broomsticks to their original condition are suggested by the music.

ALFRED FRANKENSTEIN, *San Francisco Symphony Orchestra*

ANTONIN LEOPOLD DVORAK

(Born in Meulhausen, near Kralup, Bohemia, September 8, 1841—died in Prague, May 1, 1904)

THE CZECH name of Dvorak's birthplace is Nelahozeves, on the Voltava, and whether it still exists depends upon whether the Nazis made contact with it. At last accounts, the ruins were there but little else.

Antonin was the eldest son of Frantisek Dvorak, the local butcher and innkeeper. His mother, Anna, was the daughter of Josef Zdenek, steward of Uh-near-Chrzin, an estate in the district of Slanaske.

The boy grew up healthy and high-spirited. The only person in this rusticated Czech village capable of giving him the rudiments of a musical education was the Czech cantor, Josef Spitz, an excellent organist.

Learning first the basic elements of violin-playing well enough to help his father in his capacity as village musician, the boy finally went to live with an uncle in a nearby village. Here he learned German and carried on his music. In his sixteenth year, he undertook systematic study at Prague, "profiting greatly by contact with Smetana and Bendl and struggling heroically onward until, in 1875, he gained financial assistance from the Viennese government."

His Slavonic Dances established his reputation as a composer, although a previous patriotic cantata brought him to the attention of musicians. The success of this work was striking, for in it he first made use of the national idiom. But the popularity of the dances spread his name far and wide among the lay public.

The friendship at this time of several famous musicians helped his career immeasurably. Among them was Brahms, who had been appointed one of the judges to pass upon works submitted for an annual pension. The duets of Dvorak fascinated him and enlisted his immediate enthusiasm. He soon kindled the interest of the other judges to such an extent that Dvorak won the prize.

In 1892 he was invited to become director of the National

Conservatory of New York. He accepted and filled the position until 1895. He passed two summers in a Bohemian colony in Iowa, where a good part of the Fifth Symphony was composed, also some chamber music and song. He returned to Bohemia and headed the Prague Conservatory. He died there suddenly on May 1, 1904.

Carnival Overture

The year 1891 was a momentous one for that "wild-man-of-the-woods," Antonin Dvorak. In January, at the age of fifty, he began teaching for the first time when he accepted the post of professor of composition and instrumentation and form, at the Prague Conservatory. In the spring, he journeyed to England where, at Cambridge, he received the honorary degree of Mus.D., a recognition that was echoed at home when the Prague University, not to be outdone, conferred the degree of Ph.D. During the summer months, the grateful Dvorak turned his mind to the writing of thank-you notes, which, with him, took the form of music.

The result was a sort of three-decker musical sandwich, consisting of as many overtures, the collective title being, *Nature, Life and Love*. The top layer, as it were, was titled: *In Nature's Realm*, and was dedicated to the University of Cambridge. The middle layer, or "filling" of the sandwich, was the *Carnival Overture* (originally titled *Bohemian Carnival*) and that was dedicated to the Prague University. His thank-you notes completed, but his pen still full, he dashed off the bottom layer, *Othello*. This done, he turned his full attention to enjoying the epidemic of celebration that broke out in his beloved Bohemia over the observance of his fiftieth birthday on September 8.

While Dvorak planned the three overtures to be done at one hearing (they were so done at their Prague premiere on April 28, 1892, and at their first American performance in the fall of that year, the composer conducting both performances) they were published separately, two years later, as Opus 91, 92 and 93, in the order given above, of which the first and last have been lost in the busy shuffle of time.

Carnival is a gay, exuberant work, expertly scored and always

effective. Few works carry the emotional impact of the very opening pages when the entire orchestra, short only piccolo and harp,
fairly leaps upon the brilliant main theme.

GUSTAV KLEMM, *Baltimore Symphony Orchestra*

Symphony No. 5 in E minor (Opus 95, "From the New World")

The tide of controversy that swirled about the *New World
Symphony* after its first performance by the Philharmonic Society
of New York, under Anton Seidl, on December 18, 1893, can have
small interest for the casual listener of today.

Yet the point of whether the *New World Symphony* was really
"American" in its import and thematic derivation, or Bohemian in
color and design, occasioned some bitter feuds in the small world
of music and musicians. The late Henry Krehbiel, a close friend of
Dvorak during those days of his American residence as head of the
New York Conservatory of Music, was a constant adviser in the
composition of this work.

In a letter to the English critic, H. C. Colles, Mr. Krehbiel
contends that Dvorak, while intensely interested in slave songs and
in certain patriotic ditties like "Yankee Doodle," adapted none of
these expedients to create an "American" symphony and that the
music is an expression of Dvorak's own idiom. Therefore, Krehbiel
adds, it can be called Bohemian rather than American.

Karel Hoffmeister, pupil and biographer of Dvorak, seems inclined to agree with Mr. Krehbiel. Hoffmeister speaks of the
"splendid sonority" of the work and explains that "because at
this time Dvorak was more disposed to homophonic methods, the
contrapuntal treatment is less predominant than in former works.
. . . The Fifth Symphony depicts Dvorak's restless life and all the
varied impressions of the New World. . . . Whatever melodic fragments he may have seen fit to use in his Fifth Symphony, to those
who are familiar with the folk music of the Central-European
Slavs this work will always seem, in melodic material and
rhythmic treatment, more akin to the Slavonic than the Afro-
American world."

Dvorak produced five symphonies published during his lifetime. Two others (E flat, 1872; D minor, 1874) were issued post-

humously. Dr. Percy Goetschius remarks that "they possess no special importance." The five are designated as follows:

No. 1, D major (Opus 60); No. 2, D minor (Opus 70); No. 3, F major (Opus 76); No. 4, G minor (Opus 88); No. 5, E minor (Opus 95, *From the New World*).

JULIAN SEAMAN, *Elizabeth (N.J.) Philharmonic Society*

Concerto for violoncello in B minor (Opus 104)

Dvorak completed his Violoncello Concerto in 1895. The project of composing it was probably suggested to the Bohemian master by his friend Hans Wihan, to whom the work is dedicated. Wihan. . . . was a pupil of the Conservatorium in Prague. In 1874 he became concertmaster of the private orchestra of Prince Dervies, at Nice, and later (in 1876) concertmaster of Bilse's orchestra in Berlin. He took the position of solo violoncellist at the Munich Opera in 1880 and seven years later became teacher of violoncello playing in the Conservatorium of Prague. He founded the Bohemian String Quartet in 1892.

Some of the Violoncello Concerto was composed before Dvorak left New York to return to Bohemia, and advice was given to him in the matter of passage-writing for the instrument by Alwin Schroeder, but it is certain that Wihan had something to do with the "effects" which are contained in the solo part of the work. "I have now," wrote Dvorak to his publisher, Simrock, June 28, 1895, "the 'Cello Concerto, score and parts (the principal part with fingering and bowing indications has been made by Professor Wihan himself.)"

Simrock accepted the concerto and a *Te Deum,* which Dvorak had offered for sale, and communicating with the firm, asking them to state the price which they would give for the works, the composer writing in September 1895, said that he was arranging piano accompaniment from the score. "The Concerto," he added, "I must dedicate to my friend, Wihan."

It would seem, however, that Wihan desired to have more to do with Dvorak's Concerto than its composer wished. Dvorak was afraid that his friend might even induce the publishers to accept his ideas concerning the work without first obtaining his consent.

The Bohemian master wrote therefore on October 3 to Simrock, thus:

"My friend Wihan and I have differed as to certain things. Many of the passages do not please me, and I must insist that my work be printed as I have written it. In certain places the passages may, indeed, be printed in two versions—a comparatively easy and a more difficult one. Above all, I give you my work only if you will promise me that no one—not even my friend Wihan—shall make any alteration in it without my knowledge and permission— also no cadenza such as Wihan has made in the last movement— and that its form shall be as I have felt it and thought it out. The cadenza in the last movement is not to exist either in the orchestral or the piano score; I informed Wihan, when he showed it to me, that it is impossible so to insert one. The Finale closes gradually *diminuendo*—like a breath—with reminiscences of the first and second movements; the solo dies away to a *pianissimo,* then there is a *crescendo,* and the last measures are taken up by the orchestra, ending stormily. That was my idea, and from it I cannot recede."

In November 1895, Dvorak received a letter from the Philharmonic Society of London, inviting him to conduct one of its concerts. It was not, however, until March that the composer made his appearance in the British metropolis.

On the nineteenth of that month, he conducted his first performance of the new Violoncello Concerto, the soloist having been Leo Stèrn. In addition to the Concerto, Dvorak conducted his symphony in G and his Biblical songs. The latter, originally composed for voice and piano, were orchestrated specially for this concert, and they were sung by Mrs. Katherine Fisk. In addition to these works, Beethoven's E flat Concerto for piano was played by Emil Sauer. . . .

FELIX BOROWSKI, *Chicago Symphony Orchestra*

Slavonic Dances (Opus 45 and Opus 72)

It was Johannes Brahms who suggested to his publisher, Simrock, that he ask the young Dvorak to compose some Slavonic Dances, more or less in the style of Brahms' own very successful

Hungarian Dances. Dvorak responded eagerly to the suggestion and composed his first set of eight in rapid succession. He employed the characteristic rhythms of Czech folk dances but the melodies and harmonies were his own. In this respect he differed from Brahms, who confined himself almost entirely to actual Gypsy melodies. He used the medium of the piano duet for his dances as Brahms had done, but he began to orchestrate them immediately and did not leave them for others to transcribe as did Brahms with all but three of the Hungarian Dances.

Swiftly composed and immediately published, Dvorak's dances quickly made their way around the musical world . . . Simrock soon pressed Dvorak for more of such salable items . . . But it was not until July 1886 that Dvorak was ready with eight more Slavonic Dances . . . Simrock immediately asked him to orchestrate the new dances. This took six months longer and apparently caused the composer some annoyance, for he wrote that the instrumentation "sounds like the devil." It was perhaps difficult for Dvorak to find once again melodies so peculiarly naive and natural as those that had given the first series of dances their elemental freshness. In the second set he was tempted more to write dance-poems than straightforward dances, and he looked beyond Czech folk forms to those of other Slavic peoples . . .

GEORVE HENRY LOVETT SMITH, *Cleveland Orchestra*

SIR EDWARD WILLIAM ELGAR

(Born in Broadheath, England, June 2, 1857—died
in Worcester, February 23, 1934)

SON OF AN organist and a musical family, at sixteen Elgar entered a solicitor's office in London, but after three years decided to abandon law for music. Back he went to Broadheath and began to study—theory and several instruments. He returned to London in 1877, to study violin with Adolf Pollitzer, but the fifth lesson convinced him he would never be a virtuoso.

Back he went to Worcester, near his home, to be a bandmaster and conduct a glee club. He took a short holiday in Germany, then was appointed organist of St. George's Cathedral.

His career as a composer may be attributed somewhat to the influence of his wife, Caroline Alice Roberts, whom he married in 1889. "In 1891," writes David Ewen, "he settled in Malvern and, having deserted all other musical occupations, turned to composition. Two years later 'The Black Knight,' a choral work, was performed in Worcester." Other choral works followed, with moderate success.

His first and probably most important works were the "Enigma" Variations for orchestra and the oratorio "The Dream of Gerontius." Subsequent compositions, up to the outbreak of the First World War, brought his name to the front rank of English composers. During the war he served as a special constable in the Hampstead Volunteer Reserve.

His wife died in 1920 and Elgar, who had "leaned heavily on her advice, criticism and encouragement," decided to give up composing. Consequently, nothing came from his pen until 1929, when he was induced to compose a hymn of prayer for the recovery of King George V, then seriously ill.

He was appointed Master of the King's Music in 1924 and was knighted in 1934. He began a third symphony but died at his home before it was completed.

Variations for Orchestra (Opus 35, "Enigma")

The seventy-fifth anniversary of Sir Edward Elgar's birth was widely celebrated last year (1932), especially in England. Interesting comment was rife on the emergence of English music from its nineteenth century obscurity, and of the part which Sir Edward Elgar had played in this emancipation.

The Variations were composed in 1899, and performed in London under Hans Richter in June of that year. There are fourteen variations and the work is dedicated "to my friends pictured within." Elgar's own comment is as follows: "It is true that I have sketched for their own amusement and mine, the idiosyncrasies of my friends, not necessarily musicians; but this is a personal matter and need not have been mentioned publicly. The Variations should stand simply as a piece of music. The Enigma I will not explain, its 'dark saying' must be left unguessed, and I warn you that the apparent connection between the Variations and the Theme is often of the slightest texture; further, through and over the whole set another and larger theme 'goes' but is not played. . . . So the principal Theme never appears, even as in some late dramas—e.g., Maeterlinck's *L'Intruse* and *Les Sept Princesses*— the chief character is never on the stage."

Each variation is headed by an initial or a fanciful name. For none of these indications has the original been certainly discovered, save for the ninth variation, entitled "Nimrod," which describes the composer's friend, A. A. Jaeger. But even admitting this, Sir Edward says: "Something ardent and mercurial, in addition to the slow movement would have been needed to portray his character and temperament. The variation is the record of a long summer evening talk, when my friend grew nobly eloquent (as only he could) on the grandeur of Beethoven and especially of his slow movements."

If the reader will measure the increase in satisfaction which is due to the identification of its object, and compare it with the pleasure he has from "Ysobel" (the sixth) or "Dorabella" (the tenth), whose personalities have never been identified, he will probably be willing to give up speculating and enjoy the music.

DONALD FERGUSON, *Minneapolis Symphony Orchestra*

March: *Pomp and Circumstance*

The title of *Pomp and Circumstance* was bestowed by England's distinguished and self-taught composer, Sir Edward Elgar, upon a set of six military marches which he wrote because he was "appalled at the lack of interesting and spirited music" for marching.

Nowadays, however, the popularity of just one of these

marches has led most musicians to forget the other five, and to apply the title of the set to this one alone. It is frequently sung, too, under the title of "Land of Hope and Glory" and in that form, has become almost as popular in England as "God Save the King."

Although Elgar was the son of an organist, most of his musical education was self-acquired and he learned to play the organ and other instruments with very little outside help. Not until he married, in 1889, did his compositional career start in earnest and then he had the great good fortune to marry a woman who was even more to him—in inspiration and friendly understanding criticism—than wonderful Elisabet von Herzogenberg was to bachelor Brahms.

As most concertgoers know, Elgar's fame rests largely upon the "Enigma" Variations, a brilliant piece of orchestral writing in which each variation paints a portrait of a musical friend, the whole being (as he once expressed it) a "counterpoint on a theme that is never played." Other of his important works include a violin concerto and an oratorio, *The Dream of Gerontius*.

Yet some of his most important pieces may be the little ones, such as the poetic "salut d'Amour," which is frequently heard coming from the silken bows of string orchestras playing "dinner music."

GEORGE SCHAUN, *Baltimore Symphony Orchestra*

GEORGES ENESCO

(Born in Dorohiu, Romania, August 19, 1881—now
living in New York)

GEORGES ENESCO has come to be regarded as a musical ambassador-at-large from his native Romania. Two things impress one upon first acquaintance. First his fantastic modesty; second, his bewildering competence as a musical scholar, instrumentalist, conductor and composer. Musicians long have considered him to be one of the really great masters of the present day.

For he is a musicologist of searching and comprehensive talents, a gifted and impressive pianist, an extraordinary 'cellist and a respected performer upon nearly every instrument of the modern orchestra. The violin is his especial metier, and he is widely known as a conductor and composer.

The violin fitted naturally into his small hands, a farm boy in the Moldavian hills, and he was heard to improvise and imitate the folk tunes of his people long before he could tell one note from another, or knew the slightest rudiments of formal music.

He entered the Vienna Conservatory at the age of seven and was graduated with high honors. From there he went on to study at the Conservatoire in Paris under Massenet, Gedalge and Gabriel Fauré. Then followed an interval of virtuoso violin playing all over Europe, during which he acquired a glittering reputation as an interpreter of Mozart.

At the age of seventeen he made his debut as a composer with a performance of "Poeme Romain" at one of the Concerts Colonne in 1898. Soon after this event, he was appointed Court Violinist to the Queen of Romania, Carmen Sylva, herself an accomplished musician.

At the beginning of the First World War, Enesco returned to Romania, to share the sufferings and privations of his fellow countrymen. After the war he conducted in Bucharest, composed and organized concerts of contemporary music. His remarkable versatility became apparent at this time.

He came to the United States for the first time in 1922-1923 as guest conductor of the Philadelphia Orchestra.

For a number of years, Yehudi Menuhin studied with Enesco. This young violinist says of him: "He is the man to whom I owe everything and he is the one man who never says so. I used to spend three or four months every year with him during which he criticized my playing, helped with interpretations and so on. I know of no person who is so complete as he is. There are no shadows in him, he is all right. If miracles could be performed, I mean real miracles, supernatural manifestations, he could perform them."

Many of his more serious works have become established in the standard orchestral repertoire, including the *Romanian Rhapsodies*. He has been working over a third symphony first completed in the winter of 1913-1914 for orchestra, organ and chorus. He has begun a new sonata for violin and piano devised especially, he says, for Menuhin, his former pupil, "whom I love as my own son."

One of his latest creations is the four-act lyrical tragedy, *Oedipus Rex,* which had its premiere in March 1938, at the Paris Opera.

He will be remembered as a conductor by those who may have frequented the Hall of Fame at the New York World's Fair in 1939, when he led the Philharmonic-Symphony Society of New York under the auspices of the Romanian High Commission in a concert devoted exclusively to contemporary Romanian music.

Enesco has this word for young composers:

"I compose very slowly because I believe that is the best way. If you work slowly and carefully, even if you do not achieve great results, you at least achieve sincere ones."

Romanian Rhapsody No. 1 in A (Opus 11)

. . . . As a composer his [Enesco's] works cover the musical field (chamber music, a four-act lyrical tragedy, two symphonies, two orchestral suites, etc.) but none of them enjoys a greater popularity than the first of his three *Romanian Rhapsodies,* a dazzling composition compounded of folk tunes drawn from the rich lore of his native land.

While the popularity of his rhapsody must be gratifying to the composer, it is quite possible that his pleasure is somewhat dampened when he realizes that, through his publisher's carelessness, the work is not copyrighted in the United States, where its many performances net him exactly nothing in the way of financial return.

GUSTAV KLEMM, *Baltimore Symphony Orchestra*

Romanian Rhapsody No. 2 in D (Opus 11)

Georges Enesco is best known for his *First Romanian Rhapsody*. The distinguished Romanian composer, violinist and conductor has written technically and musically more important works, but this work has done for him, in a sense, what the C-sharp minor prelude did for Rachmaninoff.

In this score (*Rhapsody No. 2*). . . . the voice of Romania, the dance tunes of gypsies and the songs of peasants speak unmistakably and captivating. Brilliant, dramatic contrasts, specifically national in tunes and color, this orchestra piece, notwithstanding modern instrumentation, is idealized folk music from the composer's native country. It is interesting to observe that this music, like the people of Romania, combines Slavonic strains with those of Asia and Arabia and, again, seems to have a touch of the Spanish.

BRUNO DAVID USSHER, *Los Angeles Philharmonic Orchestra*

MANUEL DE FALLA

(Born in Cádiz, Spain, November 23, 1876—died in
Alta Gracia, Argentina, November 14, 1946)

THE NEW spirit of music in Spain might be said to repose in Manuel de Falla. He has become an almost legendary figure in the annals of contemporary Spanish music, yet his musical thinking has been likened to the post-Debussy school of Ravel.

Born in Cádiz, that beautiful white city near the mouth of the Guadalquivir, he first learned the rudiments of music from his mother, a gifted pianist and a musician of the highest taste and feelings.

His talent was apparent and developed rapidly and at an early age he was sent to the Royal Conservatory in Madrid, where he studied under the composer Filipe Pedrell and the pianist José Trago. It may have been Pedrell who turned his attention to native Spanish music.

He began serious composition after graduation from the Conservatory and in 1905 composed a lyric drama, *La Vida Breve,* which won first prize in a competition for national opera conducted by the Real Academia de Bellas Artes.

Two years later he went to Paris, to stay seven years and absorb the atmosphere of its musical life, coming in frequent contact with leading French composers, particularly Claude Debussy. He returned to Spain in 1924.

"During the Civil War in Spain," says David Ewen, "Falla allied himself with the Franco forces, because he saw in the Franco nationalist movement a check to the antireligious activities that had been taking place throughout Spain. In 1938, Falla visited South America, where he conducted concerts of his own works. He has since made his home. . . . near Cordoba, in Argentina" (1942).

Three Dances from the ballet—*The Three Cornered Hat*

The three-cornered hat was the badge of office (in Don Pedro de Alarcón's novel of the 1870's) of a flirtatious *corregidor,* or magistrate, who had the village miller thrown into jail for no sounder reason than that he, the *corregidor,* might spend a pleasant interlude with the miller's wife. That lady, who enjoyed a joke, entertained her guest with seductive charm, but adroitly planned that, in his pursuit of her, he should fall into the mill pond. The would-be lover, chagrined at his wetting, but not yet despairing of his amour, had to hang up some of his clothes to dry, and meantime lay down to rest on the miller's bed. In that compromising situation, snoring, he was found by the miller who, in revenge, departed in the intruder's official finery (including the three-cornered hat) leaving behind a note to the effect that "your wife is no less beautiful than mine."

This thoroughly Spanish anecdote, which has been the basis

of four operas, was translated into terms of the dance by Martinez Sierra for Diaghilev's Russian Ballet, which first performed it at the Alhambra in London, July 23, 1919. Massine, Karsavina and Woisikowsky were the principal dancers; Pablo Picasso designed the settings and costumes; Ernest Ansermet conducted de Falla's music. The "Three Dances" drawn from the ballet were first heard in America at the hands of Pierre Monteux and the Boston Symphony in 1921. . . .

The English critic Edwin Evans has written of the "expressive directness" and the "remarkable unity" of this "lucid and luminous score," which he aptly refers to as a miniature music-drama. "The essential quality of the music is sharp, rhythmic definition, as clear, and, if you like to put it that way, as hard, as the landscape appears in the strong light of the South. There is nothing blurred either by compromise or by misty sentiment which belongs to the Northern atmosphere."

Manuel de Falla, most distinguished of all the Spanish composers of our time, exiled himself from the land of which he is so sensitive an interpreter at the height of the Spanish civil war. With a sister who had dedicated her life to his care (this note was written in October, 1942), he lives in precarious health, in near-poverty, in the country outside Cordoba, in the Argentine. Struggling against a bronchial ailment, as much as against the fear of it, the gentle little composer spends what working time he can muster strength for in the completion of a great oratorio *Atlantida* upon which he has been working for almost ten years, and which will take four hours to perform.

The few callers at the bare little house, according to an article by Lincoln Kirstein in the *New York Herald Tribune* of October 12, 1941, find that "Don Manuel is a tiny man with large eyes burned into his bald skull. His head is very fine, with a fringe of iron gray hair like a low tonsure. His skin is waxen brown. He carries a cane like a soldier, forcing service out of it. His mouth is very narrow. He stood at the table to talk, resting his large hands on it. His features were elongated as if by a combination of spiritual discipline and disease. He has the fanatic, suppressed ascetism of St. Francis as imagined by El Greco."

This, then, is perhaps the last portrait of a man whose music —small in quantity but great in artistry—will keep his name bright in Spain, and elsewhere, as the exemplar of Spain in music. He was, in his heyday, an honored colleague of Debussy, Ravel, Dukas and the rest of a vital and productive Parisian group. He was in demand as a pianist, his stage-pieces found producers and popularity. His little opera *La Vida Breve* was written in 1905, when it won a prize from the Madrid Academy of Fine Arts, although it was not produced until 1913. *El Amor Brujo* did not succeed as an opera, but de Falla made of it a Symphonic Suite, with a mezzo-soprano obbligato, which is frequently programmed. (Its first American performance was by the Philadelphia Orchestra in 1922). Of a Suite of four *Night Pieces* in E, *Nights in the Gardens of Spain* is often heard; it is the composer's chief symphonic score.

Later works include a marionette-opera *El Retablo de Maese Pedro,* based on an episode from *Don Quixote;* a concerto for harpsichord and strings; and *Psyche* a setting of a poem by Jean Aubry for mezzo-soprano, flute, harp, violin, viola and 'cello.

R. F. L. McCombs, *Philadelphia Orchestra*

Nights in the Gardens of Spain—Symphonic Impressions for Piano and Orchestra

De Falla had conceived the plan of writing his *Nights in the Gardens of Spain* as early as 1911, although he had originally intended to call the work *Nocturnes.* The composition was finished in 1916 and the first performance was given that year in Madrid. The composer did not intend his work to be program music.

"If," he wrote, "these 'symphonic impressions' have achieved their object the mere statement of their titles should be sufficient guide to the listener. Although in this work—as in all compositions which have a rightful claim to be considered as music—the composer has followed a definite design in regard to tonal, rhythmical and thematic material, the object for which it was written is no other than to evoke the memory of places, sensations and sentiments. The themes which are used are based on rhythms, modes, cadences and ornamental figures which are peculiar in Andalusia, although they are seldom employed in their original forms; and orchestration frequently uses in a conventional manner certain effects which are peculiar to the instruments which are popular in those parts of Spain. The music does not pretend to be descriptive; but something more than the sounds of festivals and dances has inspired these 'evocations in sound,' for melancholy and mystery play their parts also."

The following orchestra is employed in the work: Two flutes, two oboes, English horn, two clarinets, two bassoons, two trumpets, three trombones, bass tuba, kettledrum, triangle, cymbals, celesta, harp, piano and strings.

1—"At Generalife." (Allegretto tranquilo e misterioso, C-sharp minor, 6-8 time). Generalife is a part of the Alhambra, the ancient fortress and palace of the Moorish monarchs of Granada. Separated from the Alhambra by a ravine, Generalife, "The Garden of the Architect," was probably in the original form of the fortress an outwork, but later it became the summer villa of the sultans of Granada.

2—"Distant Dance." (Allegretto giusto, F major, 3-4 time). This leads without pause into

3—"In the Gardens of the Sierra of Cordova." Cordova is the name of a province of Andalusia, as well as the name of its capital, situated on the banks of the Guadalquivir, some seventy-five miles northeast of Seville. Under the name of *Corduba,* the town formed the first Roman colony in Spain.

In regard to this closing section of de Falla's work, J. B. Trend wrote in *Manuel de Falla and Spanish Music* (New York, 1929):

"We have suddenly been transported to one of those large villas on the hillside above Cordova, on an evening when a party is in progress, with a *zamba* of gypsy musicians, players, singers and dancers, while somewhere under the trees is a lone trestle table with a row of *dama-juanas* (demijohns) holding two or three firkins of *manzanilla* apiece.

FELIX BOROWSKY, *Minneapolis Symphony Orchestra*

Dance from *La Vida Breve*

While the Spanish composer, de Falla, was still in his twenties
—and long before he achieved worldwide eminence by composing
the orchestral nocturnes, *Nights in the Gardens of Spain,* or the
colorful ballets, *The Three-Cornered Hat* and *Love, the Sorcerer*
—he entered a prize competition held by the Madrid Academy of
Fine Arts. Falla submitted a lyric drama in two acts, *La Vida
Breve (Life is Short),* and won the prize.

The prize, like most of those which even the most successful
musicians capture, was large enough to be worthwhile but not
enough to keep the wolf from the door for very long. Consequently, during the eight years before the opera was finally given a
first performance (at the Casino Municipale de Nice on April 1,
1913), Falla went through many a day when food and hunger
were his two most insistent thoughts. He never forgot those gnawing experiences (chiefly in Paris, where Richard Wagner and his
young wife, Minna, had likewise been short of food) and so, during his more affluent later days in Granada, he made it a point to
carry a basket of food every day from his garden-surrounded hillside
home to some of the city's poor folk.

The Spanish dance. . . . occurs in the opera's second act.
It begins *molto ritmico* (very rhythmical) and soon launches into
a bold theme proclaimed by the horns and strings, in unison. The
principal theme returns, and then this foot-tingling music is con-
cluded by a series of rich chords scored for full orchestra.

GEORGE SCHAUN, *Baltimore Symphony Orchestra*

El Amor Brujo (*Love, the Sorcerer*)

This work was written originally as a ballet pantomime with
voice and small orchestra and was first produced at the Teatro de
Lara in Madrid on April 15, 1915. The libretto was based on an
Andalusian Gypsy tale. The story deals with Candelas, who had
loved a jealous and dissolute, but fascinating gypsy. Although having led an unhappy life with him, when he dies his memory re-

mains like a hypnotic dream—a morbid, gruesome spell. Carmelo, a handsome, gallant youth woos her but she is tormented by the thought that the gypsy may return and with this spectre before her she cannot exchange the kiss of perfect love with Carmelo. The spectre, however, is outwitted when Carmelo induces Lucia, an enchanting Gypsy girl, to ensnare him with her charms. The spectre makes love to Lucia and she brings him almost to despair. In the meantime, Carmelo convinces Candelas of his love and life triumphs over death. The lovers at last exchange the kiss and defeat the evil influence of the spectre, who perishes, definitely conquered by love.

BARBARA DUNCAN, *Rochester Philharmonic Orchestra*

CÉSAR-AUGUSTE FRANCK

(Born in Liége, December 10, 1822—died in Paris, November 8, 1890)

NO CONVENTIONAL objections to a musical career on the part of his parents harried the beginnings of César Franck. His father, described as "a stern, self-willed man," decided to make musicians of his two sons by main strength if necessary. Joseph, older than César by two years, did not fare well under this tutelage, but César took to it naturally.

When César was eleven, he played the piano well enough to undertake a concert tour of Belgium, "always accompanied by his eager and watchful sire." Apparently both boys had exhausted the resources of their local teachers by 1835, whereupon Papa Franck took them both to Paris. César studied first there under Anton Reicha, a friend of Beethoven.

Franck entered the Conservatoire in 1837, and was to re-enter the same institution thirty-five years later as a professor. He won an "extraordinary" prize in sight-reading in 1838. He began organ lessons with Benoist and studied composition with Leborne and was about ready to compete for the *Prix de Rome*. But his father decided he should be a virtuoso, so he had to rove the provinces, playing music "of his own and others' making, to thrill rural audiences. . . ." The family settled permanently in Paris in 1844, and from that year until his death César Franck taught music.

Liszt was impressed by Franck's first important work, the oratorio *Ruth*. He wrote a letter in 1854:

"Many years ago I conceived a very favorable opinion of the talent of M. César Franck as a composer at a performance of his Trios (very remarkable in my opinion, and far superior to other works of the same type published these last few years). His oratorio *Ruth* also contains some very beautiful things and bears the stamp of an elevated and well-sustained style."

Franck had been appointed organist of Notre Dame de Lorette in 1848 and in February of that year, in the midst of the revolution, he married a young actress. Carl Engel relates that to reach the church "the bridal pair and guests had to climb over barricades erected by insurgents."

The couple left the parental hearth for their own home and some years later Franck became choirmaster of Sainte Clotilde, then organist at the same church, and "in the unrelieved shadow of this organ loft Franck spent the better part of his life."

He succeeded his teacher Benoist at the Conservatoire in 1872 and remained a professor there until his death. He did not often have the chance to hear his own music played and his worth was hardly recognized outside a small circle of his disciples. He revered Liszt and several of his larger symphonic poems reflected this influence, but none of these works made much of an impression. The Franck Festival of 1887, for which his pupils and friends collected funds, was far from satisfactory.

His symphony in D minor puzzled most of the Parisian critics. When he got home after the performance, he told his family:

"Oh, it sounded well; just as I thought it would."

Perhaps the first real success of his rather obscure career came in 1890, when his string quartet was played by Ysaye and his associates at a concert of the Societe Nationale, which Franck had help to found and of which he was then president.

On a day in May of that year he set out for the home of one of his pupils. An omnibus ran him down and injured him severely. For a brief time he slowly rallied, but an attack of pleurisy caused his death on November 8, 1890.

Carl Engel recalls that the funeral was simple and "the mourners included but few representatives of musical Paris. France was not aware then that a very great master had passed away."

Symphony in D minor

This Symphony was produced at the Conservatoire, Paris, February 17, 1889. The Symphony is scored for two flutes, two oboes, English horn, two clarinets, bass clarinet, two bassoons, four horns, two trumpets, two cornets, three trombones, bass tuba, tympani, harps and strings. The score is dedicated to Henri Duparc. It was composed in 1888 and completed August 22 of that year.

Vincent d'Indy (pupil of Franck) in his *Life of Franck* gives some particulars about the first performance of the Symphony in D minor. "The performance was against the wish of most members of the famous orchestra, and was only pushed through thanks to the benevolent obstinacy of the conductor, Jules Garcin. The subscribers could make neither head nor tail of it, and the musical authorities were much in the same position. I inquired of one of them—a professor at the Conservatoire, and a kind of factotum on the committee—what he thought of the work. 'That a Symphony?' he replied in contemptuous tones. 'But, my dear sir, who ever heard of writing for the English horn in a symphony? Just mention a single symphony of Haydn or Beethoven introducing the English horn. There, well, you see—your Franck's music may be whatever you please, but it will certainly never be a symphony!' This was the attitude of the Conservatoire in the year of grace 1889.

"At another door of the concert hall, the composer of *Faust*, escorted by a train of adulators, male and female, fulminated a

kind of papal decree to the effect that this symphony was the
affirmation of incompetence pushed to dogmatic lengths. For sincerity and disinterestedness we must turn to the composer himself,
when, on his return from the concert, his whole family surrounded him, asking eagerly for news.

" 'Well, were you satisfied with the effect on the public? Was
there plenty of applause?'

"To which 'Father Franck,' thinking only of his work, replied
with a beaming countenance: 'Oh, it sounded well; just as I
thought it would!' "

PHILIP HALE, *Boston Symphony Orchestra*

GEORGE GERSHWIN

(Born in Brooklyn, September 26, 1898—died in
Hollywood, July 11, 1937)

HE WAS simple, unaffected and modest, he knew himself
and had he lived to musical maturity might have created a masterpiece in his own peculiar way. As it is, his serious music has a
quality of lasting memory, despite its obvious limitations.

Gershwin composed his first popular song at fourteen, studied
the piano himself and with a neighborhood teacher, finally went
to Rubin Goldmark for lessons in harmony. The publishing house
of Remick hired him at sixteen as a pianist. He stayed there for
three years.

By that time he had a few tunes of his own to his credit—and
his first musical comedy score, *La, La, Lucille*. When he was
twenty, George White commissioned him to write the score for the
Scandals. Then came his first smash song hit "Swanee," sung everywhere by Al Jolson.

Paul Whiteman was preparing his first all-American concert for Aeolian Hall in 1923, and he engaged George to compose a large work in the jazz idiom. *Rhapsody in Blue,* orchestrated by Ferde Grofe, made Gershwin famous. Performances of this work, the sale of phonograph records and sheet music brought in a tidy income.

Walter Damrosch and the Symphony Society of New York commissioned the Concerto in F and the symphonic fantasy, *An American in Paris.* The Boston Symphony Orchestra gave the first public performance of Gershwin's *Rhapsody in Rivets* (Rhapsody No. 2) on January 29, 1932.

Gershwin had begun to think seriously about a symphony, had even sketched the first two movements, for performance by the Philharmonic-Symphony Society of New York, when he died prematurely of a brain tumor in Hollywood.

Rhapsody in Blue

While the recent distressing spate of "Pavanes," "Grand Canyon" suites and "Warsaw Concertos" is enough to make one believe nothing good could possibly come from popular inspiration, the more serious works of George Gershwin are a happy disproof of such a slander. Whether they are as great as his songs in *Lady Be Good, Girl Crazy,* and a score of Broadway successes is unimportant. What is important is that they are great, albeit imperfect, works which, without needing to be stigmatized as "middle music" can receive the suffrage of a larger and more varied section of the musical public than those of any other composer whatever. . . .

The *Rhapsody in Blue* has become a part of the American tradition and has survived lethal treatments of the greatest diversity, ranging from the desecration of choral settings to performances by quite distinguished "squares" who have approached it in the same spirit as they might the Ninth Symphony or who consider themselves free to add their own embellishments at will. The *Rhapsody in Blue* is too well-known to need much analysis, although I believe that sufficient attention has not been called to the economy of the means from which it has been built up to give an impression of luxuriant and unrestrained growth.

There are really only five theoretical ideas in the *Rhapsody*, three of which occur at the very beginning and are variants of the old trick of jazz bands of turning the final chord of a piece into the dominant seventh of the key a fourth higher. The three are:

The initial clarinet solo with its epochmaking glissando, the declamatory phrase of bass clarinet and the brass which follows immediately, the very first notes of the piano's calm but impressive entry. The fourth also occupies a place in the early part of the work, where it is heard on trumpets which call preliminary attention to themselves by a loud flutter-tongue trill.

From these four motifs and the ideas which develop from them in related patterns the first half of the *Rhapsody* is constructed, allowing three opportunities for the solo to play with this material, at times in cadenza-like fashion, at others in a spirit of capricious and good-humored irony. The last idea is the celebrated slow theme which, after its presentation once by the orchestra, and once by piano, surprisingly becomes also the theme of an Allegro section enlivened by jazzily brilliant figuration of the solo. Finally, a sort of coda presents the three ideas of the beginning, but in reverse order so that the work ends in a grandiose way on its initial note.

BATEMAN EDWARDS, *St. Louis Symphony Orchestra*

An American in Paris

An American in Paris was the result of a visit which George Gershwin made to the French capital in 1928. In that year the composer communicated the following to an interviewer for *Musical America:*

"This new piece," he said, "really a rhapsodic ballet, is written very freely and is the most modern music I've yet attempted. The opening part will be developed in typical French style, in the manner of Debussy and The Six, though the themes are all original. My purpose here is to portray the impression of an American visitor in Paris, as he strolls about the city, listens to the various street noises, and absorbs the French atmosphere.

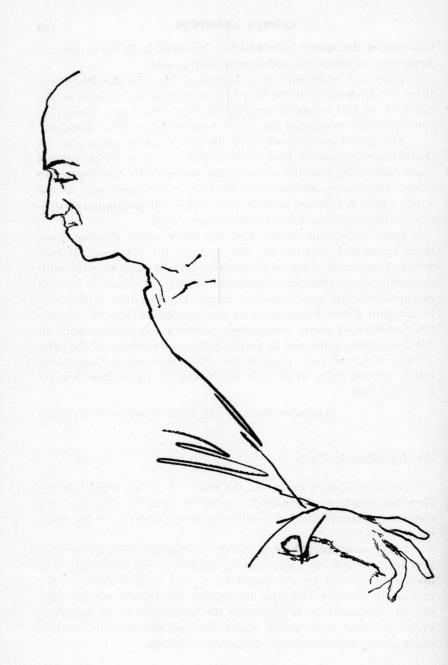

"As in my other orchestral compositions I've not endeavored to represent any definite scenes in this music," he continued. "The rhapsody is programmatic only in a general impressionistic way, so that the individual listener can read into the music such episodes as his imagination pictures for him.

"The opening gay section," he explained, "is followed by a rich 'blues' with a strong rhythmic undercurrent. Our American friend, perhaps after strolling into a café and having a couple of drinks, has suddenly succumbed to a spasm of homesickness. The harmony here is both more intense and simple than in the preceding pages. This 'blues' rises to a climax followed by a coda in which the spirit of the music returns to the vivacity and bubbling exuberance of the opening part with its impressions of Paris. Apparently the homesick American, having left the café and reached the open air, has disowned his spell of the blues and once again is an alert spectator of Parisian life. At the conclusion, the street noises and French atmosphere are triumphant!". . . .

The first performance of *An American in Paris* was given by the New York Symphony Society at Carnegie Hall in New York, December 13, 1928, under the direction of Walter Damrosch.

FELIX BOROWSKI, *Chicago Symphony Orchestra*

Concerto in F major for piano and orchestra

When Paul Whiteman introduced Gershwin's *Rhapsody in Blue* during that memorable concert of February 12, 1924, Walter Damrosch was in the audience which included more than a few potentates of the so-called legitimate concert stage.

In the article which the veteran pioneer of American orchestral music contributed to Merle Armitage's informative and fascinating book about Gershwin, the conductor does not speak of that event. Gershwin had made his mark in the annals of American theater music.

Beginning in 1920, he had written the scores for several editions of George White's *Scandals*. He had recorded a style of his own and developed it in the course of those five shows, in the *Rhapsody in Blue* and other pieces.

"It was in 1925 that I first became attracted by George Gershwin and the music he had composed for various Broadway shows. It was of such originality, both of melodic invention and harmonic progression, that I strongly felt he had in him the possibility of development on more serious lines," writes Damrosch in the Armitage book. . . . published by Longmans, Green and Company.

"I suggested to the president of the New York Symphony Society, Mr. Harry Harkness Flagler, that it might be a lovely and important inducement for his artistic future to commission Gershwin to write a piano concerto for the Symphony Society, which should have the first performance at one of our concerts, the composer to be the soloist."

Mr. Flagler agreed heartily. The premiere, December 3, 1925, demonstrated the soundness of Damrosch's judgment. He admired particularly the "second movement. . . . with its dreamy atmosphere of a summer night in a garden of our South, the music reaching a high-water mark of Gershwin's talent.". . . .

. . . . It was George Gershwin's evening and Damrosch made one of his graceful speeches from the platform. He pointed out to the enthusiastic audience that this was a concert significant not only for Gershwin but a milestone in the progress of American music. It was a subtle and finely humorous speech as even a few sentences will show:

"Various composers have been walking around jazz, like a cat around a plate of very hot soup, waiting for it to cool off so that they could enjoy it without burning off their tongues, hitherto accustomed only to the more tepid liquid distilled by the cooks of the classical school.

"Lady Jazz adorned by her intriguing rhythms, has danced her way around the world, even as far as the Eskimos of the North, and the Polynesians of the South Sea Isles. But for all her travels and her sweeping popularity she has encountered no knight who would lift her to a level that would enable her to be received as a respectable member in musical circles.

"George Gershwin seems to have accomplished this miracle. He has done it by boldly dressing this independent and up-to-date young lady in the classical garb of a concerto. Yet he has not detracted one whit from her fascinating personality. He is the prince

who has taken Cinderella by the hand and openly proclaimed her
a princess to the astonished world, no doubt to the fury of her envious sisters."

BRUNO DAVID USSHER, *Los Angeles Philharmonic Orchestra*

REINHOLD MORITZOVICH GLIERE

(Born in Kiev, Russia, January 11, 1875—now
living in Russia)

GLIERE may be considered today among the last of the great
nationalistic Russian composers. He studied at the Moscow Conservatory under Taneiev and Ippolitov-Ivanof, was regarded as a
brilliant student and won a gold medal for composition in his
graduation year.

He wandered far afield in the years before the First World
War, lived in various European cities, and finally returned to Russia and became head of the Kiev Conservatory, "bringing the
school," remarks Charles O'Connell, "through a series of troubles
to a position of security and importance."

He is highly regarded by the Soviet government and by the
Russian people. Americans know him for a symphony of prodi-
gious length and absorbing interest inspired by a group of Russian
folk tales, under the title *Ilia Mourometz,* a legendary hero supposed to have lived in the twelfth century.

His ballet, *The Red Poppy,* has become popular in this country and one frequently hears the *Russian Sailors' Dance* as a concert piece. Other works of Gliere include a suite for orchestra, two
string quartets, three string sextettes, a Ballade for 'cello, songs
and pieces for one and two pianos, and another opera, *Awakened.*

Dance of the Russian Sailors from the ballet, *The Red Poppy*

Pavot Rouge (The Red Poppy) is a ballet from which this dance is taken. The score of this one number was published separately in 1930 by the Russian state publishing bureau in Moscow.

It is a rollicking bit of music employing the full modern orchestra with many added percussion instruments.

After an introductory passage ending on a fortissimo chord, the dance begins in syncopated rhythm. Nine times this theme is developed with increasing power until it ends in a brilliant climax.

BARBARA DUNCAN, *Rochester Philharmonic Orchestra*

MIHAIL IVANOVITCH GLINKA

(Born near Smolenska, Russia, June 1, 1804—died in Berlin, February 15, 1857)

ONE MIGHT call Glinka, in a musical manner of speaking, a discontented pioneer. He was not a reformer, "in the active sense of the term," to quote M. Montagu-Nathan. "He sought the right but did not concern himself much about the wrong."

Glinka writes in his memoirs that he was born "at dawn on 20th May, 1804 (June 1 of the Western calendar) in the village of Novospasskoi, the property of my father, Ivan Nikolayevitch Glinka, who was a retired army captain."

He adds that soon after his birth his mother "was obliged to confide my upbringing to my maternal grandmother Thyokla Aleksandrovna who, having taken possession of me removed me to her room where, together with my two nurses, I spent the next three or four years, seldom seeing my parents."

His musical proclivities were so pronounced that he and his

sister, Ludmilla, were sent to study with one Varvara Feodorovna Klemmer, a governess of St. Petersburg. And Mihail received lessons on the violin from a player in the military band that his uncle conducted.

The Glinka family went to St. Petersburg in the winter of 1817 and Mihail entered the Pedagogical Institute. His parents arranged for him to study the piano with the famous Irishman, Field, precursor of Chopin. But after three lessons Field left for Moscow and Field's pupil, Oman, took over.

Mihail's health, due to the coddling of his grandmother, was precarious and his father prescribed a journey to the Caucasus for medicinal waters. The said waters did him little good, however, and he returned to Novospasskoi, upon advice of his doctor. Improved somewhat in health, and at least on the way to becoming a competent musician, he went back to St. Petersburg and his family. This was in March of 1826. His father obtained for him the offer of a secretarial post in the Ministry of Ways and Communications, and advised him to accept it, which he did, but "the work, though light, proved distasteful," yet it served to bring him contact with an influential amateur, Count Sivers, with whom he became fast friends.

An official friend of his father was able to engineer a profitable speculation—so profitable that Mihail found it unnecessary to pursue music as a professional career. The result was that Mihail became what Montagu-Nathan calls a "frenzied dilettante" and Glinka's memoirs record a series of musical revels.

But all of this dissipation took a heavy toll of an already frail constitution. Warned by his physician, Dr. Spindler, that he must spend at least three years in a warm climate, he and a friend set out for Italy in April of 1830. His wanderings all over Europe improved his composing technique, but did not result in the composition of any masterpieces. The death of his father brought him back to St. Petersburg in April of 1834, but he grew restless at the end of a month and intended to go to Moscow to join a friend and wait for a passport that would enable him to go back to Berlin. But before his departure, he met the sister of the wife of his friend, Stuneyef, Maria Petrovna Ivanovna. So he decided to give up his project of returning to Berlin and remain in St. Petersburg. He married Maria in 1835.

During the courtship, Glinka came in touch with a circle of intellectuals, including Pushkin, Gogol and Joukovsky. The latter suggested a plot for an opera and offered to write the book. He did actually complete some verses, but his only real contribution is to be found in the Trio of the Epilogue. He excused himself by saying that he had no time.

He did, however, obtain the services of the Tsarevitch's secretary, Baron Rosen, who supplied what must be considered a rather poor libretto. The opera, "Ivan Susanin," was completed in the summer of 1836 and had its first public performance in November of that year. Although the public acclaimed it, the critics demurred. In January 1837, he was appointed the choral director of the Imperial Chapel.

Russlan and Ludmilla, suggested by Prince Shakovsky and the Tsar, followed, but this was hardly a success from any standpoint, though it did provoke a deal of controversy. At Easter of 1838, he went to Little Russia to gather new voices for the Imperial Chapel. Again his dubious health intervened and he was forced to give up his duties at the end of 1839. He decided to head for Spain, but tarried in Berlin and Paris, where he met Hector Berlioz.

Some concerts he gave in Paris cost him some 1500 francs, though he obtained the published praise of Berlioz and a few other critics. He resumed his journey to Spain and passed the summer of 1845 in Valladolid. *Jota Aragonesa* and *Summer Night in Madrid* were the results of this visit. He stayed in Spain until June 1847, and then turned his face homeward, finally settling in Smolensk, where he lived with his married sister. His health grew steadily worse.

Two months later, the wanderlust seized him again and he prepared for a trip to Paris. But French disturbances made it impossible for him to get a passport, so he stayed in Warsaw until 1852. In June, he departed for Paris via Berlin, where he stopped off long enough to meet Meyerbeer. In Paris that September he began a *Ukrainian Symphony,* but put it aside.

He left Paris for Berlin in the spring of 1854, went on to Warsaw and Tsarskoe Selo, where he lived for a time with Mme. Shestakof and began writing his memoirs. Attracted by church music, he undertook his last journey abroad in 1856 to pursue his researches. In Berlin, Meyerbeer arranged a brilliant court concert in his honor at which Glinka received a tremendous ovation.

Upon leaving the concert, he caught a chill and on February 15, 1857 he died. His body was brought to St. Petersburg and deposited in the cemetery of the Alexander Nevsky Monastery.

Overture to *Russlan and Ludmilla*

Glinka founded the school of Russian nationalism and used the folk songs of his native land to vitalize his legacy to Russian music and the world.

The opera of *Russlan and Ludmilla*, first performed in 1842, exerted a great influence upon the group of Russian composers known as the "Famous Five." Rimsky Korsakoff tells in his memoirs of the enthusiasm of Liadow for the work and in many of the compositions of Balakirew, Borodin and Moussorgsky who flourished in the latter part of the nineteenth century, one can see that this opera was the model from which they drew their inspiration.

The overture to *Russlan and Ludmilla* contains very little of the music of the opera itself except for some material from the finale and a portion of the air sung by Russlan in the second act. It is constructed according to the classical mode with the usual development and recapitulation ending with a coda.

BARBARA DUNCAN, *Rochester Philharmonic Orchestra*

CHRISTOPH WILLIBALD RITTER von GLUCK

(Born in Weidenwang, Germany, July 2, 1714—
died in Vienna, November 15, 1787)

GLUCK, son of a forester employed on the estate of Prince Lobkowitz, was verily a "climber" in the sense that he used music as a ladder upon which to attain the acquaintance and patronage of the aristocracy. The "von" of nobility was purely his own invention, for in his early years no such patrician label adorned his name.

The great Händel, securely established in London, met Gluck and on hearing one of his operas was heard to remark that Gluck "knew no more of counterpoint than his cook." Doubtless his technical shortcomings were many and obvious, yet he did more to reform the entire tenure of lyric drama than any other composer up to that time.

"His father, Alexander," says Grove, "and his mother, Walpurga belonged to the household of Prince Lobkowitz and it was at his castle of Eisenburg that the future reformer of the lyric drama passed his early days. At twelve he was sent for six years to the Jesuit school at Komotow or Chamutow in Bohemia where he studied classics and had his first lessons in singing, the violin, clavecin and organ."

Prince Lobkowitz took a personal interest in the young man and invited him to stay at his house in Vienna. There he met Prince Melzi, "a distinguished amateur who engaged him for his private band, took him to Milan and placed him with G. B. Sammartini to complete his studies in harmony."

He began to turn out operas with an incredible facility. Most of these were well-received and he was invited in 1745 to London, as composer for the opera at the Haymarket. But his efforts in London were not successful, chiefly because most of the works he produced "had not even originality to recommend them."

Gluck was too shrewd and genuine an artist to ignore criticism, however it may have wounded his vanity. Consequently, his visit to London, somewhat mortifying to his self-esteem, forced him to change his style.

He went to Paris and there heard the operas of Rameau. "Returning to Vienna by way of Hamburg and Dresden towards the end of 1746," says Grove, "he applied himself to the study of aesthetics as connected with music, and of the language and literature of various countries, taking care at the same time to frequent the most intellectual society within his reach."

Perhaps the first result of these studies may be detected in *Semiramide* and *Felide,* the latter described as "a serenade or, more properly, a cantata in two acts, written at Copenhagen for the birthday of Christian VII."

Orfeo, produced in Vienna on October 5, 1762, the libretto by Calzabigi, "showed to all capable of forming a judgment what the aims of the reformer of the lyric stage were. After several intervening pieces, written to please various of his aristocratic patrons, he finally brought forward *Alceste,* again with Calzabigi as librettist, instead of Metastasio, with whom he had collaborated on former occasions. *Alceste* was produced on December 16, 1767 and *Paride e Elena,* two years later. Both were dedicated to the Archduchess Leopold and the Duke of Braganza.

Gluck was fifty-three when he composed *Alceste.* Ten years elapsed between the intial performance at the Berg Theater, Vienna, and the French version in Paris on April 23, 1776. The actual American premiere of this work is in doubt.

But such innovations in style and structure as Gluck put forth in *Alceste, Orfeo* and *Paride e Elena* were bound to make him some enemies among the diehards. He enjoyed a rare favor at the court in Vienna, yet so biting were the criticisms of his countrymen that Gluck decided to continue along the new path before a more sympathetic public.

"In the Bailli du Rollet, an attaché of the French embassy in Vienna," says Grove, "he found an enthusiastic partisan and a valuable auxiliary." They talked of a drama suitable to Gluck's new ideas, "in which music might be employed for enhancing the expression of the words and the pathos of the situations . . ."

They hit upon Racine's *Iphigenia* and finally devised *Iphigenia in Aulis,* partly rehearsed at the opera in Vienna and finally produced at the Paris Opera on April 19, 1774. On this occasion Gluck was his own press agent—interviews, announcements and "letters to authors whose good will it was desirable to propitiate."

His former pupil, Marie Antoinette, stood him in good stead for her protection and friendship enabled him to get his work performed. His arrival in France as one might expect, had aroused strong opposition, particularly among those determined to keep him out of the Academie de Musique. The Dauphiness insured the production of *Iphigenia en Aulis,* called him *notre cher Gluck* in a letter to her sister, Marie Christine and granted him a pension of 6000 francs "and the same sum for every fresh work he should produce on the French stage."

Then came *Orphee et Eurydice,* adapted from the original *Orfeo,* produced at the Academie on August 2, 1774, an opera that made a "profound impression" on the French musical public. This success was followed by yet another *Armide* which provoked the fury of admirers of Piccini, recently arrived in Paris. The result was an operatic war allowed to reach ridiculous lengths.

His last work for the Paris Opéra was *Echo et Narcisse,* produced on September 21, 1779. Its success was moderate although it was revived in August of 1780 "and one of the airs" says Grove "the 'Hymne a l'Amour,' has since been introduced into *Orphee.*" He was working on a final opera, *Les Danaides* when he suffered an apoplectic stroke. He turned over the libretto to his pupil Salieri and retired to Vienna. Gluck had accumulated a large fortune and lived comfortably, until a second stroke caused his death in 1787.

Ballet Suite—arranged from three operas by Felix Mottl

This Suite is derived from the operas *Alceste, Iphigenie en Aulide* and *Paride e Elena.*

1. March (*Alceste*); Minuet (*Iphigenie en Aulide*). . . .
2. Grazioso (*Paride e Elena*). . . .
3. Slavic Dance (*Iphigenie en Aulide*)

The minuet was a dance in Poitu, France. It was called *menuet* on account of the small steps—*pas menus.* The dance, it is said, was derived from the courante. It quickly made its way to court. Louis XIV danced it to music composed for him by Lully; for the minuet, originally a gay and lively dance, soon lost its vivacity when exported, and became a stately dance of the aristocracy. The Grande Encyclopedie described its characteristic as "a noble and elegant simplicity; its movement is moderate rather than rapid; and one may say that it is the least gay of all such dances." Louis XV was passionately devoted to the minuet, but his predecessor, the Grand Monarch, is said to have excelled all others.

The court minuet was a dance for two, a man and a woman.

The tempo was moderate, and at balls this dance was followed by a gavotte. Those proficient in other dances were obliged to spend three months learning the most graceful and ceremonious of all postures and dancing steps.

. . . . When Haydn was in London in 1791, he went to balls in November, and he described his adventures in his entertaining diary. He wrote of one ball: "They dance in this hall nothing but minuets. I could not stay there longer than a quarter of an hour: first, because the heat was so intense on account of so many people in a small room; secondly, on account of the miserable dance music, for the whole orchestra consisted of two violins and violoncello. The minuets were more like the Polish ones than ours or those of Italy.". . . . .

PHILIP HALE, *Boston Symphony Orchestra*

Overture to *Iphigenia in Aulis*

Iphigenia was long a favorite figure in the revival of the Greek spirit that began in the time of the Florentine Medici. . . . Racine and Goethe celebrated her anew in tragedy, as Euripides had done of old; Gluck was the greatest of the composers who treated her in the musical drama. Indeed his *Iphigenia in Aulis* marked an era in rescuing opera from mere vocal display and in consecrating it to dramatic truth.

Gluck's treatment of the legend (with Wagner's rearrangement) agrees in the main with the Greek myth. The whole idea is a striking counterpart of an ancient Biblical story.

Iphigenia was the daughter of Agamemnon, leader of the Greeks in the Trojan War. When the ships are prevented by unfavoring winds from sailing from Aulis, the oracle declares that the goddess Artemis, offended by Agamemnon, has demanded the sacrifice of his daughter.

Iphigenia had come to Aulis from Mycene with her mother Clytemnestra as the bride of Achilles. At the moment of impending sacrifice the goddess intervenes and saves the maiden, whom she carries away to distant Tauris on the Euxine Sea, there to serve as her own priestess among the savage Scythians. . . .

. . . . The opera commonly associated with Gluck's famous re-form of musical drama is his *Orpheus and Eurydice*. But though this work was written earliest of Gluck's masterpieces, it was the order of their later production in Paris, not in Vienna, that had most in-fluence on the development of opera. Thus the beginning of Gluck's bold reform in the center of the musical world, the arena of contending schools of opera, was made by the production of *Iphigenia in Aulis* in Paris in 1774. Rameau, the real founder of French opera in a serious sense, had died ten years before, leaving no one in France to sustain his traditions. In the meantime the Italian school with all its excesses, sacrificing the dramatic ele-ment to vocal virtuosity, had gained supreme sway. Though Gluck had had his artistic change of heart much earlier, and had pro-duced *Orpheus* in Vienna in 1762, followed by *Alceste* and *Paride e Elena,* he had not tried his fortunes in the final court. The quarrel in Paris of the Gluckists and the Piccinists broke out in full tempest after the performance of *Armide* in 1777. . . . In the overture of *Iphigenia in Aulis* is a touch, in the solemn suggestion of the oracle that Gluck greatly heightened in *Alceste*. There is no doubt of the direct influence here on Mozart, in *Don Giovanni*.

PHILIP H. GOEPP, *Philadelphia Orchestra*

EDVARD HAGERUP GRIEG

(Born in Bergen, Norway, June 15, 1843—died
there on September 4, 1907)

ONE MIGHT suppose that Grieg represented the very essence of Norway, and so he does—yet the fact is that Grieg's great-grand-father, Alexander Grieg (Gregg) was born in Aberdeen, Scotland, settled in Bergen as British consul and married a Norwegian, "and changed the spelling to Grieg to make the Norwegian pronunciation conform to the original."

His father, Alexander, was also British consul and a merchant, "a man of the kindest heart and most lovable nature." His mother, an admirable pianist, first taught Edvard. "And my mother was strict, inexorably strict," Grieg remembers. "Her mother-heart must surely have found joy in the fact that many things came quickly to me—evidence of the artistic nature—but she never showed the least sign of any satisfaction. On the contrary there was no joking with her, if she found me dreaming at the keyboard instead of diligently practicing my lesson."

He recollects that he first went to a school for boys and girls, and encountered a severe obstacle in arithmetic, for he considered the intervening figures between the problem and the result "of no importance." When he was ten his family moved from Bergen to a country place in nearby Landaas. He tried ingenuously to avoid school and since rains were frequent, he would stand under a dripping roof until wet through, whereupon the teacher would send him home.

At this time he wanted to be a preacher, instead of a musician. He learned poems from the school reader and declaimed them to his family at the slightest provocation.

The great violinist, Ole Bull, first turned the young Edvard from his churchly course. He was fifteen, he recalls "on a beautiful summer day" when "a man on horseback in full gallop drew rein on his fiery Arab steed, and dismounted. It was he, the good god of whom I had dreamed, but whom I had never seen—it was *Ole Bull!*"

Grieg's childish compositions were shown to the great visitor, an old friend of the family, who talked earnestly with his parents "shook me by the shoulders in a way that was peculiar to him and said: 'You must go to Leipzig and become a musician!' "

He remembers gratefully that his parents placed no obstacle in his path. The Norwegian boy of sixteen went to Leipzig, entered the Conservatory, became acutely homesick but pursued his studies diligently, even to practicing music "which I hated." Among his fellow students was Arthur Sullivan.

Grieg had a nervous breakdown from overwork in the spring

of 1860 and had pleurisy, from which he recovered "with only one good lung." He recovered at home but returned to the Conservatory before he had fully recovered his strength.

In the spring of 1862, he gave his first public concert at the Gewandhaus, playing some of his own piano compositions, and was much applauded. He returned to Bergen, gave another concert of his own music also successfully, and met Gade, friend of Mendelssohn. He also met a young musician a year older, Richard Nordraak, who was to turn the whole stream of his musical thought toward a national idiom. "Then there fell the scales from my eyes," says Grieg. "I learned first from him the Norwegian folk songs and therein recognized my own nature."

In Copenhagen he met his cousin Nina Hagerup, a singer with whom he fell in love. She returned his affection and he wrote the song, "I Love Thee" for her. But her mother objected: "He is nothing, he has nothing and makes music to which no one listens."

Nevertheless, they were married, on June 11, 1867. Grieg had moved to Christiania the year before and there the young couple set up housekeeping. Grieg became a part of the musical life of the city, gave piano lessons, conducted the orchestra of the Philharmonic Society. Liszt invited him to come to Weimar and through his efforts he obtained a state scholarship to study in Rome. But this was in the fall of 1869 and he did not meet Liszt until February 1870, when both were in Rome.

They had a later meeting to which Grieg brought his new piano concerto which Liszt played at sight, "roaring the theme" toward the close of the Finale. At the end he handed the music to Grieg and cried: "Go on, I tell you, you have the right stuff in you! And don't let them scare you!"

Grieg and his Nina gave a joint concert in Rome—she singing and Edvard playing the accompaniments to his own songs. Both played four-hands the Norwegian Dances. Sgambati remarks: "Mrs. Grieg also showed that in every sense of the word she is a true artist."

A few years after their return to Christiania the Norwegian government granted an annuity of 1600 crowns ($400) to the Griegs "for their services in behalf of the national musical art."

Henrik Ibsen asked Grieg to write incidental music to his drama, *Peer Gynt*. As originally written, the play was not intended for stage performance but Ibsen hoped to arrange a stage version.

Grieg set to work, hampered to some extent by the author's shifting moods and notions. The first performance was given at the Christiania Theater on February 24, 1876 and it was such a success that "it was given thirty-six times that year and also given in other Scandinavian cities." Grieg was absent and was told that the orchestral interludes were too subdued.

He arranged two suites published eleven years later. The orchestral score appeared in 1908, a piano score in 1918. He went to Bayreuth in 1876 to hear *The Ring,* became a profound admirer of Wagner though not, as he explains, "a Wagnerite."

"Wagner himself" he adds, "was by no means a Wagnerite."

He and Nina retired to a little house at Lofthus "on a little peninsula in the fjord," where he composed and received visitors and studied peasant songs and melodies for two years. He gave a series of concerts in Christiania and Copenhagen in 1879, and a year later became conductor of the musical society Harmonien, in Bergen.

In 1885 he built the villa Troldhaugen which remained his lifetime home. He continued to compose, made several concert trips to England and the continent, was invited to Paris by Edouard Colonne and refused because of the Dreyfuss trial. In 1900, his friend, Dr. Abraham head of the German publishing house of Peters died and then his brother John, in the same year. He mourned them deeply and for a time did not stir from his retreat. He accepted a second invitation to Paris in 1903 and won an ovation at his first concert.

His precarious health had been failing for some time, yet he continued to be active, undertaking arduous journeys, spending long hours at composing and giving frequent concerts. The Australian pianist, Percy Grainger, visited him in July of 1907, "with whom he rowed and walked—even taking him on a climb up a nearby mountain."

But a month later his doctor sent him to a hospital in Bergen and there in September he died in his sleep.

Suites from the incidental music to Ibsen's *Peer Gynt* (Nos. 1 and 2)

Of the music Grieg wrote for the stage presentation of Ibsen's play *Peer Gynt,* he made two Suites for concert use, the one most played being the first. In the play the numbers came in a different order than that of the Suite—the episode "In the Hall of the Mountain King" taking place rather early in the play. Then comes the death of Peer's mother Ase—one of the amazing scenes in dramatic literature.

"Morning" opens the first scene of Peer's African adventure, of which the Dance of Anitra (the daughter of a Bedouin chief) is an episode. The order in the Suite is: "Morning," "Anitra's Dance," and "In the Hall of the Mountain King."

In a Baltimore note by Klemm, Grieg is quoted as saying:

". . . . it was the winter or spring of 1873 that Ibsen asked me to write the music for *Peer Gynt.* I began it in the summer of 1873 in Sandiken near Bergen continued it the following winter in Copenhagen and orchestrated the whole thing at Fredensborg in Denmark during the summer of 1875. Unfortunately, I was not able to decide myself at what points the music was to be introduced and how long each number should be. All of that was determined by the Swedish theatrical director, Josephson . . . I was thus compelled to do real patchwork. In no case did I have an opportunity to say all I wanted to say. Hence the brevity of these pieces. The performance of the music by the very inadequate forces of that time was anything but good . . . It was really not until the last years of the 1880's . . . that the music won its chief success.

". . . It is greatly to be regretted that the local coloring and the philosophical mood of the dialogue present a great obstacle to the success of Ibsen's work outside of Scandinavia. In Paris . . . the music had a colossal success, but Ibsen was not understood. In Berlin . . . the work was simply a failure. And yet I hold it to be Ibsen's greatest creation. In the Fatherland, it will always be considered a monument to him and keep its place on the stage even as a folk play."

C. A. PALMER, *Detroit Symphony Orchestra*

Concerto for piano and orchestra (Opus 16)

Efforts have been made to read a strictly autobiographical program into the A minor Concerto of Grieg. That it is a burst of youthful ardor in some great flush of excitement no one can doubt. The love of nature courses through it, and a soaring emotionalism. There is a strange hymnlike intimacy in the Adagio, and Norwegian folk echoes abound, reflecting Grieg's constant preoccupation with the homeland. In any case, the facts surrounding its composition would suggest the idyllic.

It was the summer of 1868. Grieg was only twenty-five. The year before he had married Nina Hagerup, whom he met in Christiania, where he led the Philharmonic and taught. A daughter was born to them, and the Griegs planned a vacation in Denmark. Grieg's health was never too robust and here was a chance to drop a taxing routine, rest and compose only when he felt the urge. Husband, wife and baby daughter arrived in Copenhagen early in June. The child was left behind with grandparents in the Danish capital, and the Griegs set out for Sölleröd, an hour's journey, where a cozy, two-room gardener's cottage, rented by friends, awaited them. They spent a healthy, leisurely summer. Grieg slept late, ate heartily, took long walks and enjoyed the lovely countryside. At night he met friends in an inn nearby and chatted over a glass. Several hours a day he was left alone to compose (he could never bear anyone within earshot while at work with the piano). And the A minor concerto was born. No wonder Gerard Schjelderup, stunned by its "natural impressions," saw "all Norway in its infinite variety and unity" before his eyes, comparing the Adagio to a "lonely mountain-girt tarn which lies dreaming of infinity."

As for the sober facts, the Concerto was dedicated to the pianist Edmund Neupart . . . who first played it in Copenhagen on April 3, 1869, and in Christiania the following year. . . . Neupart wrote to Grieg from Copenhagen after the world premiere: "On Saturday your divine Concerto resounded in the great hall of the Casino. The triumph I achieved was tremendous. Even as early as the cadenza in the first movement the public broke into real storm. The three dangerous critics, Gade, Rubinstein and Hartmann, sat in the stalls and applauded with all their might. I am to send you greetings from Rubinstein and say that he is astounded to have heard a composition of such genius. He would like to make your acquaintance."

The other keyboard idol of the time, Franz Liszt, had already made the acquaintance of the young man from the North. Liszt wrote to him glowingly of an early violin sonata which had come to his notice. In it he discerned "a strong, creative, inventive and well-disciplined talent which has only to follow its natural bent to reach even higher levels." He urged Grieg to visit him so that they might "know each other better." Liszt's intercession with the Norwegian government brought Grieg a grant permitting him to visit the great man in his monastery home in Rome. Grieg relates the episode in his letters home. Liszt promptly asked for the piano concerto, which had just arrived in manuscript from Leipzig. The gathering included a "Chevalier de Concilium," Winding, Sgambati, and "a German Lisztite, who goes so far in aping his idol that he even wears the gown of an abbé." Some young ladies were present, "of the kind that would like to eat Liszt, skin, hair, and all; their adulation is simply comical."

He and Winding were eager to see if Liszt would play the Concerto at sight, Grieg considering it impossible. But the incredible abbé did, and Grieg even thought the difficult cadenza went best of all, though the first movement was "too fast" and "helter-skelter." Liszt stopped at one place, left the piano and with upraised arms strode across the huge cloister floor, "literally roaring out the theme." When he got to a particular G in the score, he "stretched out his arms imperiously and exclaimed: 'G! G! not G-sharp! Splendid!' " At the end he said to Grieg warmly: "Keep it up, and don't be intimidated!" Liszt made suggestions about amplifying the orchestration which Grieg adopted but later modified in a revised version.

The pianist Oscar Meyer, reminiscing in the *Neue Musikzeitung,* Stuttgart, 1910, adds another detail to the monastic tableau: "It happened that in turning the pages Liszt missed a modulation and played an orchestral fortissimo with great pomp in the major instead of in the minor. When Grieg pointed out the error, Liszt stared at him indignantly, took a red crayon from the desk and made some vigorous marks in the notes. After repeated sidelong scowls at the composer, he went on with his playing."

ROBERT C. BAGAR and LOUIS BIANCOLLI,
Philharmonic-Symphony Society of New York

CHARLES TOMLINSON GRIFFES

(Born in Elmira, New York, September 17, 1884—
died in New York, April 8, 1920)

WHEN GRIFFES died of pneumonia and overwork at the age of 36, in a New York hospital, a bright hope was lost to American music. For he was just coming into his own as a composer of recognized worth. As R. F. L. McCombs remarked in a program note for the Philadelphia Orchestra: "He faced and solved the problem of Bread versus Creation which confronts every artist in the usual way—he tried to do both and lost."

While a student at Elmira Academy, he studied piano with Mary S. Broughton, then went to Berlin with the idea of becoming a virtuoso pianist. Among his teachers there was Engelbert Humperdinck, composer of *Haensel und Gretel,* with whom he studied composition. He returned to the United States in 1907, and began to teach music at the Hackley School, a post he held at the time of his death.

"Long hours of teaching small boys their musical ABC's," writes Mr. McCombs, "and long nights of composing, or writing out parts, which he was too poor to have copied by a professional, at last wore down his frail body."

Among the musical creations of his brief career are *The White Peacock,* and *The Pleasure-dome of Kubla Khan;* also, *Bacchanale, By a Lonely Forest Pathway, Clouds, Notturno* and a *Poeme* for flute and orchestra.

The White Peacock

The White Peacock was composed in 1915, and is the first of a group of four compositions for the pianoforte entitled *Roman Sketches.* The work was inspired by William Sharp's *"Sospiri di Roma."* The poet describes the Peacock thus:

> Cream white, and soft as the breasts of a girl,
> Moves the White Peacock, as through the noontide,

A dream of the moonlight were real for a moment.
Dim on the beautiful fan that he spreadeth,
Foldeth and spreadeth abroad in the sunlight,
Dim on the cream-white are blue adumbrations,
Shadows so pale in their delicate blueness
That visions they seem as of vanishing violets,
Fragrant white violets veined with azure,
Pale, pale as the breath of blue smoke in the woodlands.
Here, as the breath, as the soul of this beauty,
White as a cloud through the heats of the noontide
Moves the White Peacock.

R. F. L. McCombs, *Philadelphia Orchestra*

(Note: The piece was orchestrated by the composer shortly before his death. Ed.)

The Pleasure-dome of Kubla Khan

This work is based on a few descriptive lines in the famous poem of Samuel Taylor Coleridge:

In Xanadu did Kubla Khan
A stately Pleasure Dome decree;
Where Alph the sacred river ran,
Through caverns measureless to man,
Down to the sunless sea.
So twice five miles of fertile ground,
With walls and towers were girdled round.
And there were gardens bright with sinuous rills
Where blossomed many an incense-bearing tree;
And here were forests ancient as the hills,
Enfolding spots of sunny greenery.
The shadow of the dome of pleasure
Floated midway on the waves,
Where was heard the mingled measure
From the fountain and the caves.
It was a miracle of rare device,
A sunny pleasure dome with caves of ice.

"As to argument," said Griffes, "I have given my imagination free rein in the description of this strange palace as well as of purely imaginary revelry which might take place there. The vague, foggy beginning suggests the sacred river, running 'through caverns measureless to man, down to the sunless sea.' There gradually rise the outlines of the palace 'with walls and towers girdled round.' The garden with foundations and 'sunny spots of greenery' are next suggested. From inside come sounds of dancing and revelry which increase to a wild climax and then sudenly break off. There is a return to the original mood suggesting the sacred river and 'caves of ice.' "

. . . . *The Pleasure-dome of Kubla Khan* was given its first performance under the baton of Pierre Monteux at a concert of the Boston Symphony in 1919.

ALFRED FRANKENSTEIN, *San Francisco Symphony Orchestra*

GEORG FRIEDRICH HÄNDEL

(Born in Halle, Prussia, February 23, 1685—died in London, April 14, 1759)

SCATTERED documents and too few letters have left us a rather jumbled and incomplete knowledge of Händel's early life. The Händels belonged originally to Breslau and had been coopersmiths there for several generations. Valentine Händel, grandfather to Georg Friedrich, migrated to Halle, where two of his sons followed the same vocation. His third son, Georg, became a barber-surgeon.

By the time Georg Friedrich was born to the barber on February 23, 1685, Halle had relapsed from a town of some importance under the dukes of Saxony to a quiet provincial town under the protection of the Elector of Brandenburg.

Although his father had no musical inclinations whatever, young Georg Friedrich showed his talent at an early age. In fact, he was so insistent that his father forbade him to touch any musical instrument. Scholars have attributed largely to Mainwaring's imagination the oft-told tale of how he smuggled a clavichord into the garret without his father's knowledge so that he could practice on it while the family slept.

The boy was sent to the Lutheran Grammar School and probably had some instruction there in singing. Apparently he learned more than the mere rudiments of music in childhood, despite his father's opposition, and it is highly probable that his mother saw to that, encouraging her son's initial efforts and taking care that he made music in a part of the house remote from her husband's ears.

He was between seven and nine when his father, required to attend upon the reigning duke, took him to Weissenfels where the Duke Johann Adolf had taken up residence. We do know that one day, on this or some subsequent visit, he was allowed to play on the organ in the palace chapel. The duke, happening to hear, urged upon the father the necessity of having him educated for a musical career.

But the barber-surgeon, convinced that music in his family was a waste of time, had determined to make a lawyer out of young Georg. But he may have reflected shrewdly that wisdom and tact dictated that he take some heed of the duke's words. So he decided to place the boy under the instruction of Friedrich Zachow, organist of the Lutheran church in Halle.

The Elector offered to send the boy to Italy, but the elder Händel refused this offer. Instead, Georg Friedrich studied law (and some music) at the University of Halle, was duly graduated three days before his seventeenth birthday and in March 1702, was appointed organist at the cathedral, although he belonged to the Lutheran Church. The cathedral, be it said, was Calvinist.

Händel came to Hamburg, the "Venice of the North" in the summer of 1703, and formed immediately an ardent friendship with one Johann Matheson, whom he met in the Church of St. Mary Magdalene. Matheson, four years older than Händel, is described as "one of those precociously gifted, versatile attractive and rather vain young men who are endowed with so many talents that they never achieve distinction in any branch of art."

In the autumn of that year, Matheson got his friend a job in the opera band as a second violinist. Händel also earned a part of his livelihood by teaching and was engaged by the English envoy to teach his small son. On one occasion, it is related, the harpsichord player of the band failed to show up, and Händel took over, whereupon his musicianship was recognized immediately.

Matheson, apparently, could not stand the increasing success of Händel and the two friends fell out. The breach widened when Keiser began a new opera *Almira*, could not finish it and called in Händel who composed practically the entire work. Subsequent instances of jealousy led to a street duel, in which Matheson's sword broke on a button of Händel's coat. There was a reconciliation, through the intervention of a town councillor, and the rivals dined together and went on to a rehearsal of *Almira*, which was performed on January 8, 1705, with Matheson as the principal tenor.

The friendship of Matheson and Händel gradually waned. Georg Friedrich, evidently disgusted with the whole aspect of Hamburg at this time after the failure of *Nero* and two other operas, left for Italy, probably about 1707.

Although he spent three years in that beguiling land, comparatively little is known of his life there. Apparently he flitted comfortably from one capital to another—Naples, Florence, Venice and finally Rome, where he had been recommended to the young Cardinal Ottobini, then "the most generous patron of music in Rome." He also met the brilliant and gifted "young eagle," Domenico Scarlatti, besides Corelli and Pasquini.

Händel set out for London, where he arrived for his first visit in the Autumn of 1710.

Italian music, under Queen Anne, was becoming more and more popular with London concert audiences. Händel was invited to compose an opera for the Queens Theater, his reputation having preceded him from that sunny land. The result was *Rinaldo*, which established Händel's reputation in England.

When the season ended in June of 1711, Händel left London for Germany. He finally returned to Hanover and his official post. His chief function was to compose Italian chamber duets for the

Princess Caroline of Ansbach, later to be Queen of England.

He stayed in Hanover a year then obtained permission to make a second visit to London. He probably arrived for this second visit some time in October 1712. The following years, of triumph and disappointment, of striving and poverty and bankruptcy and eventual victory, were concerned vitally with the "opera wars" of London, and the fickleness of English society. He was to leave London for brief intervals, but he always returned. "Händel of London" became a musical symbol of the times.

The greatest masterpiece of his career, the oratorio *Messiah*, was composed during the summer of 1741. He had received an invitation during that summer from the fourth Duke of Devonshire, then Lord Lieutenant of Ireland, to go over to Dublin and give some concerts for the benefit of local hospitals. But *Messiah* so engrossed him that he did not leave London until November. It is considered doubtful whether he had intended *Messiah* for a Dublin premiere, yet it was performed there for the first time on April 13, 1742. A contemporary chronicle reveals that more than 700 persons attended and that about 400 pounds was realized for charity. London first heard *Messiah* on March 23, 1742 and evidently it fell flat, for there were only two repetitions in that season. Yet during ensuing centuries, *Messiah* has become a part and parcel of English musical life and the number of performances around holiday-time, in every church and hamlet of the land, is enormous.

Other oratorios followed, a succession of failures and triumphs—*Belshazzar, Judas Maccabeus, Saul, Joseph, Semele,* etc.—and Händel's sight began to dim. An earlier attack of paralysis had been dispelled by some drastic treatments at Aix, but this latest illness had come to stay. By 1751, it is generally believed, he had become stone blind.

He had paid his last visit to Germany in the summer of 1750. He was injured severely in a carriage accident between the Hague and Haarlem. He was back in London by the following year and began the composition of *Jeptha,* a tedious process interrupted by his failing eyesight. Having finished the score by August 30 of that year, he consulted a surgeon of Guy's Hospital, Samuel Sharp, who told him that his blindness could not be cured. Yet he underwent various operations, none of which was more than partially successful.

From this time on his health gradually failed, though he was able to play the organ in public now and then, and dictated some new music and the alterations of old scores to his faithful factotum, John Christopher Smith, with whom he quarreled and later became reconciled through the intervention of Smith's son, also in Händel's service.

"His last appearance in public," writes Dent, "was at the performance of *Messiah* on April 6, 1759, but at the end of it he was seized with a fainting attack, took to his bed, and died during the night between the 13 and 14 of April. He was buried in Westminster Abbey on the evening of April 20; the choirs of the Chapel Royal and St. Paul's joined the Abbey choir in singing the burial music of Dr. Croft, and it is said that three thousand people were present."

Despite the ups and downs of his career, which included bankruptcy, Händel left a fortune of more than 20,000 pounds, most of which went to his niece and goddaughter, Johanna Friderica Floerken.

Suite from the *Music for the Royal Fireworks*
(Arranged for modern orchestra by Sir Hamilton Harty)

In October 1748, the Peace of Aix-la-Chapelle was signed, bringing to an end the war of the Austrian succession. In celebration of Britain's share in this dubious victory and, perchance, of his own, also (the house of Hanover was to retain the succession in its German states as well as in Great Britain), King George II ordered a mighty public entertainment. The feature of the merrymaking was to be a dazzling display of fireworks, a novelty in those days. The exhibition was to be held in Green Park, across from the Royal Library, and the best talents of the kingdom and overseas were engaged to play and direct the spectacle. John Jerome Servandomi, the famous Italian architect and showman, was commanded to design a "machine" as a backdrop. His phantasies took the form of a Doric temple of huge proportions; a center structure, one hundred feet high, with wings to the right and to the left, which measured more than four hundred feet. A gigantic figure of Peace attended by Neptune and Mars, and a likeness of equal size of good King George delivering peace to Britannia, adorned the pavilion. A monster sun topped the whole, and there was a special gallery for musicians large enough to accomodate a hundred men.

The Composer to the Royal Chapel, Mr. Georg Friedrich Händel, was bidden to write music appropriate to the occasion. With a largess in keeping with the event, the master lavished himself upon his musical pyrotechnics. The work was conceived in two parts:

An Overture, played before the display of the fireworks, and thriftily constructed on material contained in two earlier concerti for orchestra. Romain Rolland has likened it to Beethoven's *Ritter-ballet*—"a march in D major, full of pomp and, like it, joyous, noble and sonorous." This was followed, after a "Royal Salute of 101 brass ordnance, viz., 71 six-pounders, 20 twelve-pounders, 10 twenty-four pounders etc.," by five lesser movements intended to portray and accompany one or the other of the allegorical pieces: *Bourrée; La Paix—Largo alla Siciliana* "of charming, heroic grace, lulling itself to sleep"; *La Rejouissance*—a gay and airy *Allegro* scored for the entire band; two Minuets.

The original score of the *Music for the Royal Fireworks* is merely entitled "Concerto." It was not until the work was published, in 1786, that it was given its present name. The instrumentation indicated two trumpet parts with three players to each part; three *prinzipali* (low trumpets); three horn parts with as many performers to each part; three oboe parts with twelve, eight and four players, respectively; two bassoon parts with eight for the first and four for the second part; a "serpent" part, later rewritten for contra bassoon; and three timpani. Never before had so many instruments been massed. "The brightest and most numerous assembly ever known" is how thé *General Advertiser* described the band after the public rehearsal on Vauxhall Gardens, on April 21, 1749, which was attended by twelve thousand people. "So great a resort," the *Gentlemen's Magazine* reported, "occasioned such a stoppage on London Bridge that no carriage could pass for three hours." The footmen were so numerous as to obstruct the passage, so that a scuffle ensued in which some gentlemen were wounded. Yet vaster crowds gathered in London for the celebration proper, scheduled for April 27.

"For a week before, the town was like a country fair," wrote Horace Walpole to his friend Horace Mann. "The streets were filled from morning to night, scaffolds building wherever you could or could not see, and coaches arriving from every corner of the kingdom. The immense crowds, the guards, the machine itself, which was very beautiful, were worth seeing . . .

"The next day were the fireworks, which by no means answered the expense, the length of preparation, and expectation that had been raised . . . The rockets, and whatever was thrown up into the air, succeeded mighty well; but the wheels and all that was to compose the principal part were pitiful and ill-conducted, with no change of colored fire and shapes; the illumination was mean, and lighted so slowly that scarce anybody had patience to wait the finishing, and then, what contributed to the awkwardness of the whole, was the right pavilion catching fire and being burnt down in the middle of the show. Very little mischief was done, and but two persons killed . . ."

Although neither Mr. Walpole nor the editors of the *Gentlemen's Magazine* mention Händel's music, it was a signal success. Already snugly ensconced in royal and public favor, Händel became the musical man-of-the-hour; the *Fireworks Music* made the "Hit Parade" of the day. A month later the composer included it in a program of his works played for the benefit of his pet charity, the Foundling Hospital. Even in this discreet concert version, the composition was applauded; interest in the fireworks had fizzled out with the last sputtering pinwheel.

In arranging his Suite, Sir Hamilton Harty has included all the movements of the original score save one. He has omitted the Allegro; the Overture he follows with the music, *La Paix,* calling it merely *Alla Siciliana,* then comes the *Bourrée,* and finally the *Menuetto.* In the latter, Sir Hamilton has combined the two minuets of Händel's score, using the first as the trio of the second dance.

LOUISE BECK, *Philadelphia Orchestra*

Overture in D minor, *Concerti Grossi*

On his return to London early in 1717, Händel accepted the post of *Kapellmeister* to one of the wealthiest and most ostentatious of English aristocrats, James Brydges, first Duke of Chandos. A veritable Croesus, this gentleman maintained at his estate at Cannons, in the outskirts of London, a chapel, which, in the pomp of its ceremonies and the number and prestige of its musicians, was second only to that of the Royal Court. There Händel composed a series of eleven anthems, the so-called Chandos Anthems, heroic works which foreshadow his later oratorios.

. . . . The *Concerto Grosso,* whose opening section is the present Overture in D minor, is the fifth of a set of six *Concerti Grossi* published in three editions, between 1729 and 1734, by Walsh of London. They are known as the *Concertos de hautbois,* but by courtesy only, for the solo oboe plays a very insignificant role in them. Rarely is it used as a solo instrument; its chief function seems to be to double or reinforce the violins. The date of these works is still unsettled. Some critics place them in the second Hanoverian period, others believe that they belong to the Cannons sojourn; still others consider them a reworking of youthful compositions set down while Händel was still in Halle. It seems certain that they were first performed at the wedding of Princess Anne to the Prince of Orange, in 1733.

At least three of the concerti bear witness to Händel's thrifty habit of putting his musical ideas to work. The third makes use of a fugue found in the *Suites de Pièces pour le Clavecin,* the first volume of which appeared in 1720. The fourth concerto served as the second overture to the opera *Amadigi,* composed in May 1715, while the fifth contains two bits of music that had done duty elsewhere; the theme from the Chandos Anthem, and a fugue from the clavier suites. Not content with this, Händel used the Overture in D minor as a curtain tune for his opera *Ottone,* during a performance in 1722.

The original orchestration of the *Concerto Grosso* No. 5 was for two oboes, a bassoon, the usual strings and two cembalos.

LOUISE BECK, *Philadelphia Orchestra*

Händel took a peculiar pride in his twelve *concerti grossi* for string orchestra, publishing them himself, by subscription. No. 1 is in G; No. 2, in F; No. 3, in E minor; No. 4, in A minor; No. 5, in D; No. 6, in G minor; No. 7, in B flat; No. 8, in C minor; No. 9, in F; No. 10, in D minor; No. 11, in A; and No 12, in B minor.

. . . . The twelve concerti were composed in London within three weeks, between September 29 and October 30, 1739. They were published on April 21, 1740. They are not of equal worth; Romain Rolland finds the seventh and the last three mediocre.

It must be explained that the *concerto grosso* consists essentially of a dialogue between a group of soloists, the *concertino* (trio of two solo violins and solo bass with cembalo) and the chorus of instruments, *concerto grosso.* Evidently Händel, in Rome in 1708, was impressed by Corelli's works in this field, for several of his concerti of Opus 3 are dated 1710 and 1722. Geminiani first introduced the concerto into England, and he was a friend of Händel.

JULIAN SEAMAN, *Elizabeth, N.J., Philharmonic Orchestra*

Water Music Suite

If Newman Flower had not come along to explode the legend, Händel's *Water Music* suite would still rank as one of the great peace-offerings in the history of art.

According to the long-accepted story, Händel planned the work in 1715 as a gesture of appeasement to King George I. Händel had been George's *Kapellmeister* when he was still Elector of Hanover in 1712. Händel obtained permission from his ruler to visit England. The visit proved highly lucrative and Händel failed to return to the Hanoverian post. Finally Mahomet went to the mountain. Queen Anne died in 1714, and Händel's former employer found himself proclaimed King George I of England. The King was supposedly incensed over Händel's playing truant.

Lord Burlington and Baron Kielmansegg, the Master of the King's Horse, thought up a plan of reconciliation, which was carried out. During a "royal water-party" on the Thames, the King's barge was followed by another bearing Händel and a group of musicians. The King was enchanted by the music and naturally asked its composer's name. When told it was Händel, the two were promptly reconciled.

The story would be all right except for the date. Documents unearthed by Mr. Flower revealed the barge episode as occurring in 1717, almost two years after the records show Händel and the King to have become friends again. Moreover, it is just possible the King never took Händel's truancy too hard. Händel accompanied him on a trip to Hanover in 1716, and later George fixed an annuity for life of 200 pounds on him. Queen Anne had earlier put him on her pension list.

The *Daily Courant* of July 19, 1717, describes the incident as taking place two days earlier. The King's barge moved from Lambeth down to Chelsea during what was then termed "a state progress." The river was fairly blanketed with barges, among them one conveying the musicians. "Many other barges with persons of quality attended," the London street reported, "and so great a number of boats that the whole river in a manner was covered. A City Company barge was employed for the music, wherein were fifty instruments of all sorts, who played all the way from Lambeth, while the barges drove with the tide without rowing as far as Chelsea, the finest symphonies, composed expressly for this occasion by Mr. Händel, which His Majesty liked so well that he caused it to be played over three times in going and returning.

"At eleven His Majesty went ashore at Chelsea, where a supper was prepared, and then there was another fine concert of music which lasted till two, after which His Majesty came again into his barge and returned the same way, the music continuing to play until he landed."

A report made to the Duke of Brandenburg on July 19 by his envoy Frederic Bonnet, gives further details of the expedition down the Thames besides one or two surrounding circumstances. "Some weeks ago," writes Bonnet, "the King expressed a wish to Baron von Kilmanseck to have a concert on the river, by subscription . . . The Baron addressed himself therefore to Heidegger, a Suisse by nationality, but (sic) the most intelligent agent the nobility could have for their pleasures. Heidegger answered that much as he was eager to oblige His Majesty, he must reserve the subscription for the big enterprises, to wit, the masquerades, each of which was worth from 300 to 400 guineas to him.

"Baron Kilmanseck, seeing that H.M. was vexed about these difficulties, resolved to give the concert on the river at his own expense and so this concert took place the day before yesterday."

Bonnet added that the musicians' barge kept close to the side of the king's float and that the men "played all kinds of instruments, viz., trumpets, hunting horns, oboes, bassoons, German flute, French flutes á bec, violins and basses, but without voices." Evidently a more observant reporter than the *Daily Courant* man, he even contributes the information that the music "took an hour for each performance."

Bonnet added that the musicians' barge kept close to the side of the King's float.

John Walsh first published the "Water Music" in 1720 and later, because of its growing popularity, he brought out a harpsichord edition of *Händel's Celebrated Water Musick Compleat.* Hamilton Harty chose six of the twenty pieces comprising the original "Water Music" and arranged them for modern orchestra in an edition published in 1922.

LOUIS BIANCOLLI, *Philharmonic-Symphony Society of New York*

Pastoral Symphony from *Messiah*

The manuscript of this most popular of all oratorios—now in the Royal Music Library at Buckingham Palace—bears this inscription: MESSIAH, AN ORATORIO. PART THE FIRST ANGEFANGEN DEN 22 AUGUST 1741. The end of the first part is dated August 28, 1741, and the end of Part Two, September 6, 1741. On the last page Händel again lapsed into his native tongue. It is inscribed, in his own hand: AUSGEFÜLLT DEN 14 SEPTEMBER, 1741. A little calculation will reveal that the oratorio was composed in the space of twenty-four days.

Originally announced for April 12, 1742, the first performance took place in Dublin on the following day, and it was preceded by a public rehearsal five days earlier. On March 27 this notice appeared in *Faulkner's Journal*:

"For Relief of the Prisoners in the several Gaols and for the Support of Mercer's Hospital in Stephen's Street and of the Charitable Infirmary on the Inns Quay, on Monday the 12th of April will be performed at the Musick Hall in Fishamble Street Mr. Händel's new Grand Oratorio called *The Messiah*, in which the gentlemen in the Choirs of both Cathedrals will assist, with some Concertos on the Organ by Mr. Händel.

"Tickets to be had at the Musick Hall and at Mr. Neal's in Christ Church Yard at Half-a-Guinea each. N.B.—No person will be admitted to the Rehearsal without a Rehearsal Ticket, which will be given gratis with the Ticket for the Performance when pay'd for."

The same journal reviewed the rehearsal, which was, in effect, the premiere:

"Yesterday Mr. Händel's new Grand Oratorio, called *Messiah*, was rehearsed at the Musick Hall in Fishamble Street, to a most Grand, polite and crouded Audience; and was performed so well, that it gave universal Satisfaction to all present, and was allowed by the greatest Judges to be the finest Composition of Musick that ever was heard, and the sacred Words as being properly adapted for the Occasion.

"N.B.—At the Desire of several Persons of Distinction, the above Performance is put off to Tuesday next. The Doors will be opened at Eleven, and the performance begun at Twelve. Many Ladies and Gentlemen who are well-wishers to this Noble and Grand Charity, for which the Oratorio was composed, request it as a Favour, that the Ladies who honour this Performance with their Presence, would be pleased to come without Hoops, as it will greatly increase the Charity, by making Room for more Company."

The ladies came "without Hoops" and the gentlemen, in response to another request, came without their swords, with the result that "there were above 700 people in the Room, and the Sum collected for that Noble and Pious Charity amounted to about 400 pounds, out of which 127 pounds goes to each of the three great and pious Charities."

The music of this program is the orchestral interlude—which

the terminology of the period described as a "Symphony" or "Sinfonia"—which precedes the soprano's recitative, "There were shepherds abiding in the field." With the most moving simplicity, it sets the stage for the Story of the Nativity. At the Dublin performance the interlude was only a brief one of eleven bars. Händel later expanded it to its present proportions.

Philadelphia Orchestra

ROY HARRIS

(Born in Lincoln County, Oklahoma, February 12, 1898—now Composer-in-residence, Colorado College, Colorado Springs, Colorado)

HAVING been born in a log cabin on Lincoln's Birthday would seem to stamp Roy Harris as akin in spirit, at least, to the Great Emancipator. He may have even split rails later on the family's farm in California, though it is likely that Roy was still too young to worry about adult chores.

He had a farm of his own at eighteen and a year later joined the army for the First World War. He came back to California, but decided he was no farmer. He registered at the Southern Branch of the University of California as a student of harmony. And he drove a truck to pay for it.

He learned enough in his harmony class to realize that he needed to know much more. He sought out Arthur Farwell, California composer, and asked to become a private pupil. He worked with Farwell for two years.

Probably his debut as a composer came with the selection of an *Andante for Strings* by the Philharmonic Society of New York for performance at the Lewisohn Stadium in the Summer of 1926.

That year he went abroad, to study with Nadia Boulanger in Paris. He stayed there for two additional years, having won a Guggenheim Fellowship, and composed his first major work, a concerto for piano, clarinet and string quartet, played in Paris and praised by the French press.

Having fallen ill, he came back to the United States in 1929 and a year later won a Creative Fellowship from the Pasadena Music and Arts Association. He has been a teacher of composition at the Westminster Choir School, Princeton, New Jersey; composer-in-residence at Cornell University and the same at Colorado College.

For a time, during World War II, he was head of the music division in the Office of War Information, New York. Part of his duty in that position was to arrange and supervise the recording of American music by American performers for rebroadcast overseas.

Most of his major works have been performed here and in Europe. Today he is considered among the foremost and most successful of American composers. It is significant that when the Pro Arte Quartet presented a cross section of chamber music within the last hundred years, only one work represented the twentieth century—Harris' Second String Quartet.

Says Harris of his chosen career:

"I finally decided to choose music as a lifework because it was the only language which I found to be constant. I made my choice late in life. I was twenty-eight years old."

American Overture: *When Johnny Comes Marching Home*

When this work was performed at a concert of the Los Angeles Orchestra on May 11, 1935, Mr. Harris supplied the following information:

"When I was requested to write an American overture especially for recording, I was presented with a very specific set of problems. First, the work should express a gamut of emotions particularly American in an American manner. Secondly, the form of the work being an overture should be complete in itself and yet indicate that it was only a concentrated announcement of materials and moods which could unfold in a development of much greater length. Thirdly, the work must give these impressions and yet be eight minutes in length and divided into two well-balanced equal parts.

"The moods which seem particularly American to me are a noisy ribaldry, a sadness, a groping earnestness which amounts to suppliance toward those deepest spiritual yearnings within ourselves; and finally a fierce struggle of will for power, sheer power in itself. There is little grace or mellowness in our midst. That will probably come after we have passed high noon of our growth as a people.

"With the moods of ribaldry, sadness, suppliance and willful power in mind I chose an American theme which is not only well known and loved but capable of extended development: *When Johnny Comes Marching Home.*

"This was one of my father's favorite tunes, and it was he who planted in me the unconscious realization of its dual nature. He used to whistle it with jaunty bravado as we went to work on the farm in the morning, and with sad pensiveness as we returned at dusk behind the slow, weary plodding of the horses.

"These impressions have undoubtedly influenced me in determining the use of this theme, yet the same realization of the dual character of this peculiarly fertile theme might have been arrived at by observing that it is minor in its tonality and gay in its rhythm.

"The first half of the work expresses openly and directly the ribald quality of the theme itself and its transformation into a slow, sad mood. The second half opens with a rhythmic pattern parallel to the opening of the first half and then goes directly with the mood of suppliance. For this section the traditional treatment of the contrapuntal chorale is used in which the theme in slower tempo becomes the bass. This resolves into the last section, which treats the mood struggle for power, and ends in an unresolved continuance of that struggle.

"All material throughout is either a direct statement of the theme, or characteristic fragments of the theme or variations of the theme, so that the work is abstract from the musician's point of view; i.e., it does not depend on programmatic ideas for its form or its content. But from the layman's point of view it may be considered programmatic music, I suppose.

"In the treatment of the texture and the orchestration I have tried to keep the work roughhewn, sinewy and directly outspoken, as are our people and our civilization."

Symphony No. 3 (in one movement)

Roy Harris composed his Third Symphony during the autumn of 1938, and completed the proofreading in January 1939. The first performance was at the concerts of the Boston Symphony Orchestra February 24, 1939. It was performed at a special concert of American music October 6, 1939.

The Symphony is a continuous work in one movement, of about twenty minutes' duration. The composer has provided, instead of a long prose analysis, the following structural outline of his score:

Section 1—Tragic—low string sonorities.
Section 2—Lyric—strings, horns, woodwinds.
Section 3—Pastoral—emphasizing woodwind color.
Section 4—Fugue—dramatic. . . . .
Section 5—Dramatic—tragic.

JOHN N. BURK, *Berkshire Symphonic Festival*

FRANZ JOSEPH HAYDN

(Born in Rohrau, Lower Austria, March 31, 1732—
died in Vienna, May 31, 1809)

BORN IN a lowly peasant cottage, son of a wheelwright and one of twelve children, Haydn became rich and famous, yet he never lost his affection for his humble birthplace. His father loved music, could play the harp by ear, but he could neither read nor write.

Consequently, Joseph got no musical instruction from his father—instead he went to a neighboring schoolmaster, Johann Frankh, distantly related to the family, who must be accounted as his first teacher. Frankh lived in nearby Hainburg, and Haydn went to live with him. Joseph was a shabby, hungry urchin, yet he had a sense of humor and usually engaged in some mischief.

Georg von Reutter, director of music at St. Stephen's in Vienna, came to Hainburg, seeking choir boys for the cathedral. He heard Haydn sing and decided to take him along. Franz Joseph was then eight.

In return for their singing, the boys received a general education, food and lodging, in addition to music lessons. It is recorded that Haydn made rapid progress and learned to play the clavecin and violin; also, other instruments, "although he never excelled at any of them."

Two lessons in composition from Reutter was about all the formal instruction Haydn had before he started to write music. He could not compose away from the clavier, and used to take a portable one under his arm and "seek a quiet spot where he could compose undisturbed."

His voice broke when he was sixteen and he was turned out in the street, destitute and starving, "with three wretched shirts and a worn-out coat." For a long time he ate sparingly if at all, became a street musician, singing under windows, playing at taverns and giving lessons to children. Another poor student, Spangler, invited Haydn to share his garret where he could compose.

A music-loving merchant made him a timely loan and he was able to move into slightly better lodgings. He met a singer who helped to get him an introduction to Gluck. His music was becoming known and he got better work to do. A theater manager commissioned him to write some music for a sea scene in a pantomime, but Haydn had never seen the sea and the manager had to explain how the waves rose and fell. This early creation was not very successful.

He was nearly thirty when he wrote his first symphony for a wealthy Bohemian, Count von Morzin, who kept a private orchestra of eighteen and appointed Haydn his *Kapellmeister*. This was Haydn's first real job at a fairly good salary. It enabled him to marry; an unfortunate step, for his wife, daughter of a wigmaker, was "quarrelsome . . . shrewish, jealous and extravagant. Moreover, she was utterly unmusical, so that the two had little in common."

His married life, in fact, was one long misery—a misery he bore for thirty years, when he obtained a formal separation.

In 1761, Haydn entered upon what became practically a life tenure as assistant *Kapellmeister* to Prince Paul Anton Esterhazy, and later *Kapellmeister* to Prince Nicholas, an employment that he held for nearly thirty years.

The Esterhazy family was fabulously rich and the prince had built a theater and opera house on his estate. "The appointment," remarks an anonymous biographer in a thumbnail sketch published in England by Paxton, "left Haydn plenty of time not only for composing, but for his favorite recreations, hunting and fishing. He was provided with a fine suite of rooms and a salary of 600 florins. During this period he composed 63 symphonies, 43 quartets, 28 sonatas, 17 trios and a number of smaller works."

The British violinist and impresario, Johann Peter Salomon visited Haydn in 1790 and offered him twelve hundred pounds to visit London and conduct six new symphonies. He accepted, bade a tearful farewell to his protege, Mozart (dead when next Haydn returned to Vienna), and dared the perils of the English Channel. He stayed in England more than a year, was feted and made much of by society and won the degree of Doctor of Music from Oxford. He returned to Vienna in 1792, "laden with gifts and honors."

Upon his return, he went to Bonn and met the stormy young Beethoven, to whom he gave some lessons in composition. But a second visit to England, as successful as the first, forced him to turn Beethoven over to an assistant, and Beethoven himself rebelled.

During his last visit to London, he was introduced to a widow of sixty, Madame Schroeter, who fell desperately in love with him. "Had I been free, I should certainly have married her," he remarked.

Back in Vienna, in 1797, he composed what became the Austrian national anthem, the so-called *Emperor's Hymn*. Salomon suggested an oratorio, so Haydn spent eighteen months in composing his masterpiece of vocal music, *The Creation.* Apropos the first performance in London (1800), he said:

"One moment I was as cold as ice; the next I seemed to be on fire. I thought I should have a fit."

His second great oratorio, *The Seasons,* came a year later. He was more than sixty-five when he composed both of these great works. The former has proved most popular.

The same anonymous biographer writes the following paragraph in conclusion:

"It was in connection with a performance of *The Creation* at Vienna that Haydn made his last appearance in public in March 1808, an event that gave rise to a pathetic incident. When the orchestra played the introduction to the aria, 'And there was light,' the audience broke into loud applause, and Haydn, pointing upward, said: 'It came from above.' At the close of the performance his friends, among them Beethoven, gathered round to bid him farewell and support him to the door.

"As he neared the exit he stopped, turned around, and, lifting his arms, seemed to give his benediction to the musicians. 'Never,' relates Carpani, 'was such a pathetic spectacle.'

"Haydn died just over a year later, in May 1809. Four days before his death he made his attendants carry him to his clavier, where with great effort he managed to play the *Emperor's Hymn.* This constituted his farewell to music.

" 'I believe I have done my duty, and have helped the world by my labors: let others do the same.' These were almost his last words. He was buried at Eisenstadt."

Symphony in D major (*The Clock*)

This symphony, composed in 1794, is one of the second set which Haydn wrote for London at the stipulation of the manager, Salomon. It takes its name from an accompanying figure of bassoons and plucked strings heard in the Andante, suggesting the ticking of a large clock. Haydn, it should be mentioned, composed the minuet a year earlier for a musical clock which he presented to Prince Esterhazy. In Germany the score has the alternative title, *Glocken (Bell) Symphony*.

Up to the late war, the autograph was in the Berlin State Library. Karl Geiringer, in his Haydn biography, remarks that "the Presto of the first movement and its 6-8 time are what one would expect in the finale of a symphony rather than in its initial movement." Mr. Geiringer sees in the Andante "Haydn's favorite mixture of variation and rondo form, which so strongly impressed Beethoven that one finds traces of it even in the slow movement of the Ninth Symphony . . . Particularly attractive is the entrance of the charming main theme after the dramatic episode in G minor. The *tick tack* is here taken over by a flute, so that a tiny clock seems to replace the big timepiece heard at the beginning.

"The Trio of the following minuet belongs to the type frequently used by Haydn, which does not contrast with the preceding dance but rather supplements it. Both sections are also in the same key, a fact which has induced some conductors to omit the repetition of the minuet after the trio . . ."

HERBERT F. PEYSER, *Philharmonic-Symphony Society of New York*

Symphony in G major (No. 94, *The Surprise*)

The Symphony was composed in 1791; performed for the first time on March 23, 1792, at the Hanover Square Rooms, London. The orchestration comprises two flutes, two oboes, two bassoons, two horns, two trumpets, tympani and strings.

This was the third in order of the twelve symphonies which Haydn wrote for Johann Peter Salomon to be performed at the concerts which the musician-impresario arranged for Haydn in London. This symphony, introduced at the sixth (and last) Salomon concert of Haydn's first visit, became at once popular, and known as the "favorite grand overture." Haydn repeated it during his second sojourn in London (1794 and 1795).

The incident of the sudden *fortissimo* chord introduced at the end of a *pianissimo* passage in the Andante undoubtedly captured the general fancy and contributed toward the favor in which the piece was held. It thus acquired the title in England, the

Surprise Symphony, and in Germany, the symphony "with the drum stroke." Adalbert Gyrowetz, writing his autobiography in 1848, quoted Haydn as having remarked, while playing it to him on the piano: "The women will cry out here."

It has been told that British audiences, having dined heartily before the concerts, were apt to doze through slow movements. But Haydn avowed no further intention than to titillate them with a novelty. "The first *allegro* of my symphony was received with countless 'bravos,' but the enthusiasm rose to the highest point after the Andante with the drum stroke. '*Ancora! Ancora!*' was shouted from all sides, and Pleyel himself complimented me upon the idea."

The reviewer in the *Oracle* was roused to a flight of fancy: "The second movement was equal to the happiest of this great Master's conceptions. The surprise might not be unaptly likened to the situation of a beautiful Shepherdess, who, lulled to slumber by the murmur of a distant Waterfall, starts alarmed by the unexpected firing of a fowling piece. The flute obbligato was delicious."

This loud chord which caused so much attention and discussion has been demonstrated to have been nothing more than an afterthought. A writer in the *Musical Times* (May 1, 1909), who signed himself "F. G. E.," explained that he had had access to the "original autograph," which was then in possession of Felix Moscheles. The first page of the Andante from the autograph in question is reproduced in facsimile in that issue of the *Musical Times*. After the first eight measures, which are marked *piano,* there is simply a double bar repeat sign. A large X is drawn across the page. (In the printed score the eight measures are repeated with a lighter scoring. The *FF* chord follows, given to the full orchestra.)

William Foster Apthorp, describing early Haydn performances in Boston, wrote of an occasion when Julien's Orchestra played the *Surprise Symphony* during the season of 1853-1854. Julien chose the Andante as a means of creating a sensation. "To make the 'Surprise' still more surprising, he added an enormous bass drum— the largest, I believe, ever seen in this country up to that time."

JOHN N. BURK, *Boston Symphony Orchestra*

Symphony in C major (*Toy*)

It is hardly likely that the Bavarian town of Berchtesgaden will go down in history as the place where Joseph Haydn purchased some toy instruments in 1788. Of course, the accounts of Haydn's purchase are somewhat conflicting. According to one version, the instruments were bought in a well-known toyshop in Berchtesgaden. According to another, Haydn purchased them at a toy-fair in Vienna. In any case, when he returned to the Esterhazy estate, Haydn had with him a new *Kindersinfonie*—toys and all. The story goes that the Esterhazy musicians chuckled so much over the music, that, in spite of its simplicity, they failed to keep time.

In early editions this *Toy Symphony* is entitled either *Kindersinfonie* or *Symphony Burlesque*. The toys used have varied somewhat, depending on caprice and ingenuity. Besides first and second violins and basses, the instruments used are a tambourine, a triangle, a bass drum, cymbals, a ratchet, a toy drum, a toy trumpet, a "cuckoo," a "quail" and a "bobwhite".

The three miniature movements are Allegro, Minuet and Finale, the last given at a faster tempo with each repetition.

Naturally, the *Toy Symphony* is little more than a *'jeu d'esprit'*, as J. Cuthbert Hadden states in his biography—a bagatelle "not requiring serious notice, especially in the case of Haydn, to whom humor in music was a very different matter from the handling of rattles and penny trumpets and toy drums."

Haydn probably dashed off the symphonic trifle in one of his impish moments of practical joking. Of these periodic seizures, Hadden writes sympathetically:

"A leading trait in his character was his humor and love of fun. As he remarked to Albert Dies: 'A mischievous fit comes over me sometimes that is perfectly beyond control.' "

The incident of the removal of the fellow-chorister's pigtail will at once recur to the memory. The *Surprise Symphony* is another illustration, to say nothing of the *Toy* and *Jacob's Dream*.

Mozart often experienced spells of a similar kind. One such impulse materialized as a *Musical Joke* in which the instruments not only remain blithely out of tune, but begin and stop playing when least expected. Composers will have their little joke.

Louis Biancolli, *Philharmonic-Symphony Society of New York*

Symphony in G major (No. 88, *Letter V*)

This symphony, identified by several numbers which vary confusingly from one catalogue to another, is also known as the *"Letter V" Symphony*. There is in that, however, no connotation of Victory. It is merely one of a series of Haydn's symphonies which the London Philharmonic Society listed by alphabetical designations—letter A to letter W. It is No. 13 in the Breitkopf and Haertel catalogue; No. 8 in that of Peters. In the chronological list compiled by Eusebius Mandyczewski it is No. 88.

In 1784, when Haydn was at the peak of his fame as a private composer to Prince Nicholas Esterhazy, he was approached by an emissary of the *Concert de la Loge Olympique* of Paris, a musical organization of great wealth and overpowering aristocracy. Buried in the country at Esterhaz, almost never farther afield than Vienna, the composer was in a position comparable to that of the backwoods maker of mousetraps. His wares were known and sought for in all the musical capitals of Europe. His symphonies had been played in Paris as early as 1779, and two years later his *Stabat Mater* had made a sensation at a *Concert Spirituel,* its popularity justifying several repetitions. There were Parisian publishers for a number of his works. Despite the safety and security of his comfortable drudgery for Prince Esterhazy, Haydn sometimes felt that he was unfortunate to live where he could not actively expand the market for his own music.

For the *Loge Olympique,* then, Haydn wrote two sets of symphonies. That in G major, of this program, was the first of the second set of five. It was composed at Esterhaz, probably in 1786, forwarded to Paris for performance that year or the next, and published there afterward as Opus 51, under the special title of *Repertoire de la Loge Olympique.*

Mention of that august association hints at the interesting early history of Parisian concerts, which provided a model for other cities. Performances at the Paris Opéra were forbidden on the holy days of the Church, and in 1725 a court musician named Philidor obtained a license to give concerts on such days on condition that neither French music nor operatic excerpts be included in the programs. This was the foundation of the *Concerts*

Spirituels which grew in importance (the ban on French and operatic music presently being lifted) and lasted until silenced by the French Revolution in 1789.

The cumulative influence of the *Concerts Spirituels* resulted in 1770 in the formation of a still more fashionable enterprise, the *Concerts des Amateurs,* which presented twelve concerts a year in the grand salon of Charles de Rohan-Rohan, Prince de Soubise et d'Epinoy. The participating orchestra was the largest that had been brought together in Paris—comprising forty violins, with other instruments in proportion—and its performances were of great artistic importance. In 1781, these concerts were reorganized and given the title *della Loge Olympique.* (The *Salle Olympique* had been the home of the *opéra buffa.*) It was rich as well as fashionable, able to engage renowned virtuosos as soloists and to commission new works from eminent composers. The great violinist, Viotti, served as conductor of the concerts.

In its early days the association had vague connections with Freemasonry. Subscribers to the performances were received only after a rigorous examination. Admittance was granted at solemn ritual meetings. Each one paid two louis d'or a year, and was given a decoration consisting of a silver lyre on a skyblue background, which was his badge of admittance.

Concerts, at first in the Palais Royal, were later given in the *Salle des Gardes* in the Tuileries, where a stage was set up for the performers and tiers of seats for the listeners. Marie Antoinette and her household were frequently present, and a *grande toilette* was required, not only for the audience but for the players, who wore embroidered coats with lace ruffles, swords and plumed hats, which lay beside them on benches as they played.

Their concord of sweet sounds, however, was to be drowned by the cries of the hungry, and, after July 15, 1789, by the rattle of the tumbrels over the cobblestones.

R. L. F. McCombs, *Phildelphia Orchestra Journal*

Symphony in F-sharp minor (*Farewell*)

At the time he wrote the *Farewell Symphony,* Haydn was in the employ of Prince Nicolas on the Esterhazy estate. The castle was sumptuous and equipped with the best accommodations money and exquisite taste could provide. But Haydn and the men in his orchestra were none too happy about their jobs.

They were far from their beloved Vienna, the place was damp, and the men's thoughts turned repeatedly to home and family.

Haydn appointed himself spokesman. The problem was to find the right channel of protest. Finally he hit on it. What better vehicle than a symphony with a cleverly worked-in device showing the men's dissatisfaction? At length the night of the premiere arrived. The first three movements of the new symphony went conventionally, with the prince nodding approval.

Then the fourth movement began, a *presto,* in Haydn's typical spirited style. Nothing unusual there. Suddenly the *presto* section ended and an unexpected *adagio* set in.

The prince frowned, puzzled. He was even more puzzled at what came next. The men seemed to be seized by sudden madness or rebellion. One by one they stopped playing, blew out their candles, and calmly walked off. At length, there were only two violinists left on the stage.

The prince, a keen-witted man, saw the point, and so did his guests. "If they all go, then we may as well go, too," he announced affably.

An erroneous version is often given of Haydn's motive in writing the *Farewell Symphony.* According to it, the composer intended it as an appeal to the prince not to dismiss the orchestra. It was an appeal, all right, but only for a change in residence.

ROBERT C. BAGAR, *Philharmonic-Symphony Society of New York*

Symphony in G major (No. 92, *Oxford*)

This symphony, composed in 1788, was performed at Oxford, England, on July 7, 1791. (This may not have been the first performance.)

In the summer of 1791, following Haydn's first series of concerts in London, the composer consented to go to Oxford and receive the degree of Doctor of Music from the university. He may not have longed for this honor. Other musicians before him had slighted it. According to Hawkins' remark in his *History of Music* in 1766: "This degree is not much sought after nowadays." Hawkins say that Händel expostulated over the offer of a diploma at Oxford in 1733: "Vat de dyfil I trow my money away for dat de blockhead wish? I no vant." Händel's objection was the customary fee of one hundred guineas that went with the privilege. A degree *honoris causa* did not carry a fee, and this was Haydn's case. Haydn was not particularly interested, according to C. F. Pohl, but "his friend Burney was of another opinion, and did everything possible to bring this honor upon his favorite." Haydn described the affair in a letter to Marianne von Genzinger, but the letter has been lost and we have only this written comment in his notebook: "I had to pay one and a half guineas for the bell peals at Oxforth (*sic*) when I received the doctor's degree, and half a guinea for the robe. The journey cost six guineas."

There were three concerts, each given in the Sheldonian Theater of the university, a hall seating four thousand which had been designed by Sir Christopher Wren more than a century before and modeled upon the Marcellus Theater in Rome. Much was made of these concerts. Singers and players were brought from far and wide. Each concert was in three long sections with a parade of soloists and an emphasis upon the choruses of Händel. A symphony of Haydn was performed at the beginning of the second portion on each evening. The company which assembled was "numerous and elegant." Haydn arrived too late to rehearse for the first concert, on July 6, and one of his symphonies already familiar to the players (but now unidentifiable) was played instead.

The Symphony which was to bear the title *Oxford* figured upon the second programme on July 7. But Haydn's "thesis" was apparently not actually written for the occasion. Karl Geiringer states categorically that this symphony was composed in 1788. He also states that "the score, laid out at first for an orchestra of medium size, was later enlarged by the addition of trumpets and timpani." This presumably for the Oxford performance. Dr. Hayes, professor of music at Oxford, presided at the concert; Cramer was the "leader." Haydn sat at the organ and indicated the *tempi*. The audience was highly pleased, and when an attempt was made to shorten the program, the students, the "gentlemen of the square cap," as Pohl called them, made a demonstration which forestalled that result. The *Morning Chronicle* reported: "A more wonderful composition never was heard. The applause given to Haydn, who conducted this admirable effort of his genius, was enthusiastic; but the merit of the work, in the opinion of all the musicians present, exceeded all praise." . . . .

Being a self-made musician without any appreciable academic recognition in his own land, Haydn was evidently gratified by these honors from a foreign university. In letters he signed himself *"Doctor zu Oxford."* The young Beethoven, dedicating to his teacher his first three published piano sonatas, may have wished to compliment him with the following phrasing of the dedication as announced in 1796: *"dédiées á Mr.* [!] *Joseph Haydn, Docteur en Musique."*

JOHN N. BURK, *Boston Symphony Orchestra*

Symphony in G major (No. 100, *Military*)

Composed in 1794, the *Military Symphony* was one of the second set of six commissioned by the English impresario Johann Peter Salomon for a London subscription series. Haydn's manuscript carries the date "1794." Since the Austrian composer had arrived in London early that year and taken lodgings at No. 1, Bury Street, St. James's, it may be assumed he wrote the Symphony there. It was apparently first played in the Hanover Square Rooms on May 2, 1794.

Salomon had arranged the opening concert of the new series for February 3. But Haydn was delayed and did not reach London till February 4, accompanied by Johann Elssler, his servant and copyist. The concerts did not start till February 10. In the course of the series all twelve "London" symphonies were played, Haydn having composed six for his earlier visit in 1791. Each of the twelve weekly concerts was sold out. Haydn was widely and warmly acclaimed. His aggregate income from lessons, concerts and symphonies was twelve hundred pounds; enough, according to the biographer Pohl, "to relieve him from all anxiety as to the future." Moreover, Haydn had grown as a composer. The "London" symphonies are "the greatest of his orchestral works," in the opinion of W. H. Hadow. During his last years Haydn would often say that "it was not till he had been to England that he became famous in Germany."

It had all started in 1790, shortly after the death of Prince Esterhazy, his patron-employer. Haydn had gone to Vienna to settle down, having acquired a pension from the Esterhazy family.

Before he could begin to enjoy his new comfort, up stepped this ebullient impresario from London. "My name is Salomon," he announced bluntly. "I have come from London to fetch you; we will settle terms tomorrow." Haydn's first impulse was to turn down the offer. He was tasting real freedom for the first time. But the terms were too tempting—300 pounds for an opera; 300 for six symphonies; plus 200 for copyrights; 200 for twenty compositions in other forms, and 200 pounds for a "benefit" concert. And Frau Haydn was already pestering him about that charming little house in the suburbs. Besides, Salomon assured him of flattering attention from royal and aristocratic circles and the homage of the whole British public. Salomon, for his part, was in desperate need of a celebrity of Haydn's standing, having organized a series of subscription concerts at the Hanover Square Rooms. Haydn was to be his trump card in London's growing managerial rivalry.

The contract signed, Haydn set out with Salomon and arrived in London for his first visit early in January 1791. Salomon had not exaggerated. Wherever the illustrious visitor went he was lionized. People of high rank sought his friendship. The best houses offered their hospitality. Ambassadors callled on him, and the delegates of the music societies outdid one another in bestowing honors upon him. Haydn, who never minimized the dividends of fame, proudly wrote his wife: "I could dine out every night if I wanted to."

Haydn's *Military Symphony* gets its title largely from the *allegretto* which replaces the usual *andante* as a second movement. There the bass drum, cymbals and triangle combined in what the eighteenth century termed "Turkish music." A martial note is also struck by the trumpet call occurring in the closing pages of the *allegretto*. "The trumpets sound the signal for falling into the line," says one analyst, taking the *Military* title literally. The oft-repeated theme of the movement derives from a French romanza

La gentille et jeune Lisette. Haydn found earlier use for this song in his *La Reine Symphony* and in a lute concerto written for the King of Naples. The so-called "Turkish music" can also be heard in the accompaniment to the G major second theme of the Presto finale.

LOUIS BIANCOLLI, *Philharmonic-Symphony Society of New York*

PAUL HINDEMITH

(Born in Hanau, Germany, November 16, 1895—
now on the faculty of Yale University, New Haven)

PAUL HINDEMITH is less of an influence than an idol to the pioneering young of American composers. They do not regard him as essentially German—in fact, no hint of nationalism is attached to his name, for his music would seem to be a quest, a searching for new syllables with which to speak eternal truths.

If history repeats itself, then the pattern of Hindemith's life has had notable precedent. We think of Haydn, Händel, Berlioz and, Tschaikowsky and a host of others when we learn that Hindemith's parents objected to a musical career, that he ran away from home at eleven, played the violin in dance orchestras, motion picture houses and cafes.

He managed to enter the Hoch Conservatory in Frankfort and studied under Arnold Mendelssohn and Bernhard Sekles. He was appointed concertmaster of the Frankfort Opera in 1915, conductor in 1923. He formed and played in the famous Amar String Quartet, "which toured Germany in programmes of modern chamber music."

So successfully did he compose that important works appeared

on the programs of the Donaueschingen Festival and at Salzburg.
A concerto for piano and "twelve solo instruments" seemed to
crystallize his style and enhance his growing reputation. This was
introduced at a festival of modern music in Venice. Fritz Busch
conducted the premiere of his opera *Cardillac* in Dresden. Then
came his jazz opera *Neues vom Tage* and *Mathis der Maler,* besides
chamber and orchestra works, pieces for pianola, radio and talking pictures.

He taught at the Hochschule in Berlin from 1927 to 1937
but the Nazis condemned his music as being antagonistic to "the
new Germany." Hindemith came to this country, at the invitation
of the Elizabeth Sprague Coolidge Foundation, played the viola on
concert tour and later joined the music faculty of Yale.

Nobilissima Visione
Suite from the ballet *St. Francis*

Hindemith wrote his ballet *St. Francis* for the Ballet Russe de
Monte Carlo in 1937, working closely with the choreographer,
Léonide Massine. It was first performed by that troupe in London, July 21, 1938. The present Suite which (in the composer's
words) "consists of three sections of the ballet score which are self-
sufficient and comprehensible as concert music and which do not
depend, therefore, on any supplementary stage action," was first
given in Venice in September 1938. The first American performance, the composer conducting, was by the Philharmonic Orchestra of Los Angeles on March 23, 1939.

To the programs of those performances of the "Choreographic
Legend" a preface was contributed by Francois Mauriac—*de
l'Academie Francais*:

"I must admit that when Léonide Massine spoke to me for
the first time of his project for *St. Francis,* the idea seemed to me
worse than bold—it was even sacrilegious. This is because I had
not realized that the dance, as this great artist conceived it, can express what is most beautiful and sacred in this world, the love of
God taking possession of the soul of a young man.

"Pascal has written: 'I love poverty because He, our Lord,
loved it.'

"We must think that it is in poverty and through poverty that St. Francis, that prince among young men, attained to Christ. Hindemith and Massine could not have presented the figure of the living God upon the stage—nor that of the Man-God, the Son of Man; but a young girl, no more than a child, inspired by these forces, incarnates for our eyes this adorable poverty, with whom St. Francis became entirely infatuated.

"No, I should never have believed that this passion (which I have been able to admire in many persons of youthful age), this mad craving for the poverty which Christ loved, could have been realized for us in music and dance—yet this miracle has been accomplished. It is that thing which St. Francis of Assisi well understood, the reconciling of Nature and of the spirit of mercy. The Hymn to his brother, the Sun, sets free the spirits of water, of air, of fire—so that the dance itself, exorcised from all base passions, puts young and beautiful bodies, and their leaping strength, at the service of true love."

To which preface Massine added that his choreographic legend "translates the moving simplicities and mentality of the strange world of St. Francis into the highly formalized language of the ballet."

The introduction (strings and clarinets) is taken from the eighth of the ballet's eleven episodes, entitled "Meditation." The Rondo (strings and flute) is the music of "The Marriage of Poverty," which is the tenth scene. The March with triangle drums for military color, is the fourth episode, and the Passacaglia is the closing number of the ballet as well as the Suite.

R. F. L. McCOMBS, *Philadelphia Orchestra*

Symphony—*Matthias the Painter*

This was first performed by the British Broadcasting Orchestra, in London on December 2, 1933, the composer conducting.

This symphony consists of three orchestral excerpts from an opera by Hindemith based on the life of Matthias Gruenwald (his name was more exactly Matthias Gothart Nithart), great German painter of the Reformation. The three movements derive their titles from one of the Master's greatest works—the Isenheim Altarpiece, which, before the war, was on exhibit in the museum at Colmar, in Alsace.

The "Concert of Angels" serves as the overture to the opera and its principal melody, *Es sangen drei Engel,* appears frequently in the opera. "The Entombment" is used as an orchestral intermezzo in the final scene, "The Temptation of St. Anthony" is a portion of the sixth scene.

Hindemith managed to incur the displeasure of the Nazi propaganda machine very shortly after Hitler's rise to power. The distinguished German conductor, Wilhelm Furtwaengler, took up the cudgels in defense of Hindemith and for his pains was "rusticated" for a period of time; but Furtwaengler subsequently patched up his differences with the Nazi government while Hindemith went into exile.

No less a Nazi personality than Alfred Rosenberg, Hitler's arbiter on cultural matters, wrote of the Hindemith-Furtwaengler case that "in this question we find two opposite ideologies. The one considers everything in the light of artistic endeavor. The other—the National Socialist—realizes that an artist often represents political trends."

. . . Hindemith wrote the libretto as well as the music of the opera and chose a tense moment in his country's history for his background—the peasant war of 1524, when the populace of southern Germany rebelled against the nobles and clergy and demanded a liberalization and popularization of Church and state. Thomas Muenzer, leader of the rebellion, was tried for treason and shot, but the movement continued until the Reformation was established. In the opera, Matthias Gruenwald, painting under the patronage of the liberal Cardinal Albrecht, identifies himself with the peasants' struggle for freedom from oppression. But the excesses of the revolutionary movement are too much for him and he turns from them, seeking peace in Odenwald.

There apparitions come to torment him in the night (figures from the Isenheim "Temptation of St. Anthony"). Ultimately he returns to his easel and withdraws from worldly affairs, in order to devote his remaining days to art.

JOHN S. EDWARDS, *St. Louis Symphony Orchestra*

ARAM KHATCHATOURIAN

(Born in Tiflis, Georgia, Armenia, June 6, 1902—
now living in Moscow)

SON OF an Armenian bookbinder, this rising young Soviet
composer did not begin to study music until he was nineteen. He enrolled in a Moscow music school, studied the 'cello and composition under Michael Gnessin, Vassilenko and the prolific Miaskow-
sky, all of whom gave him his first insight into the classics.

Almost at once he began to compose. His "Dance" for violin
and piano was issued in 1926 and other works followed immediately. "He has never tried to make up for lost time," says William
E. Benswanger, in a note for the Pittsburgh Symphony Orchestra,
"and his creative output is conservative in quantity."

Among his more important works are a *Poem* for piano
(1927), *Study in Ninths* (1927), a symphony celebrating the fifteenth
anniversary of the Sovietization of Armenia (1934), *Poem About
Stalin* (1938), a violin concerto (1940), a piano concerto (1935),
music for the ballet *Gayaneh* (1942), a second symphony, chamber
music and songs.

Dances from the ballet *Gayaneh*

For "outstanding merit in promoting the development of
Armenian art," Aram Khatchatourian was awarded the Order of
Lenin in 1939. Four years later came a further token of recognition for creative effort on behalf of his native Soviet republic—
the First Degree Stalin Prize. This Khatchatourian won with his
music to *Gayaneh,* a patriotic folk ballet, steeped in native lore and
idiom, about cotton pickers on a collective farm (*Kolkhoz*) in Soviet Armenia. The libretto was by K. N. Derzhavin. The premiere
of *Gayaneh* occurred in the city of Molotov on December 9, 1942,
during a visit of the Kirov Theater for Opera and Ballet of the
Leningrad State Academy, N. A. Anisimova, a noted Soviet ballerina, directed the production and danced the title role.

. . . The orchestral suite from *Gayaneh* contains thirteen sepa-

rate dances. Three of them—"Dance of the Rose Maidens," "Lullaby" and "Dance with the Sabres" (Nos. 2, 6 and 11 of the Suite)
were given their American premiere by Efrem Kurtz and the Kansas
City Philharmonic during the season of 1944-1945. The New York
concert premiere occurred at the Lewisohn Stadium on an all-
Soviet program of the Philharmonic-Symphony Orchestra conducted by Alexander Smallens. In response to prolonged applause
Mr. Smallens repeated "The Dance with the Sabres." Marked
Presto, this dance is in bold and spirited vein, with syncopated
rhythms and reminiscent flashes of the last movement of Khatchatourian's Piano Concerto. Abrupt changes of tempo add to the
wild, excited upsurge of rhythms.

Louis Biancolli, *Philharmonic-Symphony Society of New York*

Piano Concerto

Nicholas Slonimsky, a fertile source of information on Soviet
music and composers, points out that while Russian composers,
particularly those of the nationalist group in St. Petersburg, were
always attracted by the melodies of the Russian Orient, "it was
only after the Revolution that the minority nations brought forth
native composers who made use of the melodic and rhythmic resources of their countries, not in the form of exotic stylization, but
in creative reconstruction. Khatchatourian is such a composer. He
makes frequent use of Russian, Ukrainian, Georgian and Armenian dance rhythms."

The Piano Concerto is music of technical brillance, with frank
display passages in the first and last movements. "The slow middle
movement is a poetic interlude with a lilting waltz rhythm. The
Orientalism of the Concerto is revealed in the scales of eight and
nine notes, and the consequent emphasis on the small intervals
in thematic treatment." There are extended cadenzas in the first
and last movements.

The Concerto was written in 1935 and first performed in Moscow. Its freshness and exoticism soon made it popular throughout
Russia. The first American performance was on March 14, 1942

at the Juilliard School of Music in New York. Later it was on a
Philharmonic program at the Lewisohn Stadium and on the Philharmonic's regular Carnegie Hall programs, and the Boston Symphony also took it up.

WILLIAM E. BENSWANGER, *Pittsburgh Symphony Orchestra*

VICTOR ANTOINE EDOUARD LALO

(Born in Lille, France, January 27, 1823—died in
Paris, April 23, 1892)

HE CAME of a family of Spanish origin, studied first at the
Lille Conservatory, then came to Paris in 1839 to continue his
study of violin at the Conservatoire, besides taking private lessons
in harmony and counterpoint. Lalo's opera, *Fiesque,* won third
prize at the Théâtre-Lyrique, but he was over fifty and had been
composing for thirty years before the Spanish violinist, Pablo de
Sarasate, established his reputation by performing the violin concerto and the *Symphonie Espagnol.* He was decorated with the
Legion of Honor in 1880.

"His talent," writes Charles O'Connell, "was highly individual
and was influenced not so much by the course of study at the
Son-Conservatoire, as by his own concentration upon the music
and methods of such masters as Beethoven, Schubert and Schumann, for whom he had a special liking. Among his chief characteristics are an unusual grace in the expression of ideas, a piquancy
in the treatment of themes, and, above all, a dexterity and skill
in orchestration."

Symphonie Espagnol

When Sarasate, the great violinist, played the *Symphonie Espagnol* of Victor Antoine Lalo. . . . at a "popular concert" in Paris on February 7, 1875, the composer's rank among musicmakers was established; a somewhat slow establishment, it would seem, for Lalo was then over fifty years old and had been writing for nearly thirty years. It was the F major violin concerto, however, also played in Paris by Sarasate (January 18, 1874) which quickened attention for the first time. The *Symphonie Espagnol* brought this attention to its highest peak.

When Tschaikowsky heard the work, which might well be called a concerto-symphony, since it has a little of both, he wrote to Nadejda von Meck:

"Do you know the *Symphonie Espagnol* by the French composer, Lalo? . . . . The work has given me great enjoyment. It is so fresh and light, and contains piquant rhythms and melodies which are beautifully harmonized . . . Lalo is careful to avoid all that is *routinier,* seeks new forms without trying to be profound, and is more concerned with musical beauty than with tradition."

The music, in truth, is fanciful and brilliant, delicate, yet forceful, charming, but not without depth and thought. There are five movements in the original score: Allegro non troppo, Scherzando, Intermezzo, Andante and Rondo, although the Intermezzo is frequently omitted in performance.

Grove's has this to say of the composer:

"His talent was of an extremely individual kind, and was formed, not by the discipline of the Conservatoire, nor by the influence of professors but by the direct study of such masters as Beethoven, Schubert and Schumann, for whom he had a special predilection. His chief characteristics were the expressive grace of certain ideas, the piquancy of some of his themes and, above all, the richness and skill of his orchestration. Lalo was one of the most distinguished of French composers and fully deserved the decoration of the Legion of Honor conferred upon him in July 1880."

WALTER WHITWORTH, *Indianapolis Symphony Orchestra*

Overture to *Le Roi d'Ys*

Lalo's opera, *Le Roi d'Ys (The King of Ys)*, had as its source the same old Breton legend of the submerged city of Ys that inspired Debussy to write his prelude for piano, *La Cathédrale Engloutie (The Sunken Cathedral)*. The story of the opera deals with the rivalry of Margared and Rozenn, daughters of the King of Ys, for the hand of the young knight, Mylio. When Margared cannot have the man of her choice, she seeks revenge by showing the prince of a neighboring city at war with Ys how he can destroy his foes by opening the floodgates, thereby inundating the city. As Rozenn and Mylio are being married, the flood waters rush in, but the now repentant Margared warns the inhabitants in time, then throws herself into the water, whereupon the flood is miraculously abated through the intervention of St. Corentin.

The opera was begun in 1876, but it was another twelve years before it had its first performance—at the Paris-Opéra Comique on May 7, 1888. An aria from the opera was heard during the first year of its conception, however, and the Overture—which is practically the only portion of the work that is heard today—was performed several years before the premiere of the complete score.

The Overture to *Le Roi d'Ys* presents a musical portrait of the three principal characters. The slow introduction is centered around an aria of Mylio, heard here as a clarinet solo. The main section, a vigorous *Allegro,* deals primarily with the conflicting emotions of Margared. This is interrupted by an eloquent passage for the solo 'cello, depicting the gentle Rozenn. When the *Allegro* resumes, it is concerned chiefly with the subject of Margared and a reaffirmation of the Mylio theme.

PAUL AFFELDER, *Pittsburgh Symphony Orchestra*

FRANZ LISZT

(Born at Raiding, Hungary, October 22, 1811—died at Bayreuth, July 31, 1886)

"THE FABULOUS Liszt," an incredible pianist, had a flaming career,—as artist, social climber and lover—before he turned from a brilliant and worldly life and became the ascetic Catholic, the generous patriarch and the helping hand to youth. There was always a great deal of the rope dancer and trapeze flyer about Liszt, as MacDowell suggested.

Yet perhaps there is more truth in the assertion of Philip Hale that "Liszt suffered as a composer from foolish adulation and still more absurd denunciation. . . . Liszt also suffered from admiring friends who helped themselves to his musical ideas. . . ."

Like many another musician subsequently hailed as great, or at least who left a mark upon the musical sands, Liszt can be said to have sprung from the patronage of the Esterhazys, that famous Hungarian family to whom Haydn, Beethoven, Schubert and a few more owed so much. Liszt came of an obscure family in the service of that princely house.

Little is known of his early life, save that his father, a musician of some talent, gave him his first piano lessons. These first lessons were remarkably successful, for we learn that Franz made his professional debut at nine and a fund was raised immediately, among some wealthy patrons, to insure several years of further study. He gave another concert in Vienna, at the age of eleven, where Ludwig van Beethoven sat in the audience and marveled.

He tried to enter the Paris Conservatoire but was refused; whether because of his youth or the need for further academic training has never been disclosed. He found private teachers, however, who helped him a good deal and he was able to undertake a series of concert tours, all over the continent and England, establishing a reputation as the greatest pianist of the day.

His love affairs were numerous and engrossing, for he was a handsome and brilliant young man. The dash and elan of his playing, coupled with a miraculous technique and a showiness all his own, fascinated women of every station.

Two of these stand out above all others—Marie Countess d'Agoult, clever, witty and shrewd; and the plain and rather explosive Jeanne Elisabet Karolyne, Princess von Sayn-Wittgenstein. The former became his mistress, and she bore him three children, one of whom, Cosima, became the wife first of Hans von Buelow, pianist and conductor, and then of Richard Wagner.

His friendship for Wagner was sincere and of inestimable value to that troubled and egocentric genius. Wagner himself says: "I met Liszt during my earliest stay in Paris, at a period when I had renounced the hope, nay even the wish, of a Paris reputation, and, indeed, was in a state of internal revolt against the artistic life which I found there."

Liszt had come to Weimar several times to conduct and to play. His reception was fevered and at times hysterical. Nothing quite like it had ever happened before in the long history of that artistic center. He was offered the permanent post of conductor at the Court Theater in 1849, an offer which he accepted, though it meant abandoning his career as a virtuoso. He was wont to explain that his reason for doing so lay in a desire to devote his time and energy to helping the careers of other composers.

A dispute over the production of Cornelius' opera, *The Barber of Baghdad,* caused him to resign his official post in 1859. Thenceforth he went to Rome, Pesth, Paris and back to Weimar. As a boy he had wanted to enter the priesthood but had been dissuaded by his parents and his confessor. In Rome, he joined the Franciscan brotherhood and was invested with the minor orders. He was tonsured in 1879 and thereafter wore the clerical garb of the Franciscan order, and is so pictured in his later years.

Early in 1886, he went to England with singular success and that summer he could not shake off a bronchial affection which gave rise to a troublesome cough tending to weaken him alarmingly. Yet he found strength to visit Bayreuth for the wedding of Daniela von Buelow. He decided, against the advice of physicians, to attend a performance of *Tristan und Isolde* and was almost carried to Mme. Wagner's box. This was on July 4, 1886. He died three weeks later, "of weakness and inflammation of the lungs."

Liszt left a tremendous amount of music and writing—a good deal of the former is air and bombast and vulgarity. But some treasures lie among the dross—arrangements of Bach organ works, the *Hungarian Rhapsodies* and some notable examples of the symphonic poem.

Fantasie Hongroise for piano and orchestra

Liszt and the Countess d'Agoult had parted by the time he came to Kiev for a concert early in 1847. In the audience sat Jeanne Elisabet Karolyne von Sayn-Wittgenstein, then twenty-eight, of a plainness painful, as the French might put it. In fact, the lady was a bombastic, fustian creature, with a passion for strong cigars. Yet they met and Liszt earnestly cultivated their acquaintance.

It is obvious that Liszt . . . worshipped the lady's title and needed her money. And of course the princess, flattered by the attentions of the celebrated artist, about whom such delicious scandal had been whispered, was quite captivated. And it is quite probable that Liszt found a measure of relief in the worship of this new conquest. For the countess, brilliant and penetrating, long ago had seen through his shallow character as if it had been glass.

He and the Countess Marie kept up a sort of desultory correspondence, the ardent yet false cordiality of his letters eliciting little but perfunctory and half-hearted replies from her.

The fourteen *Hungarian Rhapsodies* for piano date from this period. The *Fantasie* is based on material culled from the fourteenth piano Rhapsody and orchestrated as No. 1 by the composer himself. He wrote to Marie in July, 1847, telling her of his meeting with the princess and professing extreme admiration for the countess' literary ability. He proposed that she write a preface to the *Rhapsodies,* derived from notes to be supplied by himself.

"I am greatly interested in this work," he said, "and it is absolutely necessary that the profound and intimate sense of this series of compositions shall be eloquently revealed to the public."

It is not recorded that the countess wrote the desired preface, or even that she believed in his earnest assurances of continued regard. Undoubtedly, she was right, for there is a gap in this correspondence from April 1849 to July 1855, and when it is resumed a curious change is apparent in Liszt. Henceforth, his tone is hard and businesslike and one may attribute this change to the influence of the princess.

JULIAN SEAMAN, *Elizabeth (N.J.) Philharmonic Society*

Les Preludes—Symphonic Poem No. 3

James Huneker, in his engaging book on the fabulous Franz Liszt, gives some idea of the welcome he received when, in 1841, he visited Weimar for the first time:

"The furore he created was historic. The reigning family—doubtless bored to death in the charming, placid little city—welcomed Liszt as a distraction . . . . . He was covered with jewels and orders. The upshot was that after a visit in 1842, Liszt was invited to the office of General Music Director at Weimar. This offer he accepted . . . That he needed royal favor will be seen when we recall that in 1850 he produced an opera by a banished socialist, Richard Wagner; the opera *Lohengrin*. He also needed court protection when . . . . he brought to Weimar the runaway wife of Prince Wittgenstein. . . . . Nikolaus Wittgenstein began divorce proceedings. His wife was ordered back to the Woronice estate . . . . She refused to go . . . . She loved Liszt . . . . She saw that in the glitter of this moving comet there was the stuff out of which fixed stars are fashioned and she lived near him at Weimar from 1848 to 1861."

It was during this period that Liszt wrote his twelve symphonic poems—*Les Preludes* was the third—and started a chain of discussion on the relative merits of absolute versus program music which endures to this day.

Liszt is supposed to have started sketching *Les Preludes* in 1845, although it was not produced until 1854 when, on February 23, he conducted the premiere at Weima. Two years later the score was published.

Printed as a preface to the score is the fifteenth of Alphonse Lamartine's *Nouvelles Meditations Poetiques,* reputed to have served Liszt as inspiration for *Les Preludes*. The prefatory passage,

not identical with the original poem, is usually translated as follows:

"What is life but a series of preludes to that unknown song
whose initial solemn note is tolled by Death? The enchanted dawn
of every life is love; but where is the destiny on whose first delicious joys some storm does not break?—a storm whose deadly blast
disperses youth's illusions, whose fatal bolt consumes its altar. And
what thus cruelly bruised, when the tempest rolls away, seeks not
to rest its memories in the calm of rural life? Yet man allows himself not long to taste the kindly quiet which first attracted him to
Nature's lap; but when the trumpet gives the signal, he hastens to
danger's post, whatever be the fight which draws him on its list,
that in the strife he may once more regain full knowledge of himself and all his strength."

GUSTAV KLEMM, *Baltimore Symphony Orchestra*

Hungarian Rhapsody No. 2

The *Rhapsodies* will always occupy a prominent place among
Liszt's original works. There are nineteen altogether, and a twentieth in manuscript, although the lists usually give only fifteen.
They are built either on real Hungarian melodies or tunes of the
composer's own invention imitating the gypsy style. The themes
and incidents used in them were collected by Liszt while studying
the Hungarian gypsy in his native heath.

The fruit of these observations was not confined to the set of
Hungarian Rhapsodies but blossomed forth in a book on *The
Bohemians and Their Music in Hungary.* It is usually insisted that
these musical works are not of national character, but are distinctly the reflections of the Hungarian gypsy. Liszt explains that
he called them *rhapsodies* because he wished to designate the "fan-
tastically epic elements" which they contain.

Instead of being formless, as is so generally believed, these
works are constructed on a regular plan, beginning with a *lassan,*
which is a sad wail, usually in the minor, into which is poured the
grief of the people. Then comes, as contrast, the *frischka,* which is

vivacious and the Finale is generally a *czardas,* which is untamed in its wildness. As in this one, there is a vast amount of primitive fire and dash in the compositions.

Cyril A. Palmer, *Detroit Symphony Orchestra*

Piano Concerto No. 1 in E-flat major

The pianoforte concerti of the great nineteenth century virtuoso who wound up a brilliant and colorful career in the monastic robes of an abbé are so well-known and so much the stock in trade of every performing pianist that it seems hardly necessary to say anything about them. The one on this program was sketched in fragmentary style in the early 1840's, but was not completed until 1849. Liszt revised it in 1851, and it was published in 1857.

Quite evidently he pondered over it a good long time before finally committing it to print. This sort of prepublication caution was not, and still is not, an uncommon matter among the best composers. It is too bad to have to admit this and shatter the romantic ideas of so many people who believe that a piece of music springs out of a composer's brain cells in perfect and unrevisable form, ready for press and public.

In 1849, Liszt withdrew from the role of piano virtuoso and accepted the role of permanent conductor of the Court Theater at Weimar. During his stay of twelve years he made this city the center of musical life in Germany. It was here that this Concerto was first performed in 1855 with Berlioz conducting and the composer as soloist. This and later performances were not warmly received by the orthodox music critics. Hanslick of the *Weimar Press* dubbed it the "triangle concerto," a name which has stuck ever since, because of Liszt's use of that instrument in the third movement—a device which had previously been used by Beethoven and Haydn. The Concerto lay idle for twelve years, when the pianist Sophie Menter decided to unearth it and perform it in Vienna.

Rubinstein warned her that "you are mad to attempt this concerto! No one has succeeded with it in Vienna." Nevertheless, she went ahead and played it, and with great success. The jinx was broken! Since then it has occupied a leading and well-established position in the pianist's repertoire.

It consists of four main sections, or movements, without break. Liszt's method of development in this work is that of "transformation of themes," making the form a free one, somewhat on the order of a symphonic poem. It has been said that the first theme makes the announcement: "None of you understand!"—with the critic Hanslick as its target. This seems a bit far-fetched, but it's a nice thought.

ANIS FULEIHAN, *Indianapolis Symphony Orchestra*

GUSTAV MAHLER

(Born in Kalischt, Bohemia, July 7, 1860—died in
Vienna, May 18, 1911)

MAHLER was born of poor but cultivated parents. At eight he gave piano lessons to a seven-year-old. His father, assured that Gustav was sufficiently talented to warrant the expense of a musical education, entered him in the Vienna Conservatory at fifteen and at the end of the first year the boy won two prizes—one for playing the piano, the other for composition.

For a time after leaving the Conservatory, Mahler supported himself by teaching piano, then obtained the first of several positions as conductor in smaller music centers. He was appointed assistant to Anton Seidl, then to Artur Nikisch. He became chief conductor at Budapest, finally musical director of the Vienna Opera and of the Vienna Philharmonic Society.

Conried engaged him to conduct at the Metropolitan Opera

House in New York in 1907, and in the following year the Philharmonic Society acquired his services. He literally wore himself out in these years, for the schedule was terrific and his health, never robust, sank under the strain. He served the Philharmonic for two seasons but could not finish a third.

He returned to Europe, striving vainly to restore his shattered health, and died in Vienna, ostensibly of pneumonia and an infected throat—certainly of exhaustion.

"He was of an intensely nervous nature," says Philip Hale. "His life as a conductor—and he was a great conductor, the feverish atmosphere of the opera house, his going from city to city until his ability was recognized in Vienna and later at the Metropolitan, the fact that he was a Jew who had turned Catholic; these, with musical intrigues and controversies from which he suffered, gave him no mental or aesthetic poise."

He left ten symphonies, the last unfinished and one for tenor and contralto soli and orchestra, *Das Lied von der Erde* (*Song of the Earth*), most of them for an enormous ensemble hardly practicable today at prevailing wages.

Symphony No. 1 in D major

. . . . In 1888, Mahler was second conductor to the great Nikisch at Leipzig. Though but twenty-eight, he resented the subordinate role, particularly because Nikisch left him much of the drudgery and deprived him of time for composing. Nevertheless, in this environment of unhappiness he composed the *Lieder eines fahrenden Gessellen* and later the First Symphony.

The two are closely related, inasmuch as Mahler wove the second and fourth *lieder* prominently into the symphony. His success as a conductor increased at Leipzig; still, completion of the symphony meant more than anything else. Finally in March, exhausted but relieved, he wrote to a friend:

"At last my work is finished! How I wish you were here by my side at the piano so that I might play it for you. Perhaps you are the only one to whom nothing in it will seem strange. The others will have something to wonder about. It has turned out so overwhelming—as if it issued from my heart, like a mountain stream."

Between the time of the completion of this symphony and its premiere, Mahler had been appointed to the post of director of the Royal Opera at Budapest. His life had had another measure of sorrow; his father had died in February 1889; his mother eight months later. Although the Budapest musicians did their utmost to make the new symphony comprehensible, the music fell on hostile ears. Gabriel Engel in his monograph on Mahler wrote: "The musiclovers, to whom Beethoven and Brahms were the unalterable symphonic gospel, squirmed about uneasily under the forked-lightning dynamic surprises in this new Symphony . . . . During the next three years Mahler kept his first symphonic score hidden away, much as if it had been a secret diary."

Later, Richard Strauss in 1894 became an "angel" for the Symphony and succeeded in having it made the feature of a Weimar concert.

Mahler was a violent foe of program notes. On the Budapest program the announcement said simply: "Symphonic Poem in Two Parts." (There are four movements nevertheless). For the Weimar performance on June 3, 1894, the Symphony stood under the title: "Titan Symphony," after a novel by Paul Richter. He had evidently recanted about program notes because the program bore the following remarkable description attributed to the composer:

"Part 1—The days of youth. Youth flowers and thorns. (1) Spring without end. The introduction represents the awakening of nature at early dawn. (2) A Chapter of Flowers (Andante). (The movement was omitted after the Weimar performance.) (3) Full sail! (Scherzo).

"Part 2—Human Comedy. (4) Stranded. A Funeral March á la Callot. (A French engraver of the seventeenth century.)

"The following remarks may serve as explanation if necessary: The author received the external stimulus to this piece from a pictorial parody well-known to all children in South Germany, 'The Hunter's Funeral Procession.' The animals accompany the dead forester's coffin to the grave. The hares carry flags; in front is a band of Gypsy musicians and musicmaking cats, frogs, crows, etc.; and deer, stags, foxes and other four-footed and feathered

denizens of the forest accompany the procession in comical postures. In the present piece the imagined expression is partly ironically gay, partly gloomily foreboding and is immediately followed
by (5) *Dall'Inferno al Paradiso* (Finale), the sudden outbreak of a
profoundly wounded heart."

Toward the end of his life, Mahler came to the United States
and was conductor of the New York Philharmonic. Nicholas Slonimsky, the omniscient Russian-born Boston musicologist, notes the
date May 18, 1911, in his chronological book, *Music Since 1900*, as
follows:

"Gustav Mahler, the last of the great romantic composers of
Vienna, who strove to translate his spiritual struggles into symphonies of cosmic design, dies in Vienna of heart trouble, complicated by septic poisoning, resulting from inflammation of the
throat, and pneumonia, fifty days before his fifty-first birthday."

Slonimsky then reproduces extracts from New York newspapers of a few days later to show that Mahler's death resulted in
part from a broken heart, from the frustrating arguments with the
Philharmonic board over financial and artistic policies—the same
self-made enemies which plagued him throughout his life.

BATEMAN EDWARDS, *St. Louis Symphony Orchestra*

Das Lied von der Erde—
(Song of the Earth)

This, then, and the Ninth Symphony, which is again permeated with the sense of leavetaking, together illustrate the third
period of Mahler's work. A Tenth Symphony was completely
sketched—the themes and their evolutions indicated as if in full
score, but so little of the accompanying detail was provided that
the task of completion is insuperable.

The texts of the poems were done into German by Hans
Bethge, from a collection of Chinese songs called *The Chinese
Flute*. The English version was made for the first American per-
formance of the work by the Philadelphia Orchestra by Philip H.
Goepp. The performance was conducted by Stokowski, December
15-16, 1916. The first performance of the piece was conducted by

Bruno Walter in Munich on November 20, 1911, almost six months after the composer's death. Space is lacking for any description of the movements in detail. We therefore print . . . . the brief but suggestive hints which were offered in the program-book of the Boston Orchestra:

The solo voices alternate, the tenor begins. The first movement, *Allegro persante,* is scored for an orchestra that comprises piccolo, three flutes, three oboes, four clarinets, three bassoons, four horns, three trumpets, three trombones, bass drum, cymbals, triangle, bells, glockenspiel, two harps and the usual strings. The opening, a chief melody is given to the horns. There are restful episodes.

The second begins somewhat "dragging—wearily," with oboe and first violin. The harp enters on the words "Sun of love" in "Autumn Solitude."

The third movement, of Oriental color, calls for two piccolos, flutes, oboes, clarinets, bassoons, horns, one trumpet, percussion instruments etc., and strings.

Fourth movement, *Comodo dolcissimo,* with an increasingly faster pace. Percussion instruments are fully represented and the score calls for mandolin.

Movement No. 5, "saucily," but not too fast.

The last movement begins heavily; strokes of the tom-tom on the low C of the double-basses; horns, harps, low strings, with a recurring figure for oboe.

The verses of the old Chinese poets:

1—Drinking Song of Earthly Woe (tenor). Poem by Li-Tai-Po (702-763).

2—Autumn Solitude (contralto). Poem by Tschang-Tsi (800)

3—Of Youth (tenor). Poem by Li-Tai-Po (702-763).

4—Of Beauty (contralto). Poem by Li-Tai-Po (702-763).

5—The Drunkard in Springtime (tenor). Poem by Li-Tai-Po (702-763).

6— (a) Awaiting a Friend (contralto). Poem by Mong-Kow-Jin (eighth century).

(b) The Farewell of a Friend (contralto). Poem by Wang-Wei (eighth century).

DONALD FERGUSON, *Minneapolis Symphony Orchestra*

JACOB LUDWIG FELIX
MENDELSSOHN-BARTHOLDY

(Born in Hamburg, February 3, 1809—died in
Leipzig November 4, 1847)

KARL GEIRINGER, now professor of the history and theory of
music at Boston University, wrote an admirable sketch of Mendelssohn's life published in the *Christian Science Monitor* for November 8, 1947. This was the centenary year of his death, and the
date was duly celebrated far and wide in the world of musical affairs.

Geiringer began by suggesting "a Mendelssohn renaissance
seems to be under way. The time is past when music lovers stifled
a yawn at the mention of his name. 'Aren't Mendelssohn's works a
little too perfect?' some used to ask, while others complained that
they could not stand his weak sentimentality."

He continued:

"The Mendelssohn family was the ideal cradle for the production of a genius. There was first the grandfather, Moses Mendelssohn, a great philosopher . . . . His second son, Abraham, the
composer's father, was a successful banker who brought a fortune
to the family. Although he was a great friend of music, his was
not a creative talent. He liked humorously to complain that he
was 'formerly the son of his father, and now the father of his son.'

"Abraham's four children all showed musical talent. Fanny, the
eldest and the favorite of Felix, was, according to her mother, born
with 'Bach-fugue fingers.' She was a successful composer whose songs
were so highly appreciated by her brother that he included six of
them among his own works.

"Fanny married the painter, Hensel, to whom we owe some of
the best portraits of the family. Of Abraham's two youngest children, Rebekka was a fine singer and Paul an outstanding 'cellist.

"Felix Mendelssohn . . . . was an infant prodigy of such versatility of talent that it seemed uncertain for some time in which
direction he would develop. In his early teens he made so successful a translation of a Latin comedy by Terence, preserving the
meter of the original, that it was printed and adopted by German
schools.

"At the age of nine he appeared for the first time as pianist in a recital. Two years afterward he started seriously to compose, writing in his twelfth year a violin and two piano sonatas, a trio, a cantata, an operetta, and numerous smaller vocal works. The following year witnessed among other works the composition of five symphonies for string quartet and nine fugues.

"At the age of seventeen Mendelssohn wrote one of his greatest masterworks, the Overture to Shakespeare's *A Midsummer Night's Dream*, a composition unsurpassed in freshness of inspiration, or technical skill by any of his later works.

"In 1829, Mendelssohn performed a deed for which he would have to be remembered by music history, even if he had not written a single composition. The youth of twenty conducted the first performance of Bach's *St. Matthew Passion* since the passing of the Thomascantor, thus restoring to the musical world one of the greatest masterpieces of all times. In the same year Felix visited England and Scotland for the first time, and the tremendous success of this trip laid the foundation for his fame as a composer.

"Great Britain, to which he returned repeatedly afterward, became a sort of second home to him. Immortal products of the inspiration he received on these visits are the Overture *Fingal's Cave* and the *Scottish Symphony*. In 1835 Mendelssohn moved to Leipzig and started on a new activity as conductor of that city's Gewandhaus Concerts.

"His unusual gifts as an orchestra leader, his vast musical education and historic knowledge, and his importance as a creative artist made him before long the center of Leipzig's musical life and Leipzig the center of the musical life of Germany.

"Not satisfied with his work as composer, conductor and virtuoso, Mendelssohn took over a new responsibility in 1843. Under the protectorate of the King of Saxony he founded in Leipzig a Conservatoire of Music for which he secured the services of teachers of the rank of Ferdinand David, the great violinist, and Robert Schumann. Henceforth, Leipzig became his permanent home, where he lived in a very happy marriage, blessed by five children, with Cecile Jeanrenaud, the daughter of a clergyman of the French Reformed Church.

"In 1846, the composer visited England for the ninth time, to conduct there the first performance of his great oratorio, *Elijah*. The concert, which took place at Birmingham, had a tremendous success. No less than four choruses and four arias had to be encored.

"On the height of his success, however, Mendelssohn's career came to an end. The passing of his beloved sister Fanny on May 14, 1847, proved to be a catastrophe for the highly sensitive composer from which he did not recover. He died on November 4, 1847.

"Mendelssohn's first great composition was based on a comedy by Shakespeare; his last masterpiece was written for an English city. This is of symbolical significance. He loved the English people and was beloved by them. His art belongs almost more to the English-speaking countries than to his native land."

Scherzo from Octet for Strings

Mendelssohn wrote the Octet for Strings in the same year as the Overture to *A Midsummer Night's Dream,* at the incredible age of seventeen. Both works glow with a spirit of freshness and vigor from which any suspicion of immaturity is wonderfully lacking. The Scherzo of the Octet, like the much later one for the *Midsummer Night's Dream,* is in the sonata form, and because of the different medium, is even more delicate than the other. Except for a few *sforzando* notes, it is played *pianissimo* all the way through, with a prevailing rhythm of staccato sixteenth-notes in 2-4 time. The first subject in G minor is an easy-going theme over tonic and dominant harmonies. The second subject in B-flat major has a good deal of bounce to it, coupled with a delightful upswing in the melodic line. The exposition ends with a rising scale and a descent in staccato octaves.

After the development and recapitulation, in which the second subject appears in E-flat major, the final figure of the exposition is used to build a short and evanescent coda. It is interesting to note that in the last movement of the Octet, Mendelssohn slyly quotes the subject of the Scherzo and then humorously changes its nature by playing it *fortissimo*.

BATEMAN EDWARDS, *St. Louis Symphony Orchestra*

Suite from the Incidental Music to *A Midsummer Night's Dream*

One of the great marvels of music is the fact that the elfin tonal web of the *Midsummer Night's Dream* overture was written by the seventeen-year-old Mendelssohn in 1826 and that it wasn't until another seventeen years had passed that he composed the incidental music for Shakespeare's play (twelve such numbers in addition to the Overture), including the poetic Nocturne, the expressive Intermezzo and the twice-familiar Wedding March. Yet they all strike the same note of high romance and deft appropriateness and all are plainly woven from the same threads of gold and silver and pixie magic. There are only a few other instances when a composer has successfully picked up the thread of his weaving after a lapse of many years, one of the most notable being that of Wagner's resumption of *Siegfried,* after having laid it aside in favor of *Tristan und Isolde,* and other works which he thought more likely to have a hearing.

It seems hardly likely that any inhabitant of North America is unfamiliar with the world's two most famous wedding marches —the other one being, of course, the Bridal Chorus, to the strains of which Elsa and Lohengrin are so tunefully married during Act 3, Scene 1 of Wagner's *Lohengrin.* Yet despite all of its unescapable popularity, one usually hears Mendelssohn's Wedding March played by organ, piano, trio and all sorts of unbalanced combinations—anything except the thousand-voiced symphony orchestra for which he composed it . . . .

GEORGE SCHAUN, *Baltimore Symphony Orchestra*

Concert Overture—*Fingal's Cave* or *The Hebrides*

Mendelssohn was twenty years old when he visited the famous Fingal's Cave on Staffa, the smallest of the Hebrides Islands. Klingemann, the friend with whom Mendelssohn toured Scotland, wrote of the strange loneliness of the scene:

"We were put out in boats and climbed, the hissing sea close beside us, over the pillar stumps to the celebrated Fingal's Cave. A greater roar of waters surely never rushed into a stranger cavern

. . . . lying there absolutely purposeless in its utter loneliness, the wide gray sea within and without."

Mendelssohn wrote his sister:

"In order to make you understand how extraordinarily the Hebrides affected me, the following came into my mind there." He then wrote down twenty-one measures of the melody which later was to open the Overture.

The first theme of the *Fingal's Cave Overture* (in violas, 'cellos and bassoons) opens the piece and is the phrase that came into Mendelssohn's mind in the cave. It is repeated many times. A passage featured by oboes, suggested to Wagner the wailing of winds over the water. The second theme—a beautiful *cantabile* scored for bassoon and continued by clarinets—is accompanied by the warlike rhythm of the first theme. Each climax seems "to picture the lashing fury of the ocean." Both themes are used in the middle, or development section. After the usual repetition of the first section, there is a short, brilliant coda.

Philip Hale wrote:

"Here he (Mendelssohn) is poetic, picturing the wildness of the scene without too deliberate attempts at realism . . . For once Mendelssohn showed himself more than a careful manufacturer of music . . . . He had been deeply affected by the sight of Staffa and Fingal's Cave; he was not ashamed to translate his emotions into music."

LENORA COFFIN, *Indianapolis Symphony Orchestra*

Violin concerto in E minor

A little over a hundred years ago, the single violin concerto composed by Mendelssohn was played in public for the first time, at a Gewandhaus Concert. The date was March 13, 1845.

This sweet-flowing yet fiery work, for solo violin and orchestra, ranks with three others in popularity—those by Beethoven, Brahms and Tschaikowsky (all three of which, probably by pure coincidence, are in the tonality of D major). Perhaps, however, there is something more than mere coincidence in the fact that each of the four chose to write only one violin concerto—despite the prolific precedents set by Bach, Mozart and other predecessors.

Mendelssohn had begun sketching some of the Concerto's themes in 1838, and had laid it aside several times, and was again occupied in working on it in 1840, when a friend asked: "When shall we hear it?"

"In five years," replied Mendelssohn jokingly.

Other matters intervened and so (completely justifying Mendelssohn's facetious reply) it was just five years later that the premiere did take place.

This Concerto differs from the normal pattern of violin concerti in several respects. The lyrical main theme of the first movement (one which fairly leaps and dances for sheer joy of life and youth and song) is immediately played by the solo violin after a bare measure-and-a-half of orchestral preamble. Most other concerti keep the soloist silent (and perhaps a bit apprehensive over the shape of things to come) while the orchestra goes through a fairly complete statement of the themes which are to be repeated (with much rococo elaboration) by the soloist of the evening. The Beethoven Concerto even obliges the soloist (after all the portentous waiting) to start right off by playing an octave passage which is perilous in the extreme.

Having reversed the usual practice of "orchestra first, soloist second," Mendelssohn ended his big cadenza, in the first movement, by having the orchestra play the principal theme under an upper layer of figure-work embroidered by the violin.

Still another unusual feature (and one which frequently disconcerts musiclovers who wish to applaud) is the fact that the brilliant opening movement leads, without pause, into the eloquently contemplative slow movement.

Jascha Heifetz has said that the Mendelssohn Concerto "is always retired at the end of one season, and revived at the beginning of the next." The reason is simply this: Although the music is frankly "dated" it is infinitely rewarding to both soloist and audience. All its brilliant tricks "come off," thereby giving the soloist a righteous glow of technical superiority. The melodies caress the ear and linger affectionately in memory. What more, therefore, could one ask?

GEORGE SCHAUN, *Baltimore Symphony Orchestra*

Symphony No. 3 in A minor (*Scottish*)

Scotland and Italy were the lands of heart's desire in the hey-day of romanticism, and it is scarcely accidental that Mendelssohn wrote a symphony about each country. It is also highly character-istic of that time that the symphony of Berlioz which wound up under the title of *Harold in Italy* was begun as a choral piece about the death of Mary, Queen of Scots.

Mendelssohn visited England, Scotland and Wales in the sum-mer of 1829, when he was twenty years old. His companion was a young man of about his own age, named Karl Klingemann, who was secretary to the Hanoverian Legation in London. Together they "did" Scotland in the grandest spirits, and their letters about their journeys form one of the most amusing and vivid passages in the Mendelssohn literature.

Mendelssohn's first letter from Edinburgh records, among other things, that "everything here looks so stern and robust, half enveloped in a haze of smoke or fog; moreover, there is to be a bagpipe competition tomorrow; many Highlanders came in cos-tume from church victoriously leading their sweethearts in their Sunday attire and casting magnificent and important looks over the world; with long red beards, tartan plaids, bonnets and feath-ers and naked knees and their bagpipes in their hands, and they passed quietly along by the half-ruined gray castle on the meadow where Mary Stuart lived in splendor and saw Rizzio mur-dered."

The letter ends: "The Highland journey will be as follows: via Stirling, Perth, Dunkeld and the waterfalls to Blair Athol; thence on foot over the hills to Inverary, to Glancoe, the Isle of Staffa and the Isle of Islay . . . From there up the Clyde to Glas-gow, then to Ben Lomond, which with Loch Lomond forms the Highland Lion, to Loch Earn, Ben Voirlich, Loch Katrine, then to Cumberland. What further shall I tell you? Time and space are coming to an end, and everything must terminate in the refrain: 'How kind the people are in Edinburgh and how generous is the good God.' "

Two days later Mendelssohn ends a letter from Edinburgh:

"In the evening twilight we went today to the palace where Queen Mary lived and loved; a little room is shown there with a winding staircase leading up to the door; up this way they came and found Rizzio in that little room, pulled him out and three rooms off there is a dark corner where they murdered him. The chapel close to is now roofless, grass and ivy grow there, and at that broken altar Mary was crowned Queen of Scotland. Everything is broken and mouldering and the bright sky shines in. I believe I found today in that old chapel the beginning of my *Scotch Symphony*. Now farewell."

Then Mendelssohn and his companion went out to Abbotsford to beard Sir Walter Scott in his lair. The great man gave them "at best one half-hour of superficial conversation," and in his chagrin Klingemann wrote a long burlesque account of their being Sir Walter's house guests and eating his sister's marmalade.

The journey continued into more romantic country, according to the itinerary given above. At Fingal's Cave, Mendelssohn was inspired to musical description, little thinking that the result would, in years to come, spread the fame of that grotto throughout the world. Eventually, the travelers returned to London, from which place Mendelssohn wrote that the *"Reformation Symphony,* the *Scotch Symphony* and the *Hebrides* matter (*i.e., Fingal's Cave*) were all shaping themselves gradually."

But the shaping of the *Scotch Symphony* took an extraordinarily long time, and it was not until thirteen years later, in 1842, that the score was finished. Therefore, although it is the third symphony Mendelssohn projected and was accordingly numbered third by him, the "Scotch" is actually the fifth and last symphony Mendelssohn brought to completion.

In a preface to the score which was not published until 1851, five years after Mendelssohn died, the composer wrote:

"The several movements of this Symphony must follow each other immediately, and not be separated by the usual pauses. For the information of the audience its contents may be stated as follows:

Sinfonia
Introduction and Allegro Agitato.
Scherzo assai vivace.
Allegro guerriero and Finale maestoso."

Note well that this table of contents says nothing about the Scotch inspiration of the Symphony, nor was the geographical title by which it is known today placed on the programs of early performances. Schumann therefore heard the *Scotch Symphony* under the impression that it was Mendelssohn's *Italian* and wrote with great enthusiasm of its "beautiful Italian pictures, so beautiful as to compensate a hearer who had never been to Italy." Thus is landscape painting in music subject to interpretation in the ear of the hearer. But Mr. Cecil Gray has more recently found elements in common between the folkwise idiom of de Falla and the equally folkwise idiom of Sibelius; between the grim North and the languorous South; as these notes have often insisted, there are more universals than particulars in folk music.

It should be pointed out that this Symphony contains none of the traditional devices whereby Scottish atmosphere is suggested. There are no bagpipe drones, no pentatonic tunes, and although the short-long rhythm known as the "Scotch snap" appears . . . nothing much is made of it. The "Scotch snap" is by no means limited to Scottish music. Dvorak uses it constantly in the *New World Symphony* to suggest American Negro folk song. . . ."

ALFRED FRANKENSTEIN, *San Francisco Symphony Orchestra*

Symphony No. 4 in A major (*Italian*)

It is characteristic of Mendelssohn's turn of mind that, of the four purely orchestral symphonies that he published, three bear titles suggestive of places or period atmospheres. The third is the *Scotch* the fourth is the *Italian* and the fifth is called the *Reformation Symphony*. (Mendelssohn's second symphony, the *Song of Praise*, is really a cantata rather than an orchestral piece. It may be worth adding by way of a footnote that, while Mendelssohn published only five symphonies, he actually composed seventeen. The first twelve symphonies, eleven of them for strings alone, and one for full orchestra, were written during the composer's childhood and youth. He considered them student efforts, and to this day they have not been published.)

Mendelssohn was not, like the wild Frenchman Berlioz, whom he met in Rome, a composer of elaborately descriptive "program symphonies," but he was very sensible to geographical impressions and his list of works, orchestral and otherwise, is filled with reflections of his travels.

The *Italian Symphony* was begun in Italy in 1831 and had its first performance in London two years later. It was completely revised between 1835 and 1837, and in this form was not heard until two years after Mendelssohn had died. It was not published until 1851. With the possible exception of the second movement, sometimes called the "Pilgrims' March," it does not depict any specific scenes, but embodies the sum total of Mendelssohn's Italian impressions so far as they could be set down in tones. . . .

ALFRED FRANKENSTEIN, *San Francisco Symphony Orchestra*

Symphony No. 5 in D major (Opus 107, *Reformation*)

When we think of Mendelssohn's Overture to *A Midsummer Night's Dream* as having been written when he was only a lad of seventeen, we are inclined to marvel. Yet it was only four years later that he completed his *Hebrides Overture* and *Reformation Symphony*.

Though it is numbered as the fifth, this symphony was actually the second in order of composition, following Symphony No. 1 in C minor and preceding, in that order, the *Italian* (No. 4), the *Song of Praise* (No. 2) and the *Scotch* (No. 3). In addition there were twelve other symphonies—eleven of them for strings, the twelfth for full orchestra—which date from his early teens, and which remain unpublished.

The *Reformation Symphony* was reputedly commissioned for the tercentenary festival of the Augsburg Confession, which was to have been celebrated on June 25, 1830. The political upheavals of that year, however, prevented the work from being performed at that time. Credence is lent to the fact that it was commissioned for the festival by a letter the composer wrote to his sister Fanny from Weimar in May 1830, to the effect that he was having trouble finding a suitable name for the Symphony. "I am having it copied here," he wrote, "and will forward it to Leipzig (where perhaps it may be performed) with strict injunctions to them to hand it to you as quickly as possible. Find out what will be the best name for it: *Reformation Symphony, Confession Symphony, Symphony for a Church Festival, Juvenile Symphony* or anything you like."

Mendelssohn began work on the *Reformation Symphony* in September 1829, while he was in London. Shortly thereafter, he was thrown from a carriage, which overturned on him. He suffered a bad leg injury, and was laid up for two months, during which time he was unable to proceed with the composition. Immediately upon recovering, however, he resumed work on the Symphony, completing it in April 1830.

. . . Mendelssohn had some difficulty getting the Symphony performed. After it had been withdrawn from the Augsburg festivities, he sent the score to Francois Antoine Habeneck, conductor of the Paris Conservatory Orchestra. A performance was planned but when the orchestra played through the Symphony, they found it "too learned," with "too much fugato," and "too little melody." Finally, Mendelssohn himself conducted the first performance on November 15, 1832 at the Singakademie in Berlin. The concert was one of a series of three devoted entirely to his music. The score was then evidently laid aside, for it did not reappear until 1868, when it was published and when it received its second hearing—a belated Paris premiere.

It is interesting to note Mendelssohn's use of two liturgical themes in the *Reformation Symphony*. In the introduction to the first movement, he quotes the so-called *Dresden Amen,* a traditional response from the Lutheran service as conducted in Saxony and long associated with the "Court" Church in Dresden. Wagner also used the *Dresden Amen* rather extensively in *Parsifal.* Then, in the last movement of the Symphony, Mendelssohn takes as one of his themes the familiar Lutheran Chorale, *Ein feste Burg ist unser Gott (A Mighty Fortress is our God)*, presenting it in various forms of development and finally shouting it forth as a triumphant finale to the work.

PAUL AFFELDER, *Pittsburgh Symphony Orchestra*

GIAN-CARLO MENOTTI

(Born in Cadigliano, near Milan, Italy, July 7, 1911
—now living in Mt. Kisco, New York)

THE ADVENT of Menotti in this country as a rising and arresting talent among the younger composers for the lyric stage was due entirely to the good sense of a mother who sought to save her son from becoming a salon darling—feted and overpraised into a state of insupportable vanity.

Gian-Carlo, son of a retired importer and a musical mother, had entered the Conservatory in Milan at nine. He says himself that he "did not learn very much," for the simple reason that he did not bother to work. Since the age of six he had been composing songs, and he played the piano with a precocious facility. Everyone pampered and flattered him and by the time he was seventeen "his self-satisfaction was insufferable."

So his mother decided to bring him to the United States in 1928, hoping he would find new friends and a new environment. She left him at the Curtis Institute in Philadelphia. He was seventeen then, and at first he was lonely and homesick but he had the strength to continue.

Among the first of his new friends was the American composer, Samuel Barber, with whom he now shares a house in Mt. Kisco, New York, each composing steadily in his own style and according to his own inspiration.

Menotti continued his musical studies at Curtis, was graduated in due course and began to compose in earnest. His *opera buffa, Amelia Goes to the Ball,* was performed in Philadelphia, won immediate critical acclaim and joined the repertoire of the Metropolitan Opera Association in New York. Other Menotti works are *The Old Maid and the Thief* and a tragic opera, *The Island God,* the latter also performed at the Metropolitan; *The Medium* and *The Telephone,* both of which became hits on Broadway and were presented successfully in England; *The Consul* achieved a notable success here.

234

Overture to *The Old Maid and the Thief*

The Old Maid and the Thief was commissioned by the National Broadcasting Company and given its first hearing over the radio. Critical response was very favorable. *Newsweek* said: "Many forgot they were listening, they thought they were looking. Several factors contributed to the illusion. One was a smartly-paced and amusing story . . . . another factor was narrative tone sense, with a sharp ear for satirized melodic lines. A third was the composer's talent for libretto writing." *Time* singled out for commendation the "fluffy, flippant, craftsmanlike score, bristling with tart melodies and limpid orchestration."

The rather inconsequential story concerns an old maid who becomes so infatuated with a passing tramp that she sets him up in her house as a permanent guest. She is somewhat disturbed by the news that a dangerous criminal, to whose description the tramp somewhat corresponds, is loose in the neighborhood, but reflects that "to be killed by a man would really be much better than to live without one."

There is some danger that the tramp will leave and in order to hold him the old maid steals the contents of a liquor shop. (Because she was the leader of the local temperance society she felt that she was unable to buy the stuff.) When the police start a house-to-house search for the thief, the tramp makes off with the old maid's possessions, her maid and her car, reflecting as he does so that "the devil couldn't do what a woman can; make a thief of an honest man."

The Overture to this "Grotesque Opera in fourteen scenes" well exemplifies *Time's* description of the music. It makes use of no material from the body of the work, but, with its sprightly and vivacious character, somehow reminiscent of Wolf-Ferrari, it puts the auditor in a frame of mind appropriate for what is to follow.

It strings together a number of contrasting ideas, alternately incisive and ingratiating and, without formal development, repeats the first two. The coda consists of a *fugato* passage in triplets which brings the piece to a snappy conclusion.

BATEMAN EDWARDS, *St. Louis Symphony Orchestra*

Concerto for piano and orchestra

This concerto was composed in 1943 and given its first performance by the Boston Symphony Orchestra, November 2, 1945. The orchestration consists of two flutes and piccolo, two oboes, B-flat and E-flat clarinets, two bassoons, four horns, three trumpets, three trombones, and tuba, timpani, tambourine, bass drum, cymbals, snare drum and strings. The work represents, as John N. Burk remarks in the Boston Symphony's program-book, "Mr. Menotti's first notable venture in the purely instrumental domain.

"The composer has no more to say about his concerto than that he has been influenced by the preromantic instrumental style of Italy, and in particular the keyboard music of Domenico Scarlatti. Although it is not a 'vehicle' for the virtuoso, there is brilliance in the treatment. After an orchestral flourish, the piano alone discloses a rhythmical theme in a contour of triplets. The woodwinds and presently the strings enter; the piano solo presents a triple figure. There is a *tutti* passage and the orchestra joins the piano in developing the original theme. There is an extended cadenza and a coda which is a long crescendo to a *forte* close. In the second movement (*Lento* 4-4) the piano sets forth a martial theme, which the orchestra takes over. Again the piano (now solo) gives another march theme which the orchestra in turn varies. Much of the accompaniment in this movement is staccato in character. The first march returns, more broadly and emphatically treated. There is a *lento* section, a return to the first tempo and a *presto* close."

Two Interludes from the Opera, *The Island God*

Commissioned by the Metropolitan Opera Association, *The Island God* obtained its world premiere at the Metropolitan on February 20, 1942. The work is in one act, its three scenes separated by two orchestral interludes.

From the composer himself come the following words of explanation regarding the opera:

"When *The Island God* had its first performance by the Metropolitan Opera Company in 1942, it was unanimously damned with faint praise. Nevertheless, I have retained a special predilection for this unfortunate child of mine, and not only because I considered it lame. Actually, *The Island God* represents an important experiment for me and a point of departure.

"After *Amelia Goes to the Ball* and *The Old Maid and the Thief*, with their calculated effects and their formalistic patterns, I strongly felt the need of freeing myself from a formula that threatened to become a mannerism. I decided then to write an opera which would be a sincere expression of a romantic element in my personality that I had timidly hidden in my previous works. In other words, I took the chance of completely exposing myself, with the sad result that this emotional nakedness neither excited nor shocked anyone. All that people seem to remember of *The Island God* is the duet at the end of the opera and the two interludes.

"This orchestral performance (January 16, 1949) of the interludes may well be called a New York premiere, since when they were performed at the Metropolitan the audience indulged in its usual habit of carrying on conversation while the curtain was down, so that I doubt very much if anyone had a chance to hear them on that occasion. . . ."

The first Interlude is thus described in the score: "The stage, which is at first completely darkened, becomes gradually illuminated. Mist and fog roll back, revealing the island in the dazzling light of midday, the sun flaming on the sea and marble."

The second Interlude suggests the struggles of the exiles in their attempt to restore the temple, and gives hints of the impending tragedy.

ROBERT C. BAGAR, *Philharmonic-Symphony Society of New York*

Suite from the ballet *Sebastian*

Sebastian is a ballet first performed by the Ballet Internationale in the season of 1944. The tale is that of a nobleman who falls in love with a Courtesan. His sisters, outraged, resort to magic in order to detroy her. They make a wax figure in the image of the Courtesan, throw over it a veil belonging to that person, and

stick long pins into the figure—pins that pain the Courtesan herself. A Moorish servant of the sisters, himself in love with the
Courtesan, puts himself in place of the wax figure and is slain by
the vengeful stabs of the sisters.

The scenes depicted in the Suite are, first, an open Venetian
Square with a great miscellany of characters, the introduction of
the Courtesan and her lover (a Barcarolle), a street-fight between
the sisters and the Courtesan, which is interrupted by a religious
procession, culminating in the Entrance of the Doges. A little
waltz is Sebastian's first solo dance; the Courtesan struggles against
the incantations of the sisters; and the Moor, pierced by the magic
pins, gives up his life.

DONALD FERGUSON, *Minneapolis Symphony Orchestra*

DARIUS MILHAUD

(Born in Aix, France, September 4, 1892—now
living in California)

MILHAUD today is highly regarded by musicians and lay-
men alike as one of the most significant and interesting of contemporary composers. One of the original "French Six," that
group of earnest young thinkers who "felt that French music had
too long been a slave of impressionism," he has progressed to
world renown far beyond the scope of his colleagues.

He studied at the Paris Conservatoire under d'Indy, Gedalgé
and Widor, distinguishing himself as a violinist and in the difficult
arts of counterpoint and fugue. The first World War interrupted
his studies and he became an attaché of the French Legation in
Rio de Janeiro. There he met Paul Claudel, with whom he collaborated in many important works for the stage.

He returned to Paris in 1919, joined the aforesaid "Six" and when that coterie of pioneers dissolved, continued to grow in artistic stature. After the death of Ravel, he was acclaimed as the senior composer of France.

Most major orchestras of the United States began to play his works soon after his first arrival here in 1922. He settled in the United States for good in 1940 and joined the faculty of Mills College in Oakland, California. The last opera performed in Paris before the Nazi occupation was Milhaud's *Médée*.

Suite Provençal

The *Suite Provençal* was composed in 1936 and presented for the first time at the Music Festival in Venice in September of that year, the composer conducting. The Suite is scored for two flutes, two oboes, English horn, two clarinets, two bassoons, four horns, three trumpets, three trombones, tuba, tympani, percussion and the usual strings.

As the title suggests, the music bears a direct association with the composer's native Provence. The composer has written that he has employed "popular folk airs from the Provence of the eighteenth century. Some of them are from Campra [Andre Campra, born in 1660, composer of church music, operas and ballets] who was born in Aix-en-Provence, like me."

A description of the music, taken from the Boston Symphony Orchestra program (December 20-21, 1940) follows:

"The Suite consists of eight brief movements. The first starts briskly upon a folklike melody in a straightforward A major, upon a pedal bass, which is as plainly in D major. Superposition of tonalities is to recur. The second movement, *très modéré*, proceeds marchlike, but quickens to *vif*. The third, *modéré*, has another lively tune, interrupted briefly before the close by slow measures. The fourth, *vif*, is a vivacious dance in triple rhythm.

"The fifth, again *modéré*, 6-8, sets forth its tune from the trumpets, before the ensemble joins in. The sixth *vif*, in 3-4 beat, is pointed and staccato. The seventh, a short, slow movement, *lent*, has a plaintive theme—after an introduction sung by the English horn, trombones, horns and strings. The Finale, *vif*, is the largest movement. It is in 3-8 time. The full orchestra brings a lively and brilliant conclusion."

Darius Milhaud, now teaching at Mills College, Oakland, California, is one of the major personalities in modern French music. He has written a large number of works in many forms—for the theater, for orchestra, chamber music, piano, voice and piano, etc. His operas *Christophe Colombe* and *Orphée* are among the most important written in the twentieth century for the lyrical stage. Other well-known compositions include the ballets, *La Création du Monde, Le Train Bleu* and *Le Pauvre Matelot*; the orchestral works, *Saudades du Brazil,* two symphonies, *Sérénade, Deux Hymnes*; and five symphonies for small orchestra. He is also the composer of the "Fanfare" written for the sixtieth anniversary of the St. Louis Symphony Orchestra.

Among his most recent compositions is the Symphony, which he wrote in honor of the fiftieth anniversary of the Chicago Symphony Orchestra. Recent concerts were given in his honor in New York by the League of American Composers and by Mrs. Elizabeth Sprague Coolidge, famous patroness of chamber music concerts.

JOHN S. EDWARDS, *St. Louis Symphony Orchestra*

MODEST MOUSSORGSKY

(Born in Karevo, Russia, March 28, 1839—died in St. Petersburg, March 28, 1881)

ONE IS apt to remember of Moussorgsky only that he was a dilettante cavalry officer given to strong drink, that he happened to write an opera, *Boris Godounov,* by which his name is known to the musical world of today, and that he died somewhat ignominiously of dissipation, epilepsy and paralysis, in a hospital ward.

All of these details are true and none of them quite true. One forgets, for instance, the real greatness of Moussorgsky's genius which suffered continuously from the well-meant refinements of his friends, Balakirev, Borodin and Rimsky-Korsakoff. The original score of *Boris,* disclosed in concert performances here by Stokowski and Koussevitzky, revealed a ruggedness and inner strength that subsequent "editings" had almost totally destroyed.

Moussorgsky was the son of a prosperous landowner who had married a serf. In his autobiography, written in the third person, he remembers that he spent a happy childhood in which music played an important part, and that he learned the old Russian tales and many of the folk songs from his nurse.

"It was mainly his familiarity with the very spirit of the life of the people that impelled him to extemporize music before knowing even the most elemental rules of piano-playing," writes David Ewen. "His mother gave him his first piano lessons."

But the army supposedly was to be his career and he was graduated as an officer from the Military School for Ensigns and commissioned in the crack Preobrajensky Guard. But he hated military routine and during the three years he passed as an officer constantly sought for some means of escape. A fellow officer, knowing that he nurtured a passionate love for music, introduced him to Dargomijsky, who in turn led him to Balakirev and Borodin. Borodin recalls their meeting and writes:

"He was a true little fop, all spick and span in a well-fitting uniform, well-groomed, his hair carefully brushed. He spoke mincingly, interlarding his sentences with French words. He was very popular with the ladies."

Moussorgsky was soon infected by the musical enthusiasm of Borodin and Balakirev and resigned from the army in 1858 to devote himself entirely to composition. In so doing, he gave up a comfortable income for the precarious existence of an artist, doubtless sure that his wealthy father would stand in the breach.

But in 1863, family reverses compelled him to take another government post. He was described as "a careless and irresponsible worker and was dismissed from one government post after another. He remained a government employee, however, until 1879, two years before his death."

His first opera may be said to have been *The Marriage,* based on Gogol's one-act tragedy. It was performed privately in the home of César Cui with no great success. But the year before he had composed some haunting songs; a choral work, *The Rout of Sennacherib* and had made a first draft of his only orchestral work, *A Night on the Bald Mountain.* This piece usually is listed as *A Night on Bald Mountain,* a misleading designation, as Stokowski pointed out some years ago, when he conducted the Philadelphia Orchestra in what he then called *A Night on the Bare Mountain,* after Moussorgsky's own designation.

Late in 1868, he began work on the Pushkin drama of *Boris Godounov.*

He remembers fondly: "When I was writing *Boris,* I was *Boris.*" After many vicissitudes and a certain degree of astonishment on the part of the directors of the Imperial Opera, which entailed the interference of a certain popular soprano who resolved to appear in the Moussorgsky opera or not at all, the first and original version of *Boris Godounov* was performed on January 27, 1874. It met a chilly reception, and after a few more performances the opera sank to obscurity. It was rescued some years after the composer's death, edited and revised by Rimsky-Korsakoff, and suddenly took hold as one of the great lyric stage works of the world.

Striving to hide his disappointment in hard work, he began another folk-opera, *The Fair at Sorochintsk* and also sketched out *Khovanstchina.* His wavering health induced him to take refuge in a concert tour of southern Russia with the soprano, Leonova, during the summer of 1879. He returned refreshed and his spirits revived. Again he drove himself to work. But this spirit of energy was brief. A lifetime of drinking and dissipation at length took their toll. After a comparatively brief illness he died in the Nicolai Hospital, St. Petersburg, on March 28, 1881, his birthday.

Soon after Moussorgsky's death, the critic Stassov, one of his closest friends, started a movement to erect a monument to Moussorgsky over the grave in Alexander Nevsky Cemetery. The monument was erected. Under a bas-relief portrait of Moussorgsky, the following excerpt from Pimen's monologue in *Boris* was inscribed:

> So that the descendants of the orthodox
> May know the past fate of their own land.

Overture to *Khovanstchina*

As in *Boris Godounov,* Moussorgsky used an episode from Russian history (the unsuccessful conspiracy of the Prince Khovansky against the life of Peter the Great) as the basis for the plot of the opera *Khovanstchina.* The work was written between 1872 and 1875 in the main, although some portions were completed and orchestrated by Rimsky-Korsakoff several years later.

The Prelude to Act 1 was entitled "Dawn on the Moskva River" by Moussorgsky. It is a musical landscape in which the composer prepares the audience for the opening scene, the quarters of the Steltsi in Moscow in the early morning.

According to Oskar von Riesemann, author of an excellent biography of Moussorgsky, five melodic variations are the basis of the prelude, and in adopting this form, the composer has made use of "a method of musical expression long familiar to the Russian people, through their popular songs."

Each repetition of the melody brings its own variants and Moussorgsky thus achieves a remarkably subtle picture of "A landscape, somewhat melancholy and monotonous" which "seems constantly to change its appearance in accordance with the changing light."

JOHN S. EDWARDS, *St. Louis Symphony Orchestra*

A Night on the Bald Mountain
(Orchestrated after the composer's death by Rimsky-Korsakoff)

On the score of this fantasie is printed this brief program:

"Subterranean sounds of unearthly voices; appearance of the spirits of darkness, followed by that of the god Tchernobog; Tchernobog's glorification and the Black Mass; the revels; at the height of the orgies there is heard from afar the bell of a little church, which causes the spirits to disappear; dawn.". . . .

A Night on the Bald Mountain is Moussorgsky's expression of an ancient superstitious theme that has inspired composers of every country where the superstition of the Witches' Sabbath and the Black Mass exists. Liszt and Saint-Saëns have treated it in their versions of the *Danse Macabre,* Berlioz devotes the Finale of his

Symphonie Fantastique to the same theme; Wagner touches upon it in the second act of *Parsifal* at Klingsor's Castle, and so does Stravinsky in a different way in his ballet, *The Firebird.* The inscription on the score reprinted here does not require elaboration. The Bare Mountain is an eminence near Kiev, Russia, about which winds whistle in winter, suggesting to superstitious natives the presence of witches and vengeful gods sent by the Evil One.

CLAD H. THOMPSON, Kansas City Symphony Orchestra

Pictures at an Exhibition
(Orchestrated by Maurice Ravel)

Moussorgsky completed his suite of piano pieces, *Pictures at an Exhibition* on June 22, 1874. It was published in 1886. Ravel's orchestral transcription, made in the early part of 1923, was first performed on May 3, 1923 at a "Koussevitzky Concert" in Paris. The American premiere of the Ravel setting was at a concert of the Boston Symphony Orchestra, Serge Koussevitzky conducting, on November 7, 1924. . . . .

Toward the end of the winter of 1874, Modest Moussorgsky walked haltingly through the rooms of the St. Petersburg Architectural Association. On the walls was spread a memorial exhibition of some 400 drawings and watercolors by the architect Victor Hartmann, whom he had numbered among his closest friends. Hartmann's death the previous summer (July 23, 1873), at the lamentably early age of 39, had put an end to a very brief career that Moussorgsky and a mutual friend, the critic Stassov, had considered highly promising.

It was Stassov who had arranged the exhibition and appointed himself official critic of Hartmann and his accomplishment. It may have been Stassov who suggested to Moussorgsky the idea of a suite of piano pieces based on Hartmann's travel sketches, costume designs and architectural drawings—perhaps as the composer mourned his dead friend at his posthumous exhibition, treading heavily as he moved from picture to picture, stopping here and there, perhaps, to wipe away a persistent tear.

Once the idea of the suite had taken possession of Moussorgsky, he worked with unaccustomed speed. He could enjoy to the full his bent for quick characterization, his eye for picturesque detail, unhampered by the exigencies of development and the broad forms required by opera and symphonic works. "Hartmann is bubbling over, just as *Boris* did," he wrote to Stassov. "Ideas, melodies come to me of their own accord, like the roast pigeons in the story—I gorge and gorge and overeat myself. I can hardly manage to put it down on paper fast enough."

The exhibition opened late in February and Moussorgsky's suite was ready by June. This was swift indeed for a composer usually given to doubts and anxieties about the labored progress of his music.

There has been much curiosity about Hartmann and the drawing that called forth such exceptionally imaginative music. During the years that the Suite was neglected, Hartmann's drawings lay unnoticed in libraries and museums, many were scattered and many lost. The only clue to the pictures outside Russia was in Stassov's brief descriptive notes printed in the score of the suite.

Alfred Frankenstein, program annotator of the San Francisco Symphony Orchestra, has repaired this lack of information concerning Hartmann and his pictures—at least so far as research can bridge the gap of years since the Memorial Exhibition of 1874. He has obtained photographic prints of several of the sketches which Moussorgsky chose for movements of his Suite. The "Ballet of Chickens in Their Shells," "The Hut on Fowls' Legs" and "The Great Gate at Kiev" may now be seen, nearly as Moussorgsky saw them, in the illustrations that accompany Mr. Frankenstein's article, "Victor Hartmann and Modest Moussorgsky," in *The Musical Quarterly* of July 1939, together with a number of drawings that may be associated with other movements of the suite. Mr. Frankenstein also discovered an original catalogue of the exhibition, complete with "a bewildering amount of information concerning Hartmann's career."

If Hartmann's pictures hardly seem to match the flights of the composer's imagination, it is necessary to remember that Moussorgsky looked upon his friend's work with indulgence and that it was consistent with the predominant interest in Russian nationalistic tradition to which Moussorgsky and his circle were pledged. There can be no doubting the fact that Hartmann's "Slavic gingerbread" awakened in Moussorgsky a similar strain of fantastic illusion.

G. H. L. Smith, *Cleveland Orchestra*

The following are short descriptions of the ten sections of the suite, taken from the Minneapolis orchestra note by Donald Ferguson:

1—"Gnomus." A drawing representing a little gnome dragging himself along with clumsy steps by his little twisted legs.

2—"Il Vecchio Castello." A castle of the Middle Ages, before which a troubador is singing.

3—"Tuileries Gardens." Children disporting after their play. An alley in the Tuileries Gardens with a swarm of nurses and children.

4—"Bydlo." A Polish wagon with enormous wheels, drawn by oxen.

5—"Ballet of Chickens in Their Shells." A drawing made by Hartmann for the staging of a scene in the ballet *Trilby*.

6—"Samuel Goldenberg and Schmuyle." Two Polish Jews, the one rich, the other poor. ("Two Jewish melodies, one replying to the other. One of them is grave, imposing, decisively marked; the other is lively, skipping, supplicating. One cannot be deceived in the two persons; one of them, the portly one, walks square-toed, like a dog with a pedigree; the other, the thin one, hurries along, dwarfs himself, twists himself about, like a puppy. He revolves in a funny way, courts a look from the other, begs. There is no doubt about them, one sees them—and the barking of the fat one who frees himself, in two triplets, from the bore, proves that Moussorgsky could draw from the pianoforte, as from the voice, as from the orchestra, comical effects"—Pierre d'Alheim, *Moussorgsky,* presumably translated by Mr. Hale.)

7—"Limoges." The market place. Market women dispute furiously.

8—"Catacombs." In this drawing Hartmann portrayed himself, examining the interior of the Catacombs in Paris by the light of a lantern. (In the original manuscript, Moussorgsky had written above the Andante in B minor: "The creative spirit of the dead Hartmann leads me toward skulls, apostrophizes them—the skulls are illuminated gently in the interior.")

9—"The Hut on Fowls' Legs." The drawing showed a clock in the form of Baba-Yaga, the fantastical witch's hut on the legs of fowls. Moussorgsky added the witch, rushing on her way, seated on her mortar.

10—"The Gate of the Bohatyrs at Kiev." Hartmann's drawing represented his plan for constructing a gate in Kiev, in the old Russian massive style, with a cupola shaped like a Slavonic helmet.

DONALD FERGUSON, *Minneapolis Orchestra*

Excerpts from the opera *Boris Godounov*
(Symphonic synthesis by Leopold Stokowski)

In its time Moussorgsky's *Boris Godounov* got more "improved," revised and generally tampered with than any other opera, excepting, perhaps, an odd one here and there of the so-called repertory works. A pamphlet by Victor Belaieff on the subject of *Boris* and its trials requires less than a half-hundred pages for a full report of the case, and we are informed, among other things, that two of the revisions were made by Moussorgsky himself and two by Rimsky-Korsakoff—one in 1896 and the other in 1908. It was this last which made the rounds of the operatic centers, bringing to Rimsky a vicarious prominence.

But thanks to the scholarly research of Paul Lamm and Boris Asaieff, an authentic and, it is said, infinitely better version of the opera finally came forth, "in accordance with the autograph manuscripts, including hitherto unpublished scenes, fragments and variants," published in 1928, in vocal score, by the Music Section of the Russian State Publishing Department of Moscow (also brought out in England and the United States). These manuscripts, it is alleged, contain all that is true and original of Moussorgsky's work. And, finally, to go with them is the complete orchestral score with the parts, printed in 1929 in the same three countries.

Thus, the first production of the original was given its premiere at the Maryinski Theater, St. Petersburg (now the Leningrad State Opera), February 16, 1928. There was a concert given by the Philadelphia Orchestra, Leopold Stokowski conducting, at the Academy of Music in Philadelphia, November 29,

1929, at which he used the earlier of the two Moussorgsky versions, plus some scenes from the later one.

Moussorgsky called his first version of the work an opera in four acts, comprising, all told, seven scenes. His second version, as we now know it, is described as a "musical folk-drama after Pushkin and Karamzin," which consists of a prologue and four acts, these being augmented by the two Polish scenes, in addition to several shiftings of locale and, hence, continuity.

The present symphonic synthesis follows a direct line of the opera's dramatic sequence, adhering closely to both Pushkin's poem and Moussorgsky's own score. Its six sections are:

1—Outside the Novodievichi Monastery: The people ask Boris for protection—Pilgrims are heard singing in the distance—They come closer and enter the Monastery.

2—Coronation of Boris.

3—Monks chanting in the Monastery of Choudov.

4—Siege of Kazan.

5—Outside the Church of St. Basil—The Idiot foretells the fate of Russia—The starving crowd asks Boris for bread.

6—Death of Boris.

Mr. Stokowski's explanation of the Symphonic Synthesis follows:

"I am basing this transcription only on the Moussorgsky original score, not on the Rimsky-Korsakoff. Although Moussorgsky and Rimsky-Korsakoff were intimate friends and for a time lived together like two brothers, they were, as creative musicians, at opposite poles. Their approach to music was totally different. With generous intentions Rimsky-Korsakoff tried to reorchestrate and reform *Boris*. Instead, he made something far from the spirit of Moussorgsky.

"The original orchestration of Moussorgsky shows clearly what he was trying to say, but sometimes he failed to express his musical conception, because he was inexperienced in the vast, subtle, and highly differentiated world of the modern orchestra. There are exceptions to this, notably the 'Siege of Kazan,' in form a theme and variations, in spirit a fantastic scherzo. This is a masterpiece of orchestration, especially that variation which describes how Ivan the Terrible lit the fires and exploded the mines under the walls of the Tartar fortress. Moussorgsky's score is full of inspired music of symphonic quality.

"Wherever the orchestration of Moussorgsky only partly expresses the spirit of his musical conception, I have tried to help the orchestra say more completely what Moussorgsky was aiming to express. The result is something like a free modern symphony, which in this form is available to musiclovers who otherwise rarely hear this music of power and imagination and genius. Moussorgsky paints richly in tone the Russia of Pushkin, Gogol, Dostoievsky—a life which few other peoples have approached in pageantry, cruelty and sensitive perception of the beauty and the horror of which life is capable."

ROBERT C. BAGAR, *Philharmonic-Symphony Society of New York*

WOLFGANG AMADEUS MOZART

(Born in Salzburg, January 27, 1756—died in
Vienna, December 5, 1791)

SINCE music began no flame of genius has burned quite as steadily across the centuries as that of Mozart. His gift for creation was fantastic, his skill uncanny. His biographers say he was rather a common little person, given to vulgarity, improvidence and moral lapses. Yet the sweetness and gaiety of his nature, his devotion to friends and his love for his wife, Constanze Weber, may be set down to his credit.

His father, Leopold, was a sound musician employed as Court Composer to the Prince-Archbishop of Salzburg. He exploited the *Wunderkind,* Wolfgang and his sister, Anna Maria ("Nannerl") by showing them off at every court in Europe. And all the while, Wolfgang composed incessantly.

Wolfgang and his sister, "Nannerl," for whom he held a

whole-souled affection all of his short life, discovered a love for music at an early age. Wolfgang in his cradle heard the music lessons given to "Nannerl" by their father and at the age of three was picking out chords on the clavier. A year later Leopold was teaching him little pieces and at five he began to compose.

"Nannerl" was a remarkable performer on the clavier and their father decided to exploit his two prodigies. So in 1762 leaving Mama at home, Leopold and the two children set out on the first of many tours, this one to the Bavarian court at Munich. Although they were well received, apparently they did not make quite the impression on the Elector that Leopold had hoped.

Next they journeyed to Vienna, where the Empress Maria Theresa welcomed the family and the nobility honored them. Upon their return to Salzburg, Wolfgang began to compose anew and his pieces for the clavier began to be published. Furthermore, he began to play the violin in public, despite the fact that he had had no formal training on this instrument.

They set out again on June 9, 1763 for an extended tour which embraced London, Holland, Versailles, Switzerland and sundry other stops and were back in Salzburg by November of 1766.

But when they returned from this jaunt, they found that the archbishop had died and that his successor was the haughty Hieronymous von Colloredo, with whom Wolfgang was to quarrel incessantly for some years. The archbishop appointed young Wolfgang the Court *Konzertmeister* at a salary of 150 florins, with leave to pay another visit to Italy. Yet the archbishop became so irritated by the continued absences of his two musicians that he dismissed them both eventually, though Leopold was reinstated.

The Mozarts decided to visit Paris in 1777, but this time Leopold dared not leave, so Wolfgang and his mother set out together. They met with little or no success in the French capital and in many other ways the venture was unfortunate. His mother fell sick and died on July 3, and this tragedy prostrated Mozart for some time.

On the way back to Salzburg, Wolfgang stopped off at Mannheim to visit the family of Fridolin Weber, operatic prompter and coach, and the father of four daughters—Josefa, Aloysia, Constanze and Sophie. He fell in love promptly with Aloysia. Frau

Weber objected and when Wolfgang wrote to his father of this passion, that worthy added even stronger reasons for disapproving the match.

But Aloysia was worldly and ambitious, and possessed, like her sisters, of an unusual voice. At that particular period in his career, Wolfgang was becoming known slowly, yet still must be considered as an impecunious musician and Frau Weber probably induced Aloysia to conserve her affections for a more rewarding opportunity.

At this time Mozart wrote a number of concert arias for Aloysia and her sister Josefa before returning to Salzburg. The Webers followed the court to Munich and Aloysia soon lost interest in Wolfgang.

Some time later, when Wolfgang was really becoming famous in Vienna, he married Aloysia's sister, Constanze. It is likely that the scheming mother of Constanze had reversed her former attitude toward him and had furthered the courtship, yet Leopold never wavered in his opposition to any connection whatever with the Weber family and became semi-estranged from Wolfgang as a consequence of this union.

In 1779, Wolfgang became court and cathedral organist. A year later he was invited by the Elector to write an Italian opera for the carnival in Munich. The result was the first of Mozart's great operas, *Idomeneo Re di Creta,* revised in recent years by Richard Strauss and Wolf-Ferrari. The opera was a magnificent success and the Elector was heard to remark: "I was surprised that such great things could be tucked away in so small a head."

At twenty-five, Mozart found himself a free lance, having been literally booted out of the jealous archbishop's service. But the success of his opera and a mounting attention from the public did not save him from a difficult time. He was staying with the Webers. Fridolin had died and his widow, "a calculating and unscrupulous woman of low character," says Pitts Sanborn, "was conducting her household according to her own likes and dislikes." It was at this time that Wolfgang wooed and married Constanze, on August 8, 1782, despite the distaste of Leopold and Wolfgang's loving sister, "Nannerl."

The intervening years in Mozart's life constitute a record of mounting debt and intense creative work. He borrowed heavily from the good merchant Michael Puchberg, a generous friend and fellow Mason. Wolfgang's domestic life at this time was chaotic. Constanze's pregnancies were frequent, yet only two of her six children survived infancy.

However, one masterpiece after another flowed from his pen —the three great symphonies in E-flat, G minor and C major, were composed between June and August of 1788; also the greatest of his operas, such as *The Marriage of Figaro, Don Giovanni, Cosi fan tutte, Clemenza di Tito* and *Zauberfloete (The Magic Flute)* came forth in this peiod of harassment.

Suddenly the fine endurance of his constitution began to wane. He became listless and fevered by turns. Whether it was typhus, which seems to have been rampant in the vicinity at that time, or a debility brought on by overwork and nervous exhaustion, no biographer has been able to establish. Constanze was absent on one of her eternal cures when the first symptoms appeared.

She returned to find him prostrate and working desperately upon his final masterpiece. "In July 1791," explains Mr. Sanborn in his biographical sketch, "an ominous-looking stranger clad in gray, called upon Mozart and ordered from him a *Requiem Mass* for an unnamed patron. Mozart dwelt upon the mystery of this incident, until in his rundown and feverish condition it became a portent of disaster. Yet, as a matter of fact, the whole thing was no more than one Count Franz van Walsegg sending his steward to induce a composer of recognized worth to compose secretly for him a work that he fondly believed he could palm off as his own, thus establishing himself as likewise a composer of worth."

Mozart accepted the commission and the last weeks of his life were obssessed by the Requiem. But he could not finish it before he died in the evening of December 5, 1791, at the age of thirty-five. True grief and love overcame Constanze, but not a single friend of her famous husband came to her assistance and the next day the body was consigned to a pauper's grave. Today the exact place of the grave is unknown, for the body has disappeared and "there is no certainty that the skull preserved in the Mozarteum at Salzburg is really his."

We are indebted to a curious circumstance of musical history

for the fact that no Opus numbers are used to designate the chronological order of Mozart's compositions. Instead, the student encounters the letter "K," which stands for Koechel. This means that in the *Koechel Catalogue of Mozart's Works,* the piece in question is so numbered, i.e., Koechel 548 etc.

Ludwig Alois Friedrich Koechel was born in Stein, Lower Austria, on January 14, 1800, the son of Johann Georg Koechel, a revenue superintendent of Passau. He studied law in Vienna and became a qualified attorney and eventually a tutor in the family of the Archduke Carl.

His closest friend was one Franz von Scharschmid, who was appointed President of the Assizes at Salzburg. Koechel accompanied him there, lingering in some awe at Mozart's birthplace. He decided then and there to classify, thematically and chronologically, the scattered works of the young Master.

Koechel and Scharschmid returned to Vienna, and Koechel settled in a wing of the palace of the Archduke Albrecht, once his pupil. He died there on June 3, 1877.

The first draft of the catalogue was published in 1862. The basis of this initial attempt was a catalogue begun by Mozart himself and never finished. The whole work took nearly twenty years to complete. The publishing firm of Breitkopf and Haertel published a second edition in 1905.

Concerto in E-flat major for two pianos and orchestra (Koechel 365)

This composition, originally entitled *Concerto a due Cembali,* was written in Vienna in 1780. Mozart played it with Josephine (or Josefa) Aurnhammer in November 1781, and again the following spring. There is evidence that he wrote it for performance with his sister, Maria Anna—the "Nannerl" of the childish concert tours—but no evidence that the two Mozarts ever played it together in public.

Fraülein Aurnhammer was an industrious and persistent pianist who was at this period a considerable thorn in Mozart's flesh. She was his pupil, made herself useful in getting some of his music published, and had the ill grace to fall in love with him.

But Mozart, writing to his father at Salzburg, described her with notable lack of gallantry as *ein Scheusal*—a horror. He even went into unkind detail: "If an artist wished to paint the Devil in a lifelike way he would be obliged to resort to her face as a model. She is as fat as a peasant girl . . . To see her is enough to make one blind; a single look is a whole day's punishment . . . . She is the biggest bore I know."

The young woman, however, was at least without illusions. She said to Mozart: "I am not pretty; on the contrary, I am plain. I don't want to marry some clerk with three or four hundred florins, and I have no choice of anyone else. So I prefer to remain as I am and make a livelihood by my talents."

As it turned out, Fräulein Aurnhammer had both husband and career. In 1796 she married a merchant named Boesenkoenig (the size of his fortune is not a matter of record) and she was still giving yearly recitals as late as 1813. She was then referred to as "the first pianist in Vienna," but a critic reported her playing as "well schooled, accurate, but cold and old-fashioned."

The three movements of the Concerto proceed in free and cheerful style, the first Allegro with its long orchestral introduction, the Andante in song-form, the Finale a rondo. To the original accompaniment of oboe, bassoons, horns and strings Mozart later added a pair of clarinets, writing the parts on separate sheets of paper, not in the score.

The composer's biographer, Otto Jahn, says of this Concerto: "There is no intention apparent of making the two instruments independent; the players emulate each other in the delivery of the melodies and passages, sometimes together, sometimes in succession, often breaking off in rapid changes and interruptions; the melodies are sometimes simply repeated, sometimes with variations so divided between the two instruments that neither can be said to have the advantage over the other. There are somewhat greater difficulties of execution than have been useful hitherto, a few passages, for instance, in octaves and thirds, but very modest ones; the passages generally have more variety and elegance. The orchestra is simply and judiciously, but very delicately treated, the wind instruments in sustained chords, as a foundation for the clavier passages."

Philadelphia Orchestra

Piano concerto in F major (Koechel 413)

The Concerto in F major composed about 1782 for the Forte-Piano, belongs to the happiest period of Mozart's life, the time when he had just married Constanze Weber. It breathes pure joy from beginning to end. It may be described as one long Menuet—we know how much Mozart loved to dance and what a good dancer he was! The first and last movements are, in fact, Menuets. Between the two, Mozart introduces a sublime *Larghetto,* truly a *Larghetto amoroso* full of the excitement and tenderness of his adolescent love for Constanze.

Those who had the good fortune to hear Mozart play the Forte-Piano were ecstatic in describing his *bel canto* which seemed to issue from the throat of a singer rather than from the keyboard of an instrument. His playing in the virtuoso passages, which was brilliant without being loud, became in the *larghetti* impassioned yet spiritual, declamatory, lively, punctuated by interrogation and exclamation points, and by *cesuras* which marked off each phrase like an air or *recitativo,* sung with the loving intelligence only to be found in the greatest artists.

WANDA LANDOWSKA, in *Musique Galante*

Piano concerto in D major (Koechel 451)

This Concerto, the sixth of the seventeen composed by Mozart in Vienna, is dated March 22, 1784. It, the Concerto in E-flat major (K. 449), the Concerto in B-flat major (K. 450) and the Concerto in G major (K. 453) were composed for the subscription concerts in Trattner Hall and the concerts in the theater during Lent. Was Mozart the pianist; or Barbara Ployer, the daughter of a Viennese banker, and a pupil of Mozart, who purposed to introduce her to Paisiello? Mozart wrote to his father on May 24, 1784, that he could not decide whether the Concerto in B-flat major or the one in D major was the better. "The two make the player sweat, yet the one in B-flat major is the more difficult. I am eager to know which of the three concertos pleases you and my sister most; for the one in E-flat major composed on February

9, 1784 (K. 449) does not belong with them, for it is of a special
kind and written more for a small than a large orchestra . . . .
Of course it is necessary that one should hear all three with all the
parts and well performed . . ."

During Lent in 1784, Mozart gave three concerts in Trattner
Hall. (Trattner was a rich bookseller and publisher. His wife was
a pupil of Mozart.) There were 174 subscribers; the price for the
three concerts was six florins. There were two concerts at the
National Theater. We know that Mozart composed the Concerto
in E-flat major (K. 449) for Barbara Ployer; that at a concert at
Ployer's at Doebling she played the Concerto in G major (K. 543),
and with Mozart the Sonata in D major for four hands (K. 448),
while Mozart took part in the performance of his Quintet for
piano, oboe, clarinet, horn and bassoon. In all probability, Mozart
was the pianist when this Concerto in D major was produced.
Barbara played the one in E-flat major (February 9, 1784) and
the one in G major (April 12, 1784).

PHILIP HALE, *Boston Symphony Orchestra*

Piano concerto in D minor (Koechel 466)

Mozart was the first great virtuoso of the pianoforte, or, as it
was quaintly reversed in his time, the "fortepiano." His predecessors had used the piano's ancestors, the clavichord and the
harpsichord. He had, therefore, to perfect a technic (*sic*) of his
own, a system of fingering and a position of the arm. We have the
report of a contemporary that Mozart himself had small and
delicate hands which he moved so quietly and naturally on the
keyboard "that the eye was pleased as well as the ear." Beholders
wondered that he could grasp so many keys, that he could play
rubato so freely with his right hand, yet keep a strict tempo with his
left. He is said to have demanded of pupils a quiet and steady hand,
with such natural lightness and flexibility that the notes would "flow
like oil." Insisting upon clean, clear playing and tasteful expression,
he also warned players against undue speed, saying that it was far
easier to play a piece fast than slowly.

The D minor Concerto was written for Mozart's own use at a

concert February 11, 1785. It was, in fact, completed only the night before. The composer's father was in Vienna at the time and wrote to his daughter Maria Anna after the concert: "Wolfgang played a new and excellent piano-concerto, which the copyist was copying yesterday when we called, and your brother did not have time to play through the Rondo once, because he had to look over the copying."

Philadelphia Orchestra

Piano concerto in E-flat major (Koechel 482)

Mozart composed this concerto at Vienna in December 1785, the work having been completed on the sixteenth of the month. It was a busy period, for Mozart was working on his *Marriage of Figaro,* and, as Leopold Mozart wrote to his daughter . . . . he was "over head and ears in work. He has put off his pupils to the afternoon so that he may have his mornings free . . . Hitherto he has, no doubt, procrastinated in his usual easy manner and taken his own time, but now he must be in earnest." But the master did not occupy himself solely with *The Marriage of Figaro,* for he was also composing not only the E-flat major Concerto for pianoforte but two other concertos, respectively in A major and C minor, as well as a sonata for piano and violin, in E flat, a rondo for pianoforte, and the little opera, *Der Schauspieldirektor.* The concertos were written for the London subscription concerts of 1786, for which, in addition to his other occupations, Mozart had rounded up 120 subscribers.

FELIX BOROWSKI, *Chicago Symphony Orchestra*

Piano concerto in C major (Koechel 503)

Chronologically, the C major Concerto nestles midway between Mozart's two operatic masterpieces, *The Marriage of Figaro,* produced in May 1786 and *Don Giovanni,* produced late in 1787. Mozart's autograph gives December 4, 1786, as the date of completion. Like many of the other fourteen piano concertos Mozart

had composed in Vienna since 1782, the C major was written for
a concert series given by him during Advent, a season rivaling Lent
in lucrative returns for a pianist-composer in Vienna who was also
a genius. As usual, Mozart was heavily in debt. The dwelling on
the Schulerstrasse was expensive. Medical bills were mounting.
The Marriage of Figaro proved a disappointment as an immediate
revenue-raiser. To add to the emotional stress, Mozart's latest son,
Johann Thomas Leopold, born on October 18, died less than a
month later. The concert series was a sure way to raise quick
funds—and, possibly to forget. Composition came easily; performance even more easily. On December 6, only two days after finishing the C major Concerto, we find the busy little man inscribing
a fresh date of completion on the manuscript of the D major
Symphony (K. 504)! "As soon as he set pen to paper, the usual
miracle happened," writes Eric Blom. "Trouble forsook him."
Could anyone begrudge Mozart this avenue of escape?

The ill-luck that hounded Mozart during those bleak December days of 1786 did not stop there. Something of a curse has
lain on the C major Concerto. Despite the ardent espousal of
specialists, the public until recently scarcely knew this work. When
Artur Schnabel and Georg Szell first collaborated on the concerto
with the Vienna Symphony at the Grosser Konzerthaussaal in May
1934, they made an astounding discovery. There was no record of
a previous performance in Vienna since Mozart's time!

As for America, research among the program files for major
orchestras in the Music Room of the New York Public Library
revealed one definite listing—a pair of performances by Webster
Aitken with Eugene Goossens and the Cincinnati Symphony on
January 30 and 31, 1942. In recent years Nadia Reisenberg, in a
WOR broadcast series, and Clarence Adler, on WQXR and at the
Town Hall, have included it in their Mozart surveys. The rest is
silence—always barring, of course, possible private and unlisted
renderings. . . . .

The work was first published by Mozart's widow, Constanze,
at her own expense in 1798 . . . . The subsequent story of these
posthumous publications is involved and at times dismal. There
was the expected bargaining and bickering. Even Constanze's new
husband, the Danish diplomat, George N. Nissen, felt called upon
to play a part in the transactions. He suspected chicanery on the

part of the first publisher to buy up the priceless bequest. "Don't attach too much importance to his fussiness and preciseness," Constanze mollified Johann A. Andre, the buyer, after casually mentioning suspicions. "See that you preserve your present good will, which, indeed, I merit in return for what I feel as your most devoted friend and servant." It seems Nissen, who kept a careful tally of successive opus issues, thought he had detected a sinister discrepancy in Andre's numbering.

And while one of the world's greatest artistic legacies was making its way into profitable circulation, what still remained of the legator lay buried in a pauper's grave.

LOUIS BIANCOLLI, *Philharmonic-Symphony Society of New York*

Piano concerto in D major (Koechel 537)

The Concerto has come to be called the "Coronation" Concerto because Mozart played it at Frankfort on the Main during the coronation festivities of the Emperor Leopold I in October 1790.

Mozart was hard pressed for money in the last year but one of his life, and was disappointed when the new Emperor, whom he sued for a secondary post, gave him no official recognition. Salieri, as the court *Kappelmeister*; Umlauf, as his assistant, and fifteen court musicians were ordered to provide the music at the coronation ceremonies. Mozart figured that he should journey to Frankfort and give a concert on his own account, that something might be reaped from it over the expenses of the journey.

He took with him his brother-in-law, Franz Hofer, the violinist, who was to share the profits. Mozart had to pawn his silver plate to hire a coach. His letters to his wife in Vienna showed that the family finances were in a bad way. He had to urge her to push the negotiation of a large loan from the publisher Hoffmeister. The letters showed a cheerfulness which may have been the composer's way of putting a good face upon miserable circumstances, or perhaps his anxiety to keep up the spirits of his wife, who was sick and worried. . . . . .

At last the concert came off, at eleven o'clock on the morning of October 15 (1790). He played two concertos (Koechel Nos. 459 and 537), a violin sonata and a piano duet with Hofer. "Unfortunately," as he wrote to his wife on that same day, "some prince was giving a big *dejeuner* and the Hessian troops were holding a grand maneuver." Enthusiasm ran high but the receipts were low.

Alfred Einstein, in his invaluable book on Mozart, comments on this concerto: "There is no question that it was the proper work for festive occasions. It is very Mozartean, while at the same time it does not express the whole or even the half of Mozart. It is, in fact, so 'Mozartesque' that one might say that in it Mozart imitated himself—no difficult task for him. It is both brilliant and amiable, especially in the slow movement; it is very simple, even primitive in its relation between the solo and the *tutti,* and so completely easy to understand that even the nineteenth century always grasped it without difficulty. It has become, along with the D minor, the best known of Mozart's concertos. . . ."

This concerto was composed in 1788, the score bearing the date February 24 in Mozart's writing.

JOHN N. BURK, *Boston Symphony Orchestra*

Piano concerto in B-flat major (Koechel 595)

The last of Mozart's piano concertos is dated January 5, 1781 and it was first performed on March 4 of the same year. The piece is in the traditional three movements, and its orchestral score calls for one flute, two oboes, two bassoons, two horns and strings.

Eric Blom, in the *Master Musicians Series,* describes it as a "truly valedictory work, with a kind of chastened mood occasionally verging on a feeling of oppressive foreboding."

Abert in turn defines it as the best among the last group of piano concertos. He discovers a relationship between it and its predecessors in form and structure, but that it departs considerably from them in character and compass.

"One gets the impression," Abert says, "that Mozart had composed it for himself rather than for the general public, for the joyous brilliance of the old yields here to a highly personal and remarkably resigned tone, which distinguishes it sharply, for one thing, from the passionate fervor of both earlier concertos in the minor.

"Mozart here makes more reserved use of his contrapuntal art than is his wont in this form, though in this respect the working out of the first movement, for example, does not disown its period of origin. The striving for unity and inwardness of the whole idiom emerges so much the clearer."

Nine days after the completion of the B-flat Concerto, Mozart wrote a song entitled *Sehnsucht nach dem Fruehlinge,* which bears an unmistakable resemblance to the rondo theme of the concluding Allegro.

ROBERT C. BAGAR, *Philharmonic-Symphony Society of New York*

Overture to *The Magic Flute (Zauberfloete)*

Mozart's two-act opera, *The Magic Flute,* the text by Emanuel Schikaneder, was first given under the composer's direction at the Theater an der Wien. in Vienna on September 30, 1791. The subject runs on the mysteries of Freemasonry, and the libretto is probably wholly comprehensible only to members of that order. It is the one *great* opera Mozart wrote to a German text, and was the last opera he. ever wrote. It was not particularly well received at first, but soon became popular and made its way all over the musical world. It was first given in Berlin on May 12, 1794; in Hamburg on November 19, 1794; in Leipzig in 1809; and in Dresden on October 27, 1818.

A pasticcio arrangement of it, with intercalated music from some of Mozart's other operas, by Ludwig Wenzel Lachnith, to a new text by Morel de Chedeville, was brought out under the title of *les Mystères d'Isis* at the Académie de Musique in Paris on August 20, 1801; some one was so scandalized by the "infamous pasticcio" that he punningly dubbed it *les Misères d'ici.* The work was given according to Mozart's original score, but with a new text in four acts by Nuitter and Beaumont, at the Théâtre-Lyrique in Paris on February 23, 1865 . . . . Its first performance in the United States was given in Italian, in New York, on November 21, 1859.

The overture has long been famous, and may probably rank as Mozart's greatest overture. It begins (*Adagio*) with three *fortissimo* E-flat major chords for the full orchestra—trombones and all—which have some hidden Masonic significance; this introductory *Adagio* continues its stately movement for fifteen measures, and is then followed by the *Allegro*. This, the chief movement of the overture, is a brilliant and elaborate fugue. This fugue is treated with orchestral freedom, much as the one in the Finale of the *Jupiter Symphony* is. About the middle of its development it is interrupted by the great Masonic E-flat major chords of the beginning of the overture. These chords are the only thing in the overture that reappears in the opera; yet the work is by no means open to the charge of musical irrelevancy, for the theme of the fugue is eminently suggestive of the lively character of Papageno, the bird-catcher. The overture to the *Zauberfloete* was probably the one Rossini had in mind when he once said: "I've been trying for months to write some fugued overtures *à la* Mozart; but I've had to tear them all up, the great model is too overpowering! Mine were all detestable."

W. F. APTHORP, *Boston Symphony Orchestra*

Overture to *The Marriage of Figaro*

Le Nozze di Figaro, a *drama giocoso* in four acts, book after Beaumarchais' comedy *La Folle journée, ou Le Mariage de Figaro* by Lorenzo da Ponte, was composed at Vienna in 1786 and produced in that city May 1 of the same year. Mozart completed the music in six weeks. According to his father, he let time slip through his fingers and presently found himself obliged to limit his teaching to the afternoon hours that he might devote his mornings to the opera.

There were obstacles in the way of a representation. Beaumarchais' piece had aroused the opposition of Louis XVI in 1781 and the King forbade its production at the Théâtre Français in Paris or at court because of its boldness in satirizing the morals of the aristocracy. Beaumarchais brought it out, nevertheless, in 1784, with overwhelming success despite the allegations of immorality.

Others in high places followed the royal example, including Mozart's Emperor Joseph II.

It was through the tactful intercession of da Ponte that the monarch finally relented in Mozart's favor (he had deigned to value the composer highly as a writer of instrumental music, but deemed his efforts for the voice "not good for much.")

The opera was produced in the face of intrigues and cabals. Michael Kelly (who sang the role of Don Curzio) declared that "never was an opera stronger cast." The work enjoyed nine performances that year. It was temporarily eclipsed by the success of Martin's *Cosa Rara*. Today—such are the ironies of history—Martin's *Cosa Rara* is remembered solely by a melody which Mozart inserted from it in the banquet scene of *Don Giovanni*.

The overture (in the form of a sonatina) begins (*presto,* D major, 4-4) with a scampering string passage in eighth notes. The second part of the theme is a more substantial subject given to the wind. The brief overture—its time of performance is three minutes—ends with a comparatively elaborate coda.

HERBERT F. PEYSER, *Symphony Society of New York*

Overture to *Don Giovanni*

Mozart had been commissioned by the Bohemian nobility to write *Don Giovanni* and toward the end of August 1787, when he was traveling with his wife, Constanza, from Vienna to Prague, he had the score in his old worn-out music case. Only a few portions of the libretto had not been composed. There were also lacking the overture and the banquet scene of the second act. When Mozart arrived at Prague he completed the opera. One can tell, by the paper used, what was written in Vienna and what in Prague. The score, one of the most valuable musical documents, was for some time in the possession of Pauline Viardot-Garcia, a former heroine of New York opera, and then went to the Paris Conservatoire.

The history of the original libretto is also remarkable. It was long considered lost, until a copy was found in Prague and another in the Library of Congress. But the Prague libretto is in no way the first of *Don Giovanni* that was printed. Many weeks before the premiere in Prague a libretto was printed in Vienna.

It seems that the Archduchess Maria Theresa on her wedding trip was to attend the first performance of *Don Giovanni* in Prague. Since the Viennese court censor expressed doubts as to whether the princess might attend this opera in which so many incidents of dubious moral character took place, the authorities had demanded from da Ponte the libretto in advance.

Da Ponte acquiesced, but was tactful enough to present a text designed for the Pollyannas and Little Rollos of Austria at that time. Thus in the first act the champagne aria and the ball are omitted. However, the princess did not get to see *Don Giovanni* because Mozart wisely postponed the performance to save himself official embarrassment.

A contemporary of Mozart, Gottlieb August Meissner, professor of literature at the University of Prague, mentions the first performance of *Don Giovanni* in some sketches he wrote, which were published by his grandson, Alfred Meissner. The elder Meissner tells of a party at the house of Josefa Duschek, the famous Prague singer and friend of Mozart, on the day before the dress rehearsal. The cream of Prague society was present, together with the whole cast of the opera and Mozart and Casanova. Everybody was worried that Mozart had not yet written the overture to the opera— had, in fact, expressed his intention of going to the inn "Zum Tempel" for a glass of Pilsner instead of finishing the work. Casanova hit upon the idea of enticing Mozart into a pavilion of the park where there was a piano standing, and not letting him out until the overture was written down. Mozart took the trick good naturedly enough.

Whether the story is true or not we cannot tell. The manuscript, however, shows signs of haste, one might almost say of irritation, and the parts, according to testimony of contemporaries, were put, with the ink still wet, on the music stands of the musicians at the moment Mozart was mounting the conductor's box. The orchestra was given a triple fanfare and the public cried out: "Bravo, Mozart!"

PAUL NETTL, *New York Times*

Dr. Paul Stefan, on the occasion of the 150th anniversary of the first performance of *Don Giovanni* (October 29, 1787), wrote

from Vienna to *Musical America* under date of October 12, 1937:
"The story of the overture to this opera, composed at the very last moment, is familiar to all. It is alleged that it did not take form until somewhere between five and seven o'clock in the morning of the day of the performance; others believe, however, that it was composed during the night before the dress rehearsal. . . ."

Eine Kleine Nachtmusik (Koechel 525)

In Mozart's time, "occasional pieces" such as serenades, divertimenti and *cassations* often were written for some special event. The Emperor and his court, the wealthier families and better hostelries retained groups of musicians for entertainment and frequently ordered pieces to be composed for specific occasions. The fashion in which Mozart used this type of piece places it between the suite and the symphony in form and scope.

A Little Night Music is a particularly lucid example of the logic and apparent nature of the form. In structure it is a minute version of his typical sonata, quartet or symphony, made up of four movements with the usual contrasts of tempo and mood.

The first movement is in simple sonata form: first and second themes, a development section, a recapitulation and a coda (Italian for "tail," which is added to any piece or section to give a greater feeling of finality.)

The second movement, *Romanza* is actually a very simple rondo form in which a main melody of well developed length is alternated with contrasting melodic sections, called "episodes." The *Minuet* is the typical third movement of the eighteenth century symphony. The fourth movement is also a Rondo, but different from the second in mood and tempo, and of a more intricate structure, both melodically and in its key pattern.

MARRILYN BLACK, *Seattle Symphony Orchestra*

Symphony No. 35 in D major (Koechel 385, *Haffner*)

The Mozart family counted among its friends Sigmund Haffner, opulent merchant and one-time burgomaster of Salzburg. In exchange for the interest that he took in the son, Wolfgang, Haffne

eemed to feel that when his household celebrated some special occasion the young musician should furnish the music for the festiv-
ties. Accordingly, at the time of the marriage of his daughter, Elise,
n the summer of 1776, Mozart was called upon to contribute a serenade and a march for the nuptial feast. Six years later, another request for a festal composition came from the socially active Haffners.
At the time, Mozart was in Vienna paying ardent court to Constanze
Weber. . . . and he was much occupied arranging parts for wind
nstruments for his opera (*The Abduction from the Seraglio*). When
he letter from his father came asking for a work posthaste, Mozart
eplied petulantly:

"I certainly have enough to do, for by a week from Sunday
the letter is dated July 20, 1782] my opera must be arranged
or wind instruments, otherwise somebody will get the better of me
and rake in all the profits, and now I have to write a new composi-
ion! I hardly see how it can be done . . . . You can depend on
getting something from me by every post, and I will work as fast as
can and as well as such haste will permit."

Within a week a first movement was shipped off with further
omplaints about the speed with which he had to write, and with
he promise of "the two minuets, the andante, and the last movement, on Wednesday, the 31st. If I am able, I will send a march,
oo." On August 7, the march was forwarded with the comment:
"I only hope that it will arrive in time and be to your liking. The
irst allegro must be played in a fiery manner, the last part as fast
s possible.". . . . Thus, the work, which was cast in the form of
n instrumental serenade, was completed in less than a fortnight,
nd was forgotten by Mozart.

A half-year later, when he was setting up a program for a con-
ert of his music to be played on March 22, 1783, Mozart sent
or his manuscript in order to recast it as a symphony. He casually
emarked to his father, on receipt of it: "The new *Haffner Symphony* has astonished me very much; I did not remember a single
note of it. It must be very striking." So the serenade became a symphony by dropping the march and one of the minuets, and as
uch was played before the Emperor and to a crowded house with
great success.

"What gratified me most," Mozart wrote his father, "was the
presence of the Emperor, who applauded me loud and long. It is

his custom usually to send the money to the box-office before going to the theater; otherwise, in justice, I might have hoped for a larger sum, because his delight knew no bounds. He sent me twenty-five ducats."

LOUISE BECK, Philadelphia Orchestra

The original manuscript of the *Haffner Symphony* is now the permanent treasure of the National Orchestral Association in New York, presented to the Association on the occasion of its tenth anniversary by one of its directors. The manuscript was sold in 1800 by Mozart's widow, Constanze, to the Offenbach music publisher, Johann Andre. His son, Julius, inherited the manuscript in 1841 and King Ludwig II of Bavaria acquired it in 1860, a birthday gift from Mayer Karl Rothschild, consul-general in Frankfort. Ludwig, patron of Wagner, considered it his greatest musical treasure and carefully preserved it in the blue velvet case designed for it by Rothschild. It remained in the possession of the Bavarian royal house until 1935, and came to this country by way of England a year later.

Symphony in G minor (Koechel 550)

This work has been called "the greatest *little* symphony in existence." It was written during the summer of 1788, when Mozart's inventive powers were, perhaps, at their most prolific, for in two months of that summer he composed three incomparable symphonies, the E-flat major (Koechel 543), dated June 26, the present one, dated July 25 and the *Jupiter Symphony* dated August 10. That he could write at all was astounding, because his wife was ill, for one thing, and his finances were at a particularly low ebb, for another.

During those trying days he once sought from Puchberg a loan of two hundred florins, describing himself, according to that authority, as "a prey to gloomy thoughts which he must repel with all his might." It has been said that the G minor symphony "reflects something of the composer's troubles." And Mozart's biographer, Otto Jahn, discovers in the first movement "a piercing cry of anguish."

In commenting on the work, Pitts Sanborn noted that "though all of us might not go so far, there is no doubt that this Symphony is touched with ineffable sadness that sometimes crosses like a summer cloud the radiance of Mozart's sun-god temperament. And along with this there are moments of celestial tenderness. Yet, at the same time, this Symphony has its capricious and spritelike quality, which comes out in the ascending and descending pairs of thirty-second notes in the Andante, echoed distantly in the whimsicality and waywardness of certain measures of the Finale."

There is an amusing and pat little anecdote related by Apthorp, which revolves around a pianistic performance by Liszt. Says Apthorp:

"He had just played his own matchless transcription of Beethoven's *Pastoral Symphony* as only he could play it. It should be remembered that the *Pastoral*, though homely enough in its thematic material and generally simple in its development and working out, is, as a piece of orchestration, one of Beethoven's most complicated scores; it thus presents quite peculiar difficulties to the pianoforte transcriber, difficulties which Liszt has conquered in a way that can only be called marvellous.

"After Liszt had played it at the concert in question, Franz Lachner stepped up to him in the green room and said: 'You are a perfect magician! Think of playing literally everything in the second movement and with only ten fingers! But I can tell you one thing even you can't play with all your magicianship.' 'What's that?' asked Liszt. 'The first sixteen measures of Mozart's little G minor Symphony, simple as they are.' Liszt thought a moment and then said with a laugh: 'I think you are right; I should need a third hand. I should need both my hands for the accompaniment alone, with that viola figure in it!' "

ROBERT C. BAGAR, *Philharmonic-Symphony Society of New York*

Symphony in C major (Koechel 551, *Jupiter*)

Inappropriate nicknames have a habit of sticking like burrs to musical compositions. For Mozart himself, this last of his symphonies was just one of half a dozen he had written in C major.

For Ludwig Ritter von Koechel, it was merely No. 551 when, seventy-five years later, he made his indispensable catalogue of Mozart's music. The public memory, however, does not easily retain keys or Koechel numbers, and the first tag that offers itself is often put to use.

The finger of suspicion points to J. B. Cramer, famous as pianist and publisher in the early 1800's, as the godfather of the *Jupiter*. Cramer, beyond doubt, was the man who saddled the last of the piano concertos of the passionately republican Beethoven with the autocratic nickname of *Emperor*. Insensitive to the implications of either name, he merely meant his designations to signify superlative music. But the very word *Jupiter* has allowed some analysts to find thunderbolts of that deity in the triplets of the first movement, and to imagine a "godlike calm and beauty" pervading the whole. Mozart speaks more clearly in his own language.

In a few summer weeks of 1788, when he was thirty-two, Mozart wrote three symphonies which surpassed even the miracles that he himself had wrought earlier. . . . They are all, of course, in his richest, maturest orchestral style; they are all precious examples of his inventiveness and his subtlety. . . . There is no evidence to persuade us that Mozart thought of these three symphonies as a last will and testament, although he had but three more years left to him. It is rather as though he felt he had, at this point in his life, achieved maturity as an artist and mastery as a craftsman—an occasion at least as worthy of celebration as a twenty-first birthday. These symphonies are the monument with which he commemorated that crisis in his creative life.

Outer circumstances, it happened, were conducive to concentrated and unperturbed composition. The death of Gluck in the preceding November left vacant the post of Court Composer to the Emperor Joseph II. Gluck, whose fame and influence were known throughout Europe, had a salary of two thousand florins. Mozart, after certain humble petitions and canny wire-pullings were effective, was given the appointment as Court Composer, but the thrifty Emperor took the opportunity to reduce that functionary's income to eight hundred florins a year. That was a blow to Mozart's professional pride (was he indeed that much less valuable than Gluck?) as well as a blow to his financial expectations. He was at this period more wretchedly poor than usual, and the records are scrawled with his IOU's to comparative strangers.

At least the Court Composer needn't work very hard for his eight hundred florins. Joseph, though he is said to have been passionately fond of music and a most excellent and accurate judge of it, had no ear for the music of Mozart. All that he commanded from his *Kappelmeister* were a few ballroom dances—and we have as a result twelve minuets and twelve German dances for orchestra. The Viennese public followed the imperial lead in snubbing and ignoring the shining genius.

The eight hundred florins did allow Mozart and his wife Constanze to move into more comfortable lodgings. In letters dated on the days he must have been devoting to these three symphonies he tells of having better air, a little garden and above all blessed quiet. On June 27, 1788, he wrote: "I have done more work in the ten days I have lived here than in two months in my other lodgings. I should be far better here were it not for the gloomy thoughts that often come to me. I must drive them away resolutely, for I am living comfortably, pleasantly and cheaply."

Two generations later a composer and critic who was not always so restrained, Robert Schumann, said: "There are things in the world about which nothing can be said—such as Mozart's C major Symphony with the fugue, a great deal of Shakespeare and many pages of Beethoven. . . ."

R. L. F. McCombs, *Philadelphia Orchestra*

Symphony in E-flat major (Koechel 543)

Mozart wrote his last three and most celebrated symphonies in the amazingly short space of about two months. The Symphony in E-flat . . . was completed June 26, 1788, while the other two, those in G minor and C major (the *Jupiter*), were completed July 25 and August 10. Ordinarily he wrote symphonies because there was a specific opportunity for performance or a benefit concert planned. But there is no record of any such occasion in the case of these three works, and it is doubtful whether he actually ever heard them. It may be legitimate, perhaps, to suspect some sudden efflorescence of inspiration, which certainly shows in the results.

The Symphony on this program (No. 39 in the usual listing) is the only one of the three with a slow introduction. After its peremptory opening chords, there is an atmosphere of suspense created over a pedal point in the lower strings (*i.e.,* an obstinately repeated note) and leading to a passage of tense, dissonant harmonies. After a brief nostalgic episode, the Allegro inconspicuously begins with a gentle theme, almost waltzlike. Presently there is an assertive passage for full orchestra followed by an episode with high repeated notes and exciting wide skips in the violins. The second theme restores some of the placidity of the first theme, but excitement recurs to close the exposition. The development is dominated by the second theme. . . .

More in the *style galant* is the sparsely scored, and thus highly contrasting trio, which places in relief two clarinets oddly undertaking what might almost be a delicate little piano piece. (The general character, very typical of the time, is like the opening of the C major Sonata for piano, popularized by Raymond Scott as *In a Twentieth Century Drawing Room.*)

The last movement has some of the playful, folkish quality and rugged contrasts of Haydn's finales. The second theme is so much like the first that the movement gives the impression of a rondo, or of the later Beethoven constructions on a single motive.

The work is scored for flute, two clarinets, two bassoons, two horns, two trumpets and strings. Note the absence of oboes.

ARTHUR V. BERGER, *New York City Symphony Orchestra*

Violin concerto in A major (Koechel 219)

Between April 14 and December 20, 1775, Mozart composed five violin concertos, each of them in one day except the fourth which may have spread over a month. The Concerto in A major was the fifth and appeared on December 20. . . .

Jahn writes generally of the five concertos:

"The first movement, which was the most elaborate, is more suggestive still of the aria, than is the corresponding movement in the symphonies. There is the same fixed alteration between solo and *tutti* passages, the same adornment of the solo part with passages and cadenzas, and indeed the whole movement is a reminiscence of the serious aria. On the other hand the structure is more condensed and more animated. . . .

"The second movement is simple and rests essentially on the tuneful artistic delivery of the cantilene. . . . The character of the movement is generally light and pleasing, but a deeper though always a cheerful mood, sometimes makes itself felt . . .

"The last movement, is as a rule in the form of a rondo . . . In the A-major concerto the chief subject is *tempo di menuetto,* interrupted by a long *allegro,* 2-4 in A minor. . . . The clearly expressed popular tune of the interpolated passages is remarkable, and has a striking and pleasing effect."

Mozart was a witty and zestful correspondent. He refers to his violin concertos in a letter from Augsburg, of October 17, 1777. "After dinner, I played two concertos, something out of my head, and then a trio on the violin. I would gladly have played more, but I was so badly accompanied that it gave me the colic." A few days later, he takes his cousin to task for not having sent him a promised portrait, in terms that would put a modern college girl to shame:

"Potz Himmel! Croations, demons, witches, hags & cross batteries! Potz Element! Air, earth, fire & water! Europe, Asia, Africa & America! Jesuits, Augustines, Benedictines, Capucins, Minorites, Franciscans, Dominicans, Carthusians & Knights of the Cross! Privateers, regular & irregular, sluggards, rascals, scoundrels, imps & Villains all! Donkeys, bufflaloes, oxen, fools, blockheads, numbskulls & foxes! What means this? 4 soldiers & 3 shoulder-belts! Such a thick packet and no portrait!!"

The letter brought results. The portrait is now hanging in the Mozarteum in Salzburg.

ADELAIDE F. HOOKER, *New York Women's Symphony Orchestra*

Violin concerto in G major (Koechel 216)

While some doubt exists about Mozart's later violin concertos, there is none regarding the five concertos he wrote in 1775. Their authenticity is unquestioned. The concertos were written during

Mozart's Salzburg appointment in the space of nine months, from April to December. That they were composed primarily for his own use is clear. "Everyone praised my beautiful, pure tone," he writes proudly in one of his letters. That they also served the needs of *Kapellmeister* Brunetti is equally certain, though whether they all did is not known.

Dyneley Hussey considered the five concertos "magnificent examples" of Mozart's work of the Salzburg period, though he conceded that they are not completely faultless in the matter of style, noting what he called the "routinier working out." Whereas Hussey found them largely French in form and style, Pitts Sanborn maintained they revealed the 19-year-old Mozart as "an accomplished cosmopolitan." To the former Philharmonic-Symphony annotator the concertos were "German in melody and Italian in the violin technic and to a lesser degree than the melody.

Joining in the international hunt, Eric Blom went a step further by tracing Hungarian gypsy influences in the A major concerto. This theory was later sustained by Abraham Veinus, who dubbed the trio middle section of the finale an "uninhibited Hungarian rhapsody." One passage in the Rondo, a kind of *alla turca,* admits Turkey to the conference table of United Nations. . . .

We know from the manuscript of the G major concerto that it was completed by Mozart on September 12, 1775. The autograph reads: *Concerto di Violino di Wolfgango Amadeo Mozart mp. Salisburgo il 12 Septembre 1775.* As the third in the series of five it represents a bold stride forward from the preceding two, an astonishing advance that has long puzzled the Mozart scholars. . . .

LOUIS BIANCOLLI, *Philharmonic-Symphony Orchestra*

WALTER PISTON

(Born in Rockland, Maine, January 20, 1894—now
head of Music Department, Harvard University)

AN ILLUMINATING paragraph concerning the position of Walter
Piston in the development of contemporary music in the United
States is contained in Nicholas Slonimsky's book, *American Com-
posers on American Music*:

"Walter Piston owes his patronymic to his grandfather, Pistone, an Italian by birth. The final 'e' fell off when Pistone came
to America; he married an American woman and his son, Walter
Piston's father, married an American". . . .

He studied violin with the Messrs. Fiumara, Theodorowicz
and Winternitz in Boston, piano with Harris Shaw. Pursuing a
general course of education at Harvard, he studied theory and
composition in the music department there, then went to Paris for
further study with Nadia Boulanger. He is now chairman of the
Music Department at Harvard.

Most of his more important symphonic works have been performed first by the Boston Symphony Orchestra, including: Symphonic Piece (1928); Suite for Orchestra (1930); Concerto for
Orchestra (1934); and Symphony No. 1 (1938). Other works first
played elsewhere include a Concertino for Piano and Chamber
Orchestra (1937); Violin Concerto (1940); Sinfonietta (1941);
Prelude and Allegro for Organ and Strings (1943); and Symphony
No. 2 (1944). The Boston "Pops" first played his music for the
ballet *The Incredible Flutist*.

Concerto for Orchestra

This piece, which had its first performance by the Boston
Symphony Orchestra in 1934, is a "concerto" in the eighteenth
century sense. It is not written to display the virtuosity of any
single instrument.

The first movement is in sectional form built upon two
themes. As in the old *concerti grossi* and in the Brandenburg con-

certi of Bach, there is an alternation of *tutti* and *concertante* in the instrumental grouping. The instruments used in the *concertante*, however, vary throughout the movement.

The second movement (in D) is in the mood of a scherzo. After introductory rapid passages for strings (pianissimo) there is a melody for the English horn. A short middle section gives the English horn theme to the violoncello. An imitative development leads to a recapitulation of the first section in retrograde, followed by a short coda.

The third movement (in A) derives formally from the passacaglia. The theme is presented by the tuba and varied by the brass section. The following variations introduce in turn a fugato over the ostinato theme, a stretto of the theme and later a canon. It is finally given to the full orchestra.

JOHN N. BURK, *Berkshire Symphonic Festival*

Suite from the ballet: *The Incredible Flutist*

Walter Piston wrote his score for the ballet *The Incredible Flutist* in collaboration with the American dancer, Hans Wiener (Jan Veen) for performance by the Boston "Pops" Orchestra and Mr. Wiener's dancers at the "Pops" Concerts in Symphony Hall in Boston. The first performances took place on May 30 and 31, 1938. Arthur Fiedler conducted; the settings and costumes were by Marco Montedoro. The production was repeated under the same auspices on May 29 and 31, 1939. . . .

The Suite from the ballet had its first public performance on November 22, 1940 at a concert of the Pittsburgh Symphony Orchestra, Fritz Reiner, conductor. . . .

The following summary of the action of the ballet appeared in the magazine *Dance* (August 1938):

"The Siesta is over. With hearty yawn and a wide stretch, the village shakes off its drowsiness. First to wake up, the apprentice opens the shop, and life begins its uneventful flow. The merchant's daughters demonstrate their father's wares to the shoppers. The busybody and the crank have their argument. But what is this? A march is heard! The band, the circus band march in, followed by people of the circus. They're all here: the barker, the juggler, the snake dancer, the monkey trainer and her monkeys; the crystal gazer, and, of course, the main attraction, the Flutist. The Flutist is a remarkable fellow, an incredible fellow. He not only charms snakes, he also charms, believe it or not, the snake dancer. He is so romantic, the Incredible Flutist, and perhaps just a bit promiscuous, for he also charms the merchant's daughter, and they meet at eight o'clock that very evening.

"When the clock strikes eight, young couples are all over the place, and love is in the air. Even the prudish, rich widow cannot resist the charged atmosphere, and grants the merchant that kiss he's been begging for well nigh two years. But they don't fare so well. Their sustained embrace is discovered, and the poor rich widow faints right into the arms of her bewildered boy friend. But the Incredible Flutist hies to the rescue. A little dancing, a little fluting and the widow comes out of her swoon, none the worse for wear. And then—the band strikes up; the spell is broken; the circus, the Incredible Flutist and all, leave the village."

G. H. L. Smith, *Cleveland Orchestra*

SERGEI ALEXEYEVICH PROKOFIEFF

(Born in Sontsova, Southern Russia, April 23, 1891
—now living in Moscow)

PROKOFIEFF ranks with Stravinsky as one of the two most arresting and provocative of living Russian composers. He is a superb technician, a satirist and a wit in music, veritably an orchestral magician and, when he is not the Soviet propagandist and tool of Communist policies in art, a sensitive poet. His quality as an artist often approaches genius.

He began to study the piano at an early age with his mother and before long turned his hand to composition, writing an opera in his ninth year.

"At the age of five and a half," says Israel V. Mestyev, in his book on Prokofieff, "he composed his first piece of music, a *Hindu Gallop,* the result of his impressions after listening to stories about the Hindus. . . . At the age of six he had already written a waltz, a march, and a rondo, and at seven, a march for four hands. His mother led him imperceptibly into the world of music, gradually enriching his knowledge and striving to develop his independent judgment and a sincere love for music."

At eight he was taken on his first visit to Moscow, heard *Faust, Prince Igor* and *The Sleeping Beauty* at the Opera, and straightway came home and composed *The Giant,* in a piano arrangement without the vocal parts. He entered the St. Petersburg Conservatory, after some private study with Pomerantsev and Reinhold Gliere, and spent ten years in unremitting labor, during which his unusual talents developed rapidly. But the struggle with his professors to assert his own individual style was ceaseless and stubborn.

"Gradually his preference for Grieg, Rimsky-Korsakoff and Wagner gave way to an avid interest in Richard Strauss, Reger and Debussy. These latter were, of course, regarded in the Conservatory as forbidden fruit."

But a systematic study of the New Music of the West did not really set in until the return visit of Reger to St. Petersburg in 1907. Prokofieff developed also a close intimacy with Miaskovsky and the three, with the pianist, Zakharov, "spent many enjoyable evenings discussing, arguing and demonstrating their own compositions."

In these years he composed a symphony, performed at one of the student concerts, played two piano concertos at public concerts in St. Petersburg, and turned out a number of smaller pieces for the piano. He was graduated from the Conservatory in 1914 with three diplomas and the Rubinstein Prize in piano.

He composed assiduously during the First World War, including *Chout,* a ballet for Diaghilev; the *Classical Symphony* and another piano concerto. He came to America first during the period of the Russian Revolution, played everywhere as a concert pianist, and composed an opera, *The Love for Three Oranges,* on commission from the Chicago Opera Company. After the premiere, he went back to Europe, "settling in Paris, which he left at intermittent periods to serve as guest conductor and as concert pianist in leading cities in Europe and America." But he returned to his native country in 1934 and has lived there since.

Scythian Suite (*Ala and Lolli,* Opus 20)

The Prokofieff of this music is very early Prokofieff indeed. . . . As a reward for the brilliant completion of his Conservatory studies (he had won the Rubenstein first prize for piano) his mother provided him with funds for a journey to London, where he might attend the performances of the Diaghilev Ballet Russe, which was in those innocent days a heady stimulant, impartial and cosmopolitan, for all the arts. . . .

Prokofieff was introduced to Diaghilev, who listened to him play his Second Concerto and discussed plans for possible ballet music from his pen. The composer received an order from the impresario for a new ballet on Russian fairy-tale or prehistoric themes. He was by this time quite committed to follow in Stravinsky's footsteps. But Stravinsky had indeed been but falling in with a mild Russian vogue for what Israel Nesteyev calls "Scythianism"—which might be loosely translated into American as "Tarzanism." At any rate, it was in this same vein that Prokofieff and the poet, Sergei Gorodetsky worked out a ballet pantomime called *Ala and Lolli.*

A rough version of the piano score was finished in the autumn of the same year, 1914, and the next January, Prokofieff took it to Diaghilev in Italy, where he met a number of the modernist composers who clustered about the Ballet Russe and where he played his Second Concerto in Rome. Diaghilev, however, rejected *Ala and Lolli* on the grounds that the plot was stilted and the music dull—*a la Tcherepnin.* He made a further and more fruitful suggestion as to utilizing Russian folk tales and folk music which resulted in *The Buffoon* or *Chout,* as the later ballet is also known.

After *The Buffoon* was finished and posted off to Diaghilev, Prokofieff turned to the rejected *Ala and Lolli* and salvaged the four movements which make up the *Scythian Suite.* As his biographer, Nesteyev, points out, it was his first large-scale and fully mature orchestral work. It was brought to performance at one of the concerts organized and directed in St. Petersburg by Alexander Siloti on January 29, 1916; some authorities say the composer conducted, but Nesteyev does not specify. It aroused the usual pro against con—Glazounov ostentatiously left the auditorium during the final "Sunrise" section—but it was repeated the next season and shortly became a familiar and popular item on Russian programs. The Chicago Orchestra introduced it to America on December 6, 1918. . . .

A pertinent footnote might be that the music of the *Scythian Suite* has been used for ballet's purposes in spite of Diaghilev's rejection. In Berlin in May 1927 it became *Die Erloesten,* with a plot full of angels and demons, as well as the redeemed, and in the following October a ballet to the music of *Ala and Lolli* was produced in Buenos Aires.

Scythia was a half-legendary land on the southern steppes of Russia bordering the Black Sea—the region indeed in which Prokofieff had grown up. It was first mentioned by Hesiod, whose comments were later imaginatively enlarged upon by Herodotus and Hippocrates. From these accounts the Scythians seem to have been a nomadic people of singularly repellent aspect and habits, subservient to whimsical and bloody-minded autocrats and confusing idolatry.

To quote Mr. Nesteyev: "After a long tussle with the ponderous and static material of Scythian mythology, Prokofieff and Gorodetsky together devised a plot. The Scythians are worshipping their favorite gods—Veles, the sun god, and Ala, his beloved daughter—when by night a cunning stranger, Chuzhbog, aided and abetted by the dark forces of evil, rises to steal Ala. His spell, however, works only in darkness; even under the pale light of the moon he is powerless. To Ala's rescue comes Lolli, the great warrior. The evil god would slay him, but in a timely intervention Veles, the sun god, smites Chuzhbog with his blinding rays."

Descriptive paragraphs printed in the score show how the movements of the Suite encompass this ingenious fable:

1—"Invocation to Veles and Ala" (Allegro feroce, 4-4). The music describes an invocation to the sun, worshipped by the Scythians as their highest deity and named by them Veles. The invocation is followed by the sacrifice to the beloved idol, Ala, daughter of Veles.

2—"The Evil God and Dance of the Pagan Monsters" (Allegro sostenuto 4-4). The evil god summons the seven pagan monsters from their subterranean realms and, surrounded by them, dances a delirious dance.

3—"Night" (Andantino, 4-4). The evil god comes to Ala in the darkness. Great harm befalls her. The moon rays fall upon Ala and the moon-maidens descend to bring her consolation.

4—"Lolli's Pursuit of the Evil God and Sunrise" (Tempestuoso 4-4). Lolli, a Scythian hero, goes forth to save Ala. He fights the Evil God. In the uneven battle with the latter, Lolli would have perished, but the sun god rises with the passing of the night and smites the evil deity. With the description of the Sunrise, the Suite comes to an end. . . ."

R. F. L. McCombs, *Philadelphia Orchestra*

Lieutenant Kije—Orchestral Suite (Opus 60)

Belgosking, the Russian film corporation, produced a successful sound-picture for which Serge Prokofieff wrote the music. The present Orchestral Suite is the result of the film music for *Lieutenant Kije,* a humorously-satiric film not yet shown in this country.

Nicholas Slonimsky, a close student and observer of Russian affairs, comments as follows on this film and the music written for it (in 1933) by Prokofieff:

"The subject of the film is based on an anecdote about Czar Nicholas I, who misread the report of his military aide so that the last syllable of the name of a Russian officer which ended *ki* and the Russian intensive expletive *je* (untranslatable by any English word) formed a nonexistent name, *Kije.*

"The obsequious courtiers, fearful of pointing out to the Czar the mistake he had made, decided to invent an officer of that name, as misread by the Czar. Hence all kinds of comical adventures and purely fictitious occurrences."

Whatever the mythical Lieutenant Kije may have added to the entertainment of Russian cinema patrons, Prokofieff's natural flair of humor and irony has transferred the moods of the film to the still more imaginative realm of music. Some exceptionally apt comment has been published by the RCA-Victor Company, when Charles O'Connell commented on the excellent recording of this Suite made by the Boston Symphony under Serge Koussevitzky. There are five movements which . . . may be taken as so many "tableaux" or "pictures."

1—"The Birth of Kije." Kije comes into existence like Pallas Athene, that mythical deity "who sprang full-panoplied from the head of Jove." Lieutenant Kije, in other words, appears at once as a full-grown, gorgeously uniformed officer of the Czar. One hears a faint call of a cornet as from a distance. It grows louder. The rasp of the snare drum becomes more distinct. Suddenly a regiment seems to swing around the corner from nowhere. It is a splendid and subtly comical impression. There is, as O'Connell points out, something amusingly broad and vulgar in the orchestration here, suggesting a pompous, rather stupid overdressed yet rather amiable fellow.

2—"Romance." In the sound-film a solo baritone voice was employed by Prokofieff. In the concert version a tenor saxophone has been substituted. The composer has printed the words of the song in the score. They need no commentary:

Heart, be calm, do not flutter;
Don't keep flying like a butterfly.

Well, what has my heart decided?
Where will we in summer rest?

But my heart could answer nothing,
Beating fast in my poor breast.

My grey dove is full of sorrow,
Moaning is she day and night.

> For her dear companion has left her,
> Having vanished out of sight,
> Sad and dull has gotten my grey dove.

3—"Kije's Wedding." Military stiffness and grotesque sentimentality plus an evident overdose of vodka are the principal in-
gredients of this scene. The music is marked *Allegro fastosa,*
the latter meaning "pompously."

4—"Troika." This is a combination of impressions, partly
folk song, partly sleighride. As before, the saxophone is substituted
for the baritone voice in the film score. There the vocalist had to
sing the following old Russian tavern ditty:

> A woman's heart is like an inn:
> All those who wish to go in,
> And they who roam about
> Day and night go in and out.
>
> Come here, I say; come here, I say,
> And have no fear with me.
> Be you bachelor or not,
> Be you shy or be you bold,
> I call you all to come here.
>
> So all those who are about
> Keep going in and coming out,
> Night and day they roam about.

5—"Burial of Kije." This, of course, is not music in the manner of the conventional dirge. The joke has gone far enough. It is
as if it were laid to rest at last. Prokofieff combines in this movement various themes heard earlier in the Suite. The Suite ends
with the faint trumpet call, heard at the start, so curiously reminiscent of the American "taps" as used by the Russian composer.

BRUNO DAVID USSHER, *Los Angeles Symphony Orchestra*

Suite from *The Love for Three Oranges*

This opera is based on a fairy tale, the story of three princesses confined by enchantment within three oranges. A prince,
afflicted with melancholy, is made to laugh by seeing a sorceress

(who is plotting his undoing) compelled to do an involuntary somersault. The melancholy is cured but the prince, by the magic art of the sorceress, is now obsessed with love for three oranges of Brobdignagian size, in which are confined three princesses. These oranges must be sought by the prince in a perilous desert. They may be opened only at the water's edge (on pain of death to the princesses), and an attendant, desperate with thirst, opens two of them amid the sandy wastes. Two princesses thus die on the spot (incidentally relieving the prince of an ultimate problem).

But the prince himself, undeterred by this dreadful warning, opens the third orange. He falls incontinently in love with the released princess, but cannot himself save her from the fate of the other two. This is accomplished, however, by certain onlookers, not real participants in the action, who watch the proceedings from either side of the stage.

The Suite, which consists of six movements selected from the music of the opera, has the following sequence:

1—"Les Ridicules"; 2—Scène Infernale; 3—Marche; 4—Scherzo; 5—"Le Prince et la Princesse"; and 6—"La Fuite."

DONALD FERGUSON, *Minneapolis Symphony Orchestra*

Peter and the Wolf

The score was completed in Moscow on April 24, 1936 and was first performed at a children's concert of the Moscow Philharmonic in the large hall of the Moscow Conservatory on May 2.

The present performance is the first outside of Russia [March 25, 1938]. The following explanation is printed in the score of *Peter and the Wolf*:

"Each character of this Tale is represented by a corresponding instrument in the orchestra: the bird, by a flute; the duck, by an oboe; the cat, by a clarinet (in a low register); the grandfather, by a bassoon; the wolf, by three horns; Peter, by the string quartet; the shooting of the hunters by the kettledrums and the bass drum. Before an orchestral performance it is desirable to show these instruments to the children and to play on them the corresponding *leitmotifs*. Thereby the children learn to distinguish the sonorities of the instruments during the performance of this Tale."

The text follows:

"Early one morning Peter opened the gate and went out on a big green meadow.

"On the branch of a big tree sat a little bird, Peter's friend. 'All is quiet,' chirped the bird gaily.

"Soon a duck came waddling around. She was glad that Peter had not closed the gate, and had decided to take a swim in the deep pond in the meadow.

"Seeing the duck, the little bird flew down upon the grass, settled next to the duck and shrugged her shoulders:

" 'What kind of a bird are you, if you can't fly?' said she. To this the duck replied:

" 'What kind of a bird are you, if you can't swim?' and dived into the pond.

"They argued and argued—the duck swimming in the pond, the little bird hopping along the shore.

"Suddenly something caught Peter's attention. He noticed a cat coming through the grass.

'The cat thought: 'The bird is busy arguing. I'll just grab her.' Stealthily she crept toward her on velvet paws.

" 'Look out!' shouted Peter, and the bird immediately flew up into the tree, while the duck quacked angrily at the cat from the middle of the pond.

"The cat crawled around the tree and thought: 'Is it worth climbing up so high? By the time I get there the bird will have flown away.'

"Grandpa came out. He was angry because Peter had gone to the meadow. 'It is a dangerous place. If a wolf should come out of the forest, then what would you do?'

"Peter paid no attention to grandfather's words. Boys such as he are not afraid of wolves.

"But grandfather took Peter by the hand, led him home and locked the gate.

"No sooner had Peter gone than a big gray wolf came out of the forest. In a twinkling the cat climbed up the tree.

"The duck quacked and in her excitement jumped out of the pond. But no matter how hard the duck tried to run she couldn't escape the wolf. He was getting nearer—nearer—catching up with her—and then he got her, and with one gulp swallowed her.

"And now, this is how things stood: the cat was sitting on one branch, the bird on another—not too close to the cat.

"And the wolf walked around and around the tree, looking at them with green eyes.

"In the meantime Peter, without the slightest fear, stood behind the gate watching all that was going on.

"He ran home, took a strong rope, and climbed up the high stone wall.

"One of the branches of the tree around which the wolf was walking, stretched out over the wall.

"Grabbing hold of the branch, Peter lightly climbed over onto the tree.

"Peter said to the bird: 'Fly down and circle around the wolf's head, only take care he doesn't catch you.'

"The bird almost touched the wolf's head with her wings, while the wolf snapped angrily at her from this side and that.

"How the bird did worry the wolf! How he wanted to catch her! But the bird was cleverer, and the wolf simply couldn't do anything about it.

"Meanwhile, Peter made a lasso and, carefully letting it down, caught the wolf by the tail and pulled with all his might.

"Feeling himself caught, the wolf began to jump wildly, trying to get loose.

"But Peter had tied the other end of the rope to the tree, and the wolf's jumping only made the rope around his tail tighter.

"Just then the hunters came out of the woods, following the wolf's trail, and shooting as they went.

"But Peter, sitting in the tree, said: 'Don't shoot! Birdie and I have already caught the wolf. Now help us take him to the zoo.'

"Imagine the triumphant procession.

"Peter at the head.

"After him, the hunters leading the wolf.

"And winding up the procession, grandfather and the cat. Grandfather tossed his head discontendedly: 'Well, and if Peter hadn't caught the wolf, what then?'

"Above them flew Birdie, chirping merrily: 'My, what fine ones we are, Peter and I! Look what we have caught!'

"And if one would listen very carefully, he could hear the duck quacking in the wolf's belly, because the wolf, in his hurry, had swallowed her alive!"

JOHN N. BURK, *Boston Symphony Orchestra*

Suite from the ballet: *Romeo and Juliet*

The ballet itself was composed in 1935 for the Bolshoi Theater in Moscow and there first performed. Prokofieff compiled two suites from this music, the first of which was performed in Moscow on November 24, 1936 under the direction of Golovanof. There was a performance in Paris on December 19. Its first hearing in this country was at a concert of the Chicago Orchestra, January 21, 1937, when Prokofieff conducted.

The Second Suite had its first performance in Soviet Russia in the spring of 1937. It was subsequently played in Paris, Prague and London. The composer conducted at the concert of the Boston Symphony, March 25, 1938.

The orchestration includes two flutes and piccolos, two oboes and English horn, two clarinets and bass clarinet, tenor saxophone, two bassoons and contra-bassoon, four horns, two trumpets and cornet, three trombones and tuba, timpani, bass drum, military drum, triangle, bells, tambourine, cymbals, maracas, harp, piano, celesta and strings.

When the ballet *Romeo and Juliet* had its trial performance in Moscow, V. V. Konin reported the event in a dispatch published in the *Musical Courier*, November 16, 1935:

"The preview of the work left the critics in dismay at the awkward incongruity between the realistic idiom of the musical language which successfully characterizes the individualism of the Shakespearean images, and the blind submission to the worst traditions of the old form, as revealed in the libretto. The social atmosphere of the period and the natural evolution of its tragic elements have been robbed of their logical culmination and brought to the ridiculously dissonant 'happy end' of the conventional ballet. This inconsistency in the development of the libretto has had an unfortunate effect, not only upon the general structure, but even upon the otherwise excellent musical score."

The two Suites which the composer compiled from his original score consist of seven numbers each.

Suite 1— (a) "Dance of the People." A tarantella performed in the public square of Verona. (b) "Scene." Music describing the adherents of the houses of Montague and Capulet, just before the outbreak of hostilities. (c) "Madrigal." The first meeting of Romeo and Juliet. (d) "Minuet." Heard at the Capulets' ball. (e) "Masques." The entrance of Romeo, disguised, in the ball scene. (f) "Romeo and Juliet." Balcony scene. (g) "The Death of Tybalt." Music accompanying the duel.

Suite 2— (a) "Montagues and Capulets." A somewhat ironical picturesque portrayal of the haughty, arrogant old noblemen, defiantly strutting about in armor, with a contrasting Trio, Juliet dancing with Paris. (b) "Juliet the Maiden." The naive, carefree young girl is admirably evoked in the main theme . . . (c) "Friar Laurence." The friar is represented by two themes, one given out by bassoons, tuba and harp; the other by 'cellos, divided in three parts. (d) "Dance." (e) "The Parting of Romeo and Juliet." This is built on the Romeo theme ("rather on the theme of Romeo's love"—S.P.) and is one of the most extensively developed movements of the suite. (f) "Dance of the West Indian Slave Girls." ("Paris presents pearls to Juliet; slave girls dance with pearls"—S.P.) (g) "Romeo and Juliet's grave." In the ballet, Juliet is not really dead and the grave is a deception. Romeo, unaware of the fact, is prostrate with grief.

JOHN N. BURK, *Boston Symphony Orchestra*

Classical Symphony (Opus 25)

The first performance of the *Symphonie Classique* was in Petrograd on April 21, 1918, the composer conducting. Prokofieff arrived in New York in September, and in December the Russian Symphony Orchestra in New York played this symphony for the first time in America. . . . The work is dedicated to Boris Assafieff, a writer on musical subjects, whose pen name is "Igor Gleboff.". . .

Written in 1916-1917, considerably before "neoclassicism" set in, this symphony in miniature surely cannot be looked upon as a pledge to past ways. It might, rather, be considered a momentary dalliance with the eighteenth century formula. It would probably be as mistaken to look for reverence in the *Symphonie Classique* as to look for irreverence in it. Let us say that the composer had a single and passing impulse to weave his own bright threads into an old pattern.

Prokofieff gives himself precisely the orchestra of Mozart or Haydn, he is punctilious in his formal procedure. He is also concise—so much so that the four movements occupy no more than thirteen minutes—about half the usual duration of the symphonies which he took as model.

D major is the prevailing key. The first movement, with clipped phrases, staccato, and to the point, sets forth its themes, its development, its recapitulation and coda, all complete. The *Larghetto* is in simple rondo form, beginning and ending with a charming pizzicato in the strings, *pianissimo,* a mere accompanying figure which nevertheless lingers in the memory. The theme and its development has a suggestion of eighteenth century ornamentation but in a less serious vein. Prokofieff departs from the letter rather than the spirit of his models in choosing a gavotte instead of the rigidly customary minuet. The Finale gives, naturally, a far greater freedom to his fancy, although he sets himself a first theme upon the common chord which his forebears might have found quite in order and to their own purposes. The working out, the recapitulation and coda are virtuously observed. The episodic byplay turns up a sauce of "modern" wit which the periwigged masters could scarcely have approved.

JOHN N. BURK, *Boston Symphony Orchestra*

SERGEI VASSILIEVITCH RACHMANINOFF

(Born in Onego, Russia, April 1, 1873—died in
Beverly Hills California March 28, 1943)

THOUGH ardently beloved by friends and family, Rachmaninoff was a sad and lonely man. And the deep affection in which he was held by the public, both here and abroad, did not seem to dissipate this innate melancholy. Psychiatrists probably would attribute his chronic depression to the despair and frustration that gripped him after his first failures as a composer. One is conscious in most of his music of mysticism and savage resignation, both of which had been labeled rather patly as pertinent to the Slavic disposition.

He came of a wealthy, land-owning family to whom music was at once an accomplishment and a recreation. He was endowed almost at birth with a precocity in this art. "Even as a child, he had a flair for it," writes a biographer, "and a perfect ear for pitch." Yet his laziness as a child was proverbial; he was almost too indolent, in fact, "to cultivate music fully."

A sudden change in the family fortunes made it impossible to send the boy to the aristocratic school his parents had chosen. Instead, he was entered at the Conservatory in St. Petersburg, where he proved to be a distinguished student, but no prodigy. It was said of him that he preferred to rely upon the brilliance of his own natural gifts, rather than bore himself with the drudgery and detail of prolonged study. Yet he managed to achieve a gold medal with his opera *Aleko,* after he had transferred to the Conservatory in Moscow, where he completed his studies in 1892. His teachers in Moscow were his relative, Alexander Siloti, pupil of Liszt, and Taneiev and Arensky. He also is said to have studied with Tschaikowsky, then active in the affairs of the Conservatory. He conceived a reverent admiration for that master, and occasional similarities and references evident in his music are thus explained.

He had attained increasing honors and responsibilities in his chosen profession before he paid his first to America in the season of 1909-1910, and became an impressive success, despite his own misgivings when the proposed tour was first discussed. He was somewhat astonished, he told me many years later, to learn that his fame had preceded him by way of a minute item of piano music, the Prelude in C sharp minor. This had gripped the public fancy, had become an integral part of the teacher's repertoire, in fact, and the name of its composer had become almost a household word.

Succeeding tours here and in Europe established him firmly as one of the towering artists of our time. He also appeared frequently as a guest conductor of American orchestras, yet his reputation as a composer of larger orchestral works developed gradually. The Second Piano Concerto and the Second Symphony first bespoke his ability in this direction and succeeding works confirmed his position as a first-rate musician.

After the First World War, he made his home here permanently and came to be regarded almost as an American institution. As Charles O'Connell remarks: "His place as a pianist is among the greatest, and as either pianist or conductor, he brings to bear upon music a technique so highly developed that it can be forgotten, and a rare and grave musicianship always refreshing and always satisfying."

He caught a severe cold during one of his concert tours and barely reached his home in California before he succumbed to pneumonia. His last recital in New York took place in Carnegie Hall in November 1942. He died in the following March.

Symphony No. 2 in E minor

The reasons for the popularity of this symphony are not far to seek. The themes are eminently melodious, and some of them are of singular beauty; there is rich coloring; there are beautiful nuances in color; there is impressive sonority; there are frequent and sharp contrasts in sentiment, rhythm and expression; there is stirring vitality. Mr. Rachmaninoff in this symphony is romantic in the old and accustomed forms. He does not surprise or perplex by experiments in harmony; his form is essentially academic and traditional. Here is another case of new wine in old leather bottles, but first of all the bottles are put in thorough order, patched, strengthened, cleaned.

. . . Mr. Rachmaninoff has written beautiful and eloquent music in this symphony. He has shown a technical skill and revealed an emotional side that he has concealed in other compositions. Whether he would show inspiration outside of traditional forms; whether he has imagination in sufficient degree to shape wondrous thoughts in a freer form and be a law not only to himself but to his hearers—these questions we shall call unnecessary.

This symphony, composed at Dresden, was played at Moscow at a concert of the Imperial Russian Music Society in the course of the season of 1908-1909. The composer conducted. The Symphony, dedicated to S. Taneiev, is scored for three flutes (and piccolo), three oboes, English horn, two clarinets, bass clarinet, two bassoons, four horns, three trumpets, three trombones, bass tuba, kettledrums, snare drum, bass drum, cymbals, glockenspiel and the usual strings. . . .

PHILIP HALE, *Boston Symphony Orchestra*

Piano concerto No. 2 in C minor (Opus 18)

Rachmaninoff's career in the United States, as conductor and soloist, is intimately bound up with the Philadelphia Orchestra. The great Russian master's American debut as conductor was made in Philadelphia, in the Academy of Music, on November 26, 1909, when he led our Orchestra in an all-Russian program. Not three weeks before, he had made his bow as soloist with the orchestra in the same venerable hall. At that time, with Max Fiedler conducting the Boston Symphony Orchestra, Rachmaninoff performed his *Concerto No. 2 in G minor.*

This work was undertaken early in 1900. The second and third movements were completed by fall, and were performed at one of the Prison Charity Concerts organized by the Princess Lieven in Moscow, on October 14, 1900. The composer was at the piano, Alexander Siloti conducted. By spring of the following year the opening movement was finished, and the whole Concerto had its first hearing during the winter of 1902, in London, at a London Philharmonic Concert. (These dates are reported by Riesemann and Lyle; they differ from those published in certain of our American symphony orchestra program notes.)

When the *Concerto in C minor* was published in 1901, there appeared on the title page a dedication to Dr. N. Dahl, which caused considerable speculation. Years later, Rachmaninoff, in his *Recollections,* relates how this came about:

In 1897, his first symphony was performed in St. Petersburg and met with such signal failure that the young composer fell into a state of apathy from which he could not rouse himself. "It is true that the performance was beneath contempt," the master confesses, "and the work in part was unrecognizable, but, apart from this, its deficiencies were revealed to me with a dreadful distinctness even during the first rehearsal. Something within me snapped. All my self-confidence broke down, and the artistic satisfaction that I had looked forward to was never realized."

This state of mind possessed the aspiring youth so completely that he resolved to give up composing altogether. "A paralyzing apathy possessed me. I did nothing at all and found no pleasure in anything. Half my days were spent on a couch sighing over my ruined life. My only occupation consisted in giving a few piano lessons in order to keep myself alive." For more than a year this depression persisted; it affected the composer's health to such a degree that his kinsmen, with whom he was living at the time, the Satins, urged him to seek health from a certain Dr. Dahl who was causing quite a stir in Moscow by the cures which he was effecting by means of autosuggestion. Anything was worth trying once, so Rachmaninoff agreed. For four months he spent hours in Dr. Dahl's consulting rooms, "day by day, in every way, growing better and better." We quote Rachmaninoff's account of his experience:

"My relatives had informed Dr. Dahl that he must by all means cure me of my apathetic condition and bring about such results that I would again be able to compose. Dahl had inquired what kind of composition was desired of me, and he was informed 'a concerto for pianoforte,' for I had promised this to people in London and had given up in despair the idea of writing it. In consequence, I heard repeated, day after day, the same hypnotic formula, as I lay half somnolent in an armchair in Dr. Dahl's consulting room. 'You will start to compose a concerto—You will work with the greatest of ease—The composition will be of excellent quality.' Always it was the same, without interruption.

"Although it may seem impossible to believe, this treatment really helped me. I began to compose at the beginning of the summer. The material grew in volume, and new musical ideas began to well up within me, many more than I needed for my concerto. By autumn I had completed two movements of the Concerto—the Andante and the Finale. These I played during the same autumn at a charity benefit concert conducted by Siloti. The two movements resulted in a gratifying success. This heightened my confidence to such an extent that I began once more to compose with great ardor. By the spring I had already completed the first movement of the concerto and the Suite for two pianos. I felt that Dr. Dahl's treatment had strengthened my nervous system to a degree almost miraculous. Out of gratitude I dedicated my Second Concerto to him."

LOUISE BECK, *Philadelphia Orchestra*

Rhapsody on a Theme of Paganini (Opus 43)

The story of this work, like that of many of Rachmaninoff's compositions, lies close to the heart of the Philadelphia Orchestra, for through the three-way collaboration of the composer as pianist, Conductor Leopold Stokowski and the musicians of the orchestra, it was given its world premiere at a concert in Baltimore's Lyric Theater, November 7, 1934. Cutting short his concert tour the previous spring, Rachmaninoff had returned to his summer home on Lake Lucerne to concentrate on this Rhapsody. It was composed between July 3 and August 24, and has since been widely performed both by Rachmaninoff himself and other famous virtuosi.

The Rhapsody consists of a short introduction and twenty-four variations. The theme itself is withheld until the first variation, when it is stated in full by the violins. Most of the variations are brief, contrasting to the utmost in mood and treatment, embroidered with engaging countermelodies and arabesques in both solo and accompaniment. One unusual feature is the addition in three variations of the somber theme from the *Dies Irae,* that portion of the Catholic Requiem Mass for the Dead which comments on the Day of Judgment. The piano first intones the solemn melody in variation seven; in variation ten the strings take it up while the piano does a whirling variant of the Paganini theme; and in the final variation the whole orchestra blares forth ominously with the *Dies Irae* while the solo instrument forges madly ahead with the original theme in a tempestuous finale.

Benno Moisseiwitsch . . . friend and admirer of Rachmaninoff, tells an anecdote about the composer's troubles in practicing the final variation for concert performance. The episode occurred in 1934 at the home of Mrs. Steinway, following one of Rachmaninoff's superb Carnegie Hall recitals. During dinner, he discussed with Moisseiwitsch a new work which he would soon introduce for the first time, a Rhapsody and Variations on a Theme by Paganini, but he seemed worried while describing it. Moisseiwitsch recounts the conversation thus:

" 'I wrote the Rhapsody down,' he said in his slow drawl, 'and it looked good. Then I went to the piano and tried it and it sounded good, but now, when I am practicing it for the concert, it all goes wrong!' He was referring to the twenty-fourth variation, and his difficulty was in getting through the chord jumps, always a formidable problem in the Paganini variations. I did not know the work at all and could not offer any suggestions but just then the Steinway butler came to my rescue. He had just entered with a tray full of a wonderful array of liqueurs. Everyone helped himself to a drink, but Rachmaninoff, as was his custom, refused. Here I stepped in, saying: 'Sergei Vassileivich, do have a glass of this beautiful crême de menthe.'

"He waved the butler aside and said to me: 'You know I never drink any alcohol.'

" 'Yes, I know that,' I replied, 'but do you know that crême de menthe is the best thing in the world for jumps.'

" 'Do you mean it?' he asked dubiously.

" 'Definitely,' I replied. So he called back the butler and helped himself to a generous portion of crême de menthe. Afterwards, when we joined the ladies in the drawing room, he sketched some of his variations, including a faultless execution of the one with the jumps. I reminded him of my inspired suggestion, and he thanked me very seriously for my help.

"Eyewitness accounts and Rachmaninoff's own assertions have it that he always had a glass of crème de menthe before playing the Rhapsody in public. Hence the superscription to the final variation: 'The Crème de Menthe Variation'!"

DONALD L. ENGLE, *Philadelphia Orchestra*

The Isle of the Dead

Rachmaninoff himself conducted the first performance of his symphonic poem in 1909 at a concert of the Moscow Philharmonic. Its American premiere occurred at a concert of the Theodore Thomas Orchestra in Chicago on December 3, 1909.

Böcklin's famous picture was painted in 1880, though it was not till the summer of 1909 that Rachmaninoff saw it in Paris and resolved on the spot to suggest its macabre moods and implications in music.

Of the painting itself, Böcklin had earlier written to a friend that "it must produce such an effect of stillness that anyone would be frightened to hear a knock at the door." Several other composers, among them Anders Hallen and Prince Joachim Albrecht of Prussia have also attempted to translate the Swiss master's picture into music.

Böcklin's *Toteninsel* was not wholly a creation of his imagination. There is evidence that the sight of the brooding Ponza Islands, which lie north of the Gulf of Naples, impressed him deeply, one in particular—the remaining half of what had once been a volcano peak.

"The waves in the course of centuries shaped a little haven," wrote Philip Hale. "Birds brought the seeds of cypress trees. The trees in time shot up in the ledges. At last man came, and made paths and hollowed chambers and threw up a rough wall as a protection against the waves.

"The island even then was as solemn as a pyramid. It was a hidden nook for the dead that wished to lie undisturbed. Böcklin expressed this rest of the dead in a place remote and forgotten by the world. The sea is still, there is no cry of the bird, no fluttering, no voice.

"The boat approaching the little harbor of the island with its towering blue-green cypresses and awful rocks is rowed noiselessly by the ferryman. The white and quiet figure near the coffin—is it some mourner or is it a priest"?

Dedicated to Nicholas von Sturve, Rachmaninoff's Symphonic Poem is scored for three flutes, piccolo, two oboes, English horn, two clarinets, bass clarinet, two bassoons, six horns, three trumpets, three trombones, tuba, kettledrums, bass drum, cymbals, harp and strings.

LOUIS BIANCOLLI, *Philharmonic-Symphony Society of New York*

MAURICE JOSEPH RAVEL

(Born in Ciboure, France, March 7, 1875—died in
Paris December 28, 1937)

RAVEL has become something of a legendary figure in the purlieus of modern orchestration. A musical descendant of Debussy and of Vincent d'Indy, ascetic and romanticist in one, a pictorialist and master of the iridescent school, he has exerted an enormous influence upon the subsequent technique of all orchestration.

Despite the glamour of his work, the meticulous precision of his style and the subtlety of his orchestral coloring, Maurice Ravel led a rather colorless life. No momentous passion of his soul overwhelmed his art, nor did he speak in his music of an inner tempest that rocked his soul. On the contrary, he has been described as "a channel through which music flowed," the detached and superlative craftsman untroubled by personal emotion.

He was a dapper little man. I remember that when he appeared in the now-defunct Century Theater in New York, during the winter of 1929, he seemed almost insignificant in presence and stature, and that I thought him an indifferent pianist. His air of simplicity gave an impression of being affected for the occasion.

"He was completely unbusinesslike," writes Madeleine Goss, "and did not even want pupils to pay for their lessons; made barely enough from his compositions and concerts to live in comfortable but modest style." At home and among his friends, he showed a rare charm. "All leading musicians of the day found their way at one time or another to the 'doll's house' at the top of the hill in Montfort l'Amaury. There were gay parties with hours of music and endless discussion."

Enrolled at the Paris Conservatoire in 1889, he studied composition with Gabriel Faure, "who exerted a profound influence upon him." Four years after beginning his lessons with Faure, he composed a cantata, *Mirrha,* which won the second *Prix de Rome.* The pianist Ricardo Viñés introduced his first important piano pieces, *Jeux d'Eau* and *Pavanne pour une Infante Defúnte,* in 1902. Two years later his Quartet in F major, played in Paris, "made a striking impression."

The *Histoire Naturelles* raised a furore of controversy in 1907, leading critics denouncing Ravel as "an imitator of Debussy." A few demurred, however, pointing out certain individual virtues entirely divorced from Debussy. Apparently he won the issue, attaching in the process of argument a new multitude of adherents, and in the next three years composed a series of remarkable works which served to establish him firmly as an important figure in French music.

These works included the orchestral *Rapsodie Espagnole,* the one-act opera *L'Heure Espagnole,* and the *Mother Goose* suite for four hands. But one of the great masterpieces of modern orchestration was to come. Diaghilev commissioned him in 1910 to write the score for a proposed ballet, *Daphnis et Chloé.* It was produced on June 12, 1912 and attained an extraordinary success.

He served in the French Army during the First World War as a motorist in the Ambulance Corps. When the war ended, he returned to France and bought a villa at Montfort L'Amaury; where he lived for the rest of his life, composing *Bolero, La Valse, L'Enfant et les Sortilèges,* and a piano concerto. The one-armed pianist, Paul Wittgenstein, ordered from him a piano Concerto for the Left Hand. He also wrote a cycle of three songs, *Don Quichotte à Dulcinée* for the film starring Feodor Chaliapin.

An operation was performed to remove a brain tumor, but it was not successful and he died in Paris in 1937. News of his death came as a distinct shock to the entire musical world and his passing was mourned sincerely by the entire profession.

Ravel never regarded himself as a "modern" composer in the strictest sense of that abused term. Interviewed by David Ewen for the magazine *Etude,* Ravel said:

"Although I have always been open-minded to new ideas in music (one of my violin sonatas contains a Blues movement) I have never attempted in it to overthrow the accepted rules of harmony and composition. On the contrary, I have always drawn liberally from the masters for my inspiration (I have never ceased studying Mozart), and my music, for the most part, is built upon the traditions of the past and is an outgrowth of it. I am not a 'modern composer' with a flair for writing radical harmonies and disjointed counterpoint because I have never been a slave to any one style of composition."

Bolero

Ida Rubinstein, the noted mime, dancer and actress, commissioned Maurice Ravel to write a piece of music for a dance pantomime with a Spanish setting. The outcome was Ravel's avowedly experimental *Bolero.*

With Mme. Rubinstein as the tantalizing dancer who enacts the bolero on a tabletop in a Spanish inn, the work was produced at the Paris Opéra on November 22, 1928. The action involves a cannily worked-up crescendo of passion. The men gathered in the public room of the inn eye the dancer fixedly. As her movements grow more animated, their excitement mounts. They beat out an obbligato with their hands and pound their heels. At the peak of the crescendo, where the key abruptly shifts from C major to E major, the sharpening tension snaps. Knives are drawn and there is a wild tavern brawl.

"I am particularly desirous that there should be no misunderstanding about this work," Ravel said to the critic, M. D. Calvocoressi. "It constitutes an experiment in a very special and limited direction and should not be suspected of aiming at achieving anything different from or anything more than it actually does achieve.

"Before its first performance I issued a warning to the effect that what I had written was a piece lasting seventeen minutes and consisting wholly of 'orchestral tissue without music'—of one long, very gradual crescendo. There are no contrasts. There is practically no invention except the plan and manner of execution . . . I have carried out exactly what I intended and it is for the listener to take it or leave it."

Staged widely in Europe and America, *Bolero* was first performed in this country as a concert number at a Carnegie Hall concert of the Philharmonic-Symphony conducted by Arturo Toscanini. The date was November 14, 1929. The audience was scarcely prepared for the sensation. Few of the musicians suspected at rehearsals that they were working on a bombshell. The effect on the Carnegie audience was almost unprecedented. Many critics joined in the frantic storms of applause.

"If it had been the American custom to repeat a number at a symphonic concert," said Pitts Sanborn, "*Bolero* would surely have been encored, even at the risk of mass wreckage of the nerves!" Sanborn, ordinarily a sedate observer, for once joined the cheering throng.

"For the prime object of *Bolero* musically is the creation of nervous tension," he wrote. "A two-limbed melody of Spanish character, uttered first by the flute, after the drum has given out the rhythm, is reiterated by solo instruments in groups while the volume of sound increases steadily, inexorably.

"When it seems that human nerves can endure no more, the key shift comes with the impact of dynamite. This Philharmonic-Symphony debut made *Bolero* an American craze."

LOUIS BIANCOLLI, *Philharmonic-Symphony Society of New York*

La Valse—Poème Choréographique

Ravel completed his *La Valse, Poème Choréographique* in 1920 and played it in an arrangement for two pianos with Alfredo Casella in Vienna in November of that year. The first performance of the full score was at a Lamoureux Concert in Paris on December 12, 1920.

The score was published in 1921, and dedicated to Misia Sert, the painter who designed the scenery for Diaghileff's production of Richard Strauss' ballet *The Legend of Joseph*.

Alfredo Casella once stated that Ravel, sketching *La Valse* during the First World War, entertained indefinite ideas of a dance production of his *poème choréographique*. Whatever these ideas may have been, they came to nothing, and no other "purpose" has been suggested for this music. If the score is based upon measures that might have flowed from the pen of one of the Strausses, it is of an intent that the family would never have considered—an intent which Ravel indicates neither in his tempo indications, "Movement of a Viennese Waltz," nor in the description which is printed in the score:

"At first the scene is dimmed by a kind of whirling mist, through which one discerns, vaguely and intermittently, the waltzing couples. Little by little the vapors disperse, the illumination grows brighter, revealing an immense ballroom filled with dancers; the blaze of the chandeliers comes to full splendor. An Imperial Court about 1855." . . . .

H. T. Parker, remembering the suggestion that the poem is in three parts—"The birth of the waltz"; "The Waltz" and "The Apotheosis of the Waltz"—notes that the waltz rhythm is gradually established from "shadowy, formless spectres of dead waltzes, drifting through grey mists. . . ."

"Then ensues," he continues, "a succession, as it were, of waltzes. The waltz sensuous and languorous, the waltz playful and piquant, the waltz sentimental, the waltz showy, the waltz strenuous—the waltz in as many variants and as many garbs as Ravel's imagination and resource may compass. Like sheep-chasings, waltz succeeds waltz; yet Ravel is wide-awake in the tenseness with which he sums and characterizes each; in the vivid and artful instrumental dress every one receives.

"Of a sudden, the chain of waltzes seems to break. Fragments of them crackle and jar, each against each, in the tonal air. The harmonies roughen; there are few euphonies; through a surface brilliance, harsh progressions jut; that which has been sensuous, may, for the instant, sound ugly.

"As some say, here is the music that imaginative minds write in this world of the aftermath of war. On the surface the sensuous glow and glint of neurotic rapture—'Dance that ye may not know and feel!' Below the surface and grating rude and grim upon it, are stress and turbulence, despairs and angers equally ugly, and maybe, nigh to bursting. A troubled 'apotheosis,' then, in these culminating measures of the waltz in this world of ours."

GEORGE H. L. SMITH, *Cleveland Orchestra*

Rapsodie Espagnole

In a letter about Ravel, published in *Revue Musicale*, April 1925, André Suarez wrote: "I recognize Spain all through Ravel, in what he is, as well as in what he does. This little man, so quaint, nervous, slender, yet unyielding; that cajoling rigidity with the suppleness of laminated steel; that great nose, those sunken eyes, that angular, slim form; his manner, a little distant, but so courteous; refined in appearance, abrupt in behavior, yet without uncivility; restricted gestures; warmth of embers which forbid themselves to flare up—this is the Spanish *grillon*." (The translation of this letter has been quoted from Madeleine Goss' biography of Ravel, *Bolero*).

Long before he wrote his *Spanish Rhapsody*, Ravel had written the *Habanera* in typical Spanish idiom. He had not had it published, for some reason, so he used it as one of the movements of the Rhapsody. Since then, of course, it has been published separately, transcribed for almost every instrument, and played so frequently, that it has become almost a "Ravel theme song."

The *Spanish Rhapsody* was begun in the summer of 1907. Ravel hoped to finish it in time for the fall music season, but he always worked slowly, in the first place, and this time he worked more slowly than usual, for the task proved to be an arduous one, partly because the noise of Paris streets distracted the composer and partly because the Rhapsody was his first work on a major scale. Like a sensible person he fled from the noise, and thanks to some friends who offered him their yacht, he became a recluse. The quietude of the sea and the hermit-like life he lived enabled him to concentrate all his energies on his music. The Rhapsody was finished by early fall. It was first played at the Concerts Colonne, Paris, March 19, 1908, with E. Colonne directing the orchestra.

The Rhapsody was enthusiastically received. The second movement, a Malagueña, was repeated. . . .

One final quotation from Mrs. Goss' book, the first full-length biographical and critical study of the composer written in English: "*Rapsodie Espagnole* is essentially an orchestral study. Here for the first time the full power and color of Ravel's orchestration is in dazzling evidence. Subtle and penetrating contrasts; crescendos of breathtaking intensity, pianissimos faint as a whisper, wild dance rhythms, and heavy lethargy follow each other in bewildering succession."

WALTER WHITWORTH, *Indianapolis Symphony Orchestra*

Alborada del Gracioso

Ravel wrote a series of five piano pieces, *Miroirs,* in 1905. These bear the titles *Noctuelles, Oiseaux Triestes, Une Barque sur L'Ocean, Alborada del Gracioso* and *La Vallée des Cloches.* The third and fourth he transcribed for orchestra. The orchestral version of *Alborada del Gracioso* was first performed, from the manuscript, at a concert of the Boston Orchestral Club, George Longy, conductor, on February 16, 1921; it was published in 1923.

Alborada del Gracioso is a title to conjure with. It is purposefully seductive, purposefully elusive. The *alborada* is a morning serenade (French *aubade*) and derives its name from the Spanish word *albor,* meaning "whiteness" or "dawn." An *alborada* is a "serenade" at dawn, just as a *serenata* (from *sera,* Italian, "evening") is a "serenade" in the evening. Certainly Ravel had in mind something far more evocative than a folk piece "played on bagpipes to the accompaniment of a side drum" (as the dictionary describes it) or the rather obvious rhythms of Rimsky-Korsakoff's *alborada* in the *Spanish Caprice.*

Gracioso is the term applied to the comic character of the sixteenth century Spanish comedy. M. Jean-Aubry, writing of Ravel's work, translates the title as *Morning Song of the Gracioso* and considers *gracioso* a word that cannot be translated. "It implies a kind of buffoon full of finesse, with mind always alert, and with irony ever in readiness—rather like Figaro. For the ever-alert mind of this type of character; it would seem as if night were never present; for him it is ever the hour of the *aubade,* always the hour of smiles and delicacy. He is skilled in pleasant mockery, and is loath to vociferate. He enjoys the sweetness of living and is not unaware of its reflections. He dreams of charming memories, and long before, composed a pavane to the memory of a defunct infanta, and its delicacy and finesse are such that the idea of death is screened behind them." Thus merging the subject and its author in a conceit of its own, M. Jean-Aubry adds that "this early piece revealed, long ago, Maurice Ravel's taste for delicately chiseled work, and a slight leaning to witty affection."

G. H. L. SMITH, *Cleveland Orchestra*

Suites from the ballet: *Daphnis et Chloé*

Daphis and Chloé was Ravel's contribution to the repertoire of the Diaghilev Ballet Russe. It was first produced in Paris in 1910 with choreography by Michael Fokine, with Nijinsky and Karsavina in the name parts, Adolph Bolm and Enrico Cecchetti in the other roles, and Pierre Monteux conducting.

The elaborate plot was adapted by Fokine from the famous Greek pastoral novel of the same name written in the Fourth Century A. D., by a highly mysterious author named Longus. Daphnis and Chloé are shepherd lovers. Their adventures are too many and involved to detail here. Suffice it to say that at one stage in the action of the ballet Chloé is carried off by pirates. The First Suite contains the music of Daphnis' prayer to Pan for her safekeeping, a choral interlude and the dance in the pirates' camp.

The Second Suite contains the music that accompanies Chloé's return, the pantomime of Daphnis and Chloé in honor of Pan, and the general dance of rejoicing.

Suite No. 1—The setting of the "Nocturne" is the entrance to the temple of Pan from which, but a moment before, Chloé has been kidnapped. Daphnis has come too late to save her, and has thrown himself upon the ground. Then comes the "Nocturne," the action of which is described as follows in the score:

"A little flame shines suddenly above the head of one of the statues in the grotto. The nymph moves and descends from her pedestal. A second and a third nymph join her and they begin a slow, mysterious dance. They perceive Daphnis, bend over him and wipe away his tears. They arouse him and conduct him to the altar stone. Little by little the form of the god becomes visible. Daphnis prostrates himself in supplication."

The "interlude" follows without pause. It is sung by a wordless chorus, behind the scenes. Calls of trumpet and horn come in behind the chorus and lead into the "Warlike Dance."

"A dim light. We are in the camp of the pirates. A rugged coast, the sea in the background, with rocks to the right and left. A *trireme* is near the shore, and cypresses grow about. We see the pirates running here and there, laden with booty. Torches are brought in, which at the end throw a lurid light on the scene."

Suite No. 2: "Daybreak." No sound but the murmur of rivulets fed by the dew that trickles from the rocks. Daphnis lies stretched before the grotto of the nymphs. Little by little the day dawns. The songs of birds are heard. Afar off a shepherd leads his flock. Another shepherd crosses the back of the stage. Herdsmen enter, seeking Daphnis and Chloé. They find Daphnis and awaken him. In anguish, he looks about for Chloé. She at last appears encircled by shepherdesses. The two rush into each other's arms. Daphnis observes Chloé's crown. His dream was a prophetic vision, the intervention of Pan is manifest. The old shepherd, Lammon, explains that Pan saved Chloé in remembrance of the nymph Syrinx, whom the god loved.

"Pantomime." "Daphnis and Chloé mime the story of Pan and Syrinx. Chloé impersonates the nymph wandering over the meadows. Daphnis as Pan appears and declares his love for her. The nymph repulses him, the god becomes more insistent. She disappears among the reeds. In desperation he plucks some stalks, fashions a flute, and on it plays a melancholy tune. Chloé comes out and by her accent imitates the accents of the flute. (This movement goes without pause into the following:)

"General Dance." "The dance grows more and more animated. In mad whirlings Chloé falls into the arms of Daphnis. Before the altar of the nymphs he swears on two sheep his fidelity. Young girls enter; they are dressed as Bacchantes and shake their tambourines. Daphnis and Chloé embrace tenderly. A group of young men comes on the stage. Joyous tumult. A general dance. Daphnis and Chloé."

ALFRED FRANKENSTEIN, *San Francisco Symphony Orchestra*

Le Tombeau de Couperin

As is often the case with Ravel, the title of this work embodies several subtle references, and translation is therefore impossible.

It was common practice for French composers of the seventeenth century to write collections of instrumental pieces in memory of their departed colleagues; the generic name for such collections was *tombeau,* a word which literally means "tombstone." Couperin himself composed several *tombeaux,* the best known of which is the *Concert instrumental sous le titre de Apothéose composé a la mémoire immortelle de l'incomparable Monsieur de Lully.*"

Ravel wrote his *Tombeau de Couperin* in 1917, after three years of service in the French Army. Originally, it was a piano suite in six movements, each of them dedicated to the memory of a companion-at-arms who had been killed by the Germans on the Western Front. This was a time when, as a result of the war, French composers were acutely conscious of their French musical heritage—when, for instance, Ravel's most famous contemporary was calling himself "Claude Debussy, musicien Français," and was composing a set of instrumental sonatas invoking the spirit of Couperin, if not his actual forms and textures.

The orchestral *Tombeau de Couperin* consists of a Prelude and three dance movements like those of the classic Suite. The Minuet needs no discussion. The "Forlane" is a gay Italian dance usually in 6-4 or 6-8 time; its name suggests that it may have originated in Forli, but it is particularly associated with Venice. The "Rigaudon" is a lively French dance in 2-4 or 4-4 time.

ALFRED FRANKENSTEIN, *San Francisco Symphony Orchestra*

Pavane pour une Infante defunte

This little masterpiece is an arrangement for orchestra of an early composition for piano. Who the Infanta was, for whom Ravel here assumed the function of a Bossuet is not stated. Neither would it serve any purpose to identify her; for the music has wider than individual references. But the strain, gentle and unforced, is attuned to a patrician grief. The Pavane (which may have got its name from Padua, or may also have been originally a Spanish dance) was a dignified and stately step—not associated with death, of course, but of a gravity not unsuitable, nevertheless. And it was Ravel's imagination to see many things of high significance as capable of interpretation in that idealized portrayal of motion with music, more than any other art can convey.

The melody is high and tenuous, it moves with dignity and grace, almost as if there were no tragedy to mourn; but twice this high composure is overmastered and the frail body droops and loses its step; and seeing this, we realize how high the tension was, even from the beginning.

DONALD FERGUSON, *Minneapolis Symphony Orchestra*

Suite: Ma Mère l'oye (Mother Goose)

These "Five Children's Pieces" were originally composed for piano duet, and for the delight of two children, Mimie and Jean Godebski, to whom they were dedicated. They were first performed by two tiny pianists, Christine Verger, aged six, and Germaine Duramy, aged ten, at a concert of the Independent Musical Society

of Paris. This was in 1910. A year later Ravel made a little ballet
out of the Suite. In the ballet, in addition to the original pieces,
there was a Prelude, introducing the five tableaux, and an
Apotheosis, entitled: "The Fairy Garden." The Prelude is omitted
from the orchestral suite.

1—"Pavane of the Sleeping Beauty." This slow movement
is only twenty bars long. It is all made of the opening phrase for
flute, horns and violas.

2—"Hop o' My Thumb." The movement is marked *trés modéré* and is in very irregular rhythm. The theme is announced
by the oboe in the fourth bar and is continued in the English
horn. After some contrasting matter, the first theme returns. Ravel
quotes, in the score, from a version of the tale by Perrault which
involves the episode of the lost boy, trying to find his way home
by means of scattered bread crumbs which the birds have already
eaten.

3—"Laideronette, Empress of the Pagodas." This is a little
march. After eight bars of introduction, the theme appears in the
piccolo, another appears in the oboe followed by the flute. There
is a sort of Trio whose subject is in oboe, celesta and harp, after
which the March returns. Laideronette is a princess, cursed in her
cradle by the fairy Magotine with the most repulsive ugliness.
Living alone in the forest, she meets a green serpent who, it
turns out, was also cursed by the same fairy. Laideronette is ship-
wrecked on a shore inhabited by "Pagodas"—little people whose
bodies are porcelain, crystal, emerald etc. The ruler of the land
is the green serpent. The two are changed to their proper shapes,
are married, and live happily ever after.

4—"The Conversation of Beauty and the Beast." This is a
waltz movement, whose melody is given out by the clarinet. This
is "Beauty." The "Beast" is presently impersonated by the double
bassoon. The two subjects, after a conversation whose purport is
not difficult to imagine, are combined, and at the end the solo violin shows what a lovely creature the Beast really was.

5—"The Fairy Garden." The music is based on the opening
theme. There is, of course, no story, this being the composer's own
epilogue to the Suite.

DONALD FERGUSON, *Minneapolis Symphony Orchestra*

OTTORINO RESPIGHI

(Born in Bologna July 9, 1879—died in Rome,
April 18, 1936)

WHEN HE died of a heart ailment in Rome, at the age of fifty-six, Respighi had had a long and distinguished career. He paid four visits to the United States, the last being in 1932.

His opera, *The Sunken Bell*, was presented at the Metropolitan Opera in New York on November 24, 1928, with Elisabeth Rethberg, Nanette Guilford, Giovanni Martinelli and Ezio Pinza in the leading roles.

For a week during the winter of 1932, he was guest conductor of the Philharmonic and led the premiere of a "mystery" tryptich for concert performance, *Maria Egiziaca*. He described the work as "a mystery play put to music—a combination of the theater and the opera for the concert public."

At this time he conceived a marked affection for "tin-pan alley." Paul Whiteman, he said, was "my hero. I love the way he conducts his band. He has grace. And his music is wonderful, the jazz that is the true American style, and for which I have the greatest respect."

He composed his first work for band in memory of John Philip Sousa, who had died the previous month. This work, "Huntingtower Ballad," was played at a memorial concert for the famous bandmaster in Washington, April 17, 1932.

Respighi began his musical education in 1892, at the Liceo Musicale, in Bologna, and was graduated with first honors in violin and composition. Wavering between the enticements of a virtuoso's career, as opposed to the ascetic pleasures of composition, he resolved upon the latter course and decided to pursue his studies further. He thereupon went to St. Petersburg and the Conservatory, to sit at the feet of Rimsky-Korsakoff. That Master taught him finish and suavity and orchestral courtesy, and he departed for Berlin, determined to polish up his violin technique with the help of Max Bruch.

He was appointed in 1913 to teach composition at the St. Cecilia Academy in Rome and ten years later was chosen by the unanimous voice of a commission, which included Puccini and Cilea, to head the same institution.

He came to the United States in 1925, as soloist with the Philharmonic under Mengelberg, in his own Concerto in the Mixolydian Mode. Josef Stransky and the same orchestra had given the first American performance of *The Fountains of Rome* on February 13, 1919. He returned to Italy in 1927.

During another visit in 1928, he attended the American premiere of his opera, *The Sunken Bell* at the Metropolitan. The work is based upon Gerhart Hauptmann's drama of the same name, first produced in the United States by E. H. Sothern and Virginia Harned.

He himself conducted the world premiere of his *Maria Egiziaca,* presented in Carnegie Hall at a special Philharmonic concert to benefit the orchestra pension fund. This was during his final American visit in 1932.

He stayed in America about a month this time, and became enamored of American jazz, in which "the rhythm came first and the music second," and remarked that "as a new form of music it is interesting to me."

Probably the most popular of his orchestral expressions in the larger forms are the three symphonic poems, *The Fountains of Rome, The Pines of Rome* and *Roman Festivals.* But he has also written many songs, chamber music, a sonata for violin and piano and arrangements of works by Monteverdi, Vitali and Bach.

Symphonic Poem: *The Fountains of Rome*

This is the first of a series of three musical pictures of the Roman scene which constitute the composer's most brilliant contribution to orchestral literature. The second is the even more frequently performed *The Pines of Rome* and the third is called *Roman Festivals.* The *Fountains* was written in 1916 and was first performed under Toscanini two years later. Although it contains no such startling passage as that in the *Pines* which pictures the inexorable march of the Roman army, as if out of the immemorial past into the immediate present, the *Fountains* is perhaps a more sensitive rendition of its subject. The composer prefixed to the score a general statement of the purpose of the music. This will suffice to guide the hearer through the somewhat intricate maze of tone:

The Fountain of the Valle Giulia at dawn; the Triton Fountain at morn; the Fountain of Trevi at midday; and Villa Medici Fountain at sunset are the four fountains in the poem. In this symphonic poem the composer has endeavored to give expression to the sentiments and visions suggested to him by four of Rome's fountains, contemplated at the hour in which their character is most in harmony with the surrounding landscape, or in which their beauty appears most impressive to the observer. The first part of the poem, inspired by the Fountain of Valle Giulia, depicts a pastoral landscape, droves of cattle pass and disappear in the fresh damp mists of a Roman dawn. A sudden loud and insistent blast of horns above the trills of the whole orchestra introduces the second part, the Triton Fountain. It is like a joyous call, summoning groups of naiads and tritons, who come running up, pursuing each other and mingling in a frenzied dance between the jets of water. Next there appears a solemn theme, borne on the undulations of the orchestra. It is the Fountain of Trevi at midday. The solemn theme, passing from the wood to the brass instruments, assumes a triumphal character. Trumpets peal; across the radiant surface of the water there passes Neptune's chariot, drawn by sea horses and followed by a train of sirens and tritons. The procession then vanishes, while faint trumpet blasts resound in the distance. The fourth part, the Villa Medici Fountain, is announced by a sad theme which rises above a subdued warbling. It is the nostalgic hour of sunset. The air is full of sound of tolling bells, birds twittering, leaves rustling. Then all dies peacefully into the quiet of the night."

DONALD FERGUSON, *Minneapolis Symphony Orchestra*

Symphonic Poem: *The Pines of Rome*

Respighi is one of the multitude of composers—good, bad and indifferent—who make you realize what enormous influence Debussy has had on the whole musical generation which followed him. Since the composer of *Pelleas* and *Iberia* was inimitable, these

later emulators have value only so far as they have been able to in-
dividualize the conception of music to which Debussy opened the
way. In all three of Respighi's compositions glorifying the grandeur that was Rome—*The Fountains, The Pines* and *Roman
Festivals*—is found a programmatic purpose much more definite
than Debussy ever suggests, and in addition, a spirit of nationalism recalling, I'm afraid, something of the political propaganda of
the late monster which ruled the fortunes of Italy. The things,
however, which occasioned the most interest and some scandal at
the time of the first performance of the *Pini di Roma* was the
mechanical reproduction of a nightingale's song—a shortcut to
realism of which Aristotle certainly would not have approved.
The preface to the score contains the following description of the
work:

1—"The Pines of the Villa Borghese." Children are at play
in the pine grove of the Villa Borghese, dancing the Italian equivalent of 'Ring-around-the-Rosy'; mimicking marching soldiers and
battles; twittering and shrieking like swallows at evening; and they
disappear. Suddenly the scene changes to—

2—"The Pines Near a Catacomb." We see the shadows of the
pines, which overhang the entrance to the catacomb. From the
depths rises a chant which re-echoes solemnly, like a hymn, and is
then mysteriously silenced.

3—"The Pines of the Janiculum." There is a thrill in the air.
The full moon reveals the profile of the pines of Gianicolo's Hill.
A nightingale sings (represented by a gramophone record of a
nightingale song, heard from the orchestra).

4—"The Pines of the Appian Way." Misty dawn on the Appian Way. The tragic country is guarded by solitary pines. In-
distinctly, incessantly, the rhythm of innumerable steps. To the
poet's fantasy appears a vision of past glories; trumpets blare, and
the army of the Consul advances brilliantly in the grandeur of a
newly risen sun toward the Appian Way, mounting in triumph to
the Capitoline Hill.

BATEMAN EDWARDS, *St. Louis Symphony Orchestra*

Symphonic Poem: *Roman Festivals*

The least debatable and hence by no means the most provocative genius of contemporary [1930] Italy is Ottorino Respighi. .... His views on the subject of modernism were expressed in an interview given to a representative of *Musical America* when, in December 1925, he first arrived in New York.

"Atonality?" he said. "Thank Heaven that's done for! The future course of music? Who can say? I believe that every composer should first of all be individual. As for dissonance, it has its place as a medium of tone-color. It is the same with polytonality. For its own sake it is abhorrent to me, but as a means to expression it has important uses.

"When I say that atonality is 'done for,' I meant it is so far as modern Italian musicians are concerned. In some sense all the contemporary—Pizzetti, Alfano, de Sabata, Tommassini, Casella, Castelnuovo-Tedesco, Malipiero and others—had their beginning in impressionism. We stem from this school, but for some years we have not been of it. The Italian genius is for melody and clarity. Today there is noticeable a return to the less sophisticated music of our past—in harmony to the Church modes, and in form to the suite of dances and other charming forms. This is no doubt good, provided all cling to our individualities and really express them."

In the *Pines* we have not so much an objective picture as an employment of characteristic strains of melody for the evocation of the "sense" of four different and typical Roman scenes, of different periods. In the present work, although the different periods are again presented, and although the spirit of each is conveyed by different melodic types, the very nature of the subject makes imperative the recognition of the scene itself, along with the emotional character proper to it.

Thus the score is prefaced by four short verbal descriptions of the four sections of the poem ....

1—"Circenses." A threatening sky hangs over the Massimo Circus, but it is the people's holiday: *Ave Nero!* The iron doors are unlocked, the strains of a religious song and the howling of wild beasts float on the air. The crowd rises in agitation; unperturbed, the song of the martyrs develops, conquers, and then is lost in the tumult ....

2—"The Jubilee." The pilgrims trail along the highway, praying. Finally appears from the summit of Mount Mario, to ardent eyes and gasping souls, the holy city: Rome! Rome! A hymn of praise bursts forth, the churches ring out their reply. . . . ."

3—"The October Festival." The October Festival in the Roman *Castelli* covered with vines; hunting echoes, tinkling of bells, songs of love. Then in the tender evenfall arises a romantic serenade . . .

4—"The Epiphany." The night before Epiphany in the Piazza Navona; a characteristic rhythm of trumpets dominates the frantic clamour; above the swelling noise float, from time to time, rustic motives, *saltarello,* cadenzas, the strains of a barrel organ, of a booth and the appeal of the proclaimer, the harsh song of the intoxicated and the lively *stornello* in which is expressed the popular feelings: "We are Romans, let us pass! . . . ."

DONALD FERGUSON, *Minneapolis Symphony Orchestra*

NICOLAI ANDREIVITCH RIMSKY-KORSAKOFF

(Born in Tikhvin, Russia, March 18, 1855—died
in St. Petersburg, June 21, 1908)

THE GRANDMOTHERS of Rimsky-Korsakoff were his most important assets. He attributed to his mother's mother his love of folk song; from his father's mother he claimed to have derived a tendency toward music in general, folk music in particular.

His father was sixty, his mother forty-five when he was born; his only brother was twenty-two years older then himself. Andrei, the composer's father, once civil governor of the Volynsky government, had been living in retirement for nine years at the time of Nicolai's birth.

The composer's memoirs best illumine the details of his early years. "The first signs of musical ability," he writes, "showed themselves in me very early. Before I was two I could distinguish all the melodies my mother sang to me; at three or four I was an expert at beating time on a drum to my father's piano playing." He had his first regular lessons at six, from a neighbor, an old lady. He cannot remember whether she was a good teacher, only that he was a bad pupil. "I played inaccurately and was weak at counting," he recalls.

A succession of amateur teachers, in varying degrees of semi-competence, did nothing to alter his lukewarm inclination toward music. Gradually, a single idea began to obsess him. He wanted to be a sailor. His brother, cruising in the Far East, wrote fascinating letters, exciting the boy's imagination beyond measure.

In July of 1856, his father took him to St. Petersburg and enrolled him in the Corps of Naval Cadets. "He seems to have been a good cadet," says Calvocoressi, "and to have been popular with his comrades, though he evidently found the discipline irksome at first."

Fortunately, some friends of his brother then were living in St. Petersburg, the Golovins, and he was allowed to spend each weekend with them. He was introduced to Italian opera in the Golovin household. In the season of 1859-1860 came his first symphony concerts—Beethoven, Mendelssohn and Glinka's *Jota Aragonese*. Then he heard *Russlan* and *Ludmilla* at the Marinski Theater and life, for the moment, was full.

Luckily, "Niki" and Voin, the elder brother, were devoted to each other, even when they found themselves in love with the same girl. "It is delightful," writes Calvocoressi, "to read in the elder brother's reports to their parents of his wise and careful handling of Niki's calf-love, his amused delight in the boy's little gallantries and his taking advantage of the affair to make Niki smarten himself and improve his French."

Meanwhile, his father died, and his mother and uncle moved to St. Petersburg to live with Voin. The latter was appointed director of the Naval College where Niki was a pupil. The dubious Ulich had been supplanted by a capable teacher, F. A. Canille, who brought Bach's fugues to young Korsakoff's attention, gave him choral melodies to harmonize and encouraged him to compose.

His brother made him give up his lessons with Canille, a bitter disappointment. But he met Balakirev in 1861 at Canille's home, also César Cui. He came to be a constant visitor to Balakirev's home, where he encountered the twenty-two-year-old Moussorgsky. Balakirev took a strong fancy to him and opened the eyes of his young friend to "the world of culture outside music."

In the depths of his ignorance, as he confesses, he had begun a symphony in the bizarre key of E-flat minor, and Balakirev insisted that he should go on with it. He finished the first movement, and with Balakirev's help began to orchestrate it. He also wrote the Scherzo and Finale, but before the work could progress further, he was graduated from the Naval College and appointed to the clipper *Almaz*.

A three-years' cruise was in prospect and Niki was in despair at the thought of leaving his new circle of friends. But Voin's common sense ruled the day. "He saw no evidence that his brother was anything more than an intelligent amateur" and decided that a legitimate career in another sphere must not be sacrificed for a whim.

He and Balakirev kept up a fevered correspondence during this long voyage, and he was urged to complete the slow movement of his symphony, but the correspondence almost waned and Nicolai gradually gave up all thought of becoming a serious musician. He wanted only to see the world.

But the ship was ordered home by way of the Pacific, and Rimsky-Korsakoff saw something of New York, Rio de Janeiro, Nice, Toulon, Marseilles, Genoa and Spezia, gambled at Monte Carlo, lost, and returned to Kronstadt a midshipman.

He saw Balakirev and caught a few fleeting glimpses of his own family, was transferred to St. Petersburg and took a furnished room there. He resumed his intimacy with Balakirev and the circle, and since his naval duties required only two or three hours of secretarial work each morning, had ample time to finish his long-dormant symphony.

The symphony was performed at one of Balakirev's Free

School concerts. It was well received, "and the audience were more than a little surprised when a young man in naval uniform appeared to take the applause."

Encouraged by Balakirev's praise of his talent for orchestration, he began a second symphony in B minor (1867), which came to nothing, completed a *Fantasia on Serbian Themes* for one of Balakirev's concerts and the "musical picture" of *Sadko*, the idea for which he owed to Moussorgsky.

In 1871 he was offered the post of Professor of Practical Composition and Instrumentation at the St. Petersburg Conservatory, a position for which he was totally unfitted. He had the bad judgment to accept. Yet he "bluffed his way through with astounding success," says Calvocoressi, teaching himself the while.

Yet this most incompetent of professors, by dint of shrewdness and hard work, managed to make himself a very great teacher, "the greatest composition teacher Russia has so far managed to produce."

His brother Voin died in the autumn of that year in which he first began to teach at the Conservatory, and he was sent to Italy to bring home his brother's body. In the course of this journey, he maintained an ardent correspondence with Nadejda Purgold. On his return to St. Petersburg the courtship developed and they were married June 30 (July 12) 1872, Moussorgsky acting as best man.

His wife was far more adequately trained as a musician than he, besides being a composer of recognized worth, and she rapidly became the chief formative influence in his life.

His opera, *The Maid of Pskov* was produced at the Marynski Theater on January 1 (13), 1873 and was performed nine times more before the season ended. The press did not like it, yet the revolutionary element in it so captured the fancy of young people that Borodin's students sang the rebel chorus in the second act about the corridors of the Army Medical Academy, which might have caused serious trouble for the composer, but for the official favor he enjoyed through the friendship of one Krabbe, Minister of Marine, [who, having consistently opposed Nicholas' brother, Voin, conceived a belated liking for Nicholas.]

Within the next few years, his tendencies as a composer and

one or two ventures into the forbidden field of chamber music, earned him the aversion of most of his old comrades, particularly Moussorgsky.

He edited and scored Moussorgsky's opera, *Khovanstchina;* completed another opera of his own, *The Snow Maiden* which, like *May Night,* had a bad press and a reasonable success.

Balakirev was appointed Intendant of the Imperial Chapel in 1883 and brought in Rimsky-Korsakoff as his assistant.

He was deeply affected by the death of Borodin, in February 1887, and set about finishing and orchestrating *Prince Igor,* with the assistance of Glazounoff.

He heard a performance of Wagner's complete *Ring,* when Neumann's Traveling Opera Company visited St. Petersburg. He and Glazounoff attended every rehearsal, following from the score. "Wagner's handling of the orchestra astonished both of us," he says, "and from this time onward Wagner's methods gradually permeated our orchestral writing."

In the summer of 1892, he experienced what might be suspected nowadays as the start of a nervous breakdown, while engaged in a myriad tangle of musical tasks. For a time music was strangely repugnant to him, despite the brilliant premiere of his opera, *Mlada.*

The distraction of a brief visit to Moscow gave him some relief. He determined to resign his post at the Imperial Chapel, and eventually did so nearly a year later. His little daughter, Masha, who had been ill for nearly two and a half years, grew steadily worse and the family spent the summer in Yalta, hoping that the mild climate would save her. Rimsky-Korsakoff joined them and passed the most wretched summer of his life.

The child died soon after he left to resume his duties in St. Petersburg, and he sank into gloomy apathy. When his family followed him to the capital, they found a new house. Too many poignant memories were attached to his old quarters. The death of Tschaikowsky seemed to rouse him to a sense of duty to his friend, and he insisted upon conducting the first concert of the Russian Symphony Society as a tribute. He resumed direction of the entire series and even turned again to composing. By the summer of 1894 he was working harder than ever.

He completed the editing and reorchestration of Moussorgsky's

Boris in May of 1896 and worked on *Sadko,* produced in Moscow on December 26 (January 7) 1898. It did not reach the Imperial stage of the Marynski Theater until February 1901.

During a visit to Paris, where he conducted some performances of the Diaghilev Ballet Russe, he heard Debussy's *Pelleas et Melisande* and remarked: "I will have nothing more to do with this music, lest I should unhappily develop a liking for it." He heard Strauss conduct *Salome* and met that "rebel in the courtyard," to quote the apt designation of the late Lawrence Gilman. He returned to Russia and resumed work on *The Golden Cockerel.*

The dramatic censor refused to sanction production of this work without cuts in the libretto, to which Rimsky-Korsakoff refused to agree. "So *The Cockerel* won't come out in Russia," he wrote defiantly to the publisher Jurgenson.

On his birthday, in April of 1908, he complained of his heart. He had sat up late that night discussing his book on instrumentation with Steinberg and suffered a severe attack of angina pectoris. Doses of oxygen and morphia, strict rest and diet, were ordered by the doctor. Visitors were barred. This lasted for a week, after which he was allowed to resume, in mild degree, his ordinary life. He was better for a time, then suffered a fresh attack, from which he recovered with difficulty.

His daughter Nadia was married to Maximilian Steinberg, but her father was not present at the wedding and the next day he had a third attack. A fourth attack a few days later was fatal. He was buried in the cemetery of the Novodevitchy Monastery in St. Petersburg.

Overture—*A Night in May*

This opera, based on a story by Gogol, was produced in St. Petersburg in 1880, and was the composer's second opera. The overture is based on folk songs and dances used in the opera. The story concerns the wooing of Hannah by Levko, son of Golova, headman of a village in Little Russia. Golova opposes the match, for he himself is in love with Hannah. A haunted house, a small lake and some water nymphs furnish a romantic background for the story and have a considerable effect on the action. There is a great deal of dancing and rough, boisterous comedy, mistaken identity and similar matters peculiar to opera. Everything is straightened out satisfactorily at last, and Golova resigns Hannah to his son.

PHILIP HALE, *Boston Symphony Orchestra*

"The Flight of the Bumblebee"—from *Tsar Saltan*

The Fairy Tale of Tsar Saltan, his son the Renowned and Mighty Paladin, the Prince Gvidon Saltanovich, and the Beautiful Tsarvna Lebed (Swan), an opera in four acts, seven scenes and a prologue, was composed in 1899-1900. The libretto is based on a fairy tale by Pushkin. The first production took place in Moscow in December 1900. An orchestral suite was performed a short time before the production of the opera.

This Scherzo, which is not in the suite, is in the first scene of the second act, The stage direction is: "Out of the sea comes a bumblebee and flies about the swan."

CYRIL ARTHUR PLAYER, W. K. KELSEY, *Detroit Symphony Orchestra*

Capriccio Espagnol (Opus 34)

The *Capriccio Espagnol*, composed in the summer of 1887, had its first performance at the Russian Symphony Concerts in St. Petersburg, October 31 of the same year—the composer conducting. It was performed at a popular concert under the direction of Anton Seidl at Brighton Beach, New York, in the summer of 1891. The first performance in Boston was at a concert of the Boston Symphony Orchestra, February 15, 1908.

The orchestration includes two flutes and piccolo, two oboes and English horn, two clarinets, two bassoons, four horns, two trumpets, three trombones and tuba, timpani, side drum, bass drum, cymbals, tambourine, castanets, harp and strings. . . . .

It was in the summer of 1887, at a rented villa on a lake shore of the Looga canton, that the *Capriccio* was written. The summer was principally occupied by the very sizable task of filling out a complete orchestration of *Prince Igor*. Borodin had died in the previous winter, and his colleague was fulfilling his usual role of rounding out the opera scores of others in a performable style. A long and assiduous summer was not enough to complete this considerable labor. "In the middle of the summer," writes Rimsky-Korsakoff, "this work was interrupted: I composed the *Spanish Capriccio* from the sketches of my projected virtuoso violin fantasy of Spanish themes. According to my plans, the *Capriccio* was to glitter with dazzling orchestral color and, manifestly, I had not been wrong."

The composer relates, in *My Musical Life,* of the first performance which he conducted in St. Petersburg:

"At the first rehearsal, the first movement (A major, in 2-4) had hardly been finished when the whole orchestra began to applaud. Similar applause followed all the other parts wherever the pauses permitted. I asked the orchestra for the privilege of dedicating the composition to them. General delight was the answer. The *Capriccio* went without difficulties and sounded brilliant. At the concert itself it was played with a perfection and enthusiasm the like of which it never possessed subsequently, even when led by Nikisch himself. Despite its length the composition called for an insistent encore.". . . .

JOHN N. BURK, *Boston Symphony Orchestra*

Scheherazade—Symphonic Poem (Opus 35)
(After *The Thousand Nights and a Night*)

Rimsky-Korsakoff attached this paragraph to the score:
"The Sultan Schahriar, persuaded of the falseness and faithlessness of women, has sworn to put to death each one of his wives after the first night. But the Sultana Scheherazade saved her life by interesting him in tales which she told him during one thousand and one nights. Pricked by curiosity, the Sultan put off his wife's execution from day to day, and at last gave up entirely his bloody plan.

"Many marvels were told Schahriar by the Sultana Scheherazade. For her stories the Sultana borrowed from poets their verses, from folk songs the words; and she strung together tales and adventures."

The composer relates how he has attempted to incite the imagination of his hearers rather than to enchain it by specific episodes:

"The program I had been guided by in composing *Scheherazade* consisted of separate, unconnected episodes and pictures from *The Arabian Nights*; the fantastic narrative of the Prince Kalandar, the Prince and the Princess, the Baghdad festival, and the ship dashing against the rock with the bronze rider upon it. The unifying thread consisted of the brief introductions to Movements I, II and IV and the intermezzo in Movement III, written for violin solo, and delineating Scheherazade herself as telling her wondrous tales to the stern Sultan. The conclusion of Movement IV serves the same artistic purpose.

"In vain do people seek in my suite leading motives linked always and unvaryingly with the same poetic ideas and conceptions. On the contrary, in the majority of cases, all these seeming leitmotifs are nothing but purely musical material in the given motives for symphonic development. These given motives thread and spread over all the movements of the suite, alternating and intertwining each with the other. Appearing as they do each time under different moods, the self-same motives and themes correspond each time to different images, actions and pictures.

"My aversion for the seeking of a too definite program in my composition led me subsequently (in the new edition) to do away with even those hints of it which had lain in the headings of each movement, such as: 'The Sea, and 'Sinbad's Ship,' the 'Kalandar's Narrative,' etc.

"In composing *Scheherazade* I meant those hints to direct but slightly the hearer's fancy on the path which my own fancy had traveled, and to leave more minute and particular conceptions to the will and mood of each listener. All I had desired was that the hearer, if he liked my piece as *symphonic music*, should carry away the impression that it is beyond doubt an Oriental narrative of some numerous and varied fairy-tale wonders, and not merely four pieces played one after the other and composed on the basis of themes common to all the four movements. Why, then, if that be the case, does my suite bear the name, precisely, *Scheherazade?*

Because this name and subtitle (After *The Thousand and One Nights*) connote in everybody's mind the East and fairy-tale wonders; besides, certain details of the musical exposition hint at the fact that all these are various tales of some one person (which happens to be Scheherazade) entertaining, therewith her stern husband."

JOHN N. BURK, *Berkshire Symphonic Festival*

CHARLES CAMILLE SAINT-SAËNS

(Born in Paris, October 9, 1835—died in Algiers, December 16, 1921)

SAINT-SAËNS at eighty-five, still living the full and restless life, was termed by an envious and somewhat younger colleague: "The Beethoven of French music." He was something less than that, perhaps, yet there is at once a magnificence and perfection in his music that lead one to understand the patness of the phrase.

Philip Hale, explaining that Saint-Saëns was "not satisfied with the making of music or the career of a virtuoso," calls him "organist, pianist, caricaturist, dabbler in science, enamored of mathematics and astronomy, amateur comedian, *feuilletonist*, critic, traveler, archaeologist."

He was tremendously active and diversely talented, yet he was thin, nervous, half-sick, irritable, possessed of a consuming discontent and forever wandering into strange places, as though to escape the plaudits of a world grown dull to a mind convinced of its own supremacy.

His father, a government employee, died of consumption at the age of thirty-seven and his mother, fearful that some vestige of the dreadful disease lingered in the frail body of her son, took him to live with her aunt.

"The two women," says Arthur Hervey in his biography, "now concentrated all their affection upon the little child, whose tiny frame was already said to contain germs of the same dread disease which had carried off his father. Fresh country air having been prescribed by the faculty, the baby was put to nurse at Corbeil for the two following years, at the end of which he was brought back to Paris."

He derived great pleasure from listening to the sound of striking clocks, he says, and related how "the symphony of a kettle," set each morning in front of the fire, delighted him, and at two and one-half years he was placed in front of a small piano and struck the notes lovingly one after the other, "and only left them when the sound had evaporated."

And at the age of four years and seven months he played the piano part of a Beethoven violin sonata "before a select audience in a drawing room." At seven, he began to study the piano and harmony, along with Latin, geometry and subjects of equal weight. At ten he made his formal debut as a pianist, at the Salle Pleyel in Paris on May 6, 1846, playing the entire program, difficult and exhausting, from memory.

But his guardians were wise, and after this sensational effort, he was withdrawn from public life to resume his schooling and began to study the organ at the Conservatoire under Benoist.

In December 1852 he was appointed organist of the Church of Saint Merry, a post which he held for five years. Then he gained the same position at the Church of the Madeleine, succeeding the famous Lefébure Wély, who had resigned. It was a great stroke of luck for so young a man, for this was the most fashionable church in Paris.

This post brought an income of 3000 francs a year, and he retained it until 1877, when he was succeeded by his friend Théodore Dubois, who in turn had as his successor Gabriel Fauré. "Various important appointments followed as teacher and instrumentalist, and his name gradually became well established. He tried a second time for the *Prix de Rome* but again was rejected. But three years later, he won over a hundred competitors in a contest sponsored by the Imperial government "on the occasion of the International Exhibition of 1867 for the best setting of a cantata . . ."

Berlioz, on the jury, wrote to a friend of his delight in the success of "his young friend, Camille Saint-Saëns, one of the greatest musicians of our epoch." Camille was decorated with the Legion of Honor in 1868.

He had to wait until 1877 before this opera Le. Timbre d'Argent was produced at the Opéra National Lyrique and then "a somewhat incoherent libretto prevented more than a moderate success. The good offices of Liszt were responsible for the premiere of his most famous opera, Samson et Dalila at Weimar in 1878 and more than twelve years elapsed before it reached Paris.

In the years immediately following the Franco-Prussian War, he worked incessantly and at top speed. He required but eight days to finish his Requiem, a prophetic work, for shortly thereafter domestic tragedy darkened his days. The eldest of his two children, a boy of two, fell from a window and was killed. Then his second son, a baby of seven months, also died. He sought solace in work, and his output at this time was enormous.

His health began to sag under the stress of strenuous work, concert tours and rehearsals and he went to Algeria for a rest. But he returned too soon, we are told, and had to extend the cure at Cauterets.

His health restored, he set to work on a five-act opera with Benvenuto Cellini as the central figure. In deference to Berlioz, who had already composed an opera by this name, he called the new work Ascanio.

He went to Cambridge in 1893 to receive an honorary degree of Doctor of Music—an honor conferred at the same time upon Max Bruch, Tschaikowsky, Boito and Grieg. All were present but Grieg.

Despite the pressure of advancing years, he continued to compose feverishly and to travel afar upon all possible occasions. He went to Buenos Aires; to Saigon; to Norfolk, Connecticut, for the annual Festival; to Birmingham, England; to the Canary Islands and his beloved Algeria for rest and meditation.

He attended the Jubilee Festival in his honor in London on

June 2, 1913. He celebrated his eighty-fifth birthday on October 9, 1920 and in the course of the next year, on one of his Algerian sojourns, Saint-Saëns fell ill and died.

Omphale's Spinning Wheel

Sometimes called the classicist of the romantic period, Saint-Saëns is the perfect foil to the French composers of the Franck-d'Indy group, with his eclecticism, his objectivity, his cleverness, his love for the things of this world. Perhaps typical of his spirit is his own remark: "The artist who does not feel completely satisfied by elegant lines, by harmonious colors, and by a beautiful succession of chords does not understand the art of music."

While he contributed extensively to the field of program music, he always avoided any (to him) excessive emotional expression or tone painting.

Le Rouet d'Omphale, which appeared in 1872, treats an episode in the legendary life of the Greek hero Hercules. Banished from the kingdom because of a quarrel which had resulted in the death of an opponent, he is condemned to penal servitude as a slave for the Lydian Queen, Omphale. Dressed in woman's attire, he performs the menial duties of a serving maid, including the operating of the spinning wheel.

The composer appended to the score an amusing denial of the realism patent in the music. "The subject of this symphonic poem is feminine seductiveness, the triumphant struggle of weakness against force. The wheel is only a pretext, chosen solely from the point of view of the rhythm and the general attractiveness of the piece. Persons who are interested in searching out details will see at letter 'J' Hercules groaning in the bonds which he cannot break, and at letter 'L' Omphale mocking the vain efforts of the hero."

The groans of the giant are sufficiently obvious in the rising melody in the basses in the middle of the piece. Omphale's mocking laughter is heard in an oboe solo, just before the spinning wheel rhythm is resumed.

ROBERT D. W. ADAMS, *Kansas City Philharmonic Orchestra*

Danse Macabre

Saint-Saëns composed the *Danse Macabre* in 1874, and it was first performed at a Concert du Chatelet, Colonne conductor, January 24, 1875, when the violin solo was played by Camille Lelong. The audience was so much pleased that the piece was immediately played a second time.

The composer at first thought of setting music to the poem of Henri Cazalis for a song, and this song was published, but the melody was unsingable, and Saint-Saëns used the sketch in the composition of the orchestral work.

The poem of Cazalis is translated as follows:

> Zig, zig, zig, Death in cadence,
> Striking with his head a tomb,
> Death at midnight plays a dance-tune,
> Zig, zig, zig, on his violin.

> The winter wind blows, and the night is dark;
> Moans are heard in the linden tree.
> Through the gloom white skeletons pass,
> Running and leaping in their shrouds.

> Zig, zig, zig, each one is frisking
> The bones of the dancers are heard to crack—
> But hist! of a sudden they quit the round,
> They push forward, they fly;
> The cock has crowed.

The hour of midnight has struck (harp), and Death tunes his fiddle (the E-string is tuned a half-tone lower). The dance begins in G minor with motive for flute. Death plays his tune, the dance grows wilder, and the xylophone imitates the clattering of dancers' bones.

The second theme is treated in a more languorous manner (B major). The plain song, *Dies Irae,* is introduced but skillfully disguised. The two themes are combined in the climax. And now the pace grows faster and faster, until there is a glimmer of dawn (horns) and the cock crows (oboe). Still a strain of Death's dance tune and the ghostly crowd disappears.

San Francisco Symphony Orchestra

Symphony No. 3 in C minor

This symphony was composed on commission from the Philharmonic Society of London for the concerts of its seventy-third season. Begun early in 1886, it was soon completed and it obtained its first performance in St. James's Hall, London, on May 19 of that year. The occasion was indeed a gala one for Saint-Saëns; he not only conducted his own work, but he appeared as soloist in the Beethoven Piano Concerto in G major. It is worth printing the remainder of the program at that concert which was conducted, except for the Saint-Saëns Symphony, by Sir Arthur Sullivan—obviously in one of his less satiric moods. The list contained Haydn's E flat Symphony (No. 8 of the *Salomon* series); Mozart's *Quando Miro*; the song, "Couplets du Mysoli," from Felicien David's *La Perle du Brésil,* and the Prelude to Wagner's *Die Meistersinger.*

The usual pros and cons took place concerning the merits of the work. Most of the professional critics, however, commended it as a piece of music, fuming, at the same time, against the composer's departure from established ideas of construction. One of them wrote: "Those advanced in the new school as far as M. Saint-Saëns professes to be, should invent new titles for their works. As we have said, there is a great deal to admire in this glowing orchestral rhapsody, but we distinctly decline to term it a 'symphony' "—which about explains the general to-do.

The C minor Symphony was given its first hearing in France at a Conservatoire concert in Paris, January 9, 1887. (Charles Gounod, who was present, is alleged to have said to a friend, as he pointed to Saint-Saëns: "There is the French Beethoven.") The Philharmonic Society of New York played it for the first time on February 19, 1887, under the direction of Theodore Thomas. . . .

The composer, eminently aware that much might be made of the piece's nonconformance with stricter precepts, readied an analysis of it for the world premiere. In that he pointed out that the Symphony "is divided into two parts, after the manner of Saint-Saëns' Fourth Concerto for Piano and Orchestra and Sonata for Piano and Violin. Nevertheless, it includes practically the traditional four movements: the first, checked in development, serves as an introduction to the *adagio,* and the *scherzo* (presto) is connected, after the same manner, with the *finale.* The composer has thus sought to shun in a certain measure the interminable repetitions which are more and more disappearing from instrumental music."

The score of the C minor Symphony carries the inscription: "To the memory of Franz Liszt." The Abbé died a good two months after the premiere, so that those observers who read into certain pages the grief of Saint-Saëns at the passing of his celebrated friend were entirely wrong. Besides, the program at the introductory performance stated simply that the Symphony was composed expressly for the Philharmonic Society of London, implying, of course, dedication.

ROBERT C. BAGAR, *Philharmonic-Symphony Society of New York*

Le Carnival des Animaux

Like Emily Dickinson's poetry, *The Carnival of Animals* was quite evidently written for the solitary pleasure of its creator, though Saint-Saëns did let a few of his friends in on the secret at a privately held Mardi Gras concert, where it was played. Not until after his death was the work played in public, since he had expressly prohibited public performance until then—perhaps feeling that certain bits of satire might be recognized and resented by the particular "animals" he had lampooned. Only one movement of the work—the enchantingly lovely section called "The Swan"—escaped the prohibition; but it, by reason of its curving tranquility, became well-known during his lifetime.

Those who pride themselves on their knowledge of music should listen closely, nevertheless, to make sure that they will not miss a number of musical quotations contained in the score. These include a theme from one of Saint-Saëns' own works, the symphonic poem, *Danse Macabre;* two melodies from Offenbach's *Orpheus in Hades;* a theme from the Ballet of the Sylphs in Berlioz' *Damnation of Faust;* a fragment from the Scherzo of Mendelssohn's *Midsummer Night's Dream* music; some French folk songs; and a fragment of melody from Rossini's *Barber of Seville.*

The instrumentation, besides the usual orchestral instruments, includes prominent parts for two pianos, which frequently occupy the spotlight in true duo-piano fashion.

1—Introduction and Royal March of the Lion. The King of Beasts, suggested by some chromatic rumbling in the bass, is heralded by a fanfare which suggests that something uncommonly important is about to take place. Quite likely, this was just Saint-Saëns' ironic way of poking a bit of fun at the public parade of important (and would-be important) personages.

2—Hens and Cocks. The symphony orchestra's infinite resources here supply just the right sounds for this barnyard vignette.

3—Mules. Since the music is played entirely by the two pianos, and without change of rhythm or dynamics, one may safely conclude that Saint-Saëns took this means of satirizing the concert pianists who depend almost entirely upon technical brilliance.

4—Tortoises. A melody from *Orpheus in Hades*—usually played very rapidly—is here played at "tortoise" speed and, adding to the incongruity, by the lumbering double-basses.

5—The Elephants. Against a waltz rhythm set forth by two pianos, the lower strings state another lumbering melody. It is here that the phrase from Berlioz' *Damnation of Faust* is quoted.

6—Kangaroos. It may be that this "jumpy" music, played by the two pianos, was Saint-Saëns' comment on the concertgoers who hurriedly exchange bits of musical gossip and, by reason thereof, "jump to conclusions."

7—Aquarium. Of this, Charles O'Connell says: "There is pale green, translucent water in the lovely sounds that flow together to make this interesting section. Flute and violin sustain a purling melody, rippling arpeggios from the piano suggest the movement of waters; a *flic* of celesta might be the flirt of a goldfish's tail . . ."

8—Personages with Long Ears. The braying effect produced by glissando passages of the violins gives a clear indication of the identity of the personages.

9—Cuckoo in the Wood. Again the pianos have the theme, and a pretty one it is. At frequent and regular intervals the clarinet joins in by playing just two notes, suggesting not only the cuckoo but also the conversational style of those who draw forth musical opinions and then, feeling themselves on safe ground, voice the equivalent of: "Me, too!"

10—Birds. The music spirals, zooms and dips as rapid flurries of tones from piano and flute convey the feeling of bird-song and bird-flight.

11—Pianists. This musical cartoon contains thematic material which should be familiar to anyone who ever lived near a piano student.

12—Fossils. No doubt, Saint-Saëns is even taking a flight at himself, in this episode, since he quotes a passage for xylophone from his own *Danse Macabre*. Here, too, are bits of several French folk tunes, and a melodic morsel (played by the clarinet) from *The Barber of Seville*.

13—The Swan. Immediately after this treasurable solo for 'cello comes—

14—Finale. With all the smiling good humor and professional brilliance of a magician, Saint-Saëns proceeds to stage a review of all the characters encountered in his *Carnival*.

GEORGE SCHAUN, *Baltimore Symphony Orchestra*

ARNOLD SCHOENBERG

(Born in Vienna, September 13, 1874—now living in Hollywood)

ARNOLD SCHOENBERG is known to the average musiclover for only one composition, *Verklaerte Nacht* (*Transfigured Night*), a work of his earliest period. Yet Schoenberg is one of the most dominant personalities creating music today and as a teacher and innovator has influenced countless contemporary musicians and composers. Many of the trends of modern music are traceable directly to him.

Born in Vienna in 1874, he showed early evidence of talent and, untrained, composed short duets to play for his violin lessons, begun at the age of eight. He remained self-taught in composition until a friend took his music to Alexander von Zemlinsky, who offered to teach him.

At the end of 1901 he moved to Berlin, where he conducted several operettas at the Bunten Theater, and taught at Stern's Conservatory. The same year, he married Zemlinsky's sister, Mathilde.

All of Schoenberg's music written before 1908 falls into what is known as his "tonal" period.

In 1906, he finished his first First Chamber Symphony and started the Second.

Almost simultaneous with his appointment to the Imperial School of Music in Vienna, in 1910, he started his *Treatise on Harmony*. This analysis of composition, which has gone through three revisions, has been hailed with hosannas and hisses. Some musicologists look on it as a musical Bible. Others, like James Gibbons Huneker, the noted music critic, think it should be "universally treated as the product of a madman."

After finishing the *Treatise on Harmony* in 1911, Schoenberg started work on "Pierrot Lunaire." This music, six months in the writing, was premiered in Berlin in the Autumn of 1912. The next year, 1913, was an important one for Schoenberg. His song cycle, "Gurre-Lieder," received its first performance in Vienna on February 23, and he completed his monumental dramatic work "Die Glueckliche Hand" ("The Lucky Hand"), which, however did not receive its premiere until eleven years later, October, 1924.

From 1913 to the 1920's Schoenberg traveled throughout Europe, conducting his own works in Amsterdam, Berlin, Paris and elsewhere. He continued to teach privately.

With the rise of Hitler to power in 1933, like many other artists, he left Germany, first going to Paris and then coming to the United States. When he arrived here the League of Composers, the Library of Congress and other organizations welcomed him by presenting concerts of his own music.

Shortly after he arrived he went to Boston to teach and then was asked to join the faculty of the University of Southern California in Los Angeles, where he has been since 1936.

S. B.

Verklaerte Nacht (Transfigured Night—Opus 4)

The present composition was written originally for a string sextet. However, the composer, aware of the work's rather wide scope, added a double bass part to it, besides making some revisions for the sake of orchestral balance and unity. In this form it has been frequently performed by orchestras.

Verklaerte Nacht, which in translation is *Transfigured Night,* was written in 1899, when Schoenberg was a mere 25, and a pupil of Alexander von Zemlinsky. In all, it took the young Schoenberg three weeks to create this music, which is today the most often played of his works. It was born in a definitely preatonal period in the composer's life and during a time when the Wagnerian influence—emotionalism, chromatics and the rest of the magic—was at its strongest.

The inspiration for *Verklaerte Nacht* came from Richard Dehmel's poem, "Weib und der Welt," a fragment of which is printed on the flyleaf of the score. Henry Krehbiel thus paraphrased that excerpt:

"Two mortals walk through a cold, barren grove. The moon sails over the tall oaks, which send their scrawny branches up through the unclouded moonlight. A woman speaks. She confesses a sin to the man at her side: She is with child, and he is not its father. She had lost belief in happiness and, longing for life's fullness, for motherhood and mother's duty, she had surrendered herself, shuddering, to the embraces of a man she knew not. She had thought herself blessed, but now life had avenged itself upon her, by giving her the love of him she walked with. She staggers onward, gazing with lack-luster eye at the moon which follows her. A man speaks. Let her not burden her soul with thoughts of guilt. See, the moon's sheen enwraps the universe. Together they are driving over chill waters, but a flame from each warms the other. It, too, will transfigure the little stranger, and she will bear the child to him. For she has inspired the brilliant glow within him and made him, too, a child. They sink into each other's arms. Their breaths meet in kisses in the air. Two mortals wander through the wondrous moonlight.". . . .

Verklaerte Nacht consists of five sections. The second refers to the "passionate plaint of the woman, the fourth the sustained answer of the man." The first, third and fifth sections are of "more epic nature and so portray the deep feeling of the people wandering about in the cold, moonlit night."

The listener, of course, will either consider this as abstract music or he will attempt to trace in its measures the progress and implications of the poem's "argument." He is welcome to whichever choice he makes: Dehmel, Schoenberg, Krehbiel, Hale, Wellez having made theirs.

      Robert C. Bagar, *Philharmonic-Symphony Society of New York*

FRANZ PETER SCHUBERT

(Born in Vienna, January 31, 1797—died in Vienna,
November 19, 1828)

There was no more dreamy, improvident and impractical composer in all the history of music, with the possible exception of Mozart, than Franz Schubert. And, like Mozart, he had an inexhaustible and almost incredible gift for melody.

He came of peasant stock and his father was a parish schoolmaster. Nine of his brothers and sisters died in infancy. Yet he grew up with two brothers and a sister—Karl, Ferdinand and

Therese. His mother died and his father married again—and there followed Josefa, Andreas, an accountant and Anton, known as Father Hermann, a Benedictine monk.

Little Franz studied music under Michael Holzer, the parish choirmaster, who said: "When I wished to teach him anything fresh, he always knew it already."

At eleven he sang in the choir of Lichtenthal, the district where he lived, then in the Imperial Choir, where he also played in the orchestra. Probably his first piano piece was a four-hand Fantasia, "containing more than a dozen movements," says Grove. At seventeen he had almost prostrated his masters at the *Convict* with the extent of his ability.

To avoid conscription, he became a teacher in his father's school. For three years he slaved there, hating every minute of it. He was not yet eighteen at the outset and had already written his first symphony. Before he was done with this odious task of teaching he had composed his first Mass.

It was first performed on October 16, 1814 and was repeated at the Augustine Church, Vienna, ten days later, his brother Ferdinand at the organ. In the next year or two he wrote songs, the second and third symphonies, the while he taught diligently in his father's school and studied with Salieri. He saw a chance to get out of this rut, and applied for a government job at Lailbach, near Trieste, but failed to get the post.

He met Franz von Schober, "a young man of good birth and some small means," who had heard his songs and wanted to meet him. He proposed to rescue Schubert and induced him to come and live with him. Flower intimates that Schober led him into dissipation and intemperance. Schubert began to give a few lessons, but soon gave them up and the household was maintained entirely by Schober. Among other works he composed at this time, besides a cantata and part of an opera, were two symphonies—the Fourth, in C minor and the Fifth, in B-flat.

The famous Schubert Circle began to form—Shober, Mayrhofer, the Spaun boys, Vogl, Schwind and Grillparzer etc. He was forced to leave these companions in the summer of 1818, having been engaged as music teacher in the family of Count Johann Esterhazy. He spent a rather uncomfortable summer in Hungary, returned to town with the family late in the fall, but there is no evidence to suppose that he continued his musical ministrations to the Esterhazy children.

The following summer he went on a jaunt into Upper Austria with Vogl, came back to Vienna refreshed and again fell to composing furiously.

Vogl began to use his influence among managers and publishers, for Schubert found his songs and more serious music in demand. The latter took shameful advantage of his generous and impulsive nature, and his total lack of business sense. He persisted in devising music for the stage, although he had no dramatic gift in this direction and all these attempts, hampered by incredibly poor libretti, resulted in failure. The Theatre-an-der-Wien suggested a libretto for a comic opera, *The Magic Harp*. His music met with general favor, but the production proved a fiasco.

In return for being elected an honorary member of the musical society in Graz, he composed two movements of the Symphony in B minor, begun in Vienna on October 30, 1822; scored part of the Third, a scherzo, and left the rest in piano sketch. The score lay hidden for many years in Graz until Herbeck, the conductor, obtained it from Anselm Huttenbrenner, for performance at a Gesellschaft concert in 1865.

Various attempts have been made to finish the *Unfinished,* notably Sir George Grove. Some years ago a phonograph company, celebrating the Schubert Centennial, offered a prize to a contemporary composer who would perform this dubious task. The resultant furore provoked an historic retort from the late Ossip Gabrilowitsch:

"To finish the *Unfinished Symphony* would be like putting arms on the Venus de Milo!"

An excursion to Gastein, in the mountains of the East Tyrol, resulted in the completion of a "grand symphony" accepted by the Musikverein of Vienna and never performed. The score has been lost.

Schubert became seriously ill in the spring of 1823 and entered a hospital. The loss of his hair, of which he was somewhat vain, and the subsequent use of a wig must have been galling. Arthur Hutchings, in the *Master Musician Series* edited by Erik Blom, remarks that "these circumstances, and the medicines used, the constant baths, the illusory 'cure' after the first few months and the later pains in the joints, all point to venereal disease and it is noteworthy that Schubert worshipers are reticent on the subject."

The invalid recovered, wrote rueful letters to his friends and family, that his hair was "growing in" and apologizing for the wig.

From May to October of 1824, he went on a second visit to the Esterhazy estate in Hungary, again as music tutor to the Esterhazy children.

In December 1826, Beethoven lay on his deathbed. After sundry tappings for dropsy, he recovered sufficiently to read through some sixty of Schubert songs and express a desire to see Schubert's piano works and operas. He predicted that Schubert would "make a great stir in the world." Schubert and Anselm Huttenbrenner called upon the dying giant eight days before the end. Schindler was there and asked Beethoven who he would see first. "Let Schubert come," Beethoven mumbled. When Franz and Anselm stood together at the foot of the bed, the Master smiled wearily and said: "You, Anselm, have my mind; Franz, here, has my soul."

But Schubert himself was not far from the end. Poverty-stricken years passed, and one disappointment followed another.

He went to live with his brother Ferdinand, who tried to restore his health, which had deteriorated steadily. Franz planned to take lessons in counterpoint and fugue from Sechter, such was his fantastic modesty. Sechter was then the reigning authority in Vienna on this subject.

He could eat and drink nothing and an obstinate fever made him miserable. He took to his bed in sheer weakness. He was treated again for venereal disease, until unmistakable symptoms of typhus appeared. He grew rapidly weaker as the fever mounted, and his frantic struggles to get out of bed, restrained by Ferdinand, made his condition worse. At length the delirium passed, and he turned his face to the wall, clutched at it "with his poor, tired hands and said in a slow earnest voice: 'Here, here is my end.'" He died in his brother's arms, at three in the afternoon of November 19, 1828.

All his clothes and effects, and his music—more than five hundred works—realized less than eight dollars. He was buried in the churchyard of St. Lorenz and St. Gertrude, three graves away from Beethoven. Schubert now, however, lies buried in the Central Cemetery in Vienna.

Ballet Music from *Rosamunde*

The author of the libretto of Schubert's *Rosamunde* is distinguished for writing the text of two operas of different masters, both of which failed of success on the dramatic stage, though set with enduring melody. The other work is Weber's *Euryanthe,* which was produced in Vienna in the very year when Schubert, having finished the score of *Fierrebras,* wrote the music of *Rosamunde, Princess of Cypress.* The plot is described as tedious and improbable. "Schubert completed the music in five days. It consists of an Overture in D . . . ; three Entr'actes; two numbers of ballet music; a little piece for clarinets, horns and bassoons, called a 'Shepherds' Melody,' of bewitching beauty; a Romance for soprano solo and three choruses . . . The play was brought out on December 20, 1823; the Overture, though the entire orchestral part of the music had only one rehearsal of two hours, was twice redemanded; other numbers were loudly applauded, and Schubert himself was called for at the close; but it only survived one more representation, and then the parts were tied up and forgotten till the year 1867."

The discovery of the *Rosamunde* music by Sir George Grove and Sir Arthur Sullivan is hardly less momentous than Schumann's finding of Schubert's Great Symphony in C Major, or the rescue of the *Unfinished Symphony* in 1865.

The Romance, the Shepherds' chorus, the Entr'acte (in B flat) and the Air de Ballet (in G) belong to the rare treasures of music that are at once beautiful and attractive in their simplicity.

PHILIP N. GOEPP, *Philadelphia Orchestra*

Symphony in B minor (*Unfinished*)

A business session preceded the music-making scheduled for an April evening in 1823 at the meeting of the music society in the little Austrian town of Graz. A member named Jenger got to

his feet and proposed a resolution which had consequences so interesting that it is worth quoting: "Under Paragraph 8 of the statutes," he proceeded with proper formality, "I beg to present the composer, Franz Schubert of Vienna, as a nonresident honorary member, for this composer, though young, has already given promise by his work that he will some day be received as a composer of high rank, and it will certainly be a credit to this association to be the first important society to receive him as an honorary member."

Mr. Jenger's resolution brought forth a showing of hands and a muttering of *ja's,* and the secretary was instructed to send notification of this honor to its recipient. It was September, however, before the new member acknowledged his fraternal bonds with the *Steiermaerkischen Musikverein.* "Worthy Music Society!" he then wrote, "I thank you most heartily for the certificate of honorary membership which you have so kindly sent me, and which, because of long absence from Vienna, I only received a few days ago. May my ardor for music be so successful that some day I shall be completely worthy of this distinction. That I may also express my lively thanks in tones, I will take the liberty to send your society as soon as possible one of my symphonies in score. With exceptional regard for the worthy membership of the society, your most thankful and obedient servant, *Franz Schubert.*"

The score which he "took the liberty of sending" was in fact only the fragment of a symphony he had begun the year before. It was in the key of B minor, and consisted of two movements and a few measures of a third. Why it was not finished remains one of the deep mysteries of musical history. As good an explanation as any is that of Donald Tovey, simply that the remainder did not drive Schubert to the labor of writing it down. He visited Graz in 1827, but neither then nor ever did he have opportunity to hear this music, except in his mind's ear.

The further fate of the two symphonic movements has been traced by the indispensable Philip Hale for the program-books of the Boston Symphony Orchestra. Anselm and Joseph Huettenbrenner were natives of Graz who lived for a time in Vienna, and who were among Schubert's most intimate friends. It was they who had instigated the honorary membership for which this symphony was thanks. Anselm was a musician, and he returned to Graz to live in 1820. Joseph, employed in the Ministry of the Interior, remained in the capital. In 1860, Joseph wrote to Johann Herbeck, then conductor of the concerts of the *Gesellschaft der Musikfreunde,* urging him to perform a work by his brother, Anselm, and saying in the same letter that Anselm had a treasure in Schubert's B minor Symphony.

Not until 1865, did Herbeck visit the aged Anselm at Graz and ask permission to produce one of his works in Vienna. The two turned over yellowing manuscripts in his dusty workroom, and the conductor chose one of ten overtures for performance. That decided, he brought up the other matter.

"It is my purpose," he said, "to bring forward three contemporaries, Schubert, Huettenbrenner and Lachner, in one concert before the Viennese public. It naturally would be very appropriate to represent Schubert by a new work."

"Oh, I have still a lot of things by Schubert," answered the old man, and pulled a mass of papers out of an old-fashioned chest.

Herbeck immediately saw on the cover of a manuscript, *Symphony in H moll* in Schubert's handwriting. He looked it over. "This would do. Will you let me have it copied immediately, at my expense?" "There is no hurry," said Anselm. "Take it with you."

It was performed in Vienna on December 17, 1865. The program opened with Huettenbrenner's Overture in C minor (listed as "new"); then the Symphony ("MS. first time"); two old German Songs, for unaccompanied chorus, arranged by Herbeck, and Mendelssohn's *Italian Symphony.* An obscure point is the program listing of a third movement, *Presto vivace,* D major, for Schubert's Symphony, since he left only nine measures of a scherzo and those are in B minor.

Curious as these antiquarian details may be, the music is quite self-sufficient, as many generations of affectionate listeners have cause to know. It is the quintessence of Schubert, setting forth his vitality and strength, his tender or melancholy depths, his subtle way of dealing with key and color and rhythm.

R. L. F. McCombs, *Philadelphia Orchestra*

Symphony No. 7 in C major

It was in March 1828, Schubert's thirty-first year and the last of his life, that he wrote his famous Symphony in C major. Schubert turned out six in his earliest composing years, from the time that, as a pupil of sixteen at the *Konvikt* (the School of the Imperial Choir at Vienna) he filled sheets with ready music for the small school orchestra in which he was a violinist. In 1816 he wrote his Fourth (*Tragic*) Symphony and his Fifth (without trumpets and drums); in 1818, reaching his twenty-first year, he produced his Sixth in C major, still for a small orchestra. These three works, containing many of the beautiful pages characteristic of the younger Schubert, were yet modest in design, having been planned for the immediate uses of the "Society of Amateurs," the outgrowth of a friendly quartet which had long met as such in his father's house.

Having come of age, the young man turned his musical thoughts away from symphonies which he attempted only twice in the remainder of his life. (He did make, in 1821, a complete outline of a Symphony in E major, with the notation and scoring only partly filled in.) The Symphony has been announced for completion and performance in Vienna this [1933] season, by Felix Weingartner. A *Gastein Symphony*, vaguely referred to in the correspondence, remains a legend, for no trace of it has been found. In 1822 he wrote another, or at least two movements of another. The *Unfinished Symphony* may be said to be the first which Schubert wrote entirely to the prompting of his free musical inclinations, and not to the constricted measure of a group of half-skilled friends who could not muster a trumpeter or a set of kettledrums. . . .

The direct words of Schubert on his more important works are here, as elsewhere, scanty and unreliable. It is known that he presented the score to the *Musikverein* in Vienna. The parts were actually written out and distributed, and the Symphony tried in rehearsal. "The Symphony was soon laid aside," so reports Schubert's early biographer, Kreissle von Hellborn, who in 1861 first published his findings on Schubert's life after consultation with those who knew and remembered him. The score was found to be "too long and difficult, and Schubert advised them to accept and perform in its stead his Sixth Symphony (also in C)."

The tale has been doubted, but it is easy to believe—not that the composer had any qualms about the essential practicability of his score, but that he hastily withdrew his Pegasus before its wings could be entirely clipped by the pedestrian *Gesellschaft.* A Symphony in C major was performed by the Society a month after Schubert's death (December 14, 1828) and repeated in March 1829. Whether it was the great "C major" or the Sixth Symphony in the same key is a point of dispute among the authorities.

In any case, Schubert's last Symphony was unperformed in his lifetime and lay in oblivion until ten years afterward, when Schumann visited Vienna and went through a pile of manuscripts then in possession of Schubert's brother Ferdinand, fastened upon the C major Symphony, and sent a copied score with all dispatch to his friend Mendelssohn, who was then the conductor at Leipzig. Mendelssohn was enthusiastic—as enthusiastic, perhaps, as his nature permitted, although beside the winged words of Schumann on the same subject, his written opinion as expressed to Moscheles sounds cool and measured: "We recently played a remarkable and interesting symphony by Franz Schubert. It is, without doubt, one of the best works which we have lately heard. Bright, fascinating and original throughout, it stands quite at the head of his instrumental works."

The performance at the Gewandhaus (March 21, 1839) was a pronounced success and led to repetitions (there were cuts for these performances). Mendelssohn urged the score upon the secretary of the Philharmonic Society in London, and attempted to put it on a program when he visisted England. The players found this straightforward music unreasonably difficult and laughed at the oft-repeated triplets in the finale; Mendelssohn forthwith withdrew the score, which was not heard in England until many years later (April 5, 1856); even then, it was finally achieved by performances in two installments of two movements at each concert. It is said that a similar derision from the players in Paris also met Habeneck's efforts to introduce the symphony there.

. . . . The work, thus put aside in England for some fifteen years, meanwhile found its first American performance by the Philharmonic Society in New York (January 11, 1851), Mr. Eisfeld conducting. It had been published a year previous. . . .

J. N. B., *Boston Symphony Orchestra*

Symphony in E major

The completed Symphony in E major was performed by the Cleveland Orchestra, under Nikolai Sokoloff, in Carnegie Hall, New York, on Tuesday evening, December 4, 1928. A program note by Arthur Shepherd, then official annotator of the orchestra, recounts the resurrection of this symphony by Sir George Grove, who obtained the original MS. sketch from Paul Mendelssohn, brother of Felix. "I had imagined a sketch of the nature of Beethoven's," writes Sir George, "—two or three leaves of paper covered with disjointed memoranda. Judge of my astonishment and delight when on undoing the parcel I found a whole symphony in forty-eight sheets!"

Herbert F. Peyser, the American critic and former annotator of the Symphony Society of New York, was in Munich with Mr. Sokoloff during the summer of 1928. Mr. Peyser wrote to Mr. Sokoloff: " . . . . I wanted to let you know about a Schubert novelty which you may be interested in picking up for your orchestra for this coming Schubert Winter [1928-1929, the centennial of Schubert's death]. No doubt you are acquainted with the existence of the sketched-out and uncompleted Symphony in E written just a year before the *Unfinished* and constituting a bridge between the early symphonies of Schubert and his mature ones . . ."

The parts were duly copied and sent to Cleveland and the work was performed there for the first time in America on November 22 and 23. These details are set down here as an explanation of why the Symphony in B minor should be numbered 9 instead of 8, and the lost *Gastein,* if it exists, should be tagged as No. 10.

J. S.

WILLIAM HOWARD SCHUMAN

(Born in New York, August 4, 1910—now President
of the Juilliard School of Music, New York)

WHEN SCHUMAN was asked if he came of musical parents,
he said:

"Yes, I think my people were very musical. My father played
the pianola very well, and my mother could play the *William Tell
Overture* and other appropriate masterpieces by ear."

He belongs to the more vigorous school of younger American
composers. His music holds little that is either frantic or foreign.
Indeed, there is a forthright clarity, a virility of purpose about it
that captures the immediate interest of an audience. This interest
arises, perhaps, because the composer does not consider the audience as a last word in the total estimate of his work.

He was born in what Ronald F. Eyer, writing in *Musical
America,* calls "a comfortable home" in New York. He was a student in business administration at New York University, and intended to adorn the profession of advertising. Perhaps a sudden
and overpowering distaste for his immediate future impelled him
to resign in the middle of his sophomore year. "Then he walked
the streets for several hours," writes Mr. Eyer, "with no idea of
what to do next. In a chaotic state of mind, he trudged from the
school building on Washington Square to 78th Street and West
End Avenue, where he found himself in front of a conservatory
of music. On an impulse, he went in and recklessly proclaimed that
he wanted to be taught harmony."

As Mr. Eyer suggests, "that was the beginning." Really, this
procedure was not quite so casual as it appears. For he had been
playing around in student dance bands, strictly by ear, and had
even tried "one-finger experiments" at composing popular music.
This was the start of "serious musical thinking."

Things progressed from here. He had previously been inocu-
lated with the virus of symphonic music, at the instance of his
mother, and haunted the concerts of the Philharmonic-Symphony
Society in Carnegie Hall, wondering "at the ability of so many
people to bow stringed instruments in unison."

345

After a time, he began to study counterpoint with Charles Haubiel, entered Columbia University and acquired Bachelor's and Master's degrees from that venerable institution. He went to the Mozarteum in Salzburg to study conducting, finding himself composing instead, and came back to the United States in 1935, to join the faculty of Sarah Lawrence College, Bronxville, New York. His tutelage of the college chorus raised it to national status.

He was elected President of the Juilliard School in 1945. The first award bestowed by the New York Music Critics' Circle went to Mr. Schuman for his Third Symphony. His First was composed at Salzburg, the Second, completed in 1937, was introduced in Boston by Serge Koussevitzky and the Boston Symphony Orchestra. His secular cantata, *This Is Our Time,* was performed July 4, 1940 at the Lewisohn Stadium.

He believes the most important music of the day "is being written in America by Americans."

Overture—*American Festival*

. . . . The following description of the present work was furnished by Mr. Schuman on the occasion of its first performance (Symphony Hall, Boston, October 6, 1939, Serge Koussevitzky conducting.):

"The first three notes of this piece, will be recognized by some listeners as the 'call to play' of boyhood days. In New York City it is yelled on the syllables 'Wee-awk-Zee!,' to get the gang together for a game or a festive occasion of some sort. This call very naturally suggested itself for a piece of music being composed for a festive occasion. From this it should not be inferred that the Overture is program music. In fact, the idea of the music came to my mind before the origin of the theme was recalled. The development of this little bit of 'folk-material' then, is along purely musical lines.

"The first section of the work is concerned with the material discussed above and the ideas growing out of it. This music leads to a transition section and the subsequent announcement by the violas of a fugue subject. The orchestration is at first for strings alone and finally, as the fugue is brought to fruition, by the strings and woodwinds in combination.

"This climax leads to the final section of the work, which consists of opening materials paraphrased and the introduction of new subsidiary ideas. The tempo of the work is fast."

BATEMAN EDWARDS, *St. Louis Symphony Orchestra*

Symphony No. 3

Bearing the dedication, "This work is for Serge Koussevitzky," the Symphony No. 3 calls for the following orchestration: two flutes, and piccolo, three oboes and English horn, E-flat clarinet, two B-flat clarinets and bass clarinet, two bassoons, four horns, four trumpets, four trombones and tuba, tympani, snaredrum, bass drum, cymbals, xylophone and strings. The composer lists other instruments, whose use is optional. They consist of a third flute and second piccolo, a third oboe, a third bassoon and contra-bassoon, a quartet of horns and a piano. The composer suggests that "to obtain the best results, they are most desirable. . . ."

This Symphony received the initial award made by the Music Critics' Circle of New York City for the best new orchestral work played during the season 1941-1942. Its first performance was given in Boston by the Boston Symphony Orchestra, under the direction of Serge Koussevitzky, on October 18, 1941. Under the same auspices it obtained its local premiere on November 22, 1941.

Composed in January 1941, the work is in two parts, each having two connected movements. The first movement contains a Passacaglia, followed by a Fugue; the second, a Chorale and a Toccata.

Philharmonic-Symphony Society of New York

Symphony for Strings

Schuman's Symphony for Strings is the fifth which he has composed. It was written for the Koussevitzky Music Foundation, the foundation made as a memorial to Mme. Natalie Koussevitzky.

Its first performance was by this orchestra, November 1, 1943.

Since its first performance, the Symphony has been published, recorded, broadcast and performed in concerts abroad—Paris, London, Edinburgh, Berlin and Rio de Janeiro.

The first movement, *Molto agitato ed energico,* opens with a brilliant and incisive theme set forth by the violins in unison on the G strings, *fortissimo.* The theme, together with a second one of less prominence, is developed in a variety of harmonic and rhythmic patterns, while the vigor of the movement is maintained to the end. The second movement, *Larghissimo,* begins with broad chords, but in these and the melody which follows, the strings are muted. As this melody is brought to a climax with an accompanying figuration in sixteenths, the mutes are momentarily removed. The close reverts to the first part and subsides to *pianissimo.* The third movement is a *presto leggiero.* The form is in the manner of a rondo, with the theme varied at each appearance. It first develops with short *pizzicato* notes, but in its course becomes sustained and melodic, rising at last to brilliance, while the tempo is not relaxed.

JOHN N. BURK, *Boston Symphony Orchestra*

ROBERT ALEXANDER SCHUMANN

(Born in Zwickau, Saxony, June 8, 1810—died in
Endenich, near Bonn, July 29, 1856)

SCHUMANN, that charming and romantic boy, for whom his first teacher predicted great renown, yearned to be a virtuoso pianist; but an injury to his hand, of his own devising, ruined this prospect. Instead, he became one of the world's first composers, and died in a private asylum at the comparatively early age of forty-six.

His father was a bookseller, and "took a lively interest in *belles-lettres.*" He encouraged the leanings of his son toward art in every possible way. His mother, daughter of a physician, had scant sympathy with such tendencies. Schumann's first piano teacher, J. G. Kuntsch, organist of the Marienkirche, gave up his charge after a few years with the comment that his pupil "could progress alone" and was headed for a brilliant career.

Robert tells us himself that he began to compose before he was seven. He got up performances at home, with the aid of some musical companions, of vocal and instrumental music "which he arranged to suit their humble powers."

Carl Maria von Weber, appointed in 1817 to the post of *Kapellmeister* at Dresden, was willing to take on the young genius as a pupil, but the scheme fell through.

He entered the academy at Zwickau at ten, and progressed in due course to study law at the University of Leipzig. He had wanted to devote himself entirely to art at the university, but his father had died in 1826 and his mother insisted that he qualify as a lawyer. He submitted, but spent a whole half-year dallying over the distasteful prospect, relieving the tedium by practicing the piano, taking a few lessons from Wieck, father of his prospective wife, and writing poetry.

He was graduated in 1828, and formed a lasting friendship with a fellow student, Gisbert Rosen, deciding to accompany him on his way to Heidelberg. The upshot, of course, was that Robert, a year later, enrolled at the university, again with the law in view.

His legal studies must have been leisurely and half-hearted, for he found time, also, to practice the piano seven hours a day, plunge into debt and conduct himself generally like an irresponsible student. In the course of a pleasure trip to North Italy, he heard Paganini and this experience made a deep impression.

In his third year at the university, he made a serious effort to master the law, without serious result. He was now nearly twenty, and his mother was still averse to the calling of a musician. He induced her to put the decision up to Wieck. The firm stand of that pedagogue in his favor finally induced his mother to yield. He quit

Heidelberg late in the summer of 1830 to resume his studies with Wieck, hoping to become a great pianist.

Impelled by a passionate desire to achieve a perfect technique as soon as possible, Schumann devised a contrivance that crippled his whole right hand. The career of a pianist had to be abandoned, and old doubts of his calling crowded upon him. But he resolved to keep on as a composer, confident in his basic ability.

He began to study composition with Heinrich Dorn, then conductor of the opera in Leipzig, really his first formal instructor. He also fell in love with Clara Wieck, one day to be reckoned among the greatest artists of the keyboard.

He and some friends who gathered at a restaurant of evenings resolved to start a paper, *Neue Zeitschrift für Musik,* of which Schumann eventually became editor and to which he contributed many brilliant articles, concealing his identity under a variety of names—Florestan, Eusebius etc. He formed an intimate friendship with Mendelssohn, under whose guidance Leipzig rose to a position of being the most musical town in Germany. He wanted to marry Clara Wieck, but Papa Wieck opposed this plan.

He went to Vienna, visited Franz Schubert's brother, Ferdinand, from whom he received the score of the C major Symphony. Schumann sent it to Leipzig, where it was performed for the first time under Mendelssohn's direction on March 21, 1839. Schumann returned to Leipzig in April of that year. He forced Papa Wieck, by court action, to consent to his marriage with Clara. They were married on September 12, 1840, in the church of Schoenfeld, near Leipzig and, as Grove remarks, "as far as anything human can be, the marriage was perfectly happy."

His life of quiet retirement and steady work in Leipzig was to end in 1844, when he and Clara moved to Dresden. The move was intended to improve his health, for "he had overworked himself into a kind of surfeit of music, so much so that his medical attendant forbade his continually hearing it." He wrote to Ferdinand David: "Here one can get back the old lost longing for music, there is so little to hear!"

The move was not entirely successful, though the friendship of Ferdinand Hiller and of Richard Wagner, then *Kapellmeister* of Dresden, did much to restore him. He found much to admire in *Tannhäuser* and heard it often. He wanted to write an opera himself, and searched vainly for a text. He hoped for a performance in Leipzig, but all his plans came to nothing. Finally, after delay and evasion on the part of the theater management, a performance of *Genoveva* actually took place on June 25, 1850. The reception, while not actually hostile, was lukewarm and the work was not repeated.

Schumann's health improved gradually, and with it his creative ability. He and his family made a tour of Switzerland in the summer of 1851. Three years later, he and his wife revisited the Netherlands for a concert tour and the subsequent years were occupied in such journeys, with intervals of composition. The fame of his music had spread all over Europe and he was in constant demand as adviser and composer.

They were in Düsseldorf in the autumn of 1853, just before the tour of Holland, and Schumann had determined to leave this city for Vienna, when a "young and wholly unknown musician arrived, with a letter of introduction from Joseph Joachim. Johannes Brahms—for he it was—immediately excited Schumann's warmest interest by the genius of his playing and the originality of his compositions."

Always ready to smooth the way for gifted youth, Schumann once more took up his literary pen, idle these nine years, to indite the famous article *(New Paths)* for the *Zeitschrift* of October 8, 1853, in which he extolled Brahms as the artist whose vocation it would be "to utter the highest ideal expression of our time."

Eccentricities of conduct betrayed to strangers the state of his nervous disorder, and delusions clouded his mind. He thought he heard incessantly one particular note, "or voices whispering words of reproof or encouragement. Once in the night he fancied that the spirits of Schubert and Mendelssohn brought him a musical theme, and he got up and noted it down."

These attacks, though temporary, were recurrent, and he himself suggested that he be placed in an asylum.

On the afternoon of February 27, 1854, "in one of his fits of agony of mind," he slipped from the house, ran down to the bridge and plunged into the Rhine. Boatmen rescued him "and he was recognized and carried home." Symptoms of insanity now became apparent, though there were intervals of utmost clarity and calmness of mind.

Clara, distracted almost beyond endurance by these events, besought the aid and comfort of Brahms, now an intimate friend of both. With Brahms' help, she finally obtained admission for Robert into the private asylum of Dr. Richars at Endenich, near Bonn. Upon arrival there, he seemed better at first, but his malady developed into deep melancholy. But again, lucid moments recurred, when he "corresponded with his friends and received visits." Relapses, however, became longer and more frequent, until he died in Clara's arms on July 29, 1856.

Overture—*Carnaval*

There has survived through the ministrations of Diaghilev's Ballet Russe a score in manuscript of an orchestration of Schumann's *Carnaval*, inscribed as having been made by Rimsky-Korsakoff, and his three pupils, Liadov, Glazounof and Tcherepnin. Yet the orchestration was made, according to the biography of Nijinsky by Romola Nijinsky, at the order of Serge de Diaghilev for a ball in St. Petersburg after the first Paris season of his Ballet. At this time, 1909, Rimsky-Korsakoff would have been dead a year. Rimsky-Korsakoff's part in the proceedings, therefore, could only be explained by orchestral sketches which he may have made and left with his pupils. Madame Nijinsky states: "Diaghilev chose Glazounov for this extremely delicate and difficult task. The score of *Carnaval* proves that Diaghilev was right to entrust the orchestration to him, for he rendered it perfectly, and in spite of the fact that both Liadov and Tcherepnin also collaborated, the final effect was as harmonious as if it had been orchestrated by a single person." There is no mention of Rimsky-Korsakoff. The score gives no clue as to which numbers Liadov or Tcherepnin may have contributed. Schumann's music has all been used excepting "The Sphinxes."

The project for an orchestral *Carnaval* arose when, in 1909, the magazine *Satyricon* arranged for a charity ball, with an exhibition of dancing in the Sala Pavlovna. "The editor Kornfeldt," writes Madame Nijinsky, "and his friend, the poet Patiomkin, told Fokine that they were calling the party *Carnaval*. Fokine immediately thought of Schumann's enchanting early piano pieces. They translated characteristic bits of Schumann's life and letters to him, as he spoke no German, and he absorbed the atmosphere of the period. Who would do the decorations and costumes? Fokine suggested Bakst, of course. Kornfeldt said he would be perfect, but too expensive. Fokine persuaded him to do it for half his usual fee, and gave him part of his own pay, for which Bakst presented him with a painting. Bakst was enchanted with the idea, and immediately saw costumes of the time of Schumann, the Austrian *Biedermeier* period of eighty years before."

When Diaghilev's company mounted the *Carnaval* in Paris in the 1910 season, Nijinsky replaced Leontiev, the original Harlequin, and Karsavina replaced Lopokova as Colombine. Nijinsky made this one of his unforgettable parts. *Carnaval* was in the company's repertory in America, and was presented in the Boston Opera House, February 2, 1916. Colonel W. de Basil's Ballet. Russe announced the same orchestration in their production of the season of 1935-1936.

Schumann composed his *Carnaval* in 1834-1835. The set of twenty-one pieces, as published, bore the subtitle *Scenes mignonnes sur quatre notes*. The four notes which form the basis of most of the little pieces, together with the title *Estrella* over one of them, gives a clue to the direction which the composer's thoughts and affection were taking at the time. "Estrella" was Ernestine von Fricken, the fair young beauty from the town of Asch in Bohemia who had won Schumann's heart for the time being, and almost his hand. Schumann explained the riddle of the four notes to his friend Ignaz Moscheles three years later in a letter accompanying the score:

"The *Carnaval* came into existence incidentally, and is built for the most part on the notes A, S, C and H (A, E-flat, C, B; S standing for E-flat in German; H, for B natural), the name of a small Bohemian town, Asch, where I had a lady friend, but which, strange to say, are also the only musical letters in my name. The superscriptions I placed over them afterward. For is not music itself always enough and sufficiently expressive. *Estrella* is a name such as is placed under portraits to fix the picture better in one's memory; *Reconnaissance,* a scene of recognition; *Aveu,* an avowal of love; *Promenade,* a walk such as one takes at a German ball with one's partner. The whole has no artistic value whatever, the manifold states of the soul alone seem to me of interest. . . ."

. . . . The *Carnaval* appears as a sort of fantastic masquerade in which the costumed figures and the faces of Schumann's musical friends pass in fleeting review. "Chiarina" is Clara Wieck, Schumann's fellow pupil. Chopin is represented by an imitation of his style: Paganini, then the virtuoso of the hour, by a show of brilliant passage work. The final "March of the Band of David Against the Philistines," refers to the *Neue Zeitschrift für Musik* which Schumann, with other musical liberals, had just organized. The *Davidsbündler* were Schumann and his fellow editors, dedicated to the recognition of new musical trends, equally sworn to put to confusion the Philistines, the conservatives of the profession. Schumann appeared in the *Zeitschrift* in alternate guises, as Florestan, which was his quick, ardent and impulsive nature, and as Eusebius, his more reasonable, thoughtful and reflective self. . . .

JOHN N. BURK, *Boston Symphony Orchestra*

Symphony No. 1 in B flat (Opus 38)

There are some who attribute to Clara Schumann the direct inspiration of the Symphony in B flat, for it was at the end of the first winter of their marriage, on the threshold of spring, that Schumann composed it. It is certainly true that a sudden expansion of his powers, a full flowering of his genius coincided with the last year of his engagement and with his marriage to Clara on September 12, 1840—a blissful ending to a distressing period of strife, in which the long and unyielding opposition of her father, Friedrich Wieck, was overcome only by an appeal to the law courts. No parent, unless it was Elizabeth Barrett's father, ever more stubbornly opposed an ideal union of kindred artists.

The pair were quietly married in the church at Schoenfeld, a suburb of Leipzig, and took up their abode at No. 5 Inselstrasse in the attractive house which Schumann was able to provide. Here, in the fourth month of their marriage, Robert worked furiously upon his First Symphony, completing it in sketch in the space of four days.

He said in a letter (November 23, 1842) to Spohr: "I wrote

the Symphony toward the end of the winter of 1841, and, if I may
say so, in the vernal passion that sways men until they are very
old, and surprises them again with each year. I do not wish to portray, to paint; but I believe firmly that the period in which the
Symphony was produced influenced its form and character, and
shaped it as it is." He later remarked of the Symphony that "it was
born in a fiery hour."

He strove to make his intentions clear, writing to the conductor Taubert (January 10, 1843) before a performance in Berlin:
"Could you infuse into your orchestra in the performance a sort of
longing for the spring, which I had chiefly in mind when I wrote
in February 1841? The first entrance of trumpets, this I should like
to have sounded as though it were from high above, like unto a
call to awakening; and then I should like reading between the
lines, in the rest of the Introduction, how everywhere it begins to
grow green, how a butterfly takes wing; and, in the Allegro, how
little by little all things come that in any way belong to spring.
True these are fantastic thoughts, which came to me after my work
was finished; only I tell you this about the Finale, that I thought
it as the goodbye of spring."

Schumann at first intended the following mottoes for the four
movements: "The Dawn of Spring," "Evening," "Joyful Playing"
and "Full Spring."

JOHN N. BURK, *Berkshire Symphonic Festival*

Symphony No. 2 in C major (Opus 61)

The numbering of this Symphony is misleading. As a matter
of fact, it is not the second of Schumann's four but the third. In
1841, four years before he began work on this C major Symphony,
he composed and brought out a Symphony in D minor, which is
really his second. The D minor Symphony in its first estate, however, failed to satisfy him, so he withdrew it and for ten years it
slumbered on the shelf. Then he reorchestrated it and the revised
version was performed with great success. But meanwhile he had
given to the world symphonies in C and E-flat (*Rhenish*). Consequently the D minor, being the fourth published, became known

as No. 4. Thus of Schumann's symphonies only the First, in B flat, is numbered correctly.

Begun in December 1845, the C major Symphony was finished in the course of the following year, and the first performance took place in Leipzig at a Gewandhaus concert on November 5, with Mendelssohn conducting. Schumann's work on this Symphony served as an antidote to pain. At the time he was suffering from the illness which had declared itself twelve years previously and which, within another ten years, was to bring about his mental collapse and death. This time he put the enemy to rout by applying himself to composition.

In Schumann's letters there are informative references to the C major Symphony. Addressing G. D. Otten, the musical director at Hamburg, in 1849, he says: "I wrote the Symphony in December 1845, when I was still ailing; it seems to me as if one could not help hearing it in the music. It was only in the last movement that I began to feel better. But otherwise, as I said, it reminds me of a dark time."

In another letter he is more specific: "I sketched it when I was still in a state of physical suffering; nay, I say it was, so to speak, the resistance of the spirit which exercised as a visible influence here, and through which I sought to contend with my bodily state. The first movement is full of this struggle and is very capricious and refractory."

He also speaks of his "melancholy bassoon" in the Adagio. Still, when J. J. H. Verhulst of the Hague asked him whether he thought he had succeeded fully in his new Symphony, he replied eagerly: "Yes, indeed, I think it's a regular Jupiter."

. . . . A curious fact about the first Trio was told to William Foster Apthorp by Otto Dresel, who in his youth had been a pupil of Mendelssohn in Leipzig. One day he happened to be left alone in Mendelssohn's study. "While mousing around there with a boy's curiosity," Apthorp relates, "he espied on a desk an MS. score that was not in Mendelssohn's handwriting. It turned out to be the MS. of Schumann's C major Symphony—then unknown, save to the composer and a friend or two; it had evidently been sent to Mendelssohn to look over. Dresel, much interested in his unexpected find, forthwith began to read the score, and had time to read it through and replace it where he had found it, before Mendelssohn returned.

"He told me that, curiously enough, the triplet theme of the first Trio of the Scherzo was exposed and carried through by the strings alone. Yet when, some weeks later, he heard the Symphony rehearsed at the Gewandhaus, this theme was played by the woodwind and horns, just as it stands now in the published score. Dresel thought it pretty plain that Schumann transferred this theme from the strings to the wind on Mendelssohn's advice. It was not uncharacteristic of Schumann's greenness in orchestral matters at the time that he should not have thought of giving the theme to the wind—after the carnival of the violins in the Scherzo proper—without being prompted thereto by his friend." It is dedicated to Oscar I, King of Sweden and Norway.

PITTS SANBORN, *Philharmonic-Symphony Society of New York*

Symphony No. 3 in E flat (Opus 97)

This Symphony was sketched and orchestrated at Duesseldorf between November 2 and December 9, 1850. . . . Clara Schumann wrote in her diary, November 16, 1850: "Robert is now at work on something, I do not know what, for he has said nothing to me about it." It was on December 9 that he surprised her with this Symphony. Sir George Grove, for some reason or other, thought Schumann began to work on it before he left Dresden to accept the position of City Conductor at Duesseldorf; that Schumann wished to compose an important work for production at the lower Rhenish Festival.

The first performance of this symphony was in Geisler Hall, Düsseldorf, at the sixth concert of *Der Allgemeine Musikverein,* February 6, 1851. Schumann conducted from manuscript. The music was coldly received. Mme. Schumann wrote after the performance that "the creative power of Robert was again ever new in melody and form." She added: "I cannot say which one of the five movements is my favorite. The fourth is the only one that at present is the least clear to me; it is most artistically made—that I hear—but I cannot follow it so well, while there is scarcely a measure in the other movements that remains unclear to me; and indeed to the layman is this Symphony, especially in its second and third movements, easily intelligible."

The Philharmonic Society of New York produced the Symphony, February 2, 1861. The Symphony was published in October 1851. Schumann wrote (March 19, 1851) to the publisher, Simrock, at Bonn:

"I should have been glad to see a greater work published here on the Rhine, and I mean this Symphony, which perhaps mirrors here and there something of Rhenish life." It is known that the solemn fourth movement was inspired by the recollection of the ceremony at Cologne Cathedral at the installation of the Archbishop of Geissel as cardinal, at which Schumann was present. Wasielewski quotes the composer as saying that his intention was to portray in the Symphony as a whole the joyful folklife along the Rhine, "and I think," said Schumann, "I have succeeded." Yet he refrained from writing even explanatory mottoes for the movements. The fourth movement originally bore the inscription: "In the character of the accompaniment of a solemn ceremony;" but Schumann struck this out, and said: "One should not show his heart to people; for a general impression of an art work is more impressive; the hearers, then, at least, do not institute any absurd comparison." The Symphony was very dear to him. He wrote (July 1, 1851) to Carl Reinecke, who made a four-handed arrangement at Schumann's wish and to his satisfaction: "It is always important that a work which cost so much time and labor should be reproduced in the best possible manner."

PHILIP HALE, *Boston Symphony Orchestra*

Symphony No. 4 in D minor (Opus 120)

Composed in 1841 at Leipzig, this Symphony was first performed at a Gewandhaus concert on December 6 of the same year. Schumann made a revision in December 1851, at Düsseldorf, and this was performed there on March 3, 1853, at the spring festival of the lower Rhine. It was published in December 1853, as his Fourth Symphony.

Schumann wrote this Symphony a few months after the completion of his First Symphony in B-flat. The D minor Symphony was numbered four only because he revised it ten years later and did not publish it until 1853, after his three others had been written and published (the Second in 1846, the Third in 1850). This Symphony, then, was the second in order of composition. It belongs to a year notable in Schumann's development. He and Clara were married in the autumn of 1840, and this event seems to have stirred in him a new and significant creative impulse; 1840 became a year of songs in sudden and rich profusion, while in 1841 he sensed for the first time in full degree the mastery of symphonic forms. He had written two years before to Heinrich Dorn, once his teacher in composition: "I often feel tempted to crush my piano—it is too narrow for my thoughts. I really have very little practice in orchestral music now; still I hope to master it." The products of 1841 show that he worked as well as dreamed toward that end. The expectant bridegroom turned ardently from piano pieces to songs. The husband, strengthened in confidence, ennobled in spirit by the consummation of his long-delayed marriage to Clara Wieck, plunged boldly into the symphonic realm. . . .

The symphony is the most notable example of the symphonic Schumann abandoning customary formal procedure to let his romantic imagination take hold and shape his matter to what end it will. It should be borne in mind that the Symphony was first thought of by its composer as a symphonic fantasia, that it was published by him as *Introduction, Allegro, Romanze, Scherzo and Finale, in One Movement.* It was in this, the published version, that he eliminated pauses between the movements, although this does not appear in the earlier version save in the joining of the scherzo and finale. The work, save in the slow movement, has no "recapitulations" in the traditional sense, no cut and dried summations. Warming to his theme, Schumann expands to new thematic material and feels no necessity for return. The score is unmistakably of one mood. It is integrated by the threads of like thoughts. Thematic recurrence becomes inevitable, because this unity of thought makes it natural. . . .

JOHN N. BURK, *Berkshire Symphonic Festival*

Piano concerto in A minor (Opus 54)

Although we know this Concerto as the only one by Schumann for piano, it seems that he began to write a piano concerto at the age of seventeen before he was conversant with musical form, and that he tried again in 1830 at Heidelberg. As early as 1839 there is apparently a reference to the A minor Concerto in a letter sent by Schumann from Vienna to his betrothed, Clara Wieck: "My concerto is a compromise among a symphony, a concerto and a huge sonata. I see I cannot write a concerto for the virtuosos: I must plan something else."

Apparently Schumann began the first movement at Leipzig in the summer of 1841, for it was given a semipublic performance at the Gewandhaus on August 13, 1841, with Mme. Schumann (the former Fräulein Wieck) as pianist. Schumann then regarded this movement as a complete composition in itself and attempted to place it with some publisher as either a "Phantasie in A moll" or as a "Concert Allegro for Pianoforte and Orchestra," but his endeavors were in vain. Later on, Schumann decided to treat the "Phantasie" as the first movement of a full-length concerto, and in May 1845, while living in Dresden, set out to write the Intermezzo and Finale.

Mme. Schumann recorded in her diary on July 31, 1845: "Robert has finished his Concerto and has given it to the copyists." In September, she commenced her study of the work and played it at its first performance at the Hotel de Saxe, Dresden, on December 4, 1845, with Ferdinand Hiller, to whom the score had been dedicated, as conductor. Schumann must have changed his mind about the titles of the second and third movements; for when Mme. Schumann played the Concerto the following year under Mendelssohn's direction at the Leipzig Gewandhaus, the *Intermezzo* was denominated *Andantino* and the *Allegro vivace, Rondo,* although the fourth movement then, as now, was called *Allegro affettuoso. . . .*

In all probability the first performance of the Concerto in America took place in New York at a concert of the Philharmonic Society on March 6, 1859, the pianist being Sebastian Bach Mills, a native of Cirencester, England, who for many years played in New York every season. . . .

England was before the United States in making the acquaintance of this Concerto. On May 14, 1856, Mme. Schumann played it
in London at a concert of the New Philharmonic Society. When,
the following month, Mme. Schumann gave a recital in London,
reviewers were curiously at odds about her achievement. The
Musical World remarked: "The reception accorded to this accomplished lady on her first coming to England will no doubt encourage her to repeat her visit. Need we say, to make use of a homely
phrase, that she will be 'welcome as the flowers in May?' "

Quite different was the *Athenaeum* in its acerbity: "That this
lady is among the greatest female players who have ever been
heard has been universally admitted. That she is past her prime
may be now added without discourtesy, when we take leave of her,
nor do we fancy that she would do wisely to adventure a second
visit to England." Clara Schumann, not yet thirty-seven, was destined to play many more times in London, the *Athenaeum* notwithstanding, making her last professional appearance in the English capital in 1888. The musical critic of the *Athenaeum* from
1861 to 1868 was none other than the celebrated Henry Fothergill
Chorley!

A reviewer quite as famous in his day, J. W. Davidson, wrote
specifically of the Concerto as "a labored and ambitious work,"
containing many bravura passages of an utter extravagance, and
with respect to Mme. Schumann's performance he condescendingly
mentioned "the praiseworthy efforts of the gifted lady to make her
husband's curious rhapsody pass for music."

PITTS SANBORN, *Philharmonic-Symphony Society of New York*

DMITRI SHOSTAKOVITCH

(Born in St. Petersburg, September 25, 1906—now
living in Moscow)

THIS YOUNG Russian composer, whose first symphony
emerged at eighteen, has been hailed with an almost hysterical zeal
as the "boy genius" of the Soviet realm. He has been exploited
shamelessly as a medium of international propaganda, his talent
forced and distorted to satisfy the demands of political fancy, and
little time or opportunity have been afforded him in which to
develop his natural gifts.

At present, his gifts are extraordinary, his defects obvious. He
has written too much, too hastily, and has been inclined to substitute contrivance and expediency for originality and craftsmanship. But the spark is there and needs only quiet and meditation
to bring an incandescent glow.

He entered the Conservatory of his native city in 1919 and left
it in 1925, having studied under Nikolaev, Steinberg and Glazounoff. He had demonstrated in these student years a remarkable precocity in composition. In the year of his graduation, he composed
his First Symphony, still regarded as his most famous and original
work.

He has not always seen eye to eye with the government in matters artistic. His first tiff came in 1930, over a satirical opera, *The
Nose,* denounced by the Kremlin worthies as "bourgeois deca-
dence." More severe displeasure and censure followed when *Lady
Macbeth of Mzensk,* conducted by Artur Rodzinski in Cleveland
and New York, attracted wide and favorable attention. The work
was called "vulgar" by Soviet critics and Shostakovitch's treatment
"too forward."

"Since then," writes David Ewen, "Shostakovitch has rehabili-
tated himself as the most favored composer of his country, particularly with his successful Fifth Symphony. His Seventh Symphony, describing the heroic defense of Leningrad in 1941, was
introduced in America by Arturo Toscanini during the summer of
1942. . . . On March 15, 1941, Shostakovitch received the Stalin

362

Prize of one hundred thousand roubles, said to have been the highest sum of money ever to have been won by a composer for a chamber music work, for his piano quintet."

Symphony No. 1 (Opus 10)

[This] . . . . is a young man's symphony, composed in 1925, when Shostakovitch was barely twenty, and yet nothing he has written during the intervening fourteen years [1939]—and there are four more symphonies—can compare with it in sheer tone-speech and emotional conviction, barring perhaps the opera *Lady Macbeth of Mzensk*. The First Symphony bears the hallmark of a strong individuality, notwithstanding certain thematic and technical similarities to composers preceding him. It could hardly be otherwise than that a young composer should be subject to certain influences.

Officially proclaimed at one time as the "composer-laureate of the Union of Soviet Socialist Republics," Shostakovitch has not met with individual favor from Russian government authorities.

The reason for his being relegated temporarily to the background of Soviet-regulated music affairs of his native country, was that some of his scores were considered too ultramodern to meet with the common denominator tenets of that proletarian art which the men in charge of public education and cultural entertainment had wished to foster.

The First Symphony is by no means exceptional in that regard. And the Fifth Symphony last winter [1938], premiered on the air by Dr. Rodzinski, rather bespeaks Shostakovitch's return to a moderate, yet by no means less forceful style of writing.

Those who wish to find "political tenets and proletarian avowals" in this Symphony can please themselves by discovering them. The Symphony, as far as can be established, follows no program except that of the composer's mind and emotions. That they must have been of and with the problems of his country, can hardly be doubted.

As Ernest Newman has put it: "The entire man composes." In other words, Shostakovitch did not sit in his "ivory tower of day dreams" when he poured himself forth in this composition. It is a symphony of life, of his own life, as is every symphony written by any composer of strong reactions.

Shostakovitch does not follow a program in this Opus 10 as he has done in the Second Symphony, the *October Symphony,* which celebrates the anniversary of the revolution of the Russian people. The Third Symphony, too, has a "political basis." The First Symphony is not a political utterance, but undoubtedly it is created in a spirit of faith in the social tenets governing the land of his birth. But apart from these considerations, the First Symphony can be enjoyed purely and simply as music. It is of strong and quick emotional appeal. At no time is the music the obvious carrier of a sociological doctrine, as, for instance, is *Lady Macbeth,* powerful as this music is.

Notwithstanding the Soviet attitude against tastes cultivated by the bourgeois class, the instrumentation of the First Symphony calls for a large modern orchestra. Shostakovitch includes also a piano. The Symphony is so dramatic and vivid, even in the quieter portions, that the listener will readily be able to follow the emotional continuity of the score as a whole. The slow third movement leads into the dynamically varied finale by way of an unmistakable drum roll which rises to a crescendo. One can well understand Shostakovitch's success in his own land and abroad.

B. D. USSHER, *Los Angeles Symphony Orchestra*

Symphony No. 5 (Opus 47)

Shostakovitch's Fifth Symphony was first performed in Leningrad on November 21, 1937, at a celebration of the twentieth anniversary of the October Revolution. It received an ovation. It also marked an important milestone in Shostakovitch's life and signalized his "reaffirmation of the Soviet political creed in music." In simpler words, Shostakovitch was restored to favor.

A year or more before the premiere of the Fifth Symphony his opera, *Lady Macbeth* had been denounced by *Pravda,* the official Soviet organ. The opera was accused of being "un-Soviet, unwholesome, cheap, eccentric and Leftist."

The government, as the guardian of the people's welfare, felt that the arts should help in the rebuilding of the self-confidence and the solidarity of the Russian people. In the theater, criticism of Russian characters and sarcasm would produce only pessimism.

Lady Macbeth, a "tragic satire," had left audiences in deep gloom, without a note of optimism. The Moscow Composers' Union held a three-day discussion of Shostakovitch and his work. Several conductors removed his compositions from their programs. The only person who apparently had nothing to say during this storm of criticism and comment was Shostakovitch. He returned to his duties as professor at the Conservatory and quietly began his Fifth Symphony.

He withdrew his Fourth Symphony which had already had its tenth rehearsal. It was long and gloomy and introspective. He knew it would not meet the requirements of Soviet music. It has never been played in public.

Pravda approved the Fifth Symphony. The rift was forgotten. Shostakovitch was returned to favor and his Symphony hailed as a "work of great depth, with emotional wealth and content."

The Fifth Symphony opens the "second period" in Shostakovitch's music—music which is to serve the "requirements of the new aesthetic alignment." . . .

Though the instrumentation and some of the harmony in the Fifth Symphony could have been written only in the twentieth century, Shostakovitch adheres to tradition. There are the customary four movements, though he has reversed the usual order of the second and third movements. The most striking qualities are his great dramatic power; masterly variety and brilliance in the use of instruments; energy, rhythmic vitality; pungent, often dissonant harmony; long-lined melodies—nostalgic or gay or boisterous—and humor.

LENORA COFFIN, *Indianapolis Symphony*

Polka from the Ballet: *The Golden Age*

The Golden Age is a ballet and was first performed in Leningrad. At that time it was described as an "athletic ballet" as differentiated from *The Bolt* which was called an "industrial ballet."

The first American performance was in Cleveland by the Cleveland Orchestra, conducted by Artur Rodzinski, April 2, 1936.

The concert suite consists of four movements—Introduction, Adagio, Polka and Dance. The xylophone is prominent in the polka and carries the principal theme. The second theme is given to the saxophone. Solos are heard in solo violin, flute and horn and the clarinet has a cadenza. In the Dance a mood of rusticity is preserved. A large orchestra is employed.

WILLIAM BENSWANGER, *Pittsburgh Symphony Orchestra*

JAN JULIUS CHRISTIAN SIBELIUS
(Jean Sibelius)

(Born in Tavastehus, Finland, December 8, 1865—
now living near Helsingfors, Finland)

SIBELIUS is the "grand old man" of Finnish music, revered alike by people and government. Since 1890 he has enjoyed an annual grant from the national treasury, so that he need do nothing but compose.

Olin Downes, critic of the *New York Times,* may be credited with disclosing Sibelius to the musical public of the United States. Suddenly, in the early thirties, a fad for Sibelius spread everywhere, like some musical rash. A Sibelius "cult" was born and the name of Sibelius adorned orchestral and other programs in hamlet and capital, from ocean to ocean.

This sudden popularity in the new world astonished Sibelius himself. "I am glad that the people of America have found my music and like it," he remarked drily to an American reporter. He added, somewhat sadly:

"I believe there is a kind of Freemasonry among composers, owing to things having been and being so difficult for us. All of us have to reckon with the critics and the public. For my part, thanks to the experience of a long lifetime, I have learned to accept disappointment and reverses with resignation. Scarcely one of my best works has met with right comprehension when first performed . . ."

And his wife, Aino Sibelius, says:

"Music irritates my husband more than anything else. Forced to hear a stray tune, a fragment of song, or someone whistling, he will throw his work overboard and wreck the inspiration. Afterward, he must begin again from the beginning. That is why at home one never hears music. No one ever sings. No one whistles. That is, unless my husband chooses otherwise."

He is the son of an army medical officer. At an early age, he was left an orphan and subsequently was brought up by his grandparents. He was enjoined to study law, and really made some dutiful progress in this direction, although from his childhood he had determined that some day he would be a musician.

But he went to school and studied the classics, entered the University of Helsingfors and specialized in law and was duly graduated. Whereupon he threw aside his legal garments and embraced the violin. His informal studies of music in private now stood him in good stead, and he went to Martin Wegelius and Ferruccio Busoni in Helsingfors, better prepared than he knew for the task before him. Later, he sought out Adolf Becker in Berlin, then Robert Fuchs and Karl Goldmark in Vienna.

Russian oppression of the Finns fired him with a patriotic ardor and he composed, among other works, *Finlandia*. Before receiving the aforementioned grant from the Finnish government, he taught theory at the Conservatory and the orchestral school of the Philharmonic Society in Helsingfors.

In the next seventeen years he traveled incessantly, visiting various musical capitals of the world, meeting noted composers and musicians, exchanging ideas, evolving new techniques of composition. He composed the violin concerto, a string quartet and the first five symphonies.

The Norfolk Festival in Litchfield, Connecticut, imported him in 1914 to conduct nine of his own works. He visited Boston and other centers, Yale University conferred an honorary degree upon him. Several of his works were played during the commencement program.

The entire music world celebrated his seventieth birthday in 1935, and Finland declared December 8 a national holiday. These festive celebrations were repeated on his seventy-fifth birthday in 1940. At present he is harboring an Eighth Symphony, which he has decreed shall not be published or performed until after his death.

Tone Poem: *Finlandia*

Finlandia was composed in 1894 and is supposed to record "the impressions of an exile's return home after a long absence." While the themes have a decided Finnish folk-song character, Sibelius himself has stated that they are absolutely his own. The work is a remarkable tone-picture of the intense national spirit of this hardy race of the North. When first performed in Helsinki it is said to have aroused the audience to such a frenzy of enthusiasm that future performances were prohibited by the Russian government for fear of its creating anti-Russian demonstrations.

San Francisco Symphony Orchestra

Swan of Tuonela: from *Four Legends* for Orchestra

The Swan of Tuonela is the third movement of the symphonic legend, *Lemminkäinen,* which Sibelius completed in 1893. In his inscription on the original score, the composer forecasts the scene and mood of his brief tone-poem. "Tuonela, the land of Death, the hell of Finnish mythology, is surrounded by a river with black waters and rapid currents, on which the Swan of Tuonela floats, majestically singing."

To portray this legendary landscape, Sibelius has chosen an extremely somber orchestra. He omits on his instrumental palette all tones of brightness. No flutes or trumpets are used. Among the family of clarinets, only that in the bass register is occasionally employed.

For the leading tone-color the English horn is selected. This alto oboe sadly sounds over an unusual combination of blowing instruments, of dull percussion and of muted and divided strings. Since Wagner's *Tristan,* the English horn has sung the tunes of renouncement and dying in its melancholy timbre. In Sibelius' tone-picture of the island of the dead, again the English horn is the prominent solo instrument; the Swan of Tuonela is symbolized in arabesque-like motifs. The gracious bend of the theme—from the dotted whole note over a triplet, down to the lower sixth and slowly ascending again to the fifth—conjures up the knightly carriage of the swan on the black waters.

Everywhere in the brief score, auditory sensations find quick points of contact with the visual. As we hear these melancholy tone rows, it seems as though we see a Northern landscape—dark green forests, threatening granite rocks and the cold waters of icy lakes.

Sibelius once explained the intent of his music to a German publisher: "Other composers mix cocktails of many varieties. I have nothing to offer but pure cold water." We may feel in the composer's metaphoric comparison a clue to the understanding of his lonely music.

DR. FREDERICK DORIAN, *Pittsburgh Symphony Orchestra*

Valse Triste—

. . . . From the category of dramatic music comes this famous composition. In the first years of the present century, at about the same time he was writing his Second Symphony, Sibelius composed a suite of incidental music for a play, *Kuolema,* written by his brother-in-law, Eero Jaernefelt.

To admirers of more abstruse works of Sibelius, the popularity of *Valse Triste,* has sometimes proved a source of embarrassment. Cecil Grey, in his book on Sibelius, calls it "all too familiar . . . a little work which has done more to make his name known to the many and to injure his reputation in the eyes of the few, than everything else he has written put together." Looking at it with critical detachment, Grey says it appears "to be merely an original, ingenious and highly effective essay in the musical 'macabre' and nothing more."

Add to the incidental intelligence about this work the following: That although it might have brought its composer more income in royalties than all his other works put together, he sold it with the rest of the suite outright for about $25.

JOHN S. EDWARDS, *St. Louis Symphony Orchestra*

Symphony No. 1 in E minor

Sibelius, being dedicated to law, devoted himself promptly to music. With such success did he replace profession with art that almost alone he stands comfortably before the world as a man so highly appreciated by his own people that the state handsomely supports him.

As far back as 1890, Sibelius was granted an annual income of $600 by the Finnish government. On the composer's fiftieth birthday, this was increased, and ten years later a further increase was given, so that up to the time of the present European conflict (1940) Sibelius drew yearly from the government the sum of 100,000 marks. (We hope this is still true today.) In addition, an affectionate and admiring public in Finland raised an independent gift for him of 150,000 marks.

Sibelius has written seven symphonies of which the First was written in 1899. To all of this composer's work there is a suitable preface, written by Paul Rosenfeld in *Musical Portraits*:

"Others have brought the North into houses and there transformed it to music. And their art is dependent on the shelter, and removed from it, dwindles. But Sibelius has written music independent of roof and enclosure, music proper indeed to the vast open, the Finnish heaven under which it grew. And could we but carry it out into the Northern day, we would find it undiminished, vivid with all its life. For it is blood-brother to the wind and the silence, to the lowering cliffs and the spray, to the harsh crying of sea-birds and the breath of the fog, and, set amid them, would wax and take new strength from the strength of its kin . . . The orchestral compositions of Sibelius seem to have passed over black torrents and desolate moorlands, through pallid sunlight and grim primeval forests and become drenched with them. The instrumentation is all wet grays and blacks, relieved only by bits of brightness, wan and elusive as the Northern summer, frostily green as the polar lights. The works are full of the gnawing of bassoons and the bleakness of the English horn, full of shattering trombones and screaming violins, full of the sinister rolling of drums, the menacing reverberation of cymbals, the icy glittering of harps. The musical ideas of those compositions that are finally realized recall the ruggedness and hardiness and starkness of things that persist in the Finnish winter. The rhythms seem to approach the wild, unnumbered rhythms of the forest and the wind and the flickering sunlight."

HERMAN WISE, *Detroit Symphony Orchestra*

Symphony No. 2 in D

Sibelius . . . has composed seven symphonies, the Second having been written in 1901-1902. George Schneevoight, an intimate friend of Sibelius, says that the composer's intention in this Second Symphony "was to depict in the first movement, the quiet pastoral life of the Finns, undisturbed by thought of oppressions. The second movement is charged with patriotic feeling, but the thought of a brutal rule over the people brings with it timidity of soul. The third, in the nature of a scherzo, portrays the awakening of natural feeling and the desire to organize in defense of their rights. In the finale hope enters their breasts and there is comfort in the anticipated coming of a deliverer!"

BARBARA DUNCAN, *Rochester Symphony Orchestra*

Symphony No. 5 in E flat

A quarter of a century ago come October [1946], the Philadelphia Orchestra gave the first American performance of Jean Sibelius' Fifth Symphony. The adjectives employed by the bewildered music critics to characterize the new work could well be used to describe the reception given it that day—cold, bleak, austere.

Philadelphia was not alone in its ungracious welcome of the

Symphony. It had been heard for the first time outside of Finland six months earlier, at a Queen's Hall concert, London, with Sibelius conducting. The critic of the *London Times* remarked: "A comparison of the reception given the man beforehand and to the work afterward suggested that the latter left the audience a little puzzled." After commenting on the more positive statement of ideas in this Symphony, its richer and fuller coloring, and on the effects of orchestral masses, the writer continues: "There is severity about the ideas which is chilling on their first presentation and each movement closes abruptly, just at the moment when the mind has become persuaded of their earnestness." After a terse analysis of the three movements, he concludes: "Sibelius as a composer and conductor stands apart, a lonely figure seeking with difficulty to bring the ideals which are intensely real to him in touch with other minds.". . . .

The Fifth Symphony was probably first conceived in the early months of 1914, before the composer's visit to the United States. He came to America at the invitation of Carl Stoeckel, founder of the Norfolk Connecticut Festival, to conduct a concert of his own music, which included the symphonic poem, *The Oceanties,* commissioned for that occasion. By September, in spite of the hazards and turmoil of war which were surrounding him, the outline of the Symphony must have been hewn out, for Sibelius writes: "In a deep dale again. But I already begin to see dimly the mountain I shall certainly ascend . . . God opens the door for a moment and His orchestra plays the Fifth Symphony."

The work had its first performance on Sibelius' fiftieth birthday, December 8, 1915. It underwent no less than three revisions before it was published in 1921.

Louise Beck, *Philadelphia Orchestra*

FRIEDRICH (Bedrich) SMETANA

(Born in Leitomischl, Bohemia, March 2, 1824—
died in Prague, May 12, 1884)

THE GAY and sun-drenched music of Smetana, the happy zest of his rhythms, the fascination of his melodies—all these belie his tragic end. Blind and insane, he ended his days in an asylum, deaf, destitute and alone.

Yet he is revered today throughout the world as "the first (and some think the greatest)," to quote Grove, "Bohemian composer, who deliberately took his stand as an exponent of the art of his native country." Comparatively little of his considerable output is known in this country. One hears, for instance, excerpts from *The Bartered Bride*; extracts (but seldom the whole six sections) from *My Country,* a symphonic poem for orchestra; nothing whatever from two other symphonic poems—*Wallenstein's Lager Hakon Jarl*—and no hint of the *Triumph Symphony* or *Prager Karneval* has ever reached these shores.

Now and again his two string quartets are played (E minor and C major), his Trio for piano and strings and his songs reach the American ear via the radio or concert hall. He also composed a *Festival March* for the Shakespeare Tercentenary, plus music for *Richard III,* heard more frequently now, and much piano music which seems to have been neglected shamefully.

For a short time in his youth, having studied with Prokosch in Prague, he became one of that famous Weimar class over which the Abbé Liszt presided, and emerged as a highly skilled pianist.

He opened a music school of his own in Prague and married a piano student there, Katharina Kolar. They went to Sweden in 1856, where Smetana had been appointed director of the Philharmonic Society of Gothenburg. His wife died there in 1860, and a year later Smetana made a tour of Sweden, then returned to Prague.

He helped to found the National Theater in Prague and eventually became its chief conductor. He directed the premiere there of his most famous work, *The Bartered Bride*. His one tragic opera, *Dalibor,* was written for this theater and first produced there. The score was performed, in a two-piano concert version, in the Town Hall, New York, on February 26, 1944, under the direction of Paul Eisler.

During his tenure as chief conductor in Prague he had shown a keen interest in the career of a young man in his orchestra, Antonin Dvorak, and this interest had a marked influence upon the young man's career.

Increasing deafness forced Smetana to resign his post in 1874. From then on his health deteriorated steadily. He lost his sight entirely, his mind was affected and he died in an asylum in Prague.

Grove remarks of his symphonic poems:

"Though his symphonic poems are not realistic, yet there can be no doubt that they carried on the tradition of that form from the hands of Liszt, and increased its power of pictorial expression."

Overture to *The Bartered Bride*

To begin with, the title of Smetana's comic opera is *Prodana nevesta* in the original Czech and the standard German version of the work offers the label *Die verkaufte Braut,* both of which may be literally Englished to *The Sold Bride.* However, for possible reasons of euphony or cadence or just plain accident, the piece is known in English as *The Bartered Bride,* which does seem an improvement on the ultralaconic definitiveness of the other.

In any case, the opera, with a libretto by Karl Sabina, was give its world premiere in Prague May 30, 1866. Forty-three years later Giulio Gatti-Casazza produced it at the Metropolitan Opera House in the German version. On that occasion, Gustav Mahler conducted and the leading soprano role of Marie was entrusted to Emmy Destinn, both of whom were of Bohemian birth. The opera "took," as the saying goes, and it fluctuated slightly in popularity for the next three seasons.

In January 1926, it was revived at the Metropolitan, remaining on the active list for three seasons more. A later revival in February 1933, brought its sum total of performances for that season to two. All of the aforementioned productions were given in the German translation. In the meantime there had been considerable bustle all along concerning a presentation in English, but not until the "popular" spring season of 1936, did it crystallize into fact. A number of writers, grouped collectively under the name of Graham Jones, were responsible for it and it had a remarkable success, so much so that the opera in that English adaptation entered the Metropolitan's repertory of the following winter season.

The Overture, however, has ever been a favorite with American concert audiences, antedating the staging of the opera by more than twenty years . . .

The composer began work on *The Bartered Bride* in May 1863, and completed it in March 1866. At its one hundredth performance in Prague, May 5, 1882, Smetana said: "I did not compose it from any ambitious desire, but rather as a scornful defiance, for they accused me after my first opera of being a Wagnerite, one that could do nothing in a light and popular style."

In its original form the opera was in two acts without change of scene and it consisted of twenty lyric parts connected by spoken dialogue. For a projected performance at the Opéra Comique in Paris, Smetana augmented his score with a male chorus in praise of beer, an aria for Marenka, and a dance.

He divided the first act into two scenes, later ending the first scene with a polka and opening the second with a furiant (peasant dance), which made three acts of the original two. For the St. Petersburg production, given in January 1871, the composer changed the spoken dialogue into recitative, bringing the opera to its present form . . .

ROBERT C. BAGAR, *Philharmonic-Symphony Society of New York*

The Moldau—from the symphonic poems—*My Country*

Smetana wrote a cycle of six symphonic poems under the general title of *Ma Vlast* (*My Country*), between 1874 and 1879. *Vltava* (*The Moldau*), the second of the series, was begun on November 20, 1874 and completed on December 8. The first performance was at Zofin Hall, in Prague, April 4, 1874. The entire cycle was performed for the composer's benefit at Prague, November 5, 1882.

The following program is printed on the score:

"Two springs pour forth their streams in the shade of the Bohemian forest, the one warm and gushing, the other cool and tranquil. Their waves joyfully flowing over their rocky beds, unite and sparkle in the morning sun. The forest brook rushing on becomes the River Moldau, which, with its waters spreading through Bohemia's valleys, grows into a mighty stream. It flows through dense woods in which are heard the joyous sounds of the hunt, the notes of the hunter's horn sounding ever nearer and nearer. It flows through emerald meadows and lowlands, where a wedding feast is being celebrated with song and dance. At night in its shining waves are reflected many a fortress and castle—witness of bygone splendor of chivalry and the vanished martial fame of days that are no more. At the Rapids of St. John, the stream speeds on, winding its way through cataracts and hewing the path for its foaming waters through the rocky chasm into the broad river-bed in which it flows in majestic calm toward Prague, welcomed by time-honored Vysehrad, to disappear from the poet's gaze in the far distance."

Intending *Ma Vlast* (My Country) to be a symphonic tetralogy, Smetana composed the first four tone-poems in eleven months, between November 18, 1874 and October 18, 1875. But the fourth, *From Bohemia's Fields and Groves,* did not wholly satisfy him as a finale, and he began to consider adding more symphonic poems to round out the cycle and bring it to a suitable climax. Four more years were required for the full conception to mature within him. *Tabor* was composed in 1878, and *Blaník* finally completed on March 9, 1879.

Each of the six tone-poems is closely identified with Bohemian history and tradition. The first, *Vysehrad,* evokes the ancient citadel near Prague, supposed stronghold of Princess Libuse; *Sàrka,* third of the series, is named for the legendary Czech Amazon. The fourth, *From Bohemia's Fields and Groves,* pictures the folk at work and in the dance. The fifth, *Tabor,* named for a fortress of the Hussites, is based upon the Hussite chorale, "You Are Warriors of God," which is heard again in *Blaník,* last of the cycle. Blaník is the mountain on which the Hussite warriors sleep, waiting the day when they shall reappear in arms to drive out their oppressors and restore freedom and glory to the Bohemian fields.

G. H. L. SMITH, *Cleveland Orchestra*

THE WALTZING STRAUSSES

WALTZES and Strausses are analogous and the Strausses themselves were multitudinous. There were Johann the elder and the younger, Eduard, Josef, Ferdinand and Franz, Nelli and Terese and a host of relatives, remote and actual. And they all, at one time or another, wrote waltzes—and played or conducted them. Their feuds and bickerings and adventures made up a fascinating history of Viennese rhythm and fanned the dance craze that swept all of Europe from the 1840's to the late 1890's.

The father of the waltzing Strausses, Johann the elder, was born in Vienna on the fourteenth of March, 1804. He was a violinist in a cafe band, formed his own in 1825 and his music proved so infectious that he became a local fad, then a national rage. He was charged with the duty of providing music for all the court balls. He toured Europe innumerable times, played seventy-two public concerts at the coronation of Queen Victoria in 1837, returned to Vienna and the continent, went back to London for a "farewell," and was "escorted down the Thames by a squadron of boats, in one of which a band played tunes in his honor." He died of scarlet fever in Vienna on September 29, 1849. He left three sons to carry on his tradition—Johann (1825-1899), Josef (1827-1870) and Eduard (1835-1916).

Oldsters still haunt the concert halls of New York who remember the American visit of Johann the younger. Boston invited him and Strauss accepted. Pitts Sanborn, in his introduction to H. E. Jacobs' book *Johann Strauss, Father and Son,* tells of this visit:

"Probably few today remember that Johann Strauss the younger once visited the United States. He came in the year 1872 at the special request of the city of Boston, which was holding a gigantic jubilee in the interests of world peace, and had invited also Buelow and Verdi. Johann the younger, unlike his father and his brother Eduard, was by no means a good traveler. Indeed, Mr. Jacobs tells us that a neurasthenic dread of a change of locality even resulted in such behavior as his seating himself on the floor of the railway carriage and drawing the curtains during the short trip from Vienna to the Semmering."

Strauss got $100,000 for this effort, plus traveling expenses for himself, his wife and two servants. And during the ocean journey, he of all the passengers aboard was not seasick.

"The auditorium in Boston," Sanborn adds, "was designed to accommodate 100,000 and six towering policemen were needed to pilot Strauss to the platform. On the musicians' tribune, Strauss himself relates, were gathered 20,000 singers. Before them was seated the great orchestra. As conductor-in-chief, he had a hundred assistants to control these huge masses. Strauss points out in his report that even though they had had rehearsals, an artistic performance in view of the numbers was impossible. But if he had declined to conduct, he declares, it would have cost him his life!

"There he stood at the raised desk, high above all the others, facing an audience of 100,000 Americans! How, he asked himself, would the business start, how would it end? Suddenly, a cannon shot rang out, a gentle hint to begin *The Beautiful Blue Danube.* Though Strauss declares this one appearance was enough for him and that he returned to Europe as quickly as he possibly could, the fact is that in Boston he conducted thirteen more concerts and two monster balls and that he also conducted in New York before sailing."

Strauss dedicated the waltz *Voices of Spring* to the piano virtuoso, Alfred Gruenfeld. "Do you know," he said, after Gruenfeld had played it through, "that waltz is not really so beautiful as it seems when you play it?"

It is said that Gruenfeld played Strauss waltzes in a Mozartean manner, clearly and without pedal, "taking care that there was no rumbling in the bass."

J. S.

RICHARD STRAUSS

(Born in Munich, June 11, 1864—died in Garmisch-
Partenkirchen, Germany, September 8, 1949)

"THE SON of a horn-player in the orchestra of the Bavarian
Court, Richard Strauss was born at Munich, in the year that an
even more famous Richard—Richard Wagner—took up his residence in the Bavarian capital at the invitation of Ludwig II.
Strauss was only four years of age when he began to receive regular
instruction from Tombo, harpist in the Munich orchestra. From
1875 until 1880 he studied composition and orchestration with the
Court *Kapellmeister*, F. W. Meyer.

"The elder Strauss was an uncompromising classicist—Wagner
and his music were the objects of his unwavering hatred—and he
saw to it that his young son should be brought continuously under
the influence of the eighteenth and early nineteenth century masters. Thus, it came about that the works of Richard Strauss' youth
are devoid of those perturbing and audacious qualities which, clear
and admirable as they may seem now, were destined to set the
musical world by the ears in the Nineties.

"The Fates parceled out a happy destiny to Richard Strauss.
He was still a young man when the great pianist-conductor, Hans
von Buelow, interested himself in his work and made him his assistant in the conductorship of the Meiningen Orchestra. Strauss'
work there attracted wide attention and shortly he was appointed
conductor at Munich. Meanwhile he busied himself with composition and his tone-poems, *Don Juan, Death and Transfiguration,
Macbeth* etc.—works distinguished by extraordinary technical skill
and vivid imagination—brought him into instant fame. His realization that sensationalism, as well as artistic beauty, had its allure-
ment for the public, led Strauss to the composition of a number
of operas which, upon their production, caused remarkable upheavals in the world of art. Such were *Salome,* based upon Oscar
Wilde's play and produced in 1905; *Elektra* (1909), *Der Rosen-
kavalier* (1911) etc. But Strauss continued the tilling of other
musical fields. His orchestral works, *Till Eulenspiegel, Don Quixote, Thus Spake Zarathustra* and the *Sinfonia Domestica,* evoked

379

wide discussion and admiration. His songs were, and are, the treasured possessions of vocalists in every land.

"Particularly in Germany is Richard Strauss regarded as one of the great conductors of the age. His triumphs as leader of the Berlin Philharmonic Orchestra, the State Opera Orchestra, the Vienna Philharmonic Orchestra, etc., have been of phenomenal brilliancy. Nor have those triumphs been confined to Europe alone. Strauss visited America in 1904 and again in 1921, and won universal acclaim for his direction of symphonic works. It may be said in conclusion that Strauss is one of the few distinguished composers who have shown great talent for the commercial exploitation of their artistic gifts. The skill and the sagacity with which he has handled the business of disposing of his works have made him probably the wealthiest composer in Europe."

FELIX BOROWSKI

In 1933, when the Nazi government came into power in Germany, Strauss was picked to head the *Kulturkammer.* Subsequent differences with Nazi ideologies caused his removal from this office. In 1948 a denazification court cleared him, in Munich, of all charges that he had collaborated with the Hitler regime. He had been living in the villa of his son, Dr. Franz Strauss, working on yet another opera. He was eighty-five at the time of his death in September 1949.

Burleske: for piano and orchestra, in D minor

In 1885, Strauss took a position as assistant to Hans von Buelow, who was then the conductor of the orchestra at Meiningen. It has been observed that Buelow's extraordinary admiration of Brahms' works had its collateral effect on the impressionable young Strauss. And in fact certain Brahmsian influences are not to be denied in the music of *Burleske.*

Be that as it may, the piece, presented to Buelow in the winter of 1886 for appraisal and, naturally with the hope that he might find some opportunity to perform it, was rejected by him with the terse declaration: "It is unplayable!" Oddly, Strauss himself had some misgivings about it, for, after giving it a rehearsal reading or two, he slipped it into a portfolio, accompanying the deed with the comment: "Sheer nonsense!"

Four years later, though, it was fished out of its hiding place and played for the first time at a concert in the town theater of Eisenach (June 21, 1890). The solo pianist was Eugen d'Albert, to whom the piece is dedicated; the conductor, Strauss. The occasion was the twenty-seventh annual music festival of the Allgemeiner Deutscher Musikverein.

The publisher Hainauer, who attended the premiere, manifested a great interest in the number and he made its composer a flattering offer for it. But Strauss, still doubtful of its worth, wrote to his friend Alexander Ritter: "I really need the money. What shall I do? It goes against me to permit publication of a work which I have left far behind, and to which I cannot give my approval."

Strauss did know what to do, however, for he did not accede to Hainauer's request, at least, not until four years had passed, in all, eight years after the composition of *Burleske*.

Buelow's later devotion to Strauss' compositions contrasted curiously with an early judgment made before their association at Meiningen. A publisher named Spitzweg, who had brought out several pieces of the youthful Strauss, sent Buelow a few more. The latter wrote back: "Piano pieces by R. Str. have thoroughly displeased me. Immature and precocious. Compared with him Lachner had the imagination of a Chopin. I miss all the youthfulness in the invention. Not a genius, I am thoroughly convinced, but at most a talent that requires sixty to make a bushel."

ROBERT C. BAGAR, *Philharmonic-Symphony Society of New York*

Till Eulenspiegel's Merry Pranks, After the Old-Fashioned Roguish Manner: In Rondo Form (Opus 28)

At first Strauss was inclined to let the title *Till Eulenspiegel's lustige Streiche, nach alter Schelmenweise—in Rondoform* stand as sufficient explanation of his intentions. Franz Wuellner, about to perform the work in Chicago, coaxed from him a letter which revealed a little more:

"It is impossible for me to furnish a program to *Eulenspiegel*; were I to put into words the thoughts which its several incidents suggested to me, they would seldom suffice, and might even give rise to offense. Let me leave it, therefore, to my hearers to crack the hard nut which the Rogue has prepared for them. By way of helping them to a better understanding, it seems sufficient to point out the two Eulenspiegel motives, which, in the most manifold disguises, moods, and situations, pervade the whole up to the catastrophe, when, after he has been condemned to death, Till is strung up to the gibbet. For the rest, let them guess at the musical joke which a Rogue has offered them." Strauss finally noted three themes; the opening of the introduction, the horn motive of Till and the portentous descending interval of the Rogue's condemnation.

And again, Strauss was persuaded by Wilhelm Mauke, the most elaborate and exhaustive of Straussian analysts, to jot the following indications in pencil in his score:

"Once upon a time there was a *Volksnarr;* named *Till Eulenspiegel*; That was an awful hobgoblin; Off for New Pranks; Just wait, you hypocrites! Hop! On horseback into the midst of the marketwomen; With seven-league boots he lights out; Hidden in a Mouse-hole; Disguised as a Pastor, he drips with unction and morals; Yet out of his big toe peeps the Rogue; But before he gets through he nevertheless has qualms because of his having mocked religion; Till as cavalier pays court to pretty girls; She has really made an impression on him; He courts her; a kind refusal is still a refusal; Till departs furious; He swears vengeance on all mankind; Philistine Motive; After he has propounded to the Philistines a few amazing theses he leaves them in astonishment to their fate; Great grimaces from afar; Till's street tune; The court of Justice; He still whistles to himself indifferently; Up the Ladder! There he swings; he gasps for air, a last convulsion; the mortal part of Till is no more."

The first performance was at a Guerzenich concert in Cologne, November 5, 1895. Strauss had completed his score in Munich, the previous May. It had been published in September. . . .

JOHN N. BURK, *Boston Symphony Orchestra*

Don Juan: A Tone-Poem
(after Nicolaus Lenau)

Strauss . . . was twenty-four when he composed *Don Juan,*
the first of his six tone-poems and one of the most popular of his
works for orchestra. There have been many Don Juans in stories,
plays and poems. The original legendary Spanish libertine was
brought into literature in 1630 in a drama by a monk who wrote
under the name of Tirso de Molina. Zorrilla, Molière, de Musser,
Dumas, Byron, Shaw—all had their Don Juans and there were several operas glorifying him, before Mozart's *Don Giovanni* (or Don
Juan) immortalized da Ponte's libretto.

Strauss' tone-poem is based upon a poem by the Hungarian,
Nicolaus Lenau. Lenau's *Don Juan* is a new and different version.
Lenau told his biographer, L. A. Frankle: "Byron's *Don Juan* will
do me no harm. My *Don Juan* is no hot-blooded man eternally
pursuing women. It is the longing in him to find a woman who is
to him incarnate womanhood."

Lenau's *Don Juan* is a romantic idealist. He searches in vain
for his ideal woman, becomes disillusioned and dissatisfied with
himself and life. He drops his sword when fighting a duel and lets
his adversary kill him. His last words were: "My deadly foe is in
my power, and this, too, bores me as does life itself."

Strauss prefixed to the score of *Don Juan* three excerpts from
Lenau's poem. These lines give no actual events, but show "the
mood and purpose of the composer." It has been said that three
emotional phases of the story appealed to Strauss; the fiery ardor
with which Don Juan pursues his ideal; the charm of women and
the idealist's "partial atonement by death."

Strauss has said: "I have long since learned that in my composition I am unable to write without a program to guide me."
But many listeners prefer to disregard the literary program and
listen to Strauss' music purely as music. No one needs a guide to
feel "the sequence of acute emotional states." The originality of
the themes—so fitted to what the composer has to say—the rich
counterpoint and the masterly use of the orchestra are obvious.

The opening measures (*Allegro molto con brio*) are thought
to picture Don Juan in all his youthful, manly vigor—the irresist-

ible gallant, impatient in his search for adventure. These measures "culminate in a superb gesture of welcome to Love wheresoever it may be found." (Tovey)

Love episodes alternate with this "questing" music of Don Juan. Two of the romantic episodes are easily recognized. After a harp cadenza, a solo violin introduces the first episode. The second is given to a solo oboe—a famous passage. This is followed by the second *Don Juan* theme played by four horns in unison— another famous melody and "one of the most magnificent Strauss ever conceived."

The opening "questing" theme is heard again and leads into the middle section, which has been called the Carnival episode. "Don Juan has flung himself headlong into a whirlwind of enjoyment." The orchestra becomes more and more brilliant and highly colored. As the climax subsides, bits of the solo violin and solo oboe themes are heard. The orchestra recalls the *Don Juan* themes.

Near the end of the composition a tremendous climax is followed by silence—then a soft chord with a discordant trumpet tone, "shuddering string tremolo," soft drum roll and solemn brass. "The conclusion is laconic, tightlipped. There is no wild complaint . . . only abandonment of life."

Indianapolis Symphony Orchestra

Also Sprach Zarathustra

A philosophical tone-poem is an art form invented entirely by Richard Strauss. Before him, Berlioz and Liszt introduced the element of fantasy and emotional brooding into orchestral composition, but neither thought of setting Kant or Hegel to music. For his philosophical tone-poem, Strauss selected the text from Friedrich Nietzsche's *Also Sprach Zarathustra*, written during the last years before insanity overtook the philosopher. The preachment of bodily health, strong leadership and cold science, was the wishful tribute of a philosopher on the brink of physical and mental disintegration, and it is an ironic commentary that this authoritarian outlook on life has found its eventual expression years later in the movement of "strength through joy."

Richard Strauss is careful to state that his tone-poem is but a free paraphrase of Nietzsche. The score carries the following quotation from *Also Sprach Zarathustra*: "Having attained the age of thirty, Zarathustra left his home and went into the mountains. There he rejoiced in his spirit and his loneliness, and for ten years he did not grow weary of it. But at last his heart turned. One morning he got up with the dawn, stepped into the presence of the Sun, and thus spake unto him: "Thou great star! What would be thy happiness, were it not for those on whom thou shinest? For ten years thou hast come up here to my cave. Thou wouldst have got sick of thy light and thy journey but for me, mine eagle and my serpent. But we waited for thee every morning, and, receiving from thee thine abundance, blessed thee for it. Lo! I am weary of thy wisdom, like the bee that hath collected too much honey. I need hands reaching out for it. I would fain grant and distribute, until the wise among men could once more enjoy their folly, and the poor once more their riches. For that end I must descend to the depths, as thou dost at even, when, sinking behind the sea, thou givest light to the lower regions, thou resplendent star! I must, like thee, go down, as men say—men to whom I would descend. Then bless me, thou impassive eye, that canst look without envy upon overmuch happiness. Bless the cup which is about to overflow, so that the water, golden-flowing out of it, may carry everywhere the reflection of thy rapture. Lo! this cup is about to empty itself again, and Zarathustra will once more become a man. Thus Zarathustra's descent began.""

The tone-poem is separated into several sections which are marked by a change of movement, or thematic content. The most important theme, recurring time and again, is the slow upward progression, C—G—C. Its deliberate bleakness, and avoidance of the tonal third so as to leave the tonality indeterminate serves no doubt a programmatic purpose. After a solemn introduction, with a climax in C major, there is a section marked: "Of the Dwellers of the World in the Rear" (*Hinterweltern*). The horns introduce the religious theme, *Credo in unum deum,* as a quotation from Gregorian chant. In the following section, "Of Profound Yearning," there is another Gregorian quotation from the Magnificat. This corresponds to the program of the work, which reflects man's feeling for the power of God. It is interesting to note that Strauss accepts this feeling as Christian and not as pagan sun-worship.

The individual longings of man turn him into passion, illustrated in the division marked "Of Joys and Sorrows." Then follows the mournful "Song of the Grave." After religion, and passion, the interest is turned into science. Its theme, opening with the progression C—G—C, underlying the entire tone-poem, is interesting in that it covers all twelve tones of the scale, and forms four mutually exclusive triads, if we start from the upper C, and adjoin it to the last note of the theme. This technique, which lies at the bottom of the Schoenberg school, is here applied possibly for programmatic purposes, to indicate the thorough exploration in scientific research. The theme is treated frugally, illustrating man's attempt to solve the riddle of life.

The continuation of this section, marked "The Convalescent," treats the "science theme" with additional counterpoint in clipped, rhythmically diversified figures. Then comes the "Dance Song." It is a waltz, in which man finds his individual joy. The night descends; the "Song of the Night Wanderer" is heard. The bell strikes twelve. There is a conflict of the theme of the ideal expressed in the bitonality of B major in the high register, and unresolved chord in the trombones. The theme C—G—C is repeated in the double basses, and its significance is revealed: it is the world riddle.

It must be understood that Strauss himself gave little elucidation on the philosophical content of *Zarathustra,* and even denied that it was conceived as a philosophical tone-poem. The usual interpretation of Nietzsche and Strauss can be formed only from the words of the commentators, and from the analysis of Nietzsche's text. Strauss wrote the music between February 4 and August 24 of the year 1896, in Munich, and conducted the first performance himself, at Frankfurt, on November 27 of the same year.

NICOLAS SLONIMSKY, *Columbia Masterworks Program Notes*

Death and Transfiguration: Tone-Poem for Full Orchestra (Opus 24)

This tone-poem was composed at Munich in 1888-1889. It was published at Munich in April 1891. The first performance was from manuscript, under the direction of the composer, at the fifth concert of the Twenty-seventh Musicians' Convention of the Allgemeine Deutscher Musikverein in the City Theater of Eisenach, June 21, 1890. . . . On the flyleaf of the score is a poem in German. The authorship of this poem was for some years unknown. The prevailing impression was that the poem suggested the music. As a matter of fact, Alexander Ritter wrote the poem *after* he was well acquainted with Strauss' score; and, when the score was sent to the publisher, the poem was sent with it for insertion. Hausegger in his *Life of Ritter* states that Strauss asked Ritter to write it. The following literal translation is by William Foster Apthorp:

"In the necessitous little room, dimly lighted by only a candle-end, lies the sick man on his bed. Now he has sunk exhausted into sleep, and thou hearest only the soft ticking of the clock on the wall in the room, whose awful silence gives a foreboding of the nearness of Death. Over the sick man's pale features plays a sad smile. Dreams he, on the boundary of life, of the golden time of childhood?

"But Death does not long grant sleep and dreams to his victim. Cruelly he shakes him awake, and the fight begins afresh. Will to live and power of Death! What frightful wrestling! Neither bears off the victory, and all is silent once more!

"Sunk back tired of battle, sleepless, as in fever-frenzy the sick man now sees his life pass before his inner eye, trait by trait and scene by scene. First the morning red of childhood, shining bright in pure innocence! Then the youth's saucier play—exerting and trying his strength—till he ripens to the man's fight, and now burns with hot lust after the higher prizes of life. The one high purpose that has led him through life was to shape all he saw transfigured into a still more transfigured form. Cold and sneering, the world sets barrier upon barrier in the way of his achievement. If he thinks himself near his goal, a 'Halt!' thunders in his ear. 'Make the barrier thy stirrup! Ever higher and onward go!' And so he pushes forward, so he climbs, desists not from his sacred purpose. What he has ever sought with his heart's deepest yearning, he still seeks in his death-sweat. Seeks—alas! and finds it never. Whether he comprehends it more clearly or that it grows upon him gradually, he can never yet exhaust it, cannot complete it in his spirit. Then clangs the last stroke of Death's iron hammer, breaks the earthly body in twain, covers the eye with the night of death.

"But from the heavenly spaces sounds mightily to greet him what he yearningly sought for here: deliverance from the world, transfiguration of the world."

PHILIP HALE, *Boston Symphony Orchestra*

Ein Heldenleben (*A Hero's Life*—Opus 40)

When upon its appearance nearly forty years ago *Ein Heldenleben* was seen to be a piece of autobiography, there was widespread repugnance at the author's monumental conceit. A hero's life, with himself the hero, forsooth! Well, other people didn't think him a hero, some rather thought him a villain or a clown. When it was discovered that Strauss had incorporated quotations from his previous works into this score, the sarcasms grew even stronger. On top of all this, the unheard-of elaborateness of his orchestral apparatus and the shockingly dissonant character of his sonorities helped to confirm the impression of megalomania which his personality evoked.

Today we are wiser. The orchestral complexity seems to be not so impressive as it is troublesome. The dissonances are enjoyed for their expressive power, but they no longer startle. We have stopped worrying about the author's conceit: *A Hero's Life* might signify the career of any strong personality, not necessarily Strauss'. Despite the egoism, the work has a broad human significance. Interestingly enough, this most personal of Strauss' tone-poems has proven to have the most enduring vitality of his works of the same period. In the number of its public performances and in the warmth of its popular acclaim, *Ein Heldenleben* has far outdistanced the two symphonic works which immediately preceded it, namely: *Don Quixote* and *Thus Spake Zarathustra*, and likewise the one that followed it, the *Sinfonia Domestica*.

If *Till Eulenspiegel* is a sort of rondo, and *Don Quixote* a set of variations, *Ein Heldenleben* may be thought of as a huge symphonic movement, in six main sections. Sections 1 and 2 might be considered as the principal theme, section 3 the secondary theme. The "Battlefield" might pass as the development section. There is undoubtedly a return to the beginning just before section 5, and the last section may be construed as an enormous coda.

1—"The Hero." The very first motive, with its aggressive upward swing, its incalculable leaps and queer intervals, represent the hero's unshakable self-confidence and extravagance. More flowing, tender motives join with it to complete a more rounded portrait, but the assertive strain has the last word.

2—"The Hero's Adversaries." These evidently are meant to be some narrow-minded, malicious, pettifogging critics. The piccalilli of woodwind sounds that makes up this portrait is about the meanest-sounding music ever concocted. The expression marks are interesting: "Very sharp and pointed," "rasping." The bass to this passage is supplied with two tubas which several times interject a little figure in open parallel fifths which says plainly, in German: *'Das sind Quinten"* ("These are Fifths"). The allusion is to an old rule of harmonic procedure which forbids the use of successive parallel fifths—a great talking point with unimaginative critics.

The Hero's reply to his adversaries is in a saddened vein. He regains his confidence momentarily, when there appears

3—"The Hero's Helpmate." The delineation of this character is assigned to the solo violin, which launches into a number of cadenza-like passages. Seductive at first, the lady soon displays other traits. The expression marks, again, are quite revealing: 'Hypocritically gushingly," "gaily," "frivolously," "tenderly, somewhat sentimentally," "very sharply," "playfully," "amiably," "furiously," "suddenly quiet again and very feelingly," "in a rage," 'quickly scolding," "tenderly and lovingly." After this last the violin retires and the orchestra works up a gorgeous love scene full of rich and honeyed sonorities. From the depths of this bath of bliss we hear as from afar a faint echo of the adversaries' carpings. The Hero is not moved; then from behind the scene three trumpets utter a stern fanfare, the call to battle. The Hero rouses himself gradually, reinforced by his helpmate.

4—"The Hero's Battlefield." This begins properly with a fierce battery of sidedrums. The adversaries' theme, broadened and loudened by being blared on a trumpet, is pitted against the Hero's theme, while the fanfares get mixed up with both. But our Hero is victorious, his theme arises, *ff,* triumphant in its entirety on the original key. He commences upon—

5—"The Hero's Works of Peace." We hear one or two quotations from his works, but there is a long pause. *"Das sind Quinten,"* say the tubas. Against this sterile pedantry his best flashes are of no avail. But he continues along his path. If we listen well we can discern snatches of *Death and Transfiguration, Till Eulenspiegel, Don Quixote, Thus Spake Zarathustra, Don Juan, Macbeth, Guntram,* and a song, *Traum durch die Daemmerung.* Again there is a pause after this powerful array of works. *"Das sind Quinten"* is the reply again.

6—"The Hero's Release from the World." There is a last heartbreaking, violent revulsion against this stupidity, then the hero finds inward peace. He has overcome both his adversaries and his own inner contradiction. The music becomes more reflective and introspective. His own theme is heard, quietly, also that of his beloved companion. The end is harmonious.

ARTHUR LOESSER, *Cleveland Orchestra*

Don Quixote: (Introduction, Theme and Variations and Finale): Fantastic Variations on a Theme of Knightly Character (Opus 35)

Composed at Munich in 1897, *Don Quixote* was given its first performance at a Guerzenich concert, Cologne, on March 8, 1898. On that occasion it was played from manuscript. Franz Wuellner was the conductor. The composer conducted the work at a concert of the Frankfurt Museumgesellschaft ten days later.

. . . *Don Quixote* . . . is a program piece without an actual program supplied by the composer. At least, the score itself is not provided with one. Yet the work has had explanations without end, among them being one by Arthur Hahn which is remarkable both for its length—twenty-seven printed pages—and its fanciful ness. . . . The following program of *Don Quixote* is derived from an explanation accompanying the two-piano arrangement. The Introduction, ten Variations and Finale are played without pause:

Introduction. The elderly hero's fancy teems with the "impossible follies" of the romantic works he has been reading. He goes mad (as exemplified in the music by a piercing discord, on the heels of a harp glissando) and in his madness he vows that he will become a knight-errant.

Theme. Don Quixote, the Knight of the Rueful Countenance; Sancho Panza. Here the theme of the hero is announced by the solo 'cello. Sancho Panza's theme emerges first in the bass clarinet, then in the tenor tuba; later, however, it is always given to the solo viola.

Variation I: "The Knight and his Squire start on Their Journey" (In a leisurely manner, D minor, 12-8). Inspired by the beautiful Dulcinea of Toboso, the Knight attacks some "monstrous giants," who are nothing more than windmills revolving in the breeze. The sails knock him down and he is in a "very evil plight."

Variation II: "The Victorious Battle against the Host of the Great Emperor Alifanfaron" (Warlike, D major, 4-4). A huge army approaches in a swirling cloud of dust. It is a great herd of sheep, but the Knight's tottering mind perceives the flashing weapons of soldiery. He rushes in to the charge, unmindful of Sancho's warnings, and the muted brass depicts the pitiful bleating of the animals. The Knight is stoned by the shepherds and he falls to the ground.

Variation III: "Colloquies of Knight and Squire" (Moderato, D major, 4-4). Honor, glory, the Ideal Woman, these are the things Don Quixote speaks on. Sancho, the realist, holds forth for a more comfortable life, but he is ordered to hold his tongue.

Variation IV: "The Adventure with the Penitents" (Somewhat broader, D minor, 4-4). Mistaking a band of pilgrims for robbers and villains, Don Quixote attacks, only to receive a sound drubbing from them. The pilgrims depart, intoning their churchly theme, and the senseless Knight revives to the great delight of Sancho, who soon falls asleep.

Variation V: "The Knight's Vigil" (Very slow, D minor, 4-4). Don Quixote spurns sleep. He will watch by his armor, instead.

Dulcinea, in answer to his prayers, comes to him in a vision, as the theme of the Ideal Woman is heard in the horn. There is a cadenza for harp and violins followed by a rhapsodic passage.

Variation VI: "The Meeting with Dulcinea" (G major, 2-4, 3-4). Jestingly, Sancho points to a country wench as Dulcinea. There are words between the Knight and Squire; the former will not believe it, the latter swears it is so. Don Quixote then vows vengeance against the wicked magician who has wrought the transformation.

Variation VII: "The Ride through the Air" (A little quieter than before, D minor, 8-4). Blindfolded, Knight and Squire sit astride a wooden horse, which—they have been informed—will carry them aloft. Their themes surge upward and one hears the whistling of the wind about them through the chromatic flute passages, the music for the harp, a drum roll and the whine of the wind machine. However, the persistent tremolo on D in the double-basses and kettledrums tells the listener that the wooden horse has never taken flight.

Variation VIII: "The Journey in the Enchanted Park." An oarless boat, lying idle on a bank of the Ebro, is the conveyance by which Don Quixote may speed to the rescue of some important dignitary. He and Sancho embark, as the typical theme of the Knight comes through in a barcarolle. Though the boat capsizes, the two finally reach shore and give thanks for their safety.

Variation IX: "The Combat with Two Magicians" (Quickly and stormily, D minor, 4-4). Back on his horse and eager as ever for adventure, Don Quixote violently charges into a peaceful pair of monks, who are going by on their mules. In his maddened brain, the monks are mighty magicians, and the Don is elated beyond measure with their utter rout.

Variation X: (Much broader, D minor, 4-4). The greatest setback of his knightly career is suffered by the Don at the hand of the Knight of the White Moon, who is, after all, a true friend. He explains that he hoped to cure Don Quixote of his madness and, having won the duel, orders him to retire peacefully to his home for a year, "so nothing more were required of him in prejudice of his fair Dulcinea."

Finale: "The Death of Don Quixote" (Very peacefully, D major, 4-4). The worn and harried Knight is no longer bemused. The

olo 'cello expresses his true understanding of the state of things,
as he recalls his useless aims and empty maneuvers. It was all
vanity, he reflects, and he is prepared, now, for the peace that is
death.

ROBERT C. BAGAR, *Philharmonic-Symphony Society of New York*

Dance of the Seven Veils—from the opera *Salome*

The one-act drama *Salome,* written in French by Oscar Wilde,
was first published in 1893. It was performed in Paris, October
, 1896. An English translation by Lord Alfred Bruce Douglas
published in 1894 with illustrations by Aubrey Beardsley) was
rst performed in London, May 10, 1905. The play was translated
nto German by Hedwig Lachmann and had a considerable vogue
n German theaters. Strauss began his score in the summer of
903 and completed it June 20, 1905. The first performance was
iven at the Dresden Court Opera, December 9, 1905.

An opera utilizing the full Straussian orchestra, and telling its
ale with all the descriptive and colorful resource of a tone-poem,
asting two hours without break, was indeed a wonder to the
peratic world of 1905. It would have been so even without the
dded sensation of its erotic subject. Within a year, *Salome* had
een mounted upon thirty operatic stages. Heinrich Conried un-
ertook a production at the Metropolitan Opera House in New
ork on January 22, 1907, when Olive Fremstad sang the role
: Salome, and Alfred Hertz conducted. The directors of the opera
ut a stop to further performances on the ground that the first
ne was "objectionable and detrimental to the best interests of
e Metropolitan." Mr. Oscar Hammerstein ventured *Salome* at
e Manhattan Opera House on January 28, 1909, Mary Garden
ppearing in the title role, and herself performing *"The Dance
the Seven Veils* (a substitute had acted this scene for Mme.
emstad). There were fourteen performances. The opera was
vived at the Metropolitan Opera House, January 13, 1934,
ith Goeta Ljungberg as Salome.

There had been many representations of the Biblical tale of
erod and Herodias when Oscar Wilde conceived the subject in

a new light, which made it far more vivid as dramatic material. The Salome of Wilde was not the pliant tool of Herodias, merely obedient to her mother's purpose of vengeance upon John the Baptist. The daughter of Herodias whom Wilde imagined became enamored of the direful prophet, who angrily spurned her advances. She was an imperious princess, conscious of her power ready to forfeit the half of Herod's kingdom which was offered her in her determination to have the lips of the prophet submit to her own—even in a submission of death.

It was the unreasoned and fanatical passion of Salome for the wan flesh of the prophet, stilled in death, which was found disturbing and scandalous in the year 1905. The subject had appealed to Oscar Wilde as *"quelque chose de curieux et de sensuel"*. So he wrote to Sarah Bernhardt, for whom he enthusiastically envisioned the part. Wilde denied having written the play for her protesting that he was an "artist" and not an "artisan." Sarah Bernhardt agreed to appear in a production at the Palace Theater, London, in 1892, but the censor refused a license. She never acted in the play, which was produced in Paris with Lina Munte as Salome (Nouveau Théatre, October 28, 1896).

The first New York production of Strauss' *Salome* aroused a storm of public discussion, in which illustrious voices were raised in defense of the composer. . . . .

Oscar Wilde's play, which Strauss has adopted with minor excisions, is a text overladen with figures of speech, in themselves artificial and mannered, which nevertheless contribute to his atmosphere of mingled Oriental sensuality and foreboding.

The scene is the great terrace in the palace of Herod, set above the banqueting hall, where festivities are in progress. Salome comes to the terrace to escape the lustful glances of the Tetrarch. She is intrigued by the voice of the Prophet Jokanaan whom she commands the guard to bring up from the cistern in which he is imprisoned, and his indignant repulsion of her advances only piques her desire. Herodias forbids her to dance before Herod, but the willful princess defies her mother. Her slaves bring perfumes and the seven veils, and take off the sandals of Salome. Herod says: "Ah, thou art to dance with naked feet! 'Tis well! Thy little feet will be like white doves. They will be like little white flowers that dance upon the trees." But there is a poet of blood upon the terrace, where the young captain of the guard has killed himself for hopeless love of her. And Herod fears an evil omen. "No, no, she is going to dance on blood. There is blood spilt on the ground." And he exclaims in terror that the moon has become red as blood.

Recovering, he commands her to begin, waving aside the protestations of her mother. Herod lays half of the kingdom's treasury as reward at her feet, but Salome startles him by demanding the head of Jokanaan upon a silver charger. When Herodias, whom Jokanaan has cursed and denounced, learns that Salome intends the death of the Prophet, she is pleased. Herod, on the other hand, is in supersitious dread of the seer. Herod recoils, in vain, for she holds him to his oath, six times repeating her demand. He is loath to give his attendant the ring which is the seal of death. The black headsman descends into the cistern. There is an awful pause of suspense while Salome hangs eagerly over the bronze rail of the black recess. It is a moment the horror of which Strauss heightens with his power of musical suggestions. "A huge black arm, the arm of the executioner, comes from the cistern bearing on a silver shield the head of Jokanaan. Salome seizes it. Herod hides his face with his cloak. Herodias smiles and fans herself. The Nazarenes fall on their knees and begin to pray."

Salome makes an apostrophe to the head: "Ah! thou wouldst not suffer me to kiss thy mouth, Jokanaan. Well, I will kiss it now. I will bite it with my teeth as one bites a ripe fruit . . . Thou wouldst have none of me, Jokanaan. Thou rejectedst me. Thou didst speak evil words against me . . . Well, I still live, but thou art dead and thy head belongs to me . . . . All other men were hateful to me, but thou wert beautiful! Thy body was a column of ivory set upon feet of silver."

Herod rises in revulsion, and commands the slaves to put out the torches. "Hide the moon! Hide the stars! Let us hide ourselves in our palace, Herodias. I begin to be afraid." The stars disappear. A great cloud crosses the moon and conceals it completely. The stage becomes quite dark. The Tetrarch begins to climb the staircase.

The Voice of Salome: Ah! I have kissed thy mouth, Jokanaan, I have kissed thy mouth. There was a bitter taste on my lips. Was it the taste of blood? . . . . Nay; but perchance it was the taste of love . . . They say that love hath a bitter taste . . . But what matter? What matter? I have kissed thy mouth.

Herod (*Turning around and seeing Salome*): Kill that woman!

(The soldiers rush forward and crush beneath their shields Salome, daughter of Herodias, Princess of Judea.)

JOHN N. BURK, *Boston Symphony Orchestra*

Waltzes from the opera—*Der Rosenkavalier*

In the early weeks of the season of 1910-1911, Strauss (a canny showman as well as a great composer) allowed it to become known that his new opera, which he then called *Ochs von Lerchenau,* contained some waltzes. That was sensational news to a public which had winced at the astringencies of *Salome* in 1905, and of *Elektra* in 1909. The Berlin *Boersin-Courier* learned, from a "well-informed source," that the score was "absolutely unStrausslike, inasmuch as none of the excessively modern subleties predominates in the vocal parts or orchestration. On the contrary, the score is brimming over with exceedingly pleasant and catchy melodies, most of them in three-four time. Yes, melodies, incredible as this may sound in the case of Richard Strauss. One waltz, especially, which the tenor sings, is likely to become so popular that many people will believe it is the work, not of Richard, but of Johann Strauss . . ."

The opera was first given in Dresden, January 26, 1911, and quickly made the rounds in Germany and elsewhere. Its humors, now gusty and now exceedingly sly, were not at once appreciated. Its Mozartian flavor and its waltzes as well were too wide a departure from what was expected of Richard II. But its charm and its smartness won rehearings that allowed the lyric loveliness and the emotional depths of the *Komodie für Musik* to emerge.

The Waltzes of the present program do not occur in the opera as a connected passage, but are rather a collection of several that appear from time to time in the second and third acts.

R. F. L. McCOMBS, *Philadelphia Orchestra*

IGOR STRAVINSKY

(Born near St. Petersburg, June 17, 1882—now
living in Hollywood, Calif.)

FROM THE *London Daily Mail Year Book of 1933*:
"Stravinsky, Igor, the audacious and experimental Russian
Composer; the most discussed musician in Europe today, at 50.
Born near Petrograd, but has for long made his home in France.
Became famous by his ballets commissioned by Diaghilev (*e.g.
The Fire Bird, Petrouchka*, his masterpiece, and *The Rite of
Spring*). His later works are one and all of curious 'cerebral' in-
terest, though their permanent musical value is problematical. He
is a frequent visitor to London, where he has the most enthusiastic
admirers, as well as violent detractors. In Paris his influence is
enormous."

Sixteen years later in the United States, Stravinsky is still a
controversial name. From the *New York Times Book Review*,
1949:

"The careers of Debussy and Stravinsky are examples of a commonplace phenomenon in the history of music. The public, having recognized as great a work (or series of works) by a living composer, proceeds to monumentalize its discovery. A specific style becomes unalterably identified with the composer, in the same manner as a type of role is associated with a famous actor. When, in
the course of a truly creative life, the composer outgrows that
style and begins to unfold in new directions, the public resents
the change. In the case of Stravinsky, the quiet introspective quality of *Orpheus* may seem disappointing after *Petrouchka's* spectac-
ular brilliance." (H. George Lawrence)

Stravinsky was born in Oranienbaum, a suburb of St. Petersburg, on St. Igor's Day, and he was named for that saint.

His father, who was a singer at the Imperial Opera, saw to it
that the boy had a sound training in music, but had no intention
of letting his son follow a musical career. Instead, Stravinsky studied law.

When he was twenty-three, young Igor abandoned the law and

397

became a private pupil of Rimsky-Korsakoff. During this tutelage, he produced several small works, including *Fireworks,* which was heard by Diaghilev and Fokine. At the time, Fokine was creating *Les Sylphides* for Diaghilev's newly-formed Ballet Russe, and they asked Stravinsky to orchestrate the Nocturne and the Valse Brillante for the Chopin ballet.

In her book, *Choreographic Music,* Verna Arvey tells an amusing story of what happened after *Sylphides* and before Diaghilev asked Stravinsky to compose *The Fire Bird.* The Russian composer Liadov had been commissioned by Diaghilev to write the music for *The Fire Bird,* and after months of waiting, Diaghilev went to see the composer to ask how it was progressing. "It won't be long now," said Liadow. "It's well on its way. I have just bought the ruled paper." Stravinsky was commissioned to do the score.

After the successful presentation of *The Fire Bird,* Stravinsky became the focal point in musical circles. Debussy's comment on *The Fire Bird* was: "Its music is not a docile servant to the dance."

After the premiere, Stravinsky went to Geneva to rest, the Parisian applause still ringing in his ears. While there he started work on a *Konzertstuecke,* which later developed into the score of *Petrouchka,* considered by some to be his masterpiece, but dubbed by the men of the orchestra, at its Viennese premiere, as "dirty music."

It was not *Petrouchka,* however, that caused the great tempests that have raged ever since over Stravinsky, but *Le Sacre du Printemps (The Rite of Spring).* The story of the howling, screaming, fighting mobs at the Paris premiere of this ballet is now famous. Everyone was indignant, either at Stravinsky and his music, or at their neighbors and their lack of appreciation of this masterpiece of genius. It is said that at the height of the pandemonium, the aged Countess Pourtales rose in her box and shouted indignantly: "This is the first time in sixty years that anyone has dared to make a fool of me!"

The Rite of Spring always caused some kind of demonstration, active or passive, wherever it was first played. After the premiere in Boston, the *Boston Herald* printed a poem:

Who wrote this fiendish *Rite of Spring?*
What right had he to write the thing?
Against our helpless ears to fling
Its crash, clash, cling; bing, bang, bing?

After the "incident" of *Printemps,* Stravinsky wrote several smaller works—*Renard,* an intimate chamber-opera pantomime; the revised opera-into-ballet, *Song of the Nightingale; L'Histoire du Soldat; Les Noces,* a ballet of early Russian village life; and *Pulcinella,* premiered in 1923. The latter caused considerable talk and argument, whether it was Pergolesi, revamped Pergolesi, Pergolesi-Stravinsky, or if Pergolesi had any connection with it at all.

Mavra, Stravinsky's opera written in 1921, was not successful. Nineteen twenty-seven, however, saw the presentation of three of his most admired later works, the classically statuesque oratorio *Oedipus Rex;* the Greek-frieze-influenced ballet, *Apollo* and the Hans Christian Andersen fairy-tale ballet, *Le Baiser de la Fée* (The *Fairy's Kiss*), which still holds a prominent place in the repertoire of the Ballet Russe de Monte Carlo.

For the fiftieth anniversary of the Boston Symphony Orchestra in 1930, Stravinsky composed *Symphonie des Psaumes,* dedicated to, "the glory of God." It received its premiere on December 13, 1930, not in Boston, but in Brussels. The first Boston performance took place six days later.

In 1934, Stravinsky, who had lived most of his later years in France and Switzerland, became a French citizen. During that year he wrote the ballet *Persephone* for the great French dancer, Ida Rubinstein, who first presented Ravel's *Bolero.*

The Eliot North Chair at Harvard was offered to Stravinsky and he took up residence in Cambridge in 1940. Shortly thereafter he became an American citizen and in gratitude made a new orchestration of "The Star-Spangled Banner."

He now lives in Hollywood, with his second wife, Vera de Bosset Sudeikine, and his four children by a previous marriage. There in the California sunshine, he writes his music daily, and wonders whether he should wear his fur-lined overcoat.

Stravinsky's music makes its own rules. Whether he is being a romanticist, as in *The Fire Bird,* or a neo-classicist, as in *Orpheus,* Nicholas Slonimsky says, he asserts "his belief in the perpetually young form of old music" and that he has filled "the old forms with new ideas."

                                                          S. B.

Circus Polka

This piece was composed for the fifty trained elephants of the Ringling Brothers and Barnum and Bailey Circus and was danced by them (and a Ballet of fifty Beautiful Girls) during the season of 1942. At the first performance in Madison Square Garden, New York, Vera Zorina joined the troupe as "prima ballerina" and performed in the center ring. The choreography was by Balanchine. In the opinion of bandmaster Merle Evans and trainer McLain, the behavior of the elephants during the rehearsal suggested that this was "not their kind of music."

The orchestral version of the piece was finished on October 5, 1942. It was first performed under the composer's direction at an all-Stravinsky concert by the Boston Symphony Orchestra, January 14-15, 1944.

                DONALD FERGUSON, *Minneapolis Symphony Orchestra*

Score for the ballet: *Le Sacre du Printemps (The Rite of Spring)*

Stravinsky's autobiography is sparse in dates, but the happenings described in the first of the following excerpts from the book must have taken place in the spring of 1910:

"One day while I was finishing the last pages of *The Fire Bird* in St. Petersburg, I had a fleeting vision that came to me as a complete surprise, my mind at that moment being full of other things. I saw in imagination a solemn pagan rite: Sage elders, seated in a circle, watched a young girl dance herself to death. They were sacrificing her to propitiate the god of spring. Such was the theme of *The Rite of Spring*. I must confess that this vision made a deep impression on me, and I at once described it to my friend, Nicholas Roerich, he being a painter who specialized in pagan subjects. He welcomed my inspiration with enthusiasm, and he became my collaborator in this creation. In Paris, I told Diaghilev about it, and he was at once carried away with the idea, though its realization was delayed by the following events."

The "following events" were, to put it succinctly, *Petrouchka* which Stravinsky began as a little piano piece by way of diversion before tackling the *Rite*, which ultimately developed into a big ballet.

Petrouchka having been composed and produced, Stravinsky returned to *The Rite* and completed it in the early spring of 1913. Diaghilev appointed Nijinsky to create the choreography, much to Stravinsky's distress. Nijinsky, says the composer, knew nothing whatever about music, and although he was a great dancer, was inexperienced and incompetent as a choreographer. The result was endless trouble and difficulty for all concerned.

It was therefore natural that Stravinsky approached the first performance of *The Rite* in a dubious frame of mind. The event took place in the Théâtre des Champs-Elysées in Paris on May 28, 1913, and caused one of the greatest scandals in the history of modern music.

"The complexity of my score," says Stravinsky, "had demanded a great number of rehearsals, which Monteux had conducted with his usual skill and attention. As for the actual performance, I am not in a position to judge, but I left the auditorium at the first bars of the prelude, which had evoked derisive laughter. I was disgusted. These demonstrations, at first isolated, soon became general, provoking counterdemonstrations and very quickly developing into a terrific uproar. During the whole performance, I was at Nijinsky's side in the wings. He was on a chair screaming: 'Sixteen, seventeen, eighteen!'—they had their own methods of counting to keep time. Naturally, the poor dancers could hear nothing by reason of the row in the auditorium and the sound of their own dance steps. I had to hold Nijinsky by his clothes—he was furious, and ready to dash on the stage at any moment and create a scandal.

"Diaghilev kept ordering the electrician to turn the lights on or off, hoping in that way to put a stop to the noise. That is all I can remember about the first performance. Oddly enough, at the dress rehearsal, to which we had, as usual, invited a number of actors, painters, musicians, writers and the most cultured representatives of society, everything had gone off peacefully and I was very far from expecting such an outburst.

"Now, after the lapse of more than twenty years, it is naturally difficult for me to recall in any detail the choreography of *The Rite*, without being influenced by the admiration with which it met in the set known as the *avant-garde*—ready, as always, to welcome as a new discovery anything that differs, be it ever so little, from the *déjà vu*.

"But what struck me then, and still strikes me most, about the choreography was and is Nijinsky's lack of consciousness of what he was doing when he created it. He showed therein his complete inability to accept and assimilate those revolutionary ideas which Diaghilev had made his creed, and obstinately and industriously strove to inculcate. What the choreography expressed was a very labored and barren effort rather than a plastic realization flowing simply and naturally from what the music demanded. How far it was from what I had desired! . . . . "

Several pages later, Stravinsky writes as follows:

"I think it was in the month of April 1914, that both *The Rite* and *Petrouchka* were played at a concert in Paris, Monteux being the conductor. It was a brilliant renascence of *The Rite*, after the Théâtre des Champs-Elysées scandal. The hall was crowded. The audience, with no scenery to distract them, listened with concentrated attention and applauded with an enthusiasm I had been far from expecting and which greatly moved me. Certain critics who had censured *The Rite* the year before now openly admitted their mistake. This conquest of the public naturally gave me intense and lasting satisfaction."

The above paragraph is particularly significant, for *The Rite* has since made its way, almost entirely as a concert piece, and, although other choreographers have taken it in hand, it has never made a great success on the stage. . . .

Since *The Rite* is better known as a concert piece than as a ballet, and is likely to remain so, a sketch of its action taken from this or that choreography would be supererogatory. The work is in two parts, or acts, the first presumably taking place in a valley or some such open place in the daytime, the second at night inside a semicircle of rough-hewn monoliths, each surmounted by the skull of a different animal and all lighted with flickering fires. The action of the first part has to do with the assemblage of the tribes, their sports and games, and their final gathering under the leadership of a sage to dance their adoration of the earth. The second part works up to the culminating sacrifice, through various ritual dances. . . .

ALFRED FRANKENSTEIN, *San Francisco Symphony Orchestra*

Suite from the ballet: *Petrouchka*

The ballet *Petrouchka: Scènes burlesque en 4 tableaux,* scenario by Igor Stravinsky and Alexander Benois, was first produced at the Théâtre du Châtelet in Paris, June 13, 1911, by the Ballet Russe of Serge de Diaghilev.

. . . . Stravinsky in 1911, still a "find" of Diaghilev, having brought upon himself the world's attention by the production in the previous spring of his *L'Oiseau de Feu* soon became absorbed in thoughts of a primitive ballet in which a young girl would dance herself to death as a sacrificial pagan rite. Diaghilev was delighted with the idea, and visited the young composer at Clarens on Lake Geneva to see how *Le Sacre du Printemps* was progressing. Instead, he found Stravinsky deep in a new idea, a *Konzertstuecke* for piano and orchestra, in which the solo part would suggest "a puppet suddenly endowed with life, exasperating the patience of the orchestra with diabolical cascades of arpeggios." The orchestra would retaliate with "menacing trumpet blasts." The outcome is a terrible noise which reaches its climax and ends in the sorrowful and querulous collapse of the poor puppet."

In these words, Stravinsky describes in his autobiography the inception of what was to be his second ballet, pushing all thoughts of *Le Sacre du Printemps* for the time being into the background. "Having finished this bizarre piece, I struggled for hours while walking beside Lake Geneva to find a title which would express in a word the character of my music and, consequently, the personality of this creature."

These were the musical plans which Diaghilev found Stravinsky working upon. "He was much astonished when, instead of sketches of the *Sacre,* I played him the piece I had just composed and which later became the second scene of *Petrouchka.* He was so much pleased with it that he would not leave it alone and began persuading me to develop the theme of the puppet's sufferings and make it into a whole ballet. While he remained in Switzerland we worked out together the general lines of the subject and the plot in accordance with the ideas I suggested. We settled the scene of the action: The Fair, with its crowds, its booths, the little traditional theater, the character of the musician, with all his tricks; and the coming to life of the dolls—Petrouchka, his rival and the dancer—and their love tragedy, which ends with Petrouchka's death."

Mr. Edwin Evans gives the following description of the ballet:

"The action takes place at St. Petersburg in the Admiralty Square during the Carnival week, about 1830. Amid the popular merrymaking an old Showman of Oriental mien presents before the public at the fair three animated puppets: Petrouchka, the Ballerina and the Moor, who perform a lively dance. The Showman's magic has imbued them with human feelings and emotions. Of the three, Petrouchka is the most nearly human, and therefore the most sensitive. He is conscious of his grotesque exterior and bitterly resentful of the Showman's cruelty. He is romantically enamored of the Ballerina, but she is only repelled by his uncouth appearance. Compared with Petrouchka, the Moor is brutal and stupid, but he is sumptuously attired and therefore more attractive to the Ballerina, who captivates him. Petrouchka intrudes upon their love scene, but is ignominiously thrown out. Meanwhile, the fun of the fair, which has offered no interruption, has reached its height. A roistering merchant, accompanied by two gypsy girls, throws banknotes to the crowd. There are dances of coachmen and of nursemaids. A performing bear traverses the scene with his trainer in attendance. Suddenly, there is a commotion in the Showman's booth, from which Petrouchka emerges, fleeing for his life, with the Moor in pursuit. He is overtaken and struck down and he dies in the snow among the merrymakers who, mystified, call upon the police to fetch the Showman. He comes and easily convinces everyone that Petrouchka is but a puppet, a thing of wood and sawdust. The crowd disperses, but the Showman is terrified to see above his booth, the ghost of Petrouchka, threatening him and jeering at his dupes."

It will be observed that the Russian Petrouchka, for all his grotesque trappings, remains, like Pierrot, an essentially tragic figure—the more tragic that he is fated to endure his troubles without the solace of sympathy. The discomfiture of Petrouchka in his courting of the Ballerina does not differ essentially from that of the gentle, romantic-minded Pierrot at the hands of the realistic, worldly-minded Columbine, who prefers the cynical Harlequin. In fact, Petrouchka adds yet another chapter to the *Commedia dell' Arte,* that fertile and glorious tradition which the majority of Englishmen know only through its dregs, the seaside Pierrot and the Harlequinade that until recently followed the Christmas pantomime, though in recent years the pathos of Pierrot has been captured elsewhere by Charlie Chaplin.

JOHN N. BURK, *Boston Symphony Orchestra*

Suite from the Ballet: *The Fire Bird*

Stravinsky regards *The Fire Bird* as his first full-fledged work. It was produced by the Diaghilev Ballet Russe in Paris in 1910, and began the long collaboration between Stravinsky and Diaghilev which was to have such extremely important results for both artists.

The story was adapted by Michael Fokine, the choreographer, from Russian sources. In briefest outline, it tells how Prince Ivan, wandering in a dark enchanted forest, beholds a fabulous bird whose feathers are plumes of fire, eating golden fruit from a silver tree. Prince Ivan tries to catch the Fire Bird, but succeeds only in plucking one flame from her coat.

The hero wanders further into the forest until he comes to the domain of the demon known as Kastchei, the Deathless, so-called because his life does not reside within his body but in an egg hidden in his castle. He beholds the grave dance of a bevy of princesses, held in a trancelike spell through the demon's power. Suddenly Kastchei and his demons surround the prince with murderous intent, but the flame from the Fire Bird's coat protects him, and the Fire Bird herself appears at the height of the battle to lend him her assistance.

The Fire Bird leads Prince Ivan into the castle, where he finds the egg and breaks it. Instantly, the castle and the demons disappear and the princesses are released from their spell. Ultimately, the prince is married to the most beautiful of the princesses amid general rejoicing.

As was the case with *Petrouchka,* the original version of *The Fire Bird* used an exceptionally large orchestra. Nevertheless, in extracting some passages from the ballet score to form his first concert suite from this work, Stravinsky did not change the instrumentation. But in the second suite he did reduce the number of instruments called for, and he also dropped out two movements, the *adagio* and *scherzo.* (The second suite, which dates from 1919, is the one most commonly played.) In the third suite made last year (1945), he clings to the reduced orchestration, restores the movements previously omitted, and adds short link passages to bind the whole together.

The introduction suggests the atmosphere of the enchanted forest. "The Dance of the Fire Bird" accompanies the first appearance of that character as she darts alone among the trees. The *adagio* and *scherzo* are duos danced by the Fire Bird and Prince Ivan. The *rondo* is the dance of the Enchanted Princesses; it uses the rhythm and style of an old Russian round dance called the *chorovod.* The titles of the remaining two movements ("Infernal Dance," "The Fire Bird's Lullaby" and "Final Hymn") are obvious enough in their meaning and reference.

ALFRED FRANKENSTEIN, *San Francisco Symphony Orchestra*

Le Chant du Rossignol

The symphonic poem *Le Chant du rossignol* (*The Song of the Nightingale*), composed in 1917, is derived from an earlier work of Stravinsky's, an opera-ballet in three acts, based on a fairy-tale of Hans Christian Andersen, and called *Le Rossignol.* Stravinsky began the composition of this opera-ballet, or "Lyric Tale," in 1910, but after completing the first act he suddenly abandoned the project, declaring that "music can be married to gesture or to words—not to both without bigamy."

For three years he remained firm in his conviction, producing meanwhile the ballets *Petrouchka* and *Le Sacre du Printemps*; then he changed his mind and resumed work on *Le Rossignol,* which was produced at Paris in 1914.

Montagu-Nathan, in his *Contemporary Russian Composers,* seeks to explain Stravinsky's apparent abandonment of his stand for musical monogamy. The music of *Le Rossignol,* he says, "is married neither to gesture nor to words, but to ideas, which the words do indeed convey, though quite indirectly."

Le Rossignol consists of three short acts. "Music and action"—to quote Mr. Calvocoressi, author of the French translation of the text—proceed evenly and rapidly. All symbolic purport, all the undercurrents of suggestion contained in the text, are never explicitly alluded to except in the brief recondite utterances of a minor character, a fisherman, who at the beginning and at the end of the acts appears in the background to prophesy and to explain.

The symphonic poem is adapted from the second and third acts of the opera, the plot of which is, briefly, as follows:

The Nightingale has been bidden to sing at the court of the Emperor of China. Excited preparations are made for the bird's reception . . . . Arrived before the throne, the Nightingale begins to sing—his orchestral representative being, of course, the flute. His performance fills all hearts with wonder and rapture. The Emperor is moved to tears, but just as he is expressing his admiration, messengers from the Emperor of Japan arrive, bringing as an offering a mechanical Nightingale.

It is set in motion, with much whirring of machinery (clarinet, piano and harp), whereupon the real Nightingale, offended, steals away unobserved. After listening again to the mechanical bird, the Emperor wishes again to hear the real one, and when he learns that it is not to be found, in high dudgeon he banishes it forever from the court.

After a brief comment by the fisherman, the scene shifts to the Emperor's bedchamber, where the monarch lies dangerously ill. Death stands near, ready to pounce upon him, having already taken possession of his crown and sceptre. The Emperor, tortured by remorseful memories and delirious fancies, murmurs: "Music might dispel these horrors."

Suddenly, the voice of the Nightingale is heard, and the benevolent bird sets about the task of driving away death. This is accomplished by singing so alluringly of the delights of the Garden of the Dead that Death, impatient to return to his own realm, relinquishes his claim upon the Emperor and retires. The sounds of a Funeral March are then heard, as the courtiers, thinking their monarch dead, come to bear away his body in solemn state. But as they enter the imperial chamber the Emperor, his health fully restored, rises and greets them.

The work ends with a short epilogue by the fisherman:

> The light of the day dispels the night;
> Gaily a bird in the wood is singing.
> Listen well, and in his voice
> Perceive the voice of Heaven.

In his treatment of this subject Stravinsky progresses further along the path which led him from *The Fire Bird,* through *Petrouchka,* to *The Rite of Spring.* Whether or not one is able to follow him step for step, one cannot but admire his audacity and his cleverness. What he has to say, he says tersely, epigrammatically, wasting no words and going straight to the point. It has been suggested that his motto should be: "The truth—no matter how it hurts."

ERNEST LA PRADE, *Symphony Society of New York*

JOSEPH DEEMS TAYLOR

(Born in New York City, December 22, 1885—now
living in New York)

As A MUSICIAN, Deems Taylor is almost entirely self-taught. He recalls that his only teacher in harmony was "an obscure musician named Oscar Coon," from whom "I learned a lot" and "who had ventured to consider Wagner a genius in an era when it took courage and independence to do so."

A man of many talents, Mr. Taylor is a brilliant and whimsical essayist, a penetrating critic, an able composer of unquestioned ability and a capable newspaper man.

He attended the Ethical Culture School, entered New York University and composed music for four comic operas in his undergraduate years. One of these, *The Echo,* was produced subsequently by Charles Dillingham. In the years after his graduation he was appointed to the editorial boards of Nelson's and the Britannica encyclopaedias; assistant Sunday editor of the *New York Tribune,* and later correspondent in France for that newspaper; associate editor of *Collier's Weekly* and music critic of the *New York World.*

His suite for chamber orchestra, *Through the Looking Glass,* won a prize offered by Carolyn Beebe and the New York Chamber Music Society. Later, he rescored it for full orchestra and it became so successful that he was engaged by the *World* in consequence.

The Metropolitan commissioned two operas by Mr. Taylor— *The King's Henchman* (February 17, 1927) and *Peter Ibbetson* (February 7, 1931). A comic opera, *Ramuntcho,* first performed at the Academy of Music, Philadelphia, February 10, 1942, did not attain appreciable success. The Introduction and Ballet Music from this work were presented at an "Evening of Premieres" in Carnegie Hall, under the direction of Joseph Blant, on March 17, 1940.

Mr. Taylor will be remembered by the public at large as the commentator of Walt Disney's musical film, *Fantasia;* also, as the intermission commentator in the radio concerts of the Philharmonic-Symphony Society of New York, and for the essentially radio music, "What I Saw on Mulberry Street." He has also composed "Portrait of a Lady," and has written innumerable books on music. He is a former president of the American Society of Composers, Authors and Publishers.

I chanced to meet Mr. Taylor one afternoon, in the buffet of the Metropolitan, at the time he was working on *Ramuntcho.*

"Hello, Deems," said I. "What's your new opera about?"

"About one hour and fifty minutes," snapped Mr. Taylor, adding as an afterthought: "Have a drink?"

Elegy for Orchestra

Mr. Taylor . . . has prepared the following program note for his Elegy:

"It is a little difficult to write a program note for a piece that has no program. The work is, as the title implies and the dictionary defines, 'a poem or composition of a thoughtful, subjective character, generally a lament.' I can only hope that, despite its elegiac character, the music has sufficient vitality to avoid being depressed.

"The first section, marked *Lento,* introduces the dirgelike main theme, heard first as a horn solo. It is taken up by the strings, then by the full orchestra, which brings it to a climax. A long, descending subsidiary theme leads to the second section, marked *Tranquillo.* Its theme is simple and lyric in character, suggestive of youth and naiveté. It is developed at some length, but is interrupted by a grave reminder of the dirge theme. Then the lyric theme resumes, and is followed by two variants, one very lively and dancelike, the other, greatly augmented, intoned by the brass. The two variants alternate until they reach a climax that is cut across by the trombones, playing a harsh reminder of the dirge. The music subsides, and the final section begins with the dirge theme, played by all the violins, on the G-string. After a last climax, the descending theme of the first section leads to a quiet close . . ."

LENORA COFFIN, *Indianapolis Symphony Orchestra*

Through the Looking Glass: Suite for Orchestra (Opus 12)

This Suite in five movements—"Dedication," "The Garden of Live Flowers," "Jabberwocky," "Looking Glass Insects" and "The White Knight"—is based on Lewis Carroll's delightful story, *Through the Looking Glass, and What Alice Found There,* a story, as all good *Alice* fans know, that is a sequel to *Alice in Wonderland.* These same fans, by exercising their imaginations to some slight extent, will readily "see" the excerpts from the story as they are translated into sound. Mr. Taylor's talent for musical mimicry does not fail him; nor does his sense of humor fail him, as you will note when the White Knight falls from his horse . . .

The music has a "once upon a time" atmosphere. The theme is lyric, quietly romantic, and a bit wistful. It is developed to some extent, rises to something of a climax, then, sinking back to serenity, leads directly to the music depicting the garden of live flowers.

You doubtless remember how astonished Alice was, when the Tiger-Lily, to whom the child spoke in the rounded phrase remembered from her Latin book ("O, Tiger-Lily, I wish you could talk"), answered with some asperity that it could talk, that all the flowers could talk, indeed, "when there's anybody worth talking to." Not only could they talk, as they said, but they could talk a great deal louder than Alice could, or, at any rate, than she did. Their conversation is a breezy chatter without pauses for breath, as if there were no time in which to say everything that had to be said. There is an interlude of subdued sound, suggestive, perhaps, of the beauty of the garden, when it isn't filled with clattering tongues, but the interlude is soon over, and the tongues clatter more eagerly than ever.

The third movement, "Jabberwocky," was suggested by that famous poem, which didn't make sense to Alice, until Humpty-Dumpty, who had a nice flair for definitions, explained it to her. The "Jabberwock" was a "frightful beast," and Mr. Taylor has conceived a correspondingly frightful theme, announced loudly by full orchestra at the beginning of the movement, The clarinet, acting as narrator, then begins to create the atmosphere of the opening stanza, whose mood, in spite of the horrible words, is peaceful:

Twas brillig, and the slithy toves
Did gyre and gimble in the wabe;
All mimsy were the borogoves,
And the mome raths outgrabe.

Humpty-Dumpty said this stanza referred to a pleasant sort of dancing party, late in the afternoon. The clarinet gives this impression, although the scene, like the James Joycean words describing it, is not without its distortions. The Jabberwock, now delineated by the bassoon, is a constant threat, what with his gloomy mutterings in the bass register.

He took his vorpal sword in hand;
Long time the manxome foe he sought—
So rested he by the Tumtum tree,
And stood awhile in thought.

His meditations are rudely interrupted by the Jabberwock, who snorts defiance (with the help of the trombone section) and who rushes from his hiding-place. Our hero, who has been standing in "uffish thought," is startled when

The Jabberwock, with eyes of flame,
Came whiffling through the tulgey wood,
And burbled as it came.

Nothing daunted, the young man "lays to" with his "vorpal sword" and the two, like Macbeth and Macduff before them, slash at each other, both obviously remembering that Macbeth had cried: "And damned be he who first cries: 'Hold, enough!' " since neither gives any quarter. The battle emerges as a Fugue (of all things!), a very good Fugue, indeed, but not a pleasant one to hear, presumably because such battles are not pleasant to watch. The "vorpal sword" (it's a saxophone in the orchestra) finds a fatal spot, and the Jabberwock (still a bassoon) dies a lingering and convulsive death. Mr. Taylor has said that this "death passage" has been referred to "with rather excessive bitterness by bassoon players as the death of the bassoon."

The battle over, our hero properly triumphant, the gayety is resumed, complete with the ringing of church bells. The young man shouts: "O frabjous day! Callooh! Callay!" Everything is perfect.

The music for the Looking-Glass Insects needs no explanation, since the orchestra hums and swirls and darts. You can make up your mind which measures describe the Bee-elephant, the Gnat, the Rockinghorse Fly, the Snapdragon Fly, the Bread and Butter Fly and the others.

There are two child themes for the final movement. One, which Mr. Taylor calls "a sort of instrumental prance," is the White Knight's notion of himself. The other, "bland, mellifluous, a little sentimental," is what the White Knight really is. The first theme is played as the Knight comes riding toward Alice, hoping that he looks as imposing as he feels. He talks about the art of riding, but, unfortunately, ruins everything by falling off his horse. The second theme is then played, letting you know what Alice thinks the Knight is like. She apparently finds him gentle, a little broken. He climbs back into the saddle, and once more starts his lecture on the equestrian art. Alas! He falls from his horse again!

The 'cellos play the second theme at great length. The White Knight picks himself up, gets on his horse, looks at Alice, and says: "You'll stay and see me off first? . . . You'll wait and wave your handkerchief, when I get to that turn in the road? I think it'll encourage me, you see." So he rides away on his prancing horse.

Mr. Taylor's idiom is that of Strauss, modified by later experiments in harmony (temperately used, one should add). He turns his chosen anecdotes into extraordinarily vivid "program" music, charming, melodic, romantic and humorous in turn, and always fine enough to be listened to purely as music. His skill as orchestrator is expert. His ability to transfer printed phrase into musical phrase is equally expert. This Suite is delightful.

WALTER WHITWORTH, Indianapolis Symphony Orchestra

Marco Takes a Walk: Variations for Orchestra (Opus 25)

Mr. Taylor has been kind enough to submit the following description of his work:

"The piece was suggested by the reading of a small book, writ-

ten in verse, by Theodor Seuss Geisel—better known as Dr. Seuss
—called *And To Think That I Saw It On Mulberry Street*. It relates the adventures—in his own mind, at least—of an overimagina-
tive small boy on his way home from school. His father has asked
him to describe anything interesting that he sees on his way but has
also warned him to 'stop telling such outlandish tales.' All that
Marco, our hero, sees, is a horse and wagon on Mulberry Street.
He decides to make the story better by saying that a zebra was
drawing the cart. No, he'll make it a chariot—no, a reindeer, pulling a sled—no, better yet, an elephant, a blue one. Still better,
there will be a Rajah riding the elephant, and the steed will be
drawing, not a sled, but a bandwagon, with a big brass band aboard.

"Dizzy with these glorious imaginings, he starts to tell his tale.
But his father's cold eye brings him back to earth. And did he see
nothing exciting at all?

" 'Nothing,' I said, growing red as a beet.

" 'But a plain horse and wagon on Mulberry Street.'

"The music attempts to convey the moods of the various imaginary sights. It resembles Beethoven's Fifth Symphony in that
everything is evolved from a short, five-note 'motto' theme. I can
think of no other way in which it resembles Beethoven's Fifth
Symphony.

"The piece begins with a brief introduction for muted strings,
marked in the score, *Marco the Romantic*. It is based on a variant
of the main theme, which follows immediately.

" . . . The score calls for the usual orchestral combination,
its only possible innovations being the use of Chinese wood blocks
and the trumpet 'cup' mute, the latter being a child of the radio
dance bands that in tonal quality is far superior to the tinny mutes
to which the more pretentious orchestras still cling.

"The work was begun late last summer (1944), and the composer was nagged by Mr. Barlow into finishing it in time (just) for
this concert. Incidentally, if any listener were to take the piece
seriously enough to listen to it simply as a theme and variations
for orchestra, the composer would be delighted."

Louis Biancolli, *Philharmonic-Symphony Society of New York*

Circus Day

This fantasy for orchestra, subtitled *Eight Pictures from Memory,* was commissioned by Paul Whiteman in 1925, and was first performed at Carnegie Hall in November 1925. It had numerous subsequent performances by the Whiteman Orchestra in 1925, and 1926, throughout the United States and in England, Holland, France and Germany. The music was extensively revised by the composer during the summer of 1933 and has been rescored by him for a regular symphony orchestra plus a trio of saxophones. . . .

As the title indicates, the music attempts to convey one's early impressions of a day at the circus. You must not, however, think of one of the huge, three-ring affairs that divide their time among the big cities and go into winter quarters at the first sign of frost. Our regular circus is a much more humble entertainment than that. It travels about the country in trucks and busses, plays under its own tent and seldom remains in any town longer than a day or two. Its menagerie, while satisfactorily ferocious, is a small one; its performers, while intrepid, are few; also its canvasmen are not above playing in the band when their other duties permit. . . .

> LILY POLK and HELEN CHOATE, *Young People's Concerts,*
> *Philharmonic-Symphony Society of New York*

VIRGIL THOMSON

(Born in Kansas City, Mo., November 25, 1896—
now living in New York)

As THE CRITIC of the *New York Herald Tribune,* Mr. Thomson becomes pert and audacious and sometimes a little unjust; as a composer, he is almost orthodox. His melodic gift, while not extraordinary, is quite definite; his orchestral color partakes of well-known hues and reflections, yet manages to beguile the listener into pleasant reverie. His orchestral work is essentially illustrative, in that it does not stand very well alone, without rhyme or program to sustain it. Yet it is important, being of this day and age, and is heard frequently enough to warrant the present commentary.

Mr. Thomson was educated in the public schools of his native Kansas City and at Harvard University, from which he was graduated in 1922. He studied composition with Scalero and Nadia Boulanger, and is derivative of that Fontainebleau group called "the Boulangerie," which nurtured Copland, Harris and a few more craftsmen now grown up.

Mr. Thomson himself, with a candor entirely characteristic, says of his life and career:

"I was born in Kansas City, Missouri, grew up there and went to war from there. That was the other war. Then I was educated some more in Boston and Paris. In composition, I was a pupil of Nadia Boulanger. While I was still young I taught music at Harvard and played the organ at King's Chapel, Boston. Then I returned to Paris and lived there for many years, till the Germans came, in fact. Now I live in New York, where I am music critic of the *Herald Tribune*."

The Plough That Broke the Plains

. . . . . . a documentary film by Pàre Lorentz, was made in 1935 for the Farm Resettlement Administration of the United States Government. It tells the tragic story of our Great Plains, their overcultivation, the ensuing dust storms and disaster for the land, as well as for the settlers. The music of the film was written and scored by the composer in ten days during February of that year. The musical sound track was recorded at Astoria, Long Island, by Alexander Smallens, conductor, and members of the New York Philharmonic-Symphony Orchestra.

The present Suite includes about half the original score, certain background passages having been omitted that seemed to the composer unsuitable for concert execution. No alteration of any kind has been made in the excerpts that make up the Suite. They stand exactly as in the original composition. The Suite has been performed widely in the United States and in Europe, both by symphony orchestras and by student groups.

Its musical themes are partly original and partly folklore. This borrowed material is in the section entitled "Cattle," which is made up of cowboy songs, and in the final fugue, called "Devastation." The latter is based on an old song beloved of disappointed farmers in the Southwest: "I'm Gonna Leave Old Texas Now."

VIRGIL THOMSON

Suite for orchestra: *Louisiana Story*

Louisiana Story is the title of a recent film produced by Robert Flaherty, well-known in the cinematic world as the author of such documentary masterpieces as *Nanook of the North, Man of Aran* and *Elephant Boy.* The eminent composer, author and *New York Herald Tribune* critic, Virgil Thomson, was commissioned by Mr. Flaherty to write the associated musical score, from which the suite of this program is derived.

Louisiana Story is a saga of an oil-development project in that southern state, and its effect on a simple French-speaking family. The story unwinds a pair of tangled threads off the same skein, with the scene shifting between two violently contrasting aspects of mankind's eternal struggle against nature. On the one hand, there are the rough and ready oil drillers, prospecting for black gold through an alligator-infested bayou, pitting the ingenuity of their machines against Nature's reluctance to yield up her hoarded wealth. On the other hand, one's attention is focused on a superstitious native lad, who roams through the swamps with a coon for a pet, making friends with the oil men, and using his own secret magic to ward off evil "things" from werewolves to submerged mermaids. Living with his humble parents in this remote corner of civilization, the boy spends most of his time in Nature's own classroom, paddling his little boat through the sluggish waters of Petit Anse bayou, landing the largest of fish and observing the habits of murderous alligators. Through his eyes, one sees civilization encroaching upon his domain, as the marsh-buggy (a marsh-buggy is an amphibious tractor, fitted with large drumlike wheels capable of operating on either land or water. It is a standard item among oil prospectors for traversing the swampy land of the bayous), the white speedboat and the towering derrick enter the scene. Gradually, his suspicion toward these outsiders is replaced by friendship, and when all their superior knowledge fails to bring in a gusher, his miraculous little bag of salt does the trick. Or so he naively believes.

. . . . . Virgil Thomson began work on his score in January of this year (1948), completing it in time for the recording session of the Philadelphia Orchestra on April 22, 1948, at the Reeves Studios in New York.

To add local color to his musical backdrop, the composer has drawn freely from the folk idiom of the Acadian region, using as source material Irene Therese Whitfield's collection of *Louisiana French Folk Songs* (Louisiana State University Press, 1939), and recordings of Cajun tunes collected on the spot by Alan Lomax. One of these melodies has been incorporated in the Suite of this program; the rest, generally in characteristic waltz and polka rhythms, are reserved for a second suite entitled *Acadian Airs and Dances.*

With the exception of this one folk tune, the Suite with which we are concerned consists of the composed or original music in the film score, its four movements derived from a sequence of scenes in the life of the Cajun boy . . . .

R. L. F. McCombs, *Philadelphia Orchestra*

PETER ILYITCH TSCHAIKOWSKY

(Born in Votkinsk, Viatka Province, Russia, May 7,
1840—died in St. Petersburg, November 6, 1893)

ONE OF THE strangest episodes in all the history of music is
connected with the name of Tschaikowsky. For fourteen years, he
was virtually supported by a woman he saw twice but never met.
This support was withdrawn abruptly, because of a wholly imaginary "bankruptcy" and today mystery surrounds the cause of
this break, though knowing commentators and subsequent authorities have affected to explain away the unexplainable. . . . .

His father was in charge of the mines at Votkinsk, "an official
of very moderate ability and intelligence." His mother, daughter
of an epileptic French immigrant, called him "Pierre." Neither of
his parents had any aptitude for music. Peter, one of seven children, began his education with a French governess. At five, he began to take piano lessons "from a Russian girl. We know nothing
of her," adds Calvocoressi, "except that in three years her pupil
could read at sight as well as she could, which may or may not be
a tribute to her ability as a teacher."

His father retired from government service in 1848 and the
family moved to Moscow, then to St. Petersburg. Peter and his
brother Nicholas were sent to a school "where they were absurdly
overworked." The family moved again to Alapieff, where his father
had been appointed manager of some private mines. Came another governess, and utter neglect of his musical education. The
family had decided that music had an "unhealthy" effect on him.
His mother finally took him back to St. Petersburg, where he entered a preparatory school.

His first known composition, at fourteen, was a waltz for
piano, dedicated to his former governess, Anastasia Petrova. He
took a few singing lessons, at this time, for he had "an extraordinarily good soprano voice." As a pianist, he was very much the
amateur, though fond of improvisation. As a student at the School
of Jurisprudence, he proved to be scarcely better than average, and
a bad mathematician. Finally, he left the school and was appointed
a clerk in the Ministry of Justice.

He began to study with a Polish theorist, Zaremba, and when this pedant joined the faculty of the new Conservatoire, headed by Anton Rubinstein, he followed his teacher and left the service. He studied counterpoint and instrumentation, the organ and flute.

He wrote his first orchestral work in the summer of 1864, an ambitious overture based on Ostrovsky's tragedy, *The Storm*. Other works followed, as his studies progressed, and many of them were played in public, thus laying the foundation of a reputation. But his graduation piece, a cantata on Schiller's *An Die Freude*, was a failure.

He went back to Moscow, depressed and nervous, began work on his first symphony and had a nervous breakdown. But he finished the symphony in the fall of 1866, and two excerpts were played in Moscow in the spring. The reception was cool, and then Anton Rubinstein resigned, to be succeeded by Zaremba, with Balakiref as conductor.

In the course of the next few years, he produced other works, became one of the Balakiref "circle," met Berlioz, formed a warm friendship with Nicholas Rubinstein, brother of Anton, and also a pianist; got to know Rimsky-Korsakoff, Moussorgsky and a few more of the so-called "mighty handful" of St. Petersburg amateurs.

He fell in love with Désirée Artôt, pupil of the great singer, Pauline Viardot-Garcia and five years older than Peter. She was already betrothed to the Spanish baritone, Padilla-y-Ramos, and eventually married him. Tschaikowsky was not incurably affected, it seems, for he was able to enjoy without stint the triumph of his opera, *The Voyvoda*, produced in January of 1869.

The year 1877 probably was the most important in his life. It brought him a "tragic, mysterious" marriage which nearly proved fatal and the beginning of that strange connection with Nadejda von Meck. She was forty-six, widow of a rich railroad engineer, who left her with a huge fortune and eleven children. She was an eccentric, and after her husband's death shut herself entirely within her family circle. Tschaikowsky saw her once at a distance, and they met again by accident, but never exchanged a word in the fourteen years of their friendship. A somewhat ephemeral explanation may be garnered from one of Nadejda's letters interred in the Newmarch collection:

". . . . There was a time," Nadejda explained "when I was very anxious to make your personal acquaintance; but now the more you fascinate me the more I fear your acquaintanceship; I prefer to think of you from afar, to hear you speak in your music and to share your feelings through it."

One of his pupils at the Conservatoire, Antonina Ivanovna Miliukova, sent him a love-letter, "so warmly and sincerely written" that he decided to answer it. He went to see her, but confessed that all he could feel for her was "sympathy and gratitude." He feared his indifference would prove fatal to her and in a mistaken surge of chivalry, proposed. Of course, the lady accepted.

In July of 1877, they were married in Moscow. His brother Anatol was the only member of his family present. The couple passed a week in St. Petersburg, visited Antonina's mother, then separated. Peter went to his sister at Kamenka, Antonina to Moscow to make ready their home. They lived together for a few months, whereupon Peter induced Anatol to send him a faked telegram, and he fled to St. Petersburg "in a state bordering on insanity." A nervous collapse followed and Anatol took his brother to Switzerland, thence to Italy. And Nadejda, at this time, induced him to accept an annuity of some six hundred pounds, freeing him from all financial worry and enabling him to devote his entire time to creative work.

He and Anatol returned to Moscow, where Tschaikowsky resigned from the Conservatoire and went abroad again. He had reached Rome when his father died. He returned to his sister's home at Kamenka, having finished the Second Symphony, the *Italian Caprice* and some "retouching" on *Eugen Onegin,* which achieved but a moderate success. But the piece proved eventually to be immensely popular after the Czar had commanded a performance on the imperial stage.

He returned to Paris and Italy again and again, but finally determined to find a home in Russia, and settled in a house near Klin, a short distance from Moscow. This was to be his headquarters thenceforth. Roaming to Berlin in 1887, he met the Griegs and Brahms.

"Grieg charmed him," says Calvocoressi. "At first he and Brahms 'didn't really like each other;' each felt that the other dis-

liked his music, so that their relations remained only outwardly
cordial. But 'Brahms took great pains to be nice to me' and
Tschaikowsky soon found him 'very pleasant.' "

During this German tour, he learned that the Czar had
granted him a life pension of 3000 rubles (about $2200 today) a
year.

He had long dreamed of an American tour and at the instance
of Walter Damrosch accepted an offer to conduct some of his own
works at the opening of Carnegie Hall in New York. He had just
received the unpleasant news from Nadejda von Meck that as
she was "on the verge of bankruptcy"—his annuity, which constituted a third of his income, would have to be discontinued.
Although depressed and bitter at this loss, and bewildered at the
reason given, he was somewhat cheered by the fact that the royalties from his opera, *Pique-Dame* more than replaced the annuity.
Yet his bitterness increased when he found that Nadejda's financial troubles were imaginary. And Nadejda ignored his subsequent letters, in which he attempted to resume their relationship.

While waiting in Havre for his ship to sail for New York, he
learned that his beloved sister, Alexandra, had died. He wanted to
abandon the tour, but decided to go on, reflecting that he could do
no good if he returned. He found himself "more famous in America than in Europe." His success was immediate and widespread,
and he was the guest of honor at the Russian Embassy in Washington, visited Niagara Falls and gave concerts in New York, Baltimore and Philadelphia.

Weary but satisfied he sailed for home, embarked upon various tours, "got the idea" for his last symphony, which he intended to call simply *Program Symphony,* and finished it in August of 1892. At the suggestion of Modeste, his brother, he hit
upon the title of *Pathetique*.

On the evening of November 1, 1893, Tschaikowsky dined
with friends, went to the theater, and sat drinking until two in
the morning. The next day he complained of indigestion and in-
somnia, but went out to pay some calls. At luncheon that day, he
ate nothing but drank a glass of unboiled water. Cholera was then
epidemic throughout Russia. Though his illness grew worse he de-

clined to see a doctor. But Modeste sent for the Bertensons, two of
the best physicians in St. Petersburg. They diagnosed his malady
as cholera. He died at three in the morning of November 6.
Nadejda von Meck died three months later.

The Nutcracker Suite

. . . It was written in 1891, upon a commission from the Imperial Opera which included also the composition of an opera,
King René's Daughter (later known as *Iolanthe*) and the *Nutcracker* ballet. He had newly finished what he believed to be a
masterpiece of opera (*Pique Dame—The Queen of Spades*), and
was not much stimulated by the new task.

Successful concerts of his own works, which he conducted in
Paris, did not alleviate his melancholy, but he signed a contract to
conduct in America, and was just about to embark when he
learned of the death of his sister, Alexandra Davidov. No wonder
he wrote to his brother: "Today, even more than yesterday, I feel
the absolute impossibility of depicting in music 'The Sugarplum
Fairy.' "

The American scene, however, proved a tonic, and after about
a month he was back in St. Petersburg, and later in Maidonovo,
where the *Casse-Noisette* ballet and *Iolanthe* were completed. On
March 19, 1892, he conducted the first performance of the Suite
extracted from the ballet. It was an unbounded success, the audience demanding the immediate repetition of five out of the six
dances. The music is too familiar to require description.

It may still be of interest, however, to note that it was here that
Tschaikowsky first used the celesta, whose delicate tone lends such
fascination to our image of the antics of the Bonbon Fairy. The
instrument was invented in 1886 by Auguste Mustel of Paris;
and Tschaikowsky having heard it in Paris, where he conducted
one of the Colonne concerts just before his departure for America,
was not slow to realize its perfect suitability to the dainty characterization of his tiny heroine.

DONALD FERGUSON, *Minneapolis Symphony Orchestra*

Overture 1812

Tschaikowsky took a special interest in composing the *1812 Overture* and the Serenade for Strings in C major. He had this to say of each in one of his many letters:

"The Overture is of local interest and noisy. I wrote it without warmth and enthusiasm. The Serenade, on the contrary, came from an inner impulse and I put into it the best there was in me."

Likewise, when his publisher suggested that he write this Overture, for a celebration in the Kremlin Square commemorating the great Russian victory of 1812 over Napoleon, Tschaikowsky complied, though first replying that he was "not a concocter of festival pieces."

Despite this apparent lack of enthusiasm on the part of the composer, the *1812 Overture* has ample internal evidence that having embarked upon the task, Tschaikowsky went about it with all the skill at his command. It is a stirring work and has been a concert favorite for many years. At the beginning, the orchestra intones the melody associated with a Russian prayer: "God Preserve Thy People." The music then takes on more and more of a military character and includes some quotations from the "Marseillaise." Following this, one hears a Russian folk song. At the very end the listener is not left in doubt concerning the victor of the 1812 conflict, since the Czarist Russian Anthem emerges *fortissimo,* cutting through a fairly effective orchestral enunciation of the "Marseillaise."

George Schaun, Baltimore Symphony Orchestra

Overture Fantasia—*Romeo and Juliet*

Romeo and Juliet is the earliest of Tschaikowsky's works that still retains its popularity. It was completed in November 1869, when the composer was only twenty-nine. "Completed" is hardly the word, however, for after its first performance by the Imperial Music Society in Moscow, under Nicholas Rubinstein's direction, on March 16, 1870, the score underwent several revisions. It was completely rewritten in the summer of 1870, further revised later that year and published in 1871. But that was not the end of the changes; ten years later, Tschaikowsky again altered the music, shortening it somewhat, and the new edition—the one we know today—was published in 1881.

The music was obviously inspired by Shakespeare's tragedy, but it was Tschaikowsky's colleague, the composer Mily Balakireff who was directly responsible for the work's creation. A wise but overbearing and domineering man, Balakireff, who acted as advisor to a number of young Russian composers, did not hesitate to foist his ideas upon young Tschaikowsky. While walking in the woods one day in May, Balakireff not only suggested the idea of writing a piece based on the Shakespearean theme, but went so far as to outline the form and style of the composition in the greatest detail, telling Tschaikowsky what the character of each theme should be and in what key it should be written.

Tschaikowsky was grateful for the advice given him by Balakireff, but he wrote to his brother that "it is my firm belief that, in spite of all his virtues, his company would oppress me like a heavy stone if we should live together, in the same town. The narrowness of his views and the arrogance with which he holds them are especially disagreeable to me. Nevertheless, his presence has helped me in many ways."

Balakireff continued to offer criticism and advice as the composition of *Romeo and Juliet* progressed, and it is unquestionably he who was largely responsible for the numerous revisions that were made in the score. . . .

PAUL AFFELDER, *Pittsburgh Symphony Orchestra*

Fantasia for Orchestra: *Francesca da Rimini*—(after Dante)

Tschaikowsky visited Paris in the summer of 1876. He was hunting a libretto for a new opera and considered one on an episode from Dante's *Inferno*. The opera was abandoned, but the subject made a deep impression on Tschaikowsky. Its pathos and restless energy suited his own musical and emotional temperament.

In July, he wrote to his brother, Modeste: "Early this morning, I read through the fifth canto of the *Inferno* and was beset by the wish to compose a symphonic poem, *Francesca da Rimini*." In the fall, he wrote from Moscow: "I have just finished a new work, the symphonic fantasia *Francesca da Rimini*. I have worked on it with love (*con amore*) and believe my love has been successful. With regard to the 'Whirlwind,' perhaps it might correspond better to Doré's picture; it has not turned out quite what I wanted. However, a just judgment of the work is impossible as long as it is not orchestrated and it has not been played."

The Fantasia was completed in November 1876 and performed in Moscow early the next year. Tschaikowsky gave no detailed program for the work but prefaced his score with the following quotation from the fifth canto of Dante's *Inferno:*

"Dante arrives in the second circle of Hell. He sees that here the incontinent are punished, and their punishment is to be tormented continually by the cruelest winds under a gloomy air. Among these tortured ones he recognizes Francesca da Rimini who tells her story."

Francesca da Rimini, daughter of an aristocratic thirteenth century family, was given in marriage by her parents to a courtier called "the lame." He was not only deformed, but was also much older than Francesca.

"Some say that he secured Francesca for wife by trickery, she being led to suppose that Paolo (his young and handsome brother) was to be her future husband. She therefore permitted herself to love him." The husband discovers the love of his wife and brother and kills them both.

On the flyleaf of Tschaikowsky's music is also Francesca's story from the fifth canto. The following is Carlyle's English translation:

"There is no greater pain than to recall a happy time in wretchedness; and this thy teacher knows. But if thou hast such desire to learn the first root of our love, I will do like one who weeps and tells.

"One day for pastime, we read of Lancelot, how love constrained him. We were alone, and without all suspicion. Several times reading urged our eyes to meet and changed the color of our faces. But one moment alone it was that overcame us. When we read of how the fond smile was kissed by such a lover, he, who never shall be divided from me, kissed my mouth all trembling. The book, and he wrote it, was a Galeotto. That day we read in it no farther . . ."

LENORA COFFIN, *Indianapolis Symphony Orchestra*

Music for the Ballet: *The Sleeping Beauty*

Based on Perrault's famous fairy tale, Tschaikowsky's *The Sleeping Beauty* ballet dates from the summer of 1889. Its music is generally regarded as superior to that of the *Swan Lake* ballet and inferior to that of the *Nutcracker Suite*. Few ballet scores are so suitable in mood and style for the action they accompany. The music is truly melodious in Tschaikowsky's lighter vein. The fantasy is conveyed in bright, glittering colors, and, as Rosa Newmarch pointed out, the music "never descends to the commonplace level of the ordinary ballet music." There are thirty numbers in all, many of them, especially the waltz, endearing in their lilting and haunting grace. The work was first produced in St. Petersburg on January 2, 1890. In the early nineteen twenties, Diaghilev, the great ballet impresario, revived the work in London and elsewhere with immense artistic éclat. Fragments of the original ballet were used in *Aurora's Wedding*, a recent production of the Monte Carlo Ballet Russe.

In an open letter to Diaghilev on the occasion of the London production, Igor Stravinsky, who orchestrated two unscored passages omitted from the St. Petersburg premiere, expressed himself fervidly about Tschaikowsky's ballet music: "I have spent some days of intense pleasure in finding therein again and again the same feeling of freshness, inventiveness, ingenuity and vigor. And I warmly desire that your audiences of all countries may feel this work as it is felt by me, a Russian musician. . . ."

LOUIS BIANCOLLI, *Philharmonic-Symphony Society of New York*

Piano concerto No. 1 in B flat minor (Opus 23)

Tschaikowsky wrote this Concerto in 1874. It was first performed in Boston on October 25, 1875; Hans von Buelow was the soloist . . . The score, dedicated first to Nicholas Rubinstein, (was) later dedicated to Hans von Buelow . . .

When the Concerto was last heard at these concerts (February 1941) Arthur Loesser wrote about it thus:

"Tschaikowsky was not fundamentally a pianist. True, he was

able to play the instrument to a certain extent—yet its kinaes-
thetics almost never formed the starting point of his musical
ideas. However, he was for years teacher of harmony at the Moscow Conservatory, the director of which was Nicholas Rubinstein,
a brilliant pianist, hardly second to his famous brother, Anton.
Tschaikowsky was deeply devoted to his principal, and frequently
sought his advice and encouragement concerning composition.
Tschaikowsky composed the great Concerto for the pianoforte, dedicated it to Rubinstein and showed the completed work to him
for the first time in the presence of a certain Nicholas Kashkin.

"But the composer, in all friendship, did not calculate with
the form in which the pin-pricked self-love of a musician would
seek to obtain a cheap and sterile revenge. This is Kashkin's account of the meeting:

" 'Nicholas Rubinstein, it appeared, was disagreeably surprised
that Tschaikowsky, not being a pianist, had not asked his advice
about the piano part, and therefore he showed prejudice and
hostility as regards this work. Rubinstein, who read admirably at
sight, started the Concerto, and began finding fault with everything, but especially the piano technique. He played even with a
certain intentional clumsiness, finding it all unsuitably written, too
difficult, and finally declaring it altogether unplayable from this
point of view, and in need of great alteration.'

"Tschaikowsky was deeply hurt; he vowed he would not
make the slightest change in the Concerto. This, of course, was
mere wounded vanity, not musicianship. He removed the dedication, and offered the Concerto to Hans von Buelow who was
soon to leave for an American tour. Buelow was delighted with
the work and so it came about that the first performance of the
Concerto took place in Boston, October 25, 1875. However, years
later, when Rubinstein, in his grave, was unable to derive any
satisfaction therefrom, Tschaikowsky, without afflicting his self-
esteem, was able to make some alterations in the Concerto. These
were incorporated into the edition of 1889.

"It has been clear right from the start that the Concerto is a
powerful, vital piece of music, combining the immediate seductiveness of dynamic brilliance and simple melody with those
more durable virtues of sound construction and logical develop-

ment that are revealed by the searching dissections of students. It is one of the most frequently played and gladly listened to of all concertos."

G. H. L. SMITH, *Cleveland Orchestra*

Violin concerto in D major (Opus 35)

This work was begun in March 1878, at Clarens, overlooking Lake Geneva in Switzerland. It was written with the helpful advice of Joseph Kotek, a young violinist who had formerly been in the class in musical theory which Tschaikowsky conducted at the Moscow Conservatory, and who later brought about the composer's friendship with Mme. von Meck. The project of a concerto seems to have been at first a little dubious, but as the work progressed his interest grew, and he worked rapidly to complete it. On April 20, he wrote to Nadejda that the piece was finished.

"I shall now play it through several times with Kotek, who is still here, and then score it," he said. And a week later: "The first movement of the Concerto is now ready—that is, copied in a clear hand and played through. I am satisfied with it. I am not content with the *Andante,* and I shall either better it radically or compose a new one. The Finale, if I am not mistaken, is as successful as the first movement." (The original *Andante* was indeed rejected, but was published with two other pieces as Opus 42, under the title of *Meditations.*) On April 29 he wrote:

"I composed today another *Andante,* which corresponds better with the other movements, which are very complicated . . . I consider that the Concerto is now completed, and tomorrow I shall rush at the scoring of it, so that I can leave here without having this work any longer before me."

But three years and nine months were to elapse before Tschaikowsky's Concerto was played in public. It was dedicated to Leopold Auer, principal professor of violin at the St. Petersburg Conservatory, but that virtuoso could not, at that time, make up his mind to grapple with the formidable difficulties of the work. Hence, the first performance was given by Adolf Brodsky, formerly

Tschaikowsky's colleague on the staff of the Moscow Conservatory, at Vienna on December 4, 1881, and the later version is dedicated to him.

The reception was not wholly enthusiastic, even on the part of the audience, but the critics were practically unanimous in their condemnation. Of all the Viennese reviewers, the most powerful was Edward Hanslick, who carried in his soul a bitter hatred of Richard Wagner, Russian art and program music. He wrote:

"The Concerto has proportion, is musical and is not without genius, but soon savagely gains the upper hand and lords it to the end of the first movement. The violin is no longer played; it is yanked about, it is torn asunder, it is beaten black and blue. I do not know whether it is possible for anyone to conquer these hair-raising difficulties, but I do know that Mr. Brodsky martyrized his hearers as well as himself. The *Adagio* with its tender national melody, almost conciliates, almost wins us; but it breaks off abruptly to make way for a finale that puts us in the midst of the brutal and wretched jollity of a Russian kermess. We see wild and vulgar faces, we hear curses, we smell bad brandy. Friedrich Vischer once asserted in reference to lascivious painting, that there are pictures that 'stink in the eye.' Tschaikowky's Violin Concerto brings us for the first time to the horrid idea that there may be music that stinks in the ear."

But Hanslick's musical judgment was no better here than in most other instances.

DONALD FERGUSON, *Minneapolis Symphony Orchestra*

Suite No. 4: *Mozartiana* (Opus 61)

In his letters to Mme. von Meck, Tschaikowsky said: "Why do you not care for Mozart? In this respect our opinions differ, dear friend; I not only like Mozart, I adore and idolize him. To me the most beautiful opera ever written is *Don Juan*. How thankful I am that the circumstances of my musical career have not changed by a hair's-breadth the charm Mozart exercises for me. You would not believe, dear friend, what wonderful feelings come over me when I give myself up to his music. It is something quite different from the stressful delight awakened in me by Beethoven, Schumann and Chopin. My contemporaries were imbued with the spirit of modern music from their childhood and came to know Mozart in later years, after they had made acquaintance with Chopin, who reflects so clearly the Byronic despair and disillusionment. Fortunately, fate decreed that I should grow up in an unmusical family, so that in childhood I was not nourished on the poisonous food of post-Beethoven music. The same kind of fate brought me into contact with Mozart, and thus opened up to me unexpected horizons. These early impressions never can be effaced. Do you know that when I play Mozart, I feel brighter and younger, almost a youth again?"

In this Suite the composer has taken four works of Mozart (three for clavier and one for voices) and arranged them for orchestra. On a flyleaf of the score of the work he has written: "A large number of the more admirable small compositions of Mozart, for incomprehensible reasons, are very little known, not alone to the public, but even to a large proportion of musicians. The author of the arrangement of the Suite having its title *Mozartiana* desires to give a new impulse to the story of these little masterworks whose succinct forms contain incomparable beauties."

1— (Allegro) The composition upon which this work is based is a *gigue* written for clavier by Mozart in 1789.

2— (Menuet) This also is taken from a clavier composition written in 1789.

3— (Prayer) An *Ave verum* for four voices and string instruments composed in 1791 is used by Tschaikowsky for this movement.

4— (Theme and Variations) A set of ten variations upon a theme from one of Gluck's operas is the origin of this movement.

BARBARA DUNCAN, *Rochester Philharmonic Orchestra*

Marche Slav (Opus 31)

First of Tschaikowsky's works in the form, the *Marche Slav* was composed at Moscow, September 1876, for performance at a benefit concert. The other marches comprise one in honor of

General Skobolew—which, incidentally, was held in such low esteem by Tschaikowsky that he used the name, Sinopoff, on the title page—the *Festival Coronation March*; the *Jurists' March*; and a *Military March,* not counting his many other marches which are parts of larger works.

The *Marche Slav* is based chiefly on folk music from the south of Russia and from Serbia. Its main theme, in fact, is taken almost directly from the Serbian folk song, *Sunce varko ne fifas jednako* ("Come, My Dearest, Why So Sad This Morning?") Made into three sections, the work incorporates in the middle portion fragments of the ertswhile Russian national hymn, *God Save the Emperor.* . . .

RObert C. Bagar, *Philharmonic-Symphony Society of New York*

Italian Caprice (Opus 45)

This is a souvenir of Tschaikowsky's visit to Italy in 1880. Nadejda Filaretovna von Meck, his elusive, but most generous patroness, had arranged the western European premiere of "our" Fourth Symphony in Paris—at considerable expense, in keeping with the Parisian custom of those days. It was to take place on January 25. In Rome he waited to hear news of the public's reaction before himself proceeding to Paris. "While he waited," Herbert Weinstock reports in his recent biography of the Russian master, "he began, on the twenty-eighth, to compose the *Italian Caprice,* which he wanted to be something on the order of Glinka's Spanish fantasies. He completed the first draft in exactly a week and then told Nadejda Filaretovna that he foresaw a bright future for this composition."

Some of his impressions of Rome, which he found very agreeable, are in this work. A bugle call, sounded at one of the nearby barracks, is announced at the outset of the work, and two locally-sung tunes are heard successively after this opening fanfare. The last part of the work is a *tarantella,* after the popular Italian model. In the midst of this dance, at a point where the very exuberant playing of the full orchestra subsides, two oboes are heard, recalling the second of the two folk themes I have mentioned. At the close, the dance becomes quite frenzied.

ARTHUR V. BERGER, *New York City Symphony Orchestra*

Serenade for String Orchestra (Opus 48)

Some of Tschaikowsky's freshest and most melodious music is found in his orchestral suites. They display his rich gift for orchestration more completely perhaps than do any of his other compositions. The musical ideas which they contain may be slight, but Tschaikowsky exploits these so deftly, and dresses them up so piquantly by means of his brilliant scoring that the suites have come to rank among his most popular works . . .

The *Serenade* was first planned as a symphony or quartet; quite by accident, Tschaikowsky wrote his publisher, did it turn out to be a Serenade. Work was undertaken some time during 1879-1880. Writing Nadejda von Meck in October 1880, the composer said: "Just think, dear friend—My muse has been so benevolent that in a short time I have got through—before my sister's illness—two pieces, a *Festival Overture* for the Exhibition and a *Serenade* in four movements for string orchestra . . ."

Nearly a year later, Tschaikowsky again mentions the *Serenade* in his correspondence with his patroness. He wrote: "I wish with all my heart that you could hear my *Serenade* properly performed. It loses so much on the piano, and I think the middle movements—played by the violins—would win your sympathy. As regards the first and the last movements, you are right. They are merely a play of sounds and do not touch the heart. The first movement is my homage to Mozart; it is intended to be in imitation of his style, and I should be delighted if I thought I had in any way approached my model. Do not laugh, my dear, at my zeal in standing up for my latest creation. Perhaps my paternal feelings are so warm because it is the youngest child of my fancy."

The *Serenade*, which was dedicated to Constantin Albrecht, came to its first public performance in Moscow, January 28,

1882, with Erdmannsdoerfer conducting. It had been heard privately a year earlier. Almost one of the last acts of Nicholas Rubinstein before his death, in the spring of 1881, was to conduct the *Serenade*. In order to get an idea of the composition, he had the parts copied, assembled the students' orchestra, and, although so ill that he could not stand, he managed to read through the score, seated at the podium.

The *Serenade* became popular almost at once, and the critics gave it high praise. Tschaikowsky played it repeatedly on his tour of 1887-1888, which went a long way in popularizing it. The German critics and audiences grudgingly admitted its good points, but the French and English were enthusiastic. After a London performance, Tschaikowsky wrote: "The *Serenade* pleased most, and I was recalled three times, which means a good deal from the reserved London public. . . ."

LOUISE BECK, *Philadelphia Orchestra*

Symphony No. 2 in C minor (Opus 17)

The first three symphonies of Tschaikowsky are performed so seldom in comparison to the last three that the chance to hear one of them given under favorable auspices should be welcomed eagerly. The Second Symphony was begun at Kamenka in June 1872, and finished at Ussovo in August save for the scoring. That was completed in October.

The first performance took place at Moscow in January 1873, at a concert of the Imperial Russian Music Society, under the direction of Nicholas Rubinstein, and the Symphony is dedicated to the Moscow section of the Society. So great was the success of the new work that by general request it was repeated at a later concert that same season.

Of all Tschaikowsky's symphonies the Second is the most national in feeling. Much of the thematic material is said to stem from Little Russia, for which reason the critic and teacher Nicholas Kashkin saw fit to dub it the *Little Russian Symphony*.

. . . . Elemental power and brilliance mark the Finale (Moderato assai: Allegro vivo, C major, 4-4), which towers above the preceding divisions of the Symphony. Even César Cui, as a rule a bitter enemy of Tschaikowsky's music, could pronounce this movement "magnificent." A Little Russian dance tune, "The Crane," announced by the first violins, supplies the initial subject. The second, also announced by the violins, is original with Tschaikowsky. Again there is harmonic novelty. The material is worked up with irresistible verve to a dazzling finish.

The Symphony was introduced to New York City as long ago as 1883 by the Symphony Society under the direction of Leopold Damrosch. There were several performances by the Society, the last occurring in 1917 under the direction of Walter Damrosch. The Philharmonic Society gave the work only three times, on December 18, 27 and 30, 1910, under the direction of Gustav Mahler. The present performances [January 8, 1940] are the first by the combined societies. . . .

PITTS SANBORN, *Philharmonic-Symphony Society of New York*

Symphony No. 4 in F minor (Opus 36)

In the winter of 1876-1877, when Tschaikowsky began the sketches for his Fourth Symphony, he was suddenly plunged into one of those inexplicable "black moods" of his, a mood so depressing that he wrote to his friend, Klimenko: "Since last we met, I am very much changed—especially mentally. Not a kopek's worth of fun and gayety is left in me. Life is terribly empty, tedious and tawdry. My mind turns toward matrimony, or indeed any other steady bond. The only thing that has not changed is my love for composing. If the conditions of my life were different, if my desire to create were not balked at every step . . . I might write something really decent."

He did write "something really decent," of course: the Fourth Symphony. The Symphony was composed, however, at a time when Peter Ilyitch was suffering from too many mixed emotions, some of which are hinted at in the letter quoted. He did marry, as the letter suggested he would, but the marriage was brief and tragic. His wife, Antonina Miliukova, was young and pretty. She was also very much in love with her husband. Numerous obstacles interfered with their happiness, none the less, not the least of which was the composer's bewildering temperament, which was not made any more cheerful, when he discovered that Antonina had positively no respect for the truth. By the time the Symphony had been completed, the marriage was only a bad dream. The experience had been wretched, and it left its mark on the music.

Still, there was a more elating experience at hand, for this same winter saw the beginning of his strange friendship with Nadejda von Meck, his benefactress, who ultimately gave him an annual and ample income with the understanding that the two should never meet. Nicholas Rubinstein was responsible for Mme. von Meck's interest, but he probably never suspected the turn this interest would take. It was Tschaikowsky's music that attracted her at once, not Tschaikowsky himself. After Rubinstein played *The Tempest* for her, she wrote the composer: "I was in a delirium from which I could not emerge." She promptly commissioned works from him. This was in the late fall of 1876.

By May 1877, he had decided to dedicate his Symphony to Mme. von Meck, and, July 15, three days before his marriage, he wrote his benefactress (in the same letter in which he announced his impending marriage), "I shall write on the Symphony, 'Dedicated to my friend.'"

WALTER WHITWORTH, Indianapolis Symphony Orchestra

Symphony No. 5 in E minor (Opus 64)

Completed in August of 1888, Tschaikowsky's Fifth Symphony was first performed at St. Petersburg on November 17 under the composer's direction. . . .

Tschaikowsky's slight opinion of his Fifth Symphony as compared to his ardent belief in his Fourth and Sixth is a curious fact, coming as it did from the incorrigible self-analyst who had so much to say to his intimate friends about his doubts and beliefs as to the progress of his music. He never hesitated to tell, for example, when he was composing from the urge to compose and when he was forcing himself to do it; when he was writing "to order" and when he was not. . . .

As for the Fifth Symphony, Tschaikowsky seems to have been

skeptical about it from the start. "To speak frankly," he wrote to Modeste in May, "I feel as yet no impulse for creative work. What does this mean? Have I written myself out? No ideas, no inclination! Still, I am hoping to collect, little by little, material for a symphony." To Mme. von Meck, a month later—"Have I told you that I intend to write a symphony? The beginning was difficult; but now inspiration seems to have come. However, we shall see." In August, with the Symphony "half-orchestrated," the listless mood still prevailed: "When I am old and past composing, I shall spend the whole of my time in growing flowers. My age, although I am not very old [he was forty-eight]—begins to tell on me. I become very tired, and I can no longer play the pianoforte or read at night as I used to do." Three weeks later he reports briefly that he has "finished the Symphony."

The first performances, which he conducted in St. Petersburg on November 17 and 24, 1888, were a popular success, but Tschaikowsky wrote to his patroness that he considered his Symphony "a failure." He still found in it "something repellent, something superfluous, patchy and insincere, which the public instinctively recognizes." He did not accept their applause as proof of enthusiasm; they were only being polite. "Am I really played out, as they say? Can I merely repeat and ring the changes on my earlier idiom? Last night I looked through *our* Symphony the Fourth). What a difference! How immeasurably superior it is! It is very, very sad!"

But the musicians plainly liked his Symphony, both in St. Petersburg and Prague. When its success in Hamburg was outstanding, he wrote to Davidoff: "The Fifth Symphony was magnificently played, and I like it far better now, after having held a bad opinion of it for some time." This was written on the crest of its immediate success. Later, his misgivings returned . . .

JOHN BURK, *Boston Symphony Orchestra*

Symphony No. 6 in B minor (Opus 74)

Upon his return from America, in 1891, Tschaikowsky began work on a Sixth Symphony. The sketches did not measure up to his exacting standards and, although the work was partly orchestrated, he destroyed it, commenting to his nephew, Vladimir Davidoff, that it "contained little that was very fine—an empty patter of sounds without any inspiration."

He went on to tell Davidoff (to whom another, completed Sixth was to be dedicated) that when he was on the train going to Paris in December 1892, the idea came to him for a new symphony. "During my journey [he was writing the following February] while composing it in my mind, I frequently shed tears."

"Now I am home again," he went on, "I have settled down to sketch out the work, and it goes with such ardor that in less than four days I have completed the first movement, while the remainder is clearly outlined in my head. There will be much that is novel as regards form in this work. For instance, the Finale will not be a great *Allegro,* but an *Adagio* of considerable dimensions. You can imagine what joy I feel in the conviction that my day is not yet over, and I may still accomplish much. Perhaps I may be mistaken, but it does not seem likely."

Tschaikowsky planned to call his new work "A Program Symphony, No. 6," but he was going to lock in his breast the secret of what the program might be. It was "to remain an enigma to all; let them guess it who can."

At the first performance it was listed simply by its number. Next morning, before sending the score to the publisher, Tschaikowsky was still worrying about the christening. "Program Symphony" had been abandoned, and "Tragic Symphony" was being considered. His brother, Modeste, on the spur of the moment, suggested *Pathetic* and the title was hailed: "Bravo, Modi, splendid!"

The Symphony was composed, for the most part, at Tschaikowsky's country house at Frolovskoe, not far from Moscow, in the spring and summer of 1893. He interrupted his work in May for a trip to London, but was bored and depressed there, probably because of that very interruption. Frolovskoe allowed him to be near his friends in town and still gave him seclusion for work. He had a garden, with a little pond and a tiny islet. He had magnificent vistas of the sweeping Central Russian countryside, fringed by forests. He had hens to care for and feed, and even a colony of ants for which he provided insects. He employed himself from time to time flying a large kite. Although his health and spirits had been more than usually good, he made sure they would remain so by taking long walks, even in bad weather. He was fifty-three, popular, respected and in fairly easy circumstances.

Tschaikowsky had high hopes of the Sixth Symphony, described it as "the best, certainly the most sincere work I have written." To Jurgenson, the publisher, he wrote: "On my word of honor, never in all my life have I been so satisfied, so proud, so happy in the knowledge that I have written a good work."

At rehearsals, however, it appeared to make no particular impression upon the orchestra, and the composer was despondent again. He was not, it is true, a compelling or persuasive conductor. He was too diffident to demand the best results from his players and would rather have a half-way performance than a fuss. In public he suffered from nervousness, and had a peculiar delusion that in conducting, his head was liable to fall off if he did not support it with his left hand, which, of course, permitted him only the use of his right.

The first performance, which was received with politeness rather than enthusiasm, was given at a concert of the Imperial Russian Musical Society in St. Petersburg, October 28, 1893. (It was first played in the United States at a concert of the New York Symphony Society the following March . . .)

Nine days after this premiere the composer was dead. In spite of warnings of the prevalence of cholera, he drank a glass of water from the tap, too impatient to wait for it to be boiled or for mineral water to be brought. Some say the impetuous draught was gulped at a luncheon, some that it was at an after-theater supper. There are those who think it was taken with deliberately suicidal intent. There is little question that his death, following so closely upon the production of the predominantly melancholy Sixth Symphony, touched the imagination of audiences and contributed to the popularity of this last work. The inconclusive discussion of whether or not there were premonitions of death mysteriously expressed in this Requiem Symphony need not be entered into here . . .

R. F. L. McCombs, *Philadelphia Orchestra*

HEITOR VILLA-LOBOS

(Born in Rio de Janeiro, March 5, 1886—now living
in Rio de Janeiro)

ONE OF THE leading composers of South America, Villa-Lobos has begun to exercise a decided influence upon the listening habits of North American and European concert audiences. The younger element among our students and musicians find him a kindred spirit in tonal audacity and "free" expression, the middle-aged who once were young are astonished and diverted by the originality and starkness of his musical speech. He is at once a disturbance and a challenge, for he has something to say and he says it with extraordinary eloquence.

Son of a lawyer of limited means, who was also an excellent 'cellist, Heitor studied the same instrument and acquired his musical training with some difficulty, because it was necessary to contribute his share of the family expenses. So "most of the day was devoted to working in business," the remainder of his time was spent in religious schools "where he was able to undertake some theoretical work in music."

But at nineteen he decided he had studied enough, and had mastered the 'cello sufficiently to undertake concert tours of his native country. His travels through Brazil, for nearly four years, brought him in contact with the people and folk music of various regions.

He returned to Rio and married a well-known Brazilian musician, Lucilla Guimaraes. He distinguished himself as a conductor, bringing representative modern works to Brazilian audiences. His own music began to be performed everywhere—in Europe and North America—and he has appeared successfully as conductor of major orchestras throughout the world. He has now become almost a national hero of his native Brazil.

Bachianas Brasileiras No. 2

Bachianas Brasileiras are combinations of short movements, and Villa-Lobos has written five such works as a symbol of his love for the classics. The Second consists of a Prelude, Aria and Dance, to which is added a Toccatina. The last movement was composed entirely apart from the rest of the Suite, and when it was orchestrated, was added to the other three movements. The work is written for chamber orchestra. The three movements are but orchestrations of three pieces for 'cello and one for piano. In order to have them fit into the Bach atmosphere, Villa-Lobos added the titles to his original compositions. The composer says:

"This is a special kind of musical composition, based on an intimate knowledge of the great works of Bach and also on the composer's affinity with the harmonic, contrapuntal and melodic atmosphere of the folklore of the northeastern region of Brazil. The composer considers Bach a universal and rich folklore source, deeply rooted in the folk music of every country in the world. Thus Bach is a mediator among all races."

The final movement is a Toccata entitled "The Little Train." It is intended to portray a car somewhat like the Toonerville Trolley, run by steam, carrying berrypickers and other hillmen. It gasps and jangles from town to town while its whistle resounds through the hills and valleys in the province of Sao Paolo. The Toccata figure is supplied by the rhythm of the imaginary wheels of the train. The movement is a gay bit of program music, more mundane and slighter in substance than the rich, deeply moving preceding sections. Simple and naive, it is clear, natural and happy. Villa-Lobos is said to have written the movement in one hour, while bumping along the rails, and he played it the same evening with his wife, a 'cellist, in its original form as a piece for piano.

WILLIAM E. BENSWANGER, *Pittsburgh Symphony Orchestra*

What follows is that portion of a note on No. 5 that does not repeat the information above:

Bachianas Brasileiras No. 5

. . . To Villa-Lobos what Bach represents is "deeply rooted in the folk music of every country in the world." Some have suspected a slightly different motive in the choice of title. "Probably a desire to tweak solemn noses," is Paul Rosenfeld's conjecture.

In the *Bachianas Brasileiras* No. 5 the air is first intoned by the soprano on an open vowel *(vocalise)*, then the Portuguese text given below, and finally hummed:

> Afternoon . . . pink and gold; Dusk falls,
> Tingeing the surface of the sea . . .
> Without knowing why people sadden,
> Without wanting, eyes begin to weep . . .
> Unaware my soul grows faint . . .
>
> It is the serene hour in which heaven's gardens
> Open in flowers of light upon the universe.
> The birds are silent, insects are chirping sadly . . .
> A poem of the sea, each wave a verse. . . .
> Night approaches, suave and slow . . .
> A bittersweet longing troubles me.
> Afternoon . . . pink and gold; Dusk falls.
> Tingeing the surface of the sea.

Louis Biancolli, *Philharmonic-Symphony Society of New York*

WILHELM RICHARD WAGNER

(Born in Leipzig, May 22, 1813—died in Venice,
February 13, 1883)

Wagner was a petty and egocentric man, a genius of titanic proportions. As an essayist and critic, he was prejudiced and medio-cre, and not without recourses to fallacy and deceit. His love affairs were scandalous, but he had an Olympian gift for dramatic melodic grandeur.

He has written deathless pages, despite the pitiable weaknesses of his character. But for the friends devoted to his genius rather than to himself, posterity might never have cherished him.

Richard was the ninth child of Carl Friedrich Wilhelm Wagner, we are told in all proper biographies, "a civil servant of Leipzig, and his wife, Johanna Rosina Paetz. The parents were comfortable, middle-class people, with normal interest in the arts, and special fondness for the theater."

Conventional biographers, record that "the father died when Richard was five months old, leaving the family in difficult circumstances." Whereupon Ludwig Geyer, an actor who boarded with them, married Frau Wagner, which did not improve the aforesaid circumstances appreciably, considering the frequent insolvency of stagefolk, then as now.

Richard was an excellent student, if he happened to be studying something that interested him, but far too self-centered to acquire any lasting knowledge of a distasteful subject. He was sent to the Kreuzschule in Dresden in 1822, and piled up a brilliant record. But at the Nicolaischule in Leipzig he was not so successful. He studied music with Gottlieb Mueller, "who thought him self-willed and eccentric." His first production as a composer was an overture, performed in Leipzig in 1830.

In the year of his graduation (1830) he began to study composition with Theodore Weinig at the Thomaschule and a symphony was performed at one of the Gewandhaus concerts in 1833. In the following year he was appointed conductor of the opera at Magdeburg. He married an actress, Wilhelmina Planer, and accepted a post as conductor at Koenigsburg, but the theater lessee went bankrupt. Instead, Wagner went to Riga, and thereby gained the inspiration for an opera, *The Flying Dutchman*.

He paid his first visit to Paris in 1839, taking along an unfinished opera, *Rienzi*. The venture proved unfortunate, and Wagner learned to starve in earnest. He returned to Germany, finished his opera and it was produced in Dresden in 1842.

He was appointed to a conducting post at the Dresden Theatre and set to work on *Tannhäuser*, produced October 19, 1845 with moderate success, despite a brilliant cast. He became embroiled in the political turmoil of 1849, was exiled and fled to Paris, then to Zurich. He had begun *Lohengrin,* took the score with him to Paris. Though "ill, miserable and despairing," he finished it and sent it to Liszt in Weimar, where it was produced under Liszt's direction August 28, 1850.

The work was so successful that Liszt immediately appealed for a new creation and Wagner, in his retreat, began studying the *Nibelungenlied* and to lay out the plan for *Tristan.* He accepted an invitation to London, to conduct the concerts of the Philharmonic Society and attained marked success there. He went on to Italy and completed the libretto of *Tristan* in Venice.

Returning to Paris a third time, he was befriended by the Prince and Princess Metternich and *Tannhäuser* was accepted for the Grand Opera. "Magnificent preparations were made; it was rehearsed 164 times; fourteen times with the full orchestra and the scenery and dresses were placed entirely under the composer's direction. More than 8000 pounds were expended upon the venture; and the work was performed for the first time in the French language and with the new Venusberg music" on March 13, 1861.

At this performance the famous riot inaugurated by the members of the Parisian Jockey Club, jealous of all this furore and powerful patronage on behalf of a foreign musician, plus the spearhead of a clique determined upon a political suppression of Wagner, put an end to the venture. After the third presentation, the opera was withdrawn and Wagner was brokenhearted.

He settled for a time in Vienna, the haven of great musicians. *Tristan* was accepted, then abandoned after fifty-seven rehearsals "because of the incompetence of the tenor." But *Lohengrin* was produced there on May 15, 1861, and Wagner heard it for the first time.

Wagner published the libretto of *Der Ring des Nibelungen.* The young King Ludwig of Bavaria read it and thereupon invited Wagner to come to Munich and finish his work there, with an annual stipend of about 120 pounds. Needless to say, Wagner accepted with rapture, for he was all but starving and this offer seemed a bolt from the blue.

But rosy plans to build a theater and music school terminated when a court intrigue formed against him and he was forced to retire to Triebschen, near Lucerne, for the next six years. But *Tristan* and *Die Meistersinger* had been produced in Munich, also *Die Walküre* and *Das Rheingold,* before this second exile took effect. Obviously the entire *Ring,* a colossal drama, required a more spacious arena for adequate performance than any then extant in Bavaria.

Consequently, a project was launched to build a *Festspielhaus* at Bayreuth. After innumerable difficulties, it was completed in 1876. Wagner himself had laid the first stone four years before. After this, he lived permanently in Bayreuth, "in a house named Wahnfried, in the garden of which he built his tomb."

Eventually, the Prologue (*Das Rheingold*) and three music-dramas of *The Ring* were performed there at enormous expense. The success was purely artistic, for the management found itself burdened with a debt of some $30,000. Hans Richter and Wagner conducted a few benefit concerts in London to help pay this debt and the profits from performances of the *Ring* in Munich entirely cleared it off.

Before he set out for London in 1877, Wagner had finished the libretto of his last work, *Parsifal,* based upon the legend of the Holy Grail. He began the music a year later and finished it at Palermo on January 13, 1882, the year before his death. A curious circumstance occurred about this time.

In the days of his Dresden residence, Wagner had an American dentist, Dr. Newell S. Jenkins. He had become annoyed and discouraged over continued expenses at Bayreuth. Bavarian official opposition irritated him and he demanded the interest on three million marks. Failing to get it, he would go to America and under certain conditions settle there.

Dr. Jenkins explains in the private memoirs left to his children that Frau Cosima had come to him as a patient with her children. She asked him to treat her husband and he went to Bayreuth to see him. He adds: that "this was the beginning of a friendship which lasted until Wagner's death."

In the course of one of their talks, Dr. Jenkins recalls, Wagner proposed that Dr. Jenkins write to J. S. Dwight, editor of *Dwight's Musical Journal,* Boston, requesting that he (Dwight) inquire in writing upon what terms Wagner would emigrate to America. Considering the hostility of Dwight and all other proper Bostonians toward Wagner and his music, the proposal was fantastic. However,

Dr. Jenkins, perhaps with a tongue in his cheek, wrote the required letter and Dwight, curiously enough, complied. Whereupon the great Richard penned one of the most remarkable epistles of his career, addressed to Dr. Jenkins from Naples, on February 8, 1880, in which he consented to emigrate to America "with my latest works and my entire family," provided "an association" were to be formed, which would offer him $1,000,000 in cash, half to "be placed at my disposal upon my taking up residence in some state of the Union with favorable climate," and the other half to be "invested as capital in a government bank at 5 percent. Thus would America have brought me from Europe for all time." In return for these favors, Wagner would turn over all his works and dedicate his future labors "without further compensation to the American nation."

Dr. Jenkins sent this letter to Dwight and it was sought fiercely as a rare prize of journalistic enterprise by nearly every large newspaper in the East. It was returned eventually to Dr. Jenkins, without having been published in this country or abroad.

Needless to say, nothing came of this grandiloquent "offer," nor is there a record of any further discussion along this line. The letter would seem to credit an assertion voiced by Cosima that Richard never would visit the United States because he could not bear to be parted from her.

Parsifal eventually was produced at Bayreuth in July and August of 1882 under Wagner's direction. But the exertion of directing these and other performances, and the nervous exactions attendant upon rehearsals and other details of production sapped the strength of the aging master. He passed that autumn in Venice and conducted a private performance of his early Symphony on Christmas Eve. But his heart failed suddenly in the late afternoon of February 13, 1883. He was buried in the tomb he had built in the garden of Wahnfried, and King Ludwig rode out there in the dead of night to pay his last respects.

Traeume (Dreams)

Of the five songs written by Wagner as settings of poems by Mathilde Wesendonck, *Traeume* and *Im Treibhaus* were described when published as *Studien zu Tristan und Isolde*. The composition of these songs occurred in Zurich at a time when Wagner's great love-drama was taking musical shape in his thoughts, with Mathilde a constant source of inspiration. Out of *Traeume* was to develop the thematic core of the love duet in the second act, and *Im Treibhaus* lies embedded in the Introduction to Act. III. Wagner made two versions of *Traeume* on December 4 and 5, 1857. A scoring for small orchestra came later, in which form it was performed on Mathilde's birthday, December 23, 1857. Wagner led an ensemble of eighteen musicians residing in Zurich, the presentation taking place in the garden of Frau Wesendonck's villa.

When he had completed the second act of *Tristan und Isolde,* he wrote to her: "Heaven knows that this song pleases me more than the proud scene itself. It is more beautiful than anything else I have created. I tremble to the very depths of my being when I listen to it."

LOUIS BIANCOLLI, *Philharmonic-Symphony Society of New York*

A Faust Overture

It was during his early residence in Paris, 1839-1840, that Wagner composed this work, originally conceived as the first movement of a *Faust Symphony*. Wagner said he wrote it out of the inner depths of his discontent, for he composed it during a period of poverty and distress. Eight years later he wrote Liszt that the work did not please him any longer, but that if Liszt wanted to perform it, he might have it. Liszt accordingly conducted the Overture at Weimar in May of 1852 and afterward wrote the composer a letter of criticism and suggestion. "The work is quite worthy of you," Liszt began, "but, if you will allow me to make a remark, I must confess that I should like either a second middle part or else a quieter and more agreeably colored treatment of the present middle part . . . If . . . you introduced a soft, tender melodious part, modulated *a la* Gretchen, I think I can assure you that your work would gain very much."

Wagner welcomed this criticism, and replied: "You have felt quite justly what is wanting: the woman is wanting. Perhaps you would understand my tone-poem if I called it *Faust in Solitude*. At that time I intended to write an entire *Faust Symphony.* The first movement was this *Solitary Faust,* longing, despairing, cursing . . . The second movement was to introduce Gretchen, the woman. I had a theme for her, but it was only a theme. The whole remains unfinished. I wrote my *Flying Dutchman* instead . . . The theme which you desire, I cannot introduce. This would naturally involve an entirely new composition, for which I have no inclination . . ."

A few years later, Wagner changed his mind, and did rewrite the work, but still omitted a "Gretchen" motive. In January of 1855 he wrote Liszt: "I have been taken with a desire to remodel my old *Faust Overture.* I have made an entirely new score . . . and have given more expansion and importance to the middle portion. I shall give it in a few days at a concert here, under the title of *A Faust Overture.*"

After the performance (January 23, 1855, at Zurich), Wagner sent Liszt the score, stating: "You will be better pleased with the middle part. I was, of course, unable to introduce a new motive, because that would have involved a remodeling of almost the whole work . . . Gretchen, of course, could not be introduced, only Faust himself."

JOHN TASKER HOWARD, Quarter Notes—October, 1944

A Siegfried Idyl

Cosima Liszt, daughter of Franz Liszt and the Comtesse d'Agoult, was born at Bellagio, Italy, on Christmas Day, 1837. She was married to Hans von Buelow at Berlin, August 18, 1857. They were divorced in the fall of 1869.

Wagner and Cosima Liszt, divorced wife of von Buelow, were married at Lucerne, August 25, 1870. Siegfried Wagner, their son, was born at Triebschen, near Lucerne, June 6, 1869.

Wagner wrote, November 11, 1870, to Ferdinand Praeger: "My house, too, is full of children, the children of my wife, but besides there blooms for me a splendid son, strong and beautiful, whom I dare call Siegfried Richard Wagner. Now think what I must feel, that this at last has fallen to my share. I am fifty-seven years old." On the twenty-fifth of the month he wrote to Praeger: "My son is Helferich Siegfried Richard. My son! Oh, what that says to me!"

But these were not the first references to the son. In a letter to a Mrs. Wille, June 25, 1870, Wagner wrote: "Certainly we shall come, for you are to be the first to whom we shall present ourselves as man and wife. She has defied all disapprobation and taken upon herself every condemnation. She has borne to me a wonderfully beautiful and vigorous boy, whom I could boldly call Siegfried: he is now growing, together with my work, and gives me a new, long life, which at last has attained a meaning. Thus we get along without the world, from which we have retired entirely . . . But now listen:

"You will, I trust, approve of the sentiment which leads us to postpone our visit until I can introduce to you the mother of my son as my wedded wife." (Finck's *Wagner,* vol. 2, p. 246)

The *Siegfried Idyl* was a birthday gift to the composer's wife. It was composed in November 1870, at Triebschen, near Lucerne. According to Hans Richter's story, he received the manuscript score on December 4, 1870. Wagner gave a remarkably fine copy to his wife. Richter wrote out immediately the parts, and then went to Zurich, where, with the help of Oskar Kahl, concertmaster of the City Orchestra, he engaged musicians. The first rehearsal was on December 21, 1870, in the foyer of the old theatre in Zurich. The Wesendoncks were present. "The musicians were excellent," says Richter, "and the music sounded magnificently." The musicians arrived at Lucerne on December 24. Wagner conducted the rehearsal that afternoon in the hall of the Hôtel du Lac. Christmas in 1870 fell on a Sunday, and early in the morning the musicians arrived at Wagner's villa at Triebschen.

In order that the performance might be a complete surprise to Cosima, the desks were put quietly in position on the stairs, and the tuning was in the large kitchen. The little orchestra took its place on the stairs; Wagner, who conducted, at the top, then the violins, violas, woodwind instruments, horns and at the bottom the violoncello and double-bass. The conductor could not see the 'cello and bass, but the performance was faultless. The orchestra was thus composed: two first violins, two second violins, two violas (one played by Hans Richter who also played the trumpet); one violoncello, one double-bass, one flute, one oboe, two clarinets, one bassoon and two horns. Richter says he borrowed a trumpet for the few measures given it from a bandsman.

In order not to excite the suspicion of Cosima, he went daily to practice the trumpet in the barracks, which were then empty. "These daily excursions and several trips to Zurich awakened the attention of Frau Wagner, who thought I was not so industrious as formerly. The highly successful performance of the *Idyl* put an end to this misunderstanding."

The performance began punctually at 7:30 a.m. The children called the *Idyl* "the stairs music." The *Idyl* was repeated several times in the course of the day, and in the afternoon the musicians played Beethoven's Sextet without the Variations.

The *Idyl* was performed at Mannheim, December 20, 1871, in private under the direction of Wagner. It was performed March 10, 1877, in the Ducal Palace at Meiningen by the Ducal Court Orchestra and Wagner conducted. The score and parts were published in February 1878.

Siegfried was born while the composition of the music-drama, *Siegfried,* was in progress. The themes in the *Idyl* were taken from the music-drama, all save one—a folk song, *Schlaf', mein Kind, schlaf' ein;* but the development of the themes was new. . . .

PHILIP HALE, *Boston Symphony Orchestra*

Overture to the opera: *Rienzi, the Last of the Tribunes*

Wagner left Koenigsberg in the early summer of 1837 to visit Dresden, and there he read Baerman's translation into German of Bulwer's *Rienzi.* And thus was revived his long-cherished idea of making the last of the Tribunes the hero of a grand opera. "My impatience with a degrading plight now amounted to a passionate craving to begin something grand and elevating, no matter if it involved the temporary abandonment of any practical goal. This mood was fed and strengthened by a reading of Bulwer's *Rienzi.* From the misery of modern private life, whence I could nohow glean the scantiest material for artistic treatment, I was wafted by the image of a great historico-political event in the enjoyment whereof I needs must find a distraction lifting me above cares and conditions that to me appeared nothing less than absolutely fatal to art."

The overture to *Rienzi* was completed October 23, 1840. The opera was produced at the Royal Saxon Court Theater, Dresden, October 20, 1842.

Overture to the Music-Drama: *The Flying Dutchman*

As John F. Runciman remarks, here in the Overture "it is the atmosphere of the sea that counts; the roar of the billows, the '*hui!*' of the wind, the dashing and plunging . . . The sea, indeed, is the background, foreground, the whole environment of the drama . . . The smell and atmosphere of the sea maintained with extraordinary vividness to the last bar."

Paramount in the construction of the Overture are the theme of the Dutchman, with its "empty fifth," given out in the opening measures by horns and bassoons, and the descending and rising motive of Senta as Angel of Mercy, the key having changed from D minor to F major, softly intoned (*Andante*) by English horn, horns and bassoons. In the end this motive, transformed from the whispered promise of salvation to redemption triumphant, concludes the Overture in a resounding paean.

The world premiere of *The Flying Dutchman* took place at the Dresden Court Opera, where Wagner was then conducting, on January 2, 1843. When preparations for the production began, exorbitant problems of staging and interpretation confronted the composer and the company.

How to navigate two ships on one stage was even a minor consideration in comparison with the difficulty of finding the right woman to embody the visionary and heroic Norwegian girl whose sacrifice saves the wandering Dutchman from eternal damnation. Of course Senta could not be allotted with confidence to just any prima donna, and Vanderdecken himself ought to be able to account to eye and ear for Senta's prophetic fixation.

For the original Senta, Wagner was fortunate in having available a great artist, the celebrated Wilhelmine Schroeder-Devrient, but the baritone selected to create the Dutchman was another story. Indeed, Waechter had to be selected. He was the only artist in the company who would do at all. For Waechter then had the prime requisite, a voice, described as sonorous, with a metallic ring, and of such compass that both bass and baritone parts lay within his range.

Unfortunately he was an obese fellow, always embarrassed by his awkward arms and legs, and obviously no actor. By 1850, his bulk had grown to such an extent and he had become so ridiculous on the stage that Sincerus, writing two years later about the Dresden Theater, declared he had "outlived himself." Inevitably Schroeder-Devrient felt that she would be obliged to carry the new work on her own shoulders. Nor was she entirely resigned to her lot.

At one rehearsal, when Senta was about to implore Heaven that she might be the Dutchman's redeemer, Schroeder-Devrient abruptly interrupted her singing to whisper despairingly to the composer: "How can I say it when I look into those beady eyes? Good God, Wagner, what a mess you have made!"

PITTS SANBORN, *Stadium Concerts*

Overture to the Music-Drama: *Lohengrin*

In March of 1848, Wagner put the last touches upon his *Lohengrin,* and in May of that year his political activities resulted in his exile from Germany. He therefore had no supervision of the early productions of the work, nor did he hear it until May 15, 1861, in Vienna, following his pardon and return. *Lohengrin* had its first performance at the instigation of his ministering friend, Liszt, on August 28, 1850, with such forces, scarcely adequate, as the court at Weimar permitted. It found favor, and after a few years of managerial hesitation, went the rounds of the principal opera houses of Germany and Austria.

Franz Liszt, the first champion and first producer of *Lohengrin,* has described the Prelude in this way: "It begins with a broad, reposeful surface of melody, a vaporous ether gradually unfolding itself, so that the sacred picture may be delineated before our secular eyes. The effect is confided entirely to the violins (divided into eight different desks), which, after some bars of harmony, continue in the highest notes of their register. The motive is afterward taken up by the softest wind instruments; horns and bas-

soons are then added, and the way prepared for the entry of the
trumpets and trombones, which repeat the melody for the fourth
time, with a dazzling brightness of color, as if in this unique moment the holy edifice had flashed up before our blinded eyes in all
its luminous and radiant magnificence.

"But the flood light, that has gradually achieved this solar intensity, now dies rapidly away, like a celestial gleam. The trans-
parent vapor of the clouds retracts, the vision disappears little by
little, in the same variegated fragrance from the midst of which it
appeared, and the piece ends with a repetition of the first six bars,
now become more ethereal still. Its character of ideal mysticism is
especially suggested by the long *pianissimo* of the orchestra, only
broken for a moment by the passage in which the brass throw out
the marvellous lines of the single motive of the Prelude."

JOHN N. BURK, *Boston Symphony Orchestra*

Overture to the Music-Drama: *Tannhäuser*

Unlike some other operatic overtures, the Overture to *Tannhäuser* was not performed until the opera itself was produced.
Three or four years before that event Wagner had made his first
sketches for *Tannhäuser,* but his duties as conductor at the Dresden Royal Opera and the production there of his own operas
Rienzi and *The Flying Dutchman* interfered with his expanding
the sketches. When he could work at *Tannhäuser,* however, he did
so with his whole soul and "such consuming ardor," he tells us,
that the nearer he approached its end, the more he was haunted
with the notion that perhaps a sudden death would prevent him
from bringing it to completion; so that when the last note was
written he experienced a feeling of joyful elation, as if he had escaped a mortal danger.

It was on April 13, 1845, that Wagner penned the last note.
The Overture seems to have been written in the course of the
weeks immediately preceding. The world premiere took place at
the Dresden Opera on October 19, 1845, with Wagner conducting
from manuscript. His youthful niece Johanna was the saintly Elisabeth. The celebrated Wilhelmine Schroeder-Devrient appeared,

somewhat reluctantly, as Venus; Joseph Aloys Tichatschek, tenor pride of Dresden, sang the minstrel knight Tannhäuser. Wolfram, his fellow minstrel, went to young Anton Mitterwurzer, who alone of the cast pleased Wagner thoroughly. Wilhelm Georg Dettmer embodied the Landgraf Herrmann. As late as 1852, when Wagner was an exile in Switzerland, he still spoke volubly of his dissatisfaction with the performances of *Tannhäuser* at Dresden.

The Overture to *Tannhäuser* follows the method provided definitely by Weber of using themes that appear in the opera for the devising in the prelude of a condensed account of the action. . . . The rousing coda, which we hear in the concert room, is no longer heard in the opera house when the "Paris" version of *Tannhäuser* is presented. Revising the score for the historic production at the Paris Opéra on March 13, 1861, Wagner omitted the latter part of the Overture, connecting the Bacchanalian pages directly with the riotous elaborations of the greatly enriched scene in the Venus Mountain. Nowadays the Overture figures in an opera house only when *Tannhäuser* is performed according to the Dresden version (or, rather, the last of the three Dresden versions).

PITTS SANBORN, *Philharmonic-Symphony Society of New York*

Overture to the Music-Drama: *Die Meistersinger von Nürnberg*

The Prelude to *Die Meistersinger von Nürnberg* was performed for the first time at Leipzig, November 1, 1862. The opera was first performed at Munich, June 21, 1868.

The idea of the opera occurred to Wagner at Marienbad in 1845. He then sketched a scenario, which differed widely from the one finally adopted. It is possible that certain scenes were written while he was composing *Lohengrin*; there is a legend that the quintet was finished in 1845. Some add to the quintet the different songs of Sachs and Walther. Wagner wrote to a friend, March 12, 1862: "Tomorrow I at last go home to begin the composition of *Die Meistersinger.*" The libretto was completed at Paris in 1861. He worked at Biebrich in 1862 on the music. The Prelude was sketched in February of that year; the instrumentation completed in the following June. In the fall of that year he wished the public to hear fragments of his new works, as yet not performed nor published—fragments of *Siegfried, Tristan, Die Walküre,* and he added to these the Overture to *Die Meistersinger,* the entrance of the mastersingers and Pogner's address, from the same opera.

His friend, Wendelin Weissheimer (1838-1910), opera conductor at Wurzburg and Mainz, composer, teacher and essayist, organized a concert at Leipzig for the production of certain works. Buelow was interested in the scheme, and the concert was given in the hall of the Gewandhaus, November 1, 1862, as stated above.

One critic wrote of the *Meistersinger* Prelude: "The Overture, a long movement in moderate march tempo, with predominating brass, without any distinguishing chief thoughts and without noticeable and recurring points of rest, went along and soon awakened a feeling of monotony. . . ."

PHILIP HALE, *Boston Symphony Orchestra*

Prelude to the Music-Drama: *Tristan und Isolde*

Wagner began work on *Tristan und Isolde* in the summer of 1857 when he was living at Zurich. The whole work was completed at Lucerne in August 1859. Though this "Action" (*Handlung*) in three acts was not performed until June 10, 1865, when it was given by command of King Ludwig II at the Hof-und-National-Theater in Munich, the Prelude, with a concert ending devised by Hans von Buelow at Prague, "through the favor of the composer," was presented as early as March 12, 1859. Wagner afterward bracketed the Prelude and "Liebestod" ("Love Death") and conducted them at a number of concerts in 1863. It is worthy of note that in these early performances the Prelude was entitled "Liebestod" and the "Liebestod" called "Verklaerung" ("Transfiguration").

The Prelude (. . . A minor, 6-8) mounts in a long crescendo to an imposing fortissimo, whence it shrinks in a shorter decrescendo to a pianissimo. In its free and continuous development it is built up on two principal themes. The first, given out by 'cellos and in the third measure combined with a chromatically ascending phrase in the oboes, has been called both the motive of the Love

Potion and the motive of Longing. The sensuous second theme, also intoned by the 'cellos, is known as Tristan's Love Glance.

The "Liebestod," which concludes the opera, is the apotheosis in which Isolde sings her life out before her body falls dead upon the dead Tristan . . .

PITTS SANBORN, *Philharmonic-Symphony Society of New York*

The Ring of the Nibelungs

Wagner's *Ring*—to indulge in the American fondness for abbreviations—is without parallel in the realm of music, operatic or otherwise. The composer thought about, and worked on, his trilogy for twenty-six years, although not with unceasing concentration, for he interrupted the *Ring's* progress to write *Tristan und Isolde* and *Die Meistersinger*.

Wagner based his poems (he wrote his own libretti, as his custom was) on sagas of the far north countries—Scandinavia and Iceland. Oddly enough, he wrote these libretti in reverse order, beginning with what is now known as *Die Götterdämmerung*, and ending with *Das Rheingold*. The first poem, originally called "Siegfried's Death," was completed in November 1848. The score of the opera was not completed until 1874. The music for the four operas was written in the proper order, however.

The *Ring* was performed, as a whole, at Bayreuth, August 13, 14, 16, and 17, 1876. It was first performed in the United States in the Metropolitan Opera House, March 5, 6, 8 and 11, 1889. Performances of the individual operas had been given before, of course.

Listeners who found *Lohengrin* and *Tannhäuser* revolutionary were completely nonplussed by this strange, disconcerting music, which the composer insisted on calling "music-drama," instead of opera. He had his theories, and he was basing the music of the *Ring* on those theories—so he thought. If opera, he apparently said to himself, was ever to free itself from the standardized routine of recitative and aria, with now and then a quartet and a chorus (a form developed and idolized by the Italians), something drastic would have to be done. He did it.

Wagner admired and appreciated the music of Beethoven. He came to the logical conclusion that operatic music, too, could be given symphonic treatment. Consequently, he made use of innumerable themes, known as "leitmotives" and he treated these themes symphonically, developing them, restating them in slightly different guises, and sounding them always for a definite purpose. A good deal of the interest, then, was shifted from the singer to the orchestra, which was tremendously enlarged. The music, instead of coming to a full stop every time the tenor and soprano sang a "C in alt," flowed steadily from the first note of the act to the last note. Furthermore, a "scene" was completed, not when the singer had sung the last word of an aria, but when the orchestra had finished developing the themes. Because of the importance of the orchestra, and because of this symphonic method of writing opera music, there were moments when the singers remained silent, and when the orchestra commented on the stage happenings. No wonder audiences, unaccustomed to listening to anything but voices, were bewildered! They could not change the habits of a lifetime. Where were the melodies? They were in the orchestra, but audiences had never listened to the orchestra.

Nowadays, one realizes that Wagner did not follow his theories blindly, but that his music, while revolutionary in a sense, is certainly not the product of scholarly theory alone. For Wagner was a musical genius as well as a theorist, and the musical genius was driven by an inward demon stronger than that which drove the theorist.

As Ernest Newman wrote in his book, *Wagner as Man and Artist:*

"So far from the poet in him shaping and controlling the musician, it was the musician who led the poet where he would have him go; so far from drama being with him the end, and the music the means, it was music that was more than ever the end, to which the drama served only as means; and so far from Wagner being first and last a dramatist, the whole significance of his work lay precisely in the fact that he was a great symphonist . . . It was not for nothing that he always claimed descent from Beethoven rather than from even the greatest of opera writers."

WALTER WHITWORTH, *Pittsburgh Symphony Orchestra*

Excerpts from the Festival Drama: *Parsifal*

From the myriad legends relating to the Holy Grail that grew up during the Middle Ages, Wagner chose the one as told by Wolfram von Eschenbach, thirteenth-century Minnesinger, in his trilogy, *Titurel-Parzival-Loherangrin*. The lore of the Grail reaches far back into antiquity. During mediaeval times the idea crystallized, and the Grail became the *Ideal* of the pious devotions of Knighthood. This chalice from which Christ was said to have drunk at the Last Supper had been brought to Britain, and entrusted to keepers who were chaste in thought, word and act. As these knights became corrupted, the Grail disappeared, and to recover it became the task of knight-errantry. None but the pure in heart and the valorous in spirit could undertake the quest. The Perfect Innocent would be the finder.

In Wolfram von Eschenbach's version of this legend (he derived it from Chretien de Troies' great French epic, *Percevaus*) the Grail and the Sacred Spear have been given into the keeping of Titurel by the angelic hosts. This knight has built a temple for the sacred relics high on Monsalvat, in northern Spain, and he has founded an order of knighthood to stand watch over them. Amfortas has succeeded Titurel; but the former has fallen from grace because he succumbed to the wiles of Kundry, the witchwoman, and he has been wounded in battle by the magician, Klingsor, who has wrested the Sacred Spear from him. It has been foretold that a guileless youth would appear who, through compassion, would become wise, and who, resisting temptation, would regain the Spear. By its aid Amfortas would be healed. The action of Wagner's music-drama begins with the coming of Parsifal, the Perfect Innocent.

. . . Nearly two-score years elapsed between the time when Wagner first came upon the legend of the Holy Grail, and when his *Buehnenweihfestspiel* (Stage-consecrating Festival Drama) was produced at Bayreuth, on July 26, 1882. As early as 1865, Wagner sketched his *Parsifal* story to his admirer, King Ludwig of Bavaria, but it was not set down until the winter of 1876, or the spring of 1877. He brought his poem to London with him in May 1877, and read it then in its entirety to a group of friends. Work on the music was begun in December 1877, and finished in

April 1879. Orchestration was not completed until January 1882.

The July 26 performance of the festival drama was for the patrons of the Bayreuth theater; the first public performance was four days later, on July 30. Because of the sacred character of the work, Wagner expressed the wish that it should not be performed as ordinary repertory of opera houses. So, for twenty-one years the stage representation of *Parsifal* took place only at Bayreuth. Then, in 1903, some technicality having been discovered in the copyright, the first complete performance outside of Bayreuth took place on Christmas Eve, in New York. In Europe, however, *Parsifal* was not performed except in the composer's theater until after the copyright expired in 1913.

LOUISE BECK, Philadelphia Orchestra

WILLIAM TURNER WALTON

(Born in Oldham, England, March 29, 1902—now
living in England)

MR. WALTON and Constant Lambert, who once represented the rising and more elfish generation of British composers, have gone their separate ways with the years. Mr. Walton, for instance, has become a witty and beguiling essayist in music, lately imbued with the creed of dissonance, the bleak and empty line, "sans melody, sans everything."

Yet his reputation for sound and able craftsmanship rests securely upon *Facade,* the Overture to *Scapino,* viola and violin concerti, *Portsmouth Point,* a string quartet and a symphony.

He comes of a family of teachers and singers. As a child he studied the violin because he hated the piano, and he learned to sing Händel almost before he could speak. At ten he joined the chorus of Christ College, Oxford, and began to compose at thirteen. He was only sixteen when it came time for him to receive a baccalaureate degree in music, probably the youngest ever to earn such a distinction.

The International Society for Contemporary Music picked his first string quartet for performance at Salzburg in 1923, thereby bringing out his name for the first time as a composer. His next work *Facade,* a setting in witty and ironic terms of some poems by Edith Sitwell, established him securely as a composer of enormous talent.

Overture: *Portsmouth Point*

This Overture was performed for the first time at the third concert of the International Society for New Music on June 25, 1926, in the larger room of the Tonhall, Zurich, Switzerland. Volkmar Andrae of Zurich conducted the Overture. The first performance in the United States was by the Boston Symphony Orchestra, Dr. Koussevitzky, conductor, on November 19, 1926.

. . . Mr. Walton has sent to us the following note, signed "C. L.": "The title *Portsmouth Point* is taken from a print by the great English caricaturist Thomas Rowlandson (1756-1827), representing quayside in the utmost confusion. The music, which is remarkable for its exuberant melodic outline and exhilarating rhythmic syncopation, is so lucid as to render analysis superfluous. The Overture enjoys the distinction of being the only work chosen to represent England at the International Festival at Zurich in 1926."

Rowlandson's print was published by T. Tegg in 1814. The following quotation from *The Portsmouth Road: The Sailors' Highway,* by Charles G. Harper, describes the print:

"Here, where the stone stairs lead down into the water, is Portsmouth Point. Mark it well, for from this spot have embarked countless fine fellows to serve King and country afloat. What would we not give for a moment's glimpse of 'Point' (as Portsmouth folk call it, with a brevity born of everyday use) just a hundred years ago!" (This book was first published in 1895. We quote from the second and revised edition, published in 1923 by Edwin Valentine Mitchell of Hartford, Connecticut) "Fortunately, the genius of Rowlandson has preserved for us something of the appearance of Portsmouth Point at that time, when war raged over nearly all the civilized world, when wooden ships rode the waves buoyantly, when battles were the rule and peace the exception.

"The Point was in those days simply a collection of taverns giving upon the harbor and the stairs, whence departed a continuous stream of officers and men of the navy. It was a place throbbing with life and excitement—the sailors going out and returning home; the leavetakings, the greetings, the boozing and the fighting are all shown in Rowlandson's drawing as on a stage, while the tall ships form an appropriate background, like the backcloth of a theatrical scene. It is a scene full of humor. Sailors are leaning on their arms out of windows; a gold-laced officer bids goodbye to his girl, while his trunks are being carried down the stairs; a drunken sailor and his equally drunken woman are belaboring one another with all the good will in the world, and a wooden-legged sailor man is scraping away for very life on a fiddle and dancing grotesquely to get a living."

Rowlandson also shows small craft pulling off to the ships; luggage, spirit-casks, packages wheeled or shouldered. A Lady is in a sedan chair. A drunken girl is borne off on the shoulders of a sailor. . . .

PHILIP HALE, *Boston Symphony Orchestra*

Suite from *Facade*

This "Entertainment, for reciting voices and instruments," was first performed at London's Aeolian Hall on December 6, 1923. It was the first work to attract definite attention to this young English composer who, from the age of sixteen, has been entirely self-taught.

Quite aside from its musical content, the premiere presentation of *Facade* was unique. The platform was entirely covered by a curtain, specially designed by Gino Severini. On the curtain was a huge face or mask—"painted half in white, half in pink"—and from the mouth projected a megaphone. Behind the curtain was a "reciter," in this case Edith Sitwell, whose poems serve as foundation for Walton's musical talents, many of them quite humorous. In the latter connection, the audience at the premiere "had been warned that it might regard *Facade* as entertainment and that it need not repress any impulse to laugh if it felt so." Miss Sitwell was assisted at the initial performance by young Constant Lambert, another gifted English composer, who also shared the reciting chores. The words, incidentally, were spoken in strict rhythm, the pulse-value being given preference over sense-value.

Behind the curtain and grouped around the reciter was the orchestra of eight instruments—flute, piccolo, clarinet, trumpet, saxophone, bass clarinet, 'cello and percussion.

As might have been expected, the work aroused considerable comment and in 1926 the composer arranged the *Facade* music for concert performance, dividing the various items into two suites . . . *Facade* was chosen for performance at the Siena International Festival in 1928 and has done more than anything else to establish its composer in the front rank of contemporary English composers . . ."

GUSTAV KLEMM, *Baltimore Symphony Orchestra*

CARL MARIA VON WEBER

(Born in Eutin, Germany, December 18, 1786—died in London, June 5, 1826)

A BOOK on his life has been called *The Enchanted Wanderer,* a romantic cognomen that fits to the last wrinkle a restless and charming genius. An engaging and dissolute youth, he died of tuberculosis at forty, amid the foggy airs of London, leaving a heri-

tage of German romantic opera that gave Wagner much of his
early inspiration.

Carl Maria was a sickly child. He showed such musical promise that his ambitious father, sure that he had sired another Mozart, forced him to practice the violin and piano for hours, and
yanked him all over Germany to exhibit his talents. Consequently,
the boy knew no home life whatever until his twelfth year.

The death of his mother stopped these exhausting tours, and
Carl entered the choir-boys' school in Salzburg, where he studied
with Michael Haydn, younger brother of Josef. Later, Abt Vogler
topped off his musical education in Vienna.

For a time, he served as secretary of the Duke of Wuerttem-
berg in Stuttgart. Some funds entrusted to his keeping disappeared
and he and his father, though adjudged innocent, were banished.
Whereupon, Carl went to Mannheim, then to Darmstadt where he,
Meyerbeer and a few others, formed the Harmonic Society.

He was appointed conductor of the Prague Opera in 1813 and
three years later took a similar position in Dresden. "A liaison with
an unscrupulous prima donna," writes Helen Kaufman, "nearly
ruined him, but after he married Caroline Brandt, who loved and
understood him, he settled down to serious work."

Italian opera had overwhelmed Germany, as every other country in Europe, and Weber found that he would have to educate his
countrymen to hear and respect a German product. This he
achieved in part by composing two romantic operas—*Der Freischuetz* and *Euryanthe*. The overtures to both operas are heard
constantly on modern orchestra programs.

He was commissioned to write an opera, to an English text, for
production in London. Although gravely ill, he undertood the task
and *Oberon* was the result. He departed reluctantly for London,
supervised exhausting rehearsals and conducted eleven performances. But the strain was too much, and he died there of tuberculosis, fatigue and homesickness.

Showmanship and restlessness characterized his orchestral
scores. He revolutionized classic instrumentation, "blending strings
and woodwinds as they never had been blended before," and creating effects to be elaborated later by Berlioz and Wagner. His orchestral works include two symphonies in C major and six concertos
(several for clarinet, one for bassoon and one for horn).

Concertstuecke for piano and orchestra in F minor—(Opus 79)

Weber's initial sketches for this work were begun in 1815. For some unknown reason, however, he did not return to them until February 1821, at Dresden. During the eventful days preceding the production of his opera *Der Freischuetz* he labored feverishly to complete the *Concertstuecke* and, as it happened, he put the finishing touches to it on the very day of the opera's premiere in Berlin.

Before returning to Dresden, with the rhapsodic praise of *Der Freischuetz* still ringing in his ears, he conceived the idea of playing the piano and orchestra piece at a farewell concert. Arrangements were made for the event, and it took place in the auditorium of the new theater on June 25, 1821. The *Concertstuecke,* according to an entry in Weber's diary, made an "enormous success." He played it again, four days later, at another concert and the number was received (again referring to the diary) "with unbelievable applause."

The piece was published in 1823, with a dedication to Princess Marie Augusta of Saxony. Sir Julius Benedict, Weber's friend and pupil, is authority for the statement that the *Concertstuecke* is not abstract, but program music. In substantiation he submitted a plan alleged to have been followed by the composer:

"The Châtelaine sits all alone on her balcony, gazing far away into the distance. Her knight has gone to the Holy Land. Years have passed by; battles have been fought. Is he still alive? Will she ever see him again? Her excited imagination calls up a vision of her husband lying wounded and forsaken on the battlefield. Can she not fly to him and die by his side? She falls back unconscious. Over there in the forest something flashes in the sunlight nearer and nearer. Knights and squires with the cross of the Crusaders, banners waving, acclamations of the people, and there—it is he. She sinks into his arms. Love is triumphant. Happiness without end. The very woods and waves sing the song of her love; a thousand voices proclaim his victory."

ROBERT C. BAGAR, *Philharmonic-Symphony Society of New York*

Invitation to the Dance
(Orchestration by Felix Weingartner)

In 1817, Weber married Caroline Brandt, a singer at the Prague Opera. A few months later he wrote the *Invitation to the Dance,* which is dedicated to "My Caroline," and is one of the few piano compositions by Weber which have remained popular until the present time.

It seems to offer peculiar temptations to arrangers. Adolf Henselt made a new version of the *Invitation* for piano solo, and Carl Tausig put forth a virtuoso edition, "with arabesques for concert performance." Otto Dresel made a popular arrangement for two pianos, eight hands. There are arrangements for many instrumental combinations, including a version for two violins.

Berlioz made an arrangement for the Paris Opéra in 1841, and his explanation throws light on the French treatment of German opera in his day:

"I have just got back from this long trip in Germany, when M. Pillet formed the project of mounting the *Freyschuetz.* But the musical numbers in this work are preceded and followed by prose dialogue, as in our opéra-comiques, and as the usage of the opera requires that everything in the lyric dramas and tragedies of its repertory shall be sung, the spoken text had to be turned into recitative. . . . They did not fail to propose the introduction of a ballet. All my efforts to prevent it being useless, I proposed composing a choreographic scene indicated by Weber himself in his pianoforte rondo, the *Invitation to the Dance,* and scored that piece for orchestra."

CHARLES N. BOYD, *Pittsburgh Symphony Orchestra*

Overture to the opera: *Oberon*

In 1824, John Kemple, then lessee of Covent Garden Theater, asked Weber to write an opera in English for the Royal Theater. Weber chose as subject *Oberon,* that tale of fairies which had occupied English poets and dramatists since 1540, when Sir John Bourchier, Lord Berners, gave to the public, under the title, *Huon*

*de Burdeuxe; Here Begynnithe the boke of duke Huon of Bur-
deuxe and of them that issuyd fro hym,* his translation of the old
French Chanson de gest, *Huon de Bordeaux.* James Robinson
Planché was asked to furnish the libretto; this he based on a Ger-
man version of the Oberon romance by Wieland. The result was
"Oberon, or the Elf-King's Oath, a romantic opera in three acts.

Neither composer nor librettist seems to have been satisfied
with the result of their efforts. Weber wrote to Planché: "The in-
termixing of so many actors who do not sing, the omission of music
in the most important moments, all deprive our *Oberon* of the title
of opera, and will make it unfit for all other theaters in Europe" . . .
"On the other hand," Planché declared, "my great object was to
land Weber safe in the midst of an unmusical public, so I wrote a
melodrama with songs, instead of an opera such as would be required today." (His *Recollections and Reflections* appeared in
1872).

Ill and feeble, Weber set about his task, not the least of which
was to learn enough English so that he might understand the text
which he was to set to music. So much was he in earnest that he
accomplished this in less than a year. The libretto was sent to him,
act by act, to Dresden, where he was living at the time. His first
sketch, Huon's aria of the first act, was composed on January 23,
1825; the Overture, the last number to be written, was finished in
London, three days before the premiere. The autograph score
bears this note, at the end of the Overture: "Finished April 9,
1826, in the morning at a quarter to twelve, and with it the whole
opera. *Soli Deo Gloria!! C.M.V.W."*

Although dying of consumption, Weber directed the first performance, at Covent Garden, on April 12, 1826. He was under
contract to conduct the first twelve performances; he struggled
through eleven of them, directing while seated at the piano. He
was found dead in bed by his host, Sir George Stuart, on the morning of June 5, 1826.

R. L. F. McCOMBS, *Philadelphia Orchestra*

Overture to the opera: *Der Freischuetz*

Although the German romantic opera can be traced back further than Weber, still the first opera of the sort to make a great international impression and to take a place among the master-pieces of the lyric drama was undoubtedly *Der Freischuetz*. The title, by the way, has been wrongly rendered *Freeshooter* or *Sharpshooter*. It means rather a man who shoots with magic bullets.

Der Freischuetz is a musical monument of the romantic movement of the late eighteenth and early nineteenth centuries. It is full of the rediscovered feeling for nature, evoking the forest with its mystery, its haunted recesses, and its supernatural terror as a living entity. Weber's forest is the dwelling place of demons, and man sets his foot within it at his peril. But Weber, a devout believer, is also aware of the immanence of divine protection. In this opera it is the angelic candor of the character of Agatha, the heroine, and the opportune emergence of a holy hermit that save the hero, Max, from the consequences of dealing with the powers of darkness.

The Overture opens with a peaceful sylvan introduction enshrining a hymnlike melody for the horns. Presently the sinister and the supernatural enter the picture, and the powers of darkness seem about to capture the music for the uses of evil. A rapturous melody, however, associated with Agatha (the finale of her scene in Act II, "All' meine Pulse schlagen") puts them to rout and the work ends in a victorious jubilation.

The initial performance of *Der Freischuetz* took place in Berlin on June 18, 1821. The language of the American premiere (Park Theater, New York, March 2, 1825) was not the original German, but English, and the opera was provided with a subtitle, *The Wild Huntsman of Bohemia*. The original German was used at Palmo's Opera House on December 8, 1845. Meanwhile, New York had heard a French version in 1827, and in 1850 an Italian version was performed there. From March 23, 1924 on, whenever *Der Freischuetz* has been given at the Metropolitan Opera House, New York, recitatives by the conductor, Artur Bodanzky, have replaced the spoken dialogue of the original.

PITTS SANBORN, *Philharmonic-Symphony Society of New York*

Overture to the opera: *Euryanthe*

Euryanthe, grand romantic opera in three acts, the text by Wilhelmine von Chézy, the music by Carl Maria von Weber, was given for the first time at the Court Opera House in Vienna on October 25, 1823. It was produced in Berlin on December 23, 1825, and shortly afterward in Weimar and Dresden. A terribly garbled version, arranged by the notorious Castil-Blaze, with interpolations from the music of *Oberon* was brought out at the Académie de Musique in Paris on April 16, 1831. . . . *Euryanthe* was first given in New York at the Metropolitan Opera House on December 23, 1887.

Euryanthe has been called at once Weber's greatest masterpiece and his greatest fiasco. In it he departed from the traditional form of German opera, in which the musical numbers were connected by spoken dialogue, substituting musical recitative for the latter, according to Italian tradition and that of the French grand opera. The work was nowhere well received by the public, Weber's free dramatic treatment of the recitative and the *scena* being considerably in advance of the age; and the libretto was too miserably poor to be acceptable even after the music came to be better understood. The text is based on an old French romance, *Histoire de Gerard de Nevers et la belle et vertueuse Euryante de Savoie, sa mie.* Commentators have more than once pointed out the striking general similarity between the characters of Adolar and Euryanthe, and Lysiart and Eglantine in *Euryanthe,* and those of Lohengrin and Elsa, and Telramund and Ortrud in Wagner's *Lohengrin.* The Overture is the only part of the opera that has well maintained its place in the standard repertory. . . .

WILLIAM FOSTER APTHORP, *Boston Symphony Orchestra (1898)*

JAROMIR WEINBERGER

(Born in Prague January 8, 1896—now living in
Fleischmanns, N. Y.)

WEINBERGER'S reputation in this country rests upon one or
two orchestral works (such as *Under the Spreading Chestnut
Tree*) and a fascinating comic-opera, *Schwanda der Dudelsackpfeifer,* loudly cheered after the American premiere at the Metropolitan, New York, in 1931. In all of these works, a decided and highly
individual idiom is apparent, besides a superb grasp of orchestral
color and an arresting melodic line, compounded of Czech and
Central European folk tunes.

But *Schwanda* was the work that made his fame worldwide,
for it had become a musical rage in Europe shortly before the first
performance here.

He studied at the Prague Conservatory and in Germany with
Max Reger. He came to the United States first in 1922, to teach
composition at Cornell University. Then he went back to Europe,
to serve as operatic director of the National Theater in Bratislava
and to guide the musical school in Eger. His growing importance
as a composer induced him to settle in Prague for a time and devote all his energies to creative work.

The first of his works to attract some attention was a tone-
poem for orchestra, *Don Quixote.* Other operas include *Leuter
von Pokerflat,* based on stories of Bret Harte, and *A Bed of Roses,*
which earned wide acclaim abroad. He came back to this country
soon after the outbreak of the Second World War, and has been
living in retirement for some years. A Mass, his first and only venture into the field of sacred music, was performed for the first time
in the Town Hall, New York, two years ago, with only moderate
success.

Polka and Fugue from the opera: *Schwanda der Dudelsack-pfeifer*

. . . Weinberger's works have received numerous presentations in Europe, where he is a well-known figure. Most of his works have been for the stage. He has written two operas, of which *Schwanda* is one; incidental music for several Shakespearean plays and a number of works for orchestra.

The full title of the opera is *Schwanda der Dudelsackpfeifer*. It is in the nature of a musical comedy and is based on Bohemian or Czech folk music and legend. It has had great success in Europe and was produced at the Metropolitan Opera House in New York a few years ago. . . .

The Polka and Fugue are closely interwoven and in effect become a single piece. The theme of the Polka has a simple rhythm and savors of the native folk. The melody is heard in the first four measures in a swinging rhythm. The tune is plain and obvious, a simple dance being set forth.

The material of the Fugue is the same as that used in the Polka. While the latter is simple and plain, the Fugue is highly complex and formal, though based on the same material. The Fugue begins *pianissimo,* in the violins, immediately after the close of the Polka. Beautiful development takes place in the Fugue. Weinberger is lavish in his use of orchestral instruments and he draws on almost every one in setting forth these two connected compositions. There is a tremendous climax in the Fugue, in which the entire resources of the orchestra are employed.

WILLIAM S. BENSWANGER, *Pittsburgh Symphony Orchestra*

RALPH VAUGHAN WILLIAMS

(Born in Down Ampney, England, October 12, 1872
—now living in England)

VAUGHAN WILLIAMS, financially independent, like Mendelssohn before him, had no reason to devote himself to music as a vocation. Rarely gifted in music, even as a child, he had every opportunity to gain an extensive education in his chosen field. He is respected today as one of England's most representative composers. All of which might indicate, contrary to the general suspicion, that true art has nothing to do with one's pocketbook.

He studied at Trinity College, Cambridge, and at the Royal College of Music under Parry and Stanford.

The year he left the Royal College, he had a "soul-shattering" experience—he heard the Wagnerian music-dramas at Bayreuth for the first time. He stayed in Germany to study at the Berlin Academy under Max Bruch, then returned to England to receive his Doctorate of Music at Cambridge.

In his student years, Vaughan Williams conceived a lifelong passion for the folk music of England. Feeling that he still lacked a complete and sound technique, he went to Paris in 1908 to study with Maurice Ravel. This will account, perhaps for the unmistakable tint of French impressionism so often encountered in his larger works for orchestra.

Returning from service in the First World War, he joined the teaching staff of the Royal College and was appointed conductor of the London Bach Chorus. The first annual congress of the British Music Society chose the *London Symphony* (1914) as "the most significant native musical work yet produced by an Englishman."

A London Symphony

Vaughan Williams composed *A London Symphony* in the years 1912 and 1913. The first performance of the original version was given at an F. B. Ellis concert in Queen's Hall, London, March 27, 1914, Geoffrey Toye, conductor. The composer later revised his score, which required almost a full hour to perform, and the revision was first played under the direction of Adrian Boult. A second revision was made in 1920 when the score was published. The score under revision was considerably shortened, particularly in the Finale. The Symphony was performed under the direction of Albert Coates at a concert of the British Music Society in Queen's Hall, May 4, 1920. Mr. Coates also was the conductor who made the Symphony heard in America at a concert of the New York Symphony Society, December 30, 1920. . . . There was a third revision after the publication of the score with further condensations which appear in the small score subsequently published. . . . The score was published with a dedication: "To the Memory of George Butterworth." George S. K. Butterworth, a composer of orchestral pieces and songs, was killed in action in France, August 5, 1916, at the age of thirty-six.

The composer made this statement in the program of the London performance of 1920:

"The title, *A London Symphony*, may suggest to some hearers a descriptive piece, but this is not the intention of the composer. A better title would perhaps be, *Symphony by a Londoner;* that is to say, the life of London (including possibly its various sights and sounds) has suggested to the composer an attempt at musical expression; but it would be no help to the hearer to describe these in words. The music is intended to be self-impressive, and must stand or fall as 'absolute' music. Therefore, if listeners recognize suggestions of such things as 'Westminster Chimes' or the 'Lavender Cry' they are asked to consider these as accidents, not essentials of the music."

Vaughan Williams has been even more laconic about his other symphonies. The early *Sea Symphony* was an exception, because it contained its own descriptive text. But of bucolic episodes in the *Pastoral Symphony* he gave no hints whatever, and his latest is frankly absolute. When Albert Coates introduced the *London Symphony* in New York he gave out in the printed bulletins of the Symphony Society a vivid word picture. The description has been generally quoted since, and taken as having emanated at least in some part from the composer. Mr. Coates had become decidedly specific. It was natural to assume some sort of an understanding "between friends."

One recalls controversies in Germany, protests of composers such as Mahler or Strauss, who were wary of sançtioning elaborate elucidations as official, and whose friends sometimes made known more than they were intended to. "Programmistic" composers have probably felt that word pictures can be a doubtful aid. . . ."

JOHN N. BURK, *Boston Symphony Orchestra*

Fantasia on a Theme by Thomas Tallis: For double string orchestra

The first performance of the *Fantasia* took place in Gloucester Cathedral on September 6, 1910 on the occasion of the Three Choirs Festival (including the choirs of Gloucester, Worcester and Hereford) of that year. It was not published, however, until 1921. The work was introduced to this country at a concert of the Symphony Society of New York in Carnegie Hall on March 9, 1922, Walter Damrosch conducting.

. . . Thomas Tallis, in so far as is known, was born about 1505. Conjecture has it that he was a chorister at either St. Paul's Cathedral or the Chapel Royal. It has been established that he held some sort of official position at the Abbey of the Holy Cross at Waltham, in Essex, when the Abbey came to the end of its days in 1540. It may be, also that Henry VIII nominated him even before that a Gentleman of the Chapel Royal, which office he held, possibly, until his death, on Nobember 23, 1585, in the reign of Elizabeth. Since the period includes the reigns of Edward VI and Mary I, it is then quite plausible to believe that Tallis took each of the successive religious changes in stride, conforming, as it were, readily, if not devotedly.

Be that as it may, he was a Protestant in 1567, when he penned eight tunes, each founded on one of the ecclesiastical modes, for the Metrical Psalter of Matthew Parker, Archbishop of Canterbury. Because the *cantus firmus* in the original volume is in the tenor part, the following explanation appears:

"The tenor of these partes be for the people when they will sing alone, the otherpartes for greater queers [choirs] or to such as will play or sing them quietly."

One of the customs of Tallis' time was to ascribe special characteristics to the eight ecclesiastical modes, as witness their quaint description in verse:

The first is meeke: devout to see.
The second sad: in maiesty.
The third doth rage: and roughly brayth.
The fourth doth fawne: and flattery playth.
The fyfth delight: and laugheth the more.
The sixth bewaileth: it weepeth full sore.
The seuenth tradeth stoute; in forward race.
The eyghth goeth mild: in modest pace.

The tune on which the *Fantasia* is based is the third. It is not likely that it will rage or bray, as it once did, perhaps, but Tallis considered it excellent for the second Psalm:

Why fumeth in sight: the Gentile spite
In fury raging stout?

Vaughan Williams, wishing to retain all of the tune's ecclesiastical character, has utilized its authentic harmonies.

In passing, Thomas Tallis and William Byrd (his godson) obtained from Queen Elizabeth in 1575 the exclusive privilege to print music and ruled music paper. The little monopoly lasted for twenty-one years, Byrd taking over when Tallis died. Thomas Tallis was buried in the parish church at Greenwich. A brass plate bearing his epitaph was removed when the church underwent alterations early in the eighteenth century. The inscription ran:

Entered here doth ly a worthy Wyght
Who for long Tyme in Musik bore the Bell:
His Name to shew, was Thomas Tallys hyght.
In honest vertuous Lyff he did excell.
He serv'd long Tyme in Chappel with grete prayse
Fower Soveregnes Reygnes (a thing not often seen)
I mean Kyng Henry and Prynce Edward's Dayes,
Quene Mary and Elizabeth our Quene.
He maryed was, though Children he had none
And lyv'd in Love full thre and thirty Yeres,
With loyal Spowse, whose name yclyipt was Jone

Who here entomb'd him Company now bears.
As he did lyve, so also did he dy
In myld and quyet Sort (O happy Man)
To God full oft for Mercy did he cry.
Wherefore he lyves, let Death do what he can.

ROBERT C. BAGAR, *Philharmonic-Symphony Society of New York*